尾田栄一郎

"Huh...? Are you... Could you...possibly be...a god?"

"...Yes."

All right, let's begin volume 50!!

-Eiichiro Oda, 2008

Eiichiro Oda began his manga career at the age of 17, when his one-shot cowboy manga **Wanted!** won second place in the coveted Tezuka manga awards. Oda went on to work as an assistant to some of the biggest manga artists in the industry, including Nobuhiro Watsuki, before winning the Hop Step Award for new artists. His pirate adventure **One Piece**, which debuted in **Weekly Shonen Jump** in 1997, quickly became one of the most popular manga in Japan.

ONE PIECE VOL. 50
THRILLER BARK PART 5 &
SABAODY PART 1

SHONEN JUMP Manga Edition

STORY AND ART BY EIICHIRO ODA

English Adaptation/Jake Forbes
Translation/JN Productions
Touch-up Art & Lettering/Elena Diaz
Design/Fawn Lau
Editor/Alexis Kirsch

ONE PIECE © 1997 by Eiichiro Oda. All rights reserved.
First published in Japan in 1997 by SHUEISHA Inc., Tokyo.
English translation rights arranged by SHUEISHA Inc.

The stories, characters and incidents mentioned in this publication are
entirely fictional.

Printed in the U.S.A.

Published by VIZ Media, LLC
P.O. Box 77010
San Francisco, CA 94107

10 9 8 7 6 5 4
First printing, June 2010
Fourth printing, October 2014

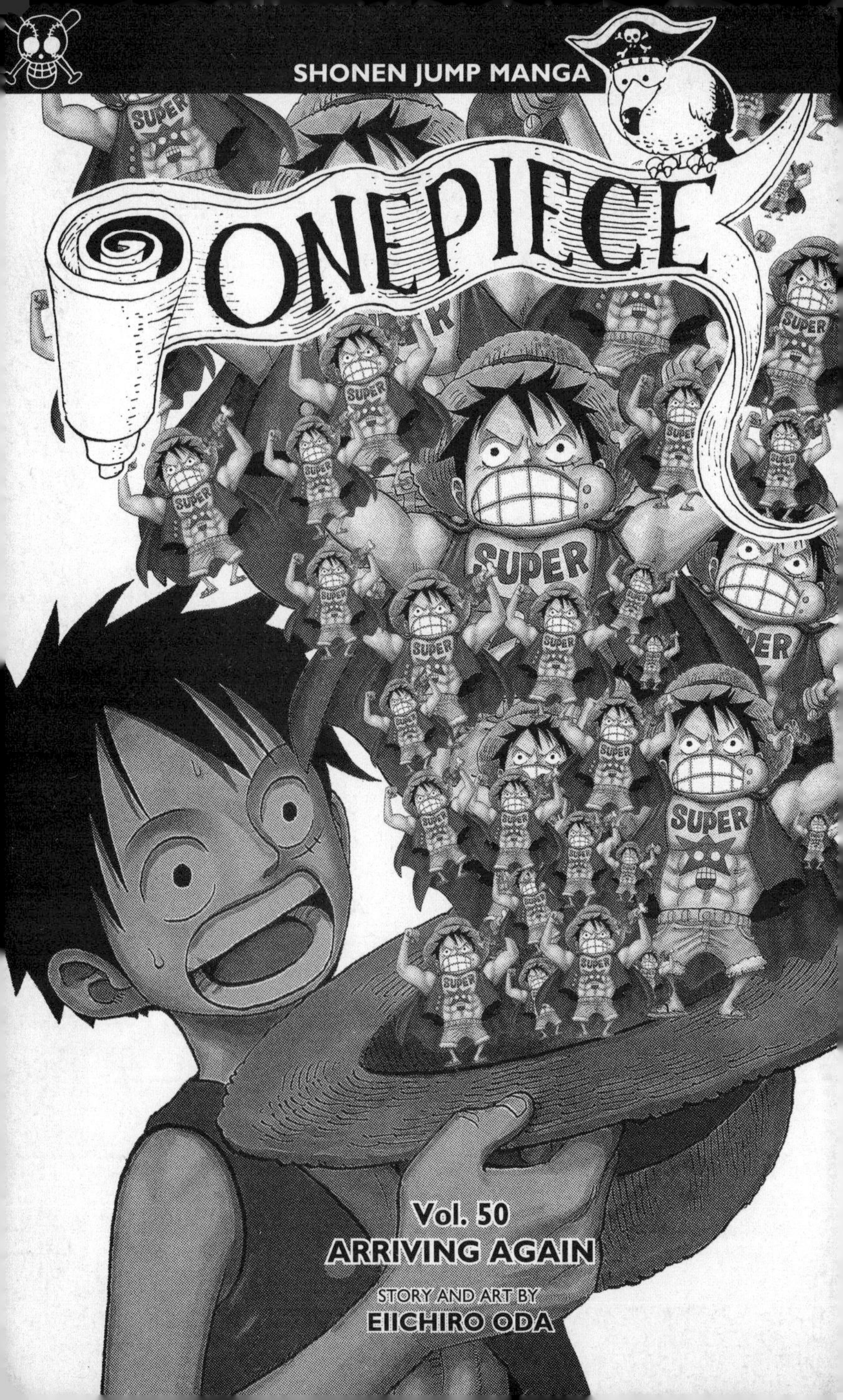
SHONEN JUMP MANGA
ONE PIECE
SUPER
Vol. 50
ARRIVING AGAIN
STORY AND ART BY
EIICHIRO ODA

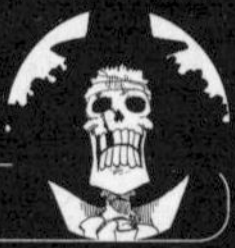

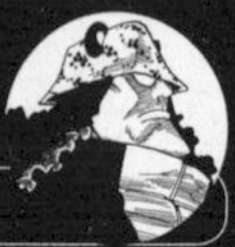

The Straw Hats

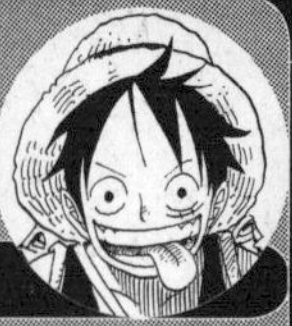

Boundlessly optimistic and able to stretch like rubber, he is determined to become King of the Pirates.

Monkey D. Luffy

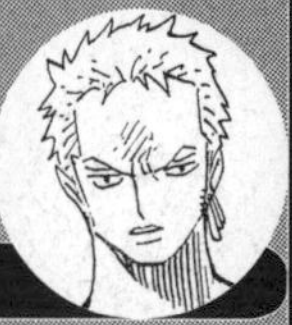

A former bounty hunter and master of the "three-sword" style. He aspires to be the world's greatest swordsman.

Roronoa Zolo

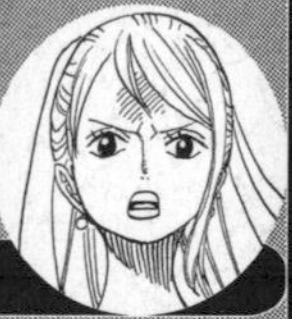

A thief who specializes in robbing pirates. Nami hates pirates, but Luffy convinced her to be his navigator.

Nami

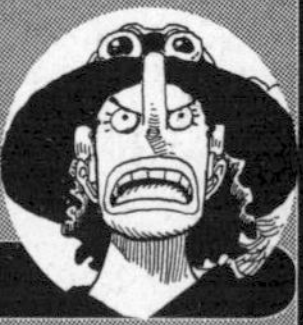

A village boy with a talent for telling tall tales. His father, Yasopp, is a member of Shanks's crew.

Usopp

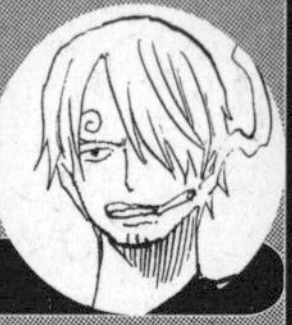

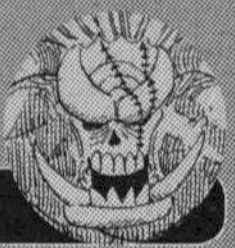

The bighearted cook (and ladies' man) whose dream is to find the legendary sea, the "All Blue."

Sanji

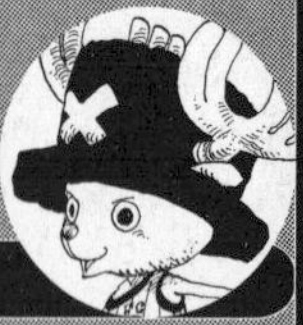

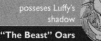

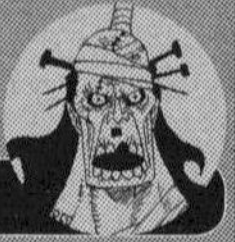

A blue-nosed man-reindeer and the ship's doctor.

Tony Tony Chopper

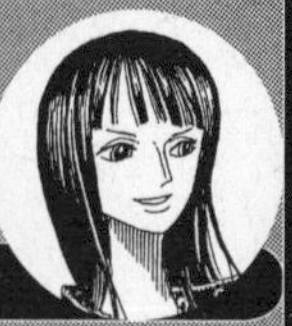

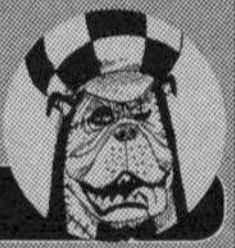

A mysterious woman in search of the Poneglyph on which true history is recorded.

Nico Robin

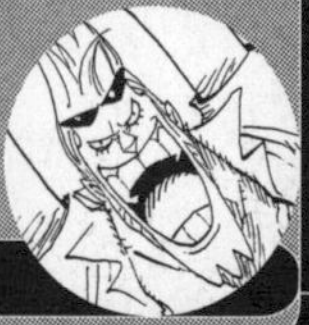

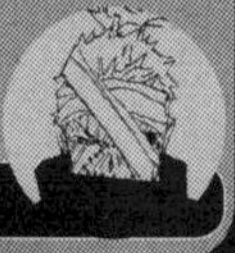

A softhearted cyborg and talented shipwright.

Franky

A musician swordsman whose shadow was stolen. He's on a quest to take it back.

Brook

The only member of the Seven Warlords of the Sea who works directly for the World Government. He's nicknamed "The Tyrant."

Bartholomew Kuma

The zombie who posseses Luffy's shadow

"The Beast" Oars

The zombie who posseses Zolo's shadow

Jigoro of the Wind

The zombie who posseses Sanji's shadow

Inuppe

The zombie who posseses Brook's shadow

Samurai Ryuma

THE STORY OF ONE PIECE

Volume 50

Monkey D. Luffy started out as just a kid with a dream—to become the greatest pirate in history! Stirred by the tales of pirate "Red-Haired" Shanks, Luffy vowed to become a pirate himself. That was before the enchanted Devil Fruit gave Luffy the power to stretch like rubber, at the cost of being unable to swim—a serious handicap for an aspiring sea dog. Undeterred, Luffy set out to sea and recruited some crewmates—master swordsman Zolo; treasure-hunting thief Nami; lying sharpshooter Usopp; the high-kicking chef Sanji; Chopper, the walkin' talkin' reindeer doctor; the mysterious archaeologist Robin; and cyborg shipwright Franky.

Having entered into the world's greatest ocean, the Grand Line, Luffy and crew replace their old ship with the *Thousand Sunny*. The Straw Hats get lost in a storm and wind up in the mysterious Florian Triangle. There, they meet Brook, a musically inclined skeleton, and a new adventure begins! *Thousand Sunny* is summoned to the ghost island, Thriller Bark, a creepy place crawling with zombies! The person who controls those zombies is one of the Seven Warlords of the Sea, Gecko Moria. He has amassed his undead army by stealing people's shadows and inserting them into the zombies that Dr. Hogback created. Luffy's shadow was taken and placed inside the "The Beast" Oars, a giant monster who feels no pain, and over the course of their battles, half the Straw Hat crew lose their shadows to Moria's wiles. If sunlight hits their bodies while they have no shadow, Luffy and the others will melt away! Just before dawn, Luffy gets an assist from the Rolling Pirate crew, who pack him full of shadows for a super-powered battle against Oars. The giant has fallen, but now Moria has absorbed all of the shadows on the island, giving him immense power! And what's going on with Bartholomew Kuma, another of the Seven Warlords…?

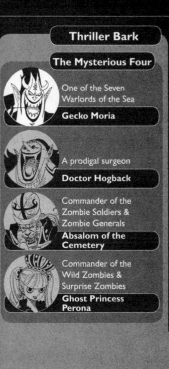

Thriller Bark

The Mysterious Four

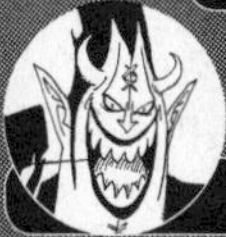

One of the Seven Warlords of the Sea

Gecko Moria

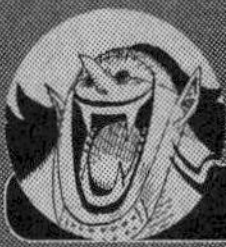

A prodigal surgeon

Doctor Hogback

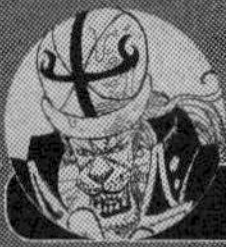

Commander of the Zombie Soldiers & Zombie Generals

Absalom of the Cemetery

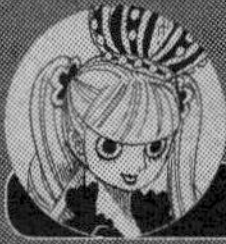

Commander of the Wild Zombies & Surprise Zombies

Ghost Princess Perona

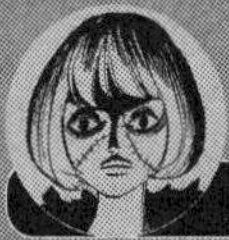

Victoria Cindry

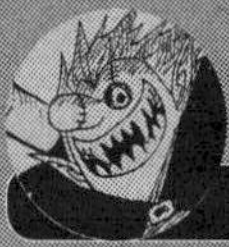

Hildon

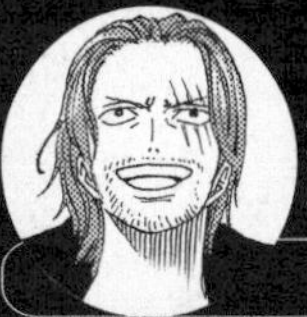

A pirate that Luffy idolizes. Shanks gave Luffy his trademark straw hat.

"Red-Haired" Shanks

Vol. 50
Arriving Again

CONTENTS

Chapter 482: MORNING IS COMING

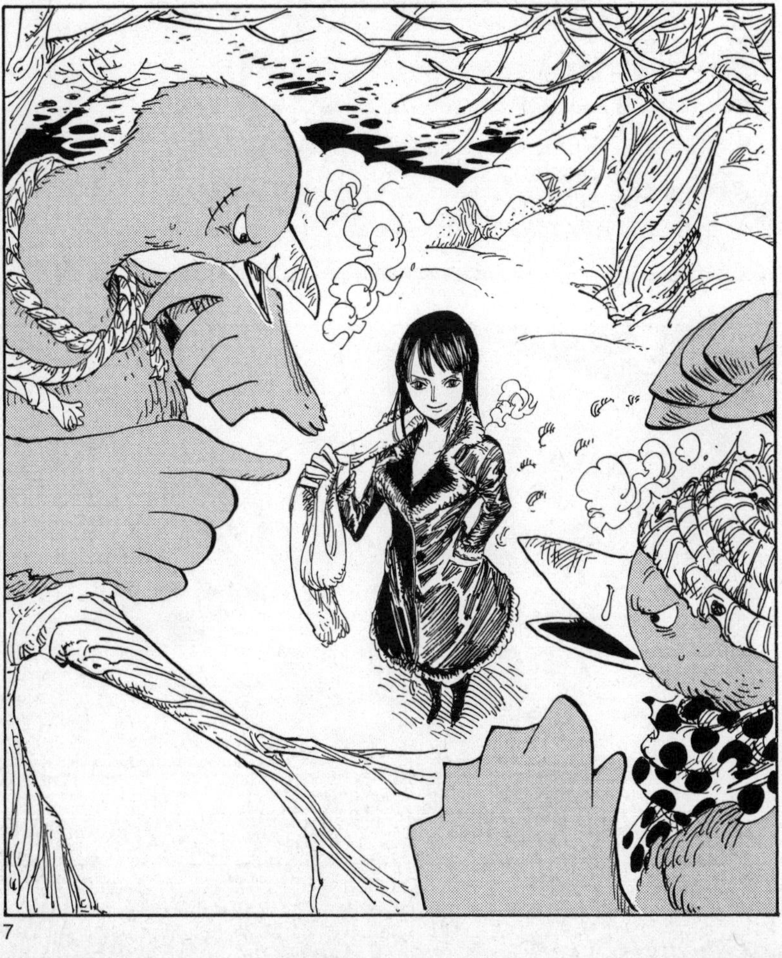

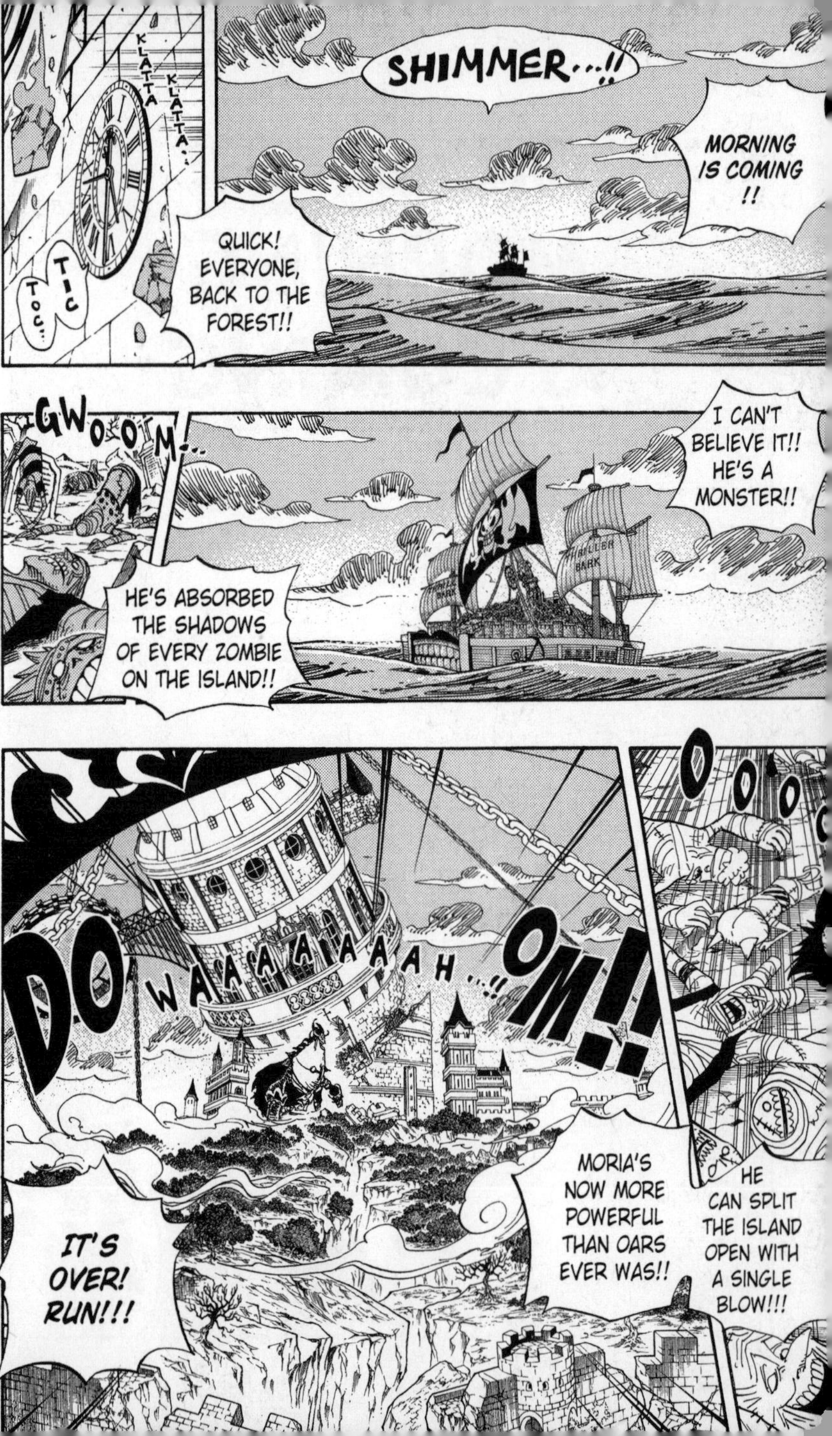

SHIMMER...!!
MORNING IS COMING!!
QUICK! EVERYONE, BACK TO THE FOREST!!
KLATTA KLATTA...
TIC TOC...
I CAN'T BELIEVE IT!! HE'S A MONSTER!!
HE'S ABSORBED THE SHADOWS OF EVERY ZOMBIE ON THE ISLAND!!
THRILLER BARK
GWOOOM...
OOOO
HE CAN SPLIT THE ISLAND OPEN WITH A SINGLE BLOW!!!
MORIA'S NOW MORE POWERFUL THAN OARS EVER WAS!!
DO WAAAAAAAH...!! OM!!
IT'S OVER! RUN!!!

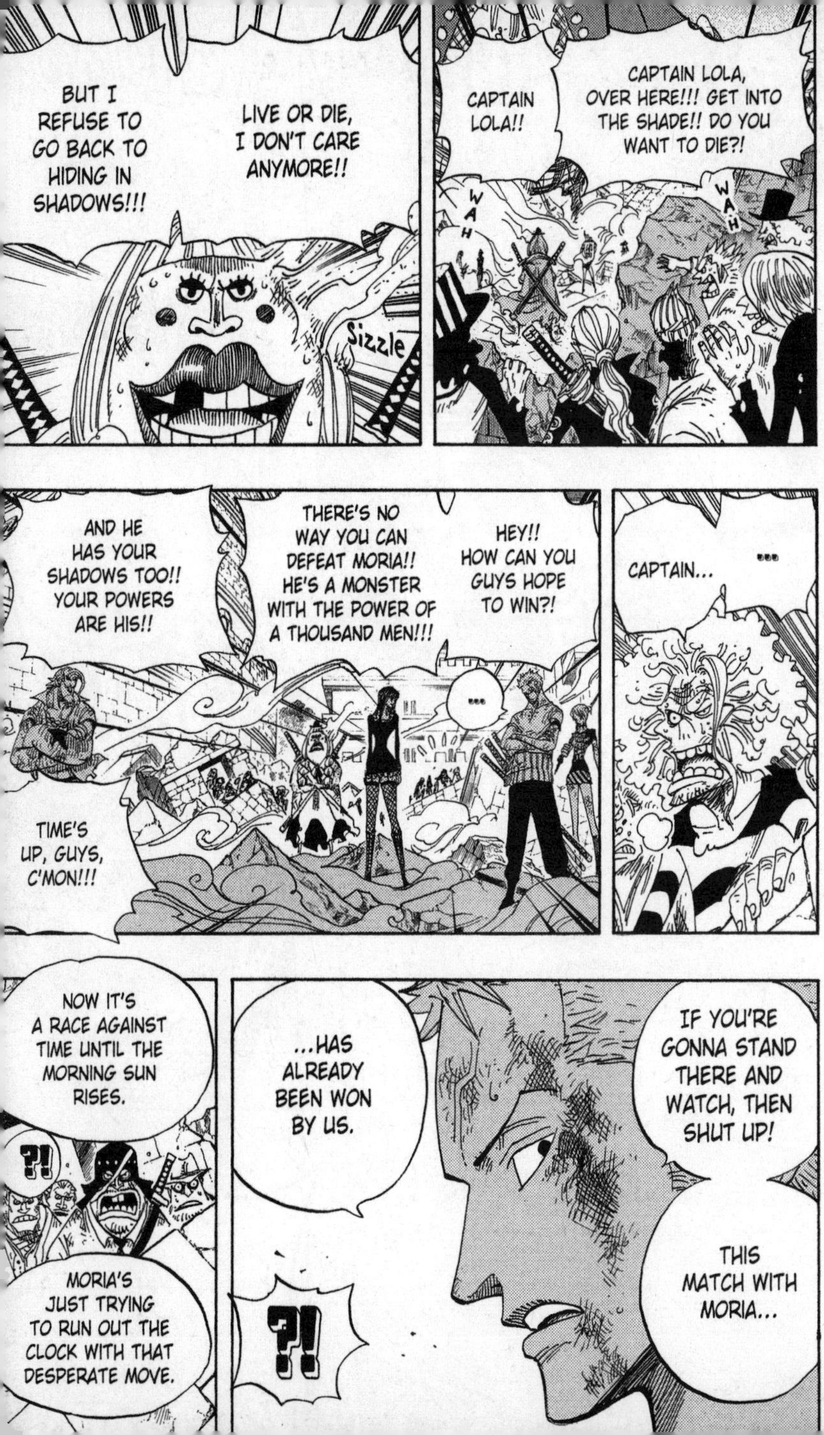
CAPTAIN LOLA, OVER HERE!!! GET INTO THE SHADE!! DO YOU WANT TO DIE?!
CAPTAIN LOLA!!
WAH
WAH
LIVE OR DIE, I DON'T CARE ANYMORE!!
BUT I REFUSE TO GO BACK TO HIDING IN SHADOWS!!!
Sizzle
...
CAPTAIN...
HEY!! HOW CAN YOU GUYS HOPE TO WIN?!
THERE'S NO WAY YOU CAN DEFEAT MORIA!! HE'S A MONSTER WITH THE POWER OF A THOUSAND MEN!!!
AND HE HAS YOUR SHADOWS TOO!! YOUR POWERS ARE HIS!!
...
TIME'S UP, GUYS, C'MON!!!
IF YOU'RE GONNA STAND THERE AND WATCH, THEN SHUT UP!
THIS MATCH WITH MORIA...
...HAS ALREADY BEEN WON BY US.
?!
NOW IT'S A RACE AGAINST TIME UNTIL THE MORNING SUN RISES.
?!
MORIA'S JUST TRYING TO RUN OUT THE CLOCK WITH THAT DESPERATE MOVE.

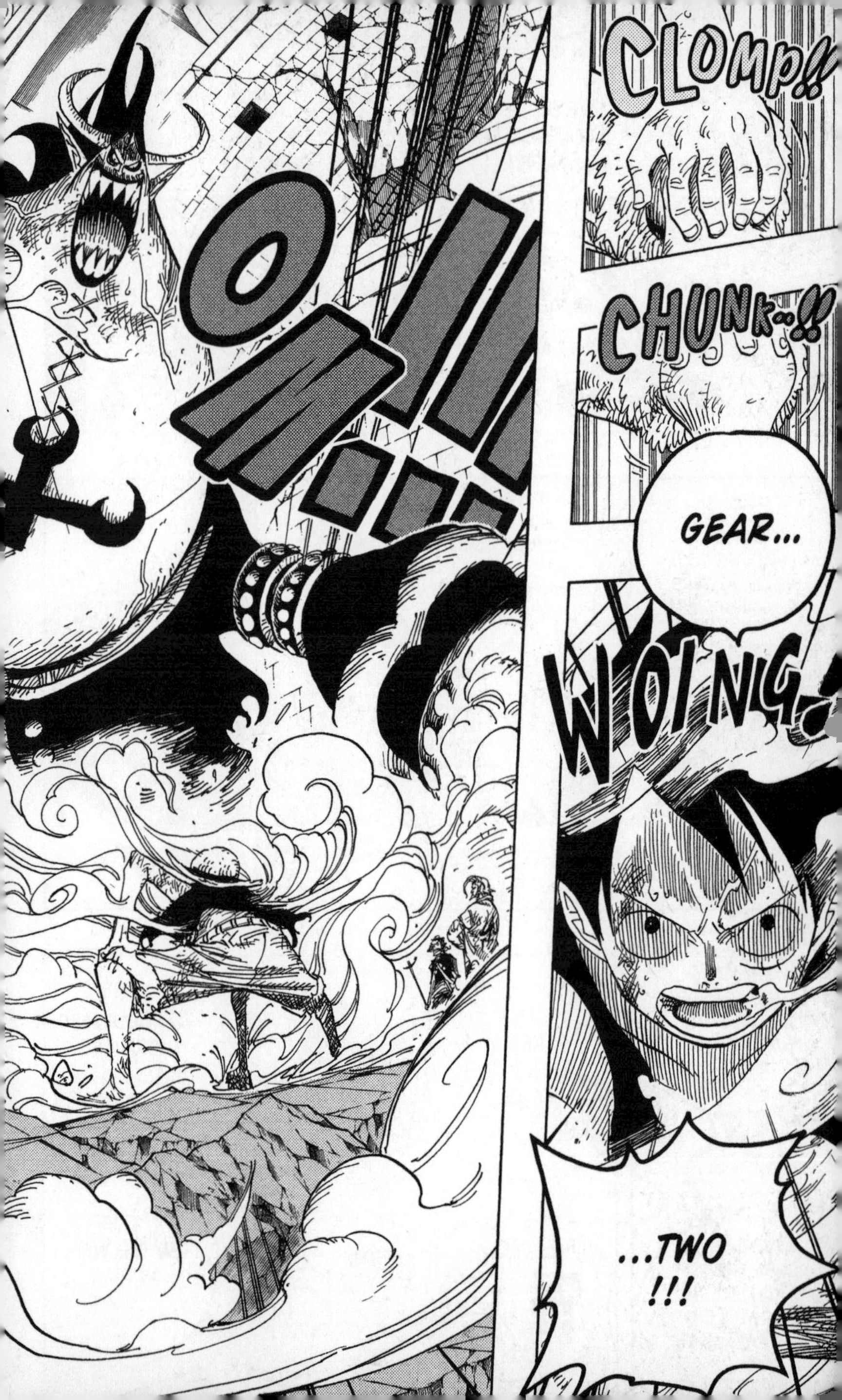
CLOMP!!
CHUNK..!!
GEAR...
WOING..!
...TWO !!!

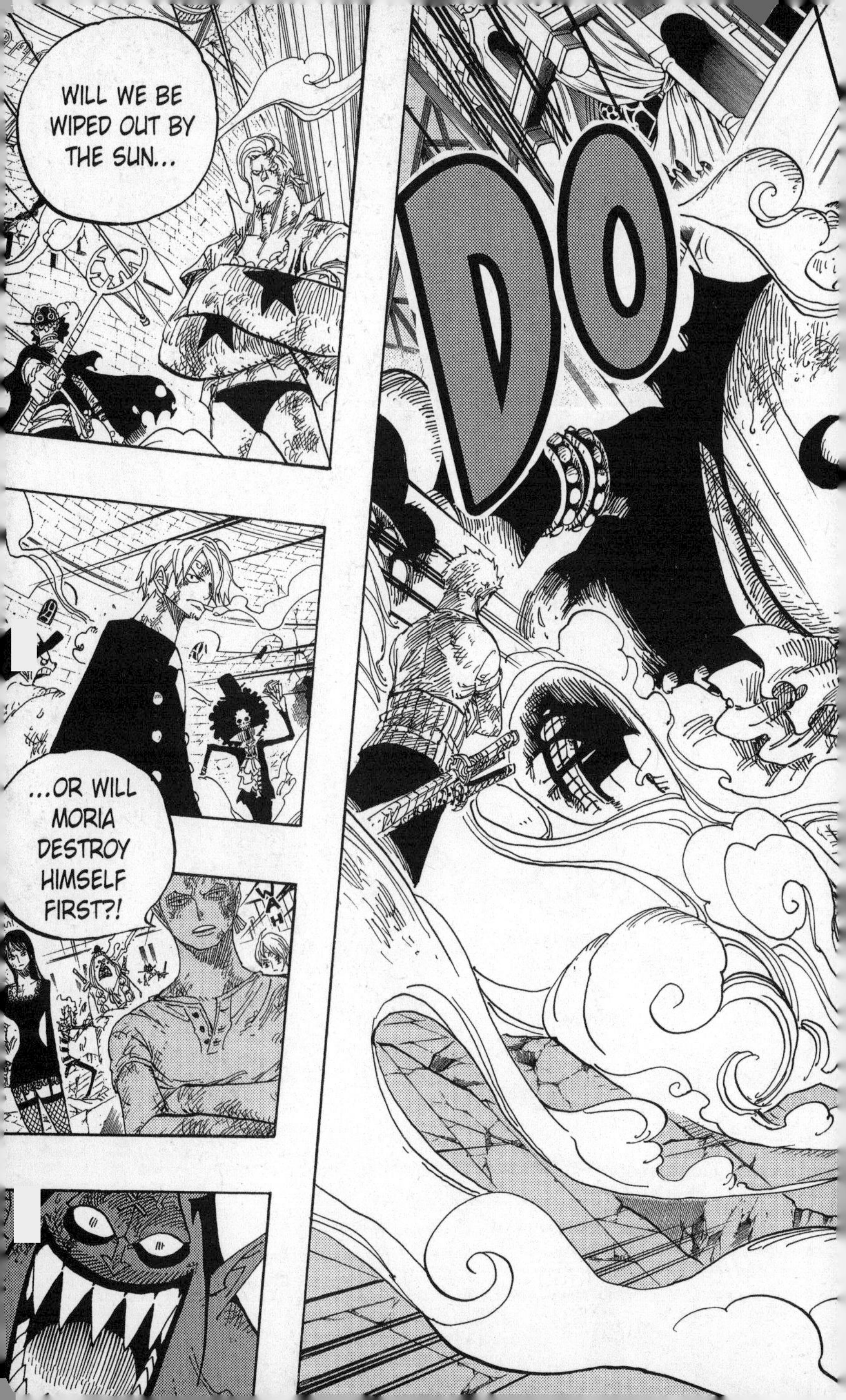
DO
WILL WE BE WIPED OUT BY THE SUN...
...OR WILL MORIA DESTROY HIMSELF FIRST?!

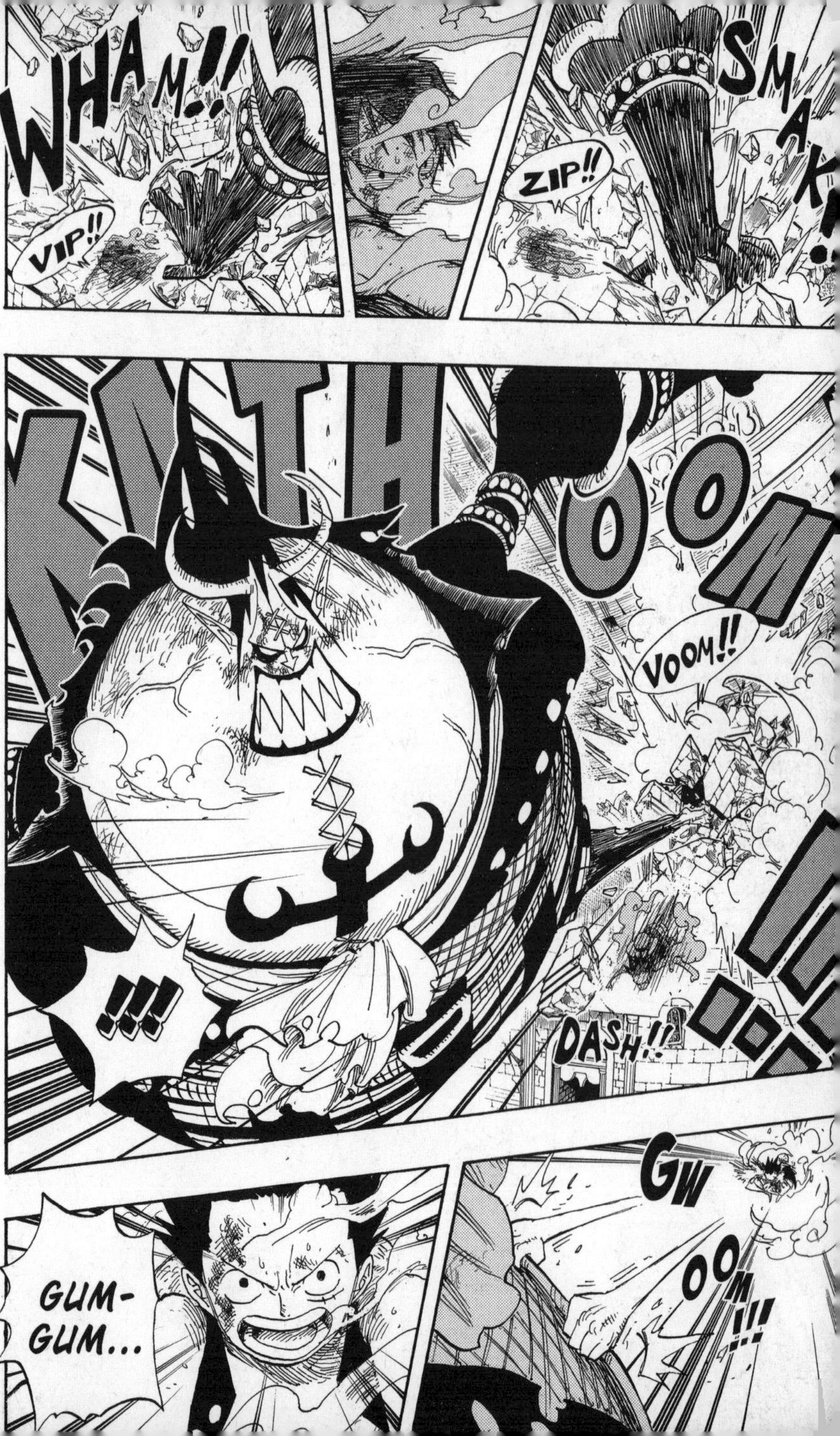
SMAK!!
ZIP!!
WHAM!!
VIP!!
VOOM!!
DASH!!
!!!
GWOOM!!!
GUM-GUM...

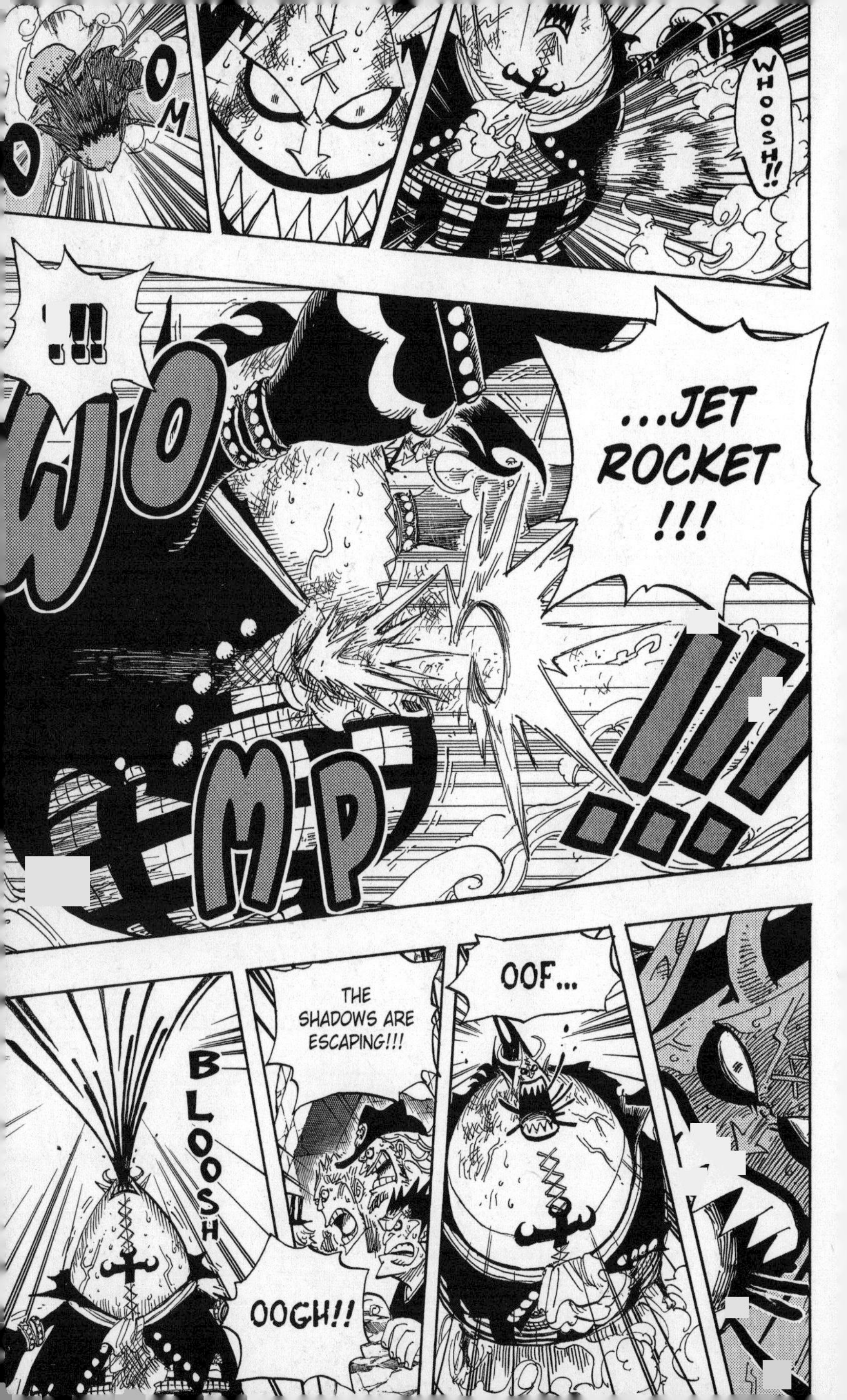
WHOOSH!!
...JET ROCKET!!!
WOMP
OOF...
THE SHADOWS ARE ESCAPING!!!
OOGH!!
BLOOSH

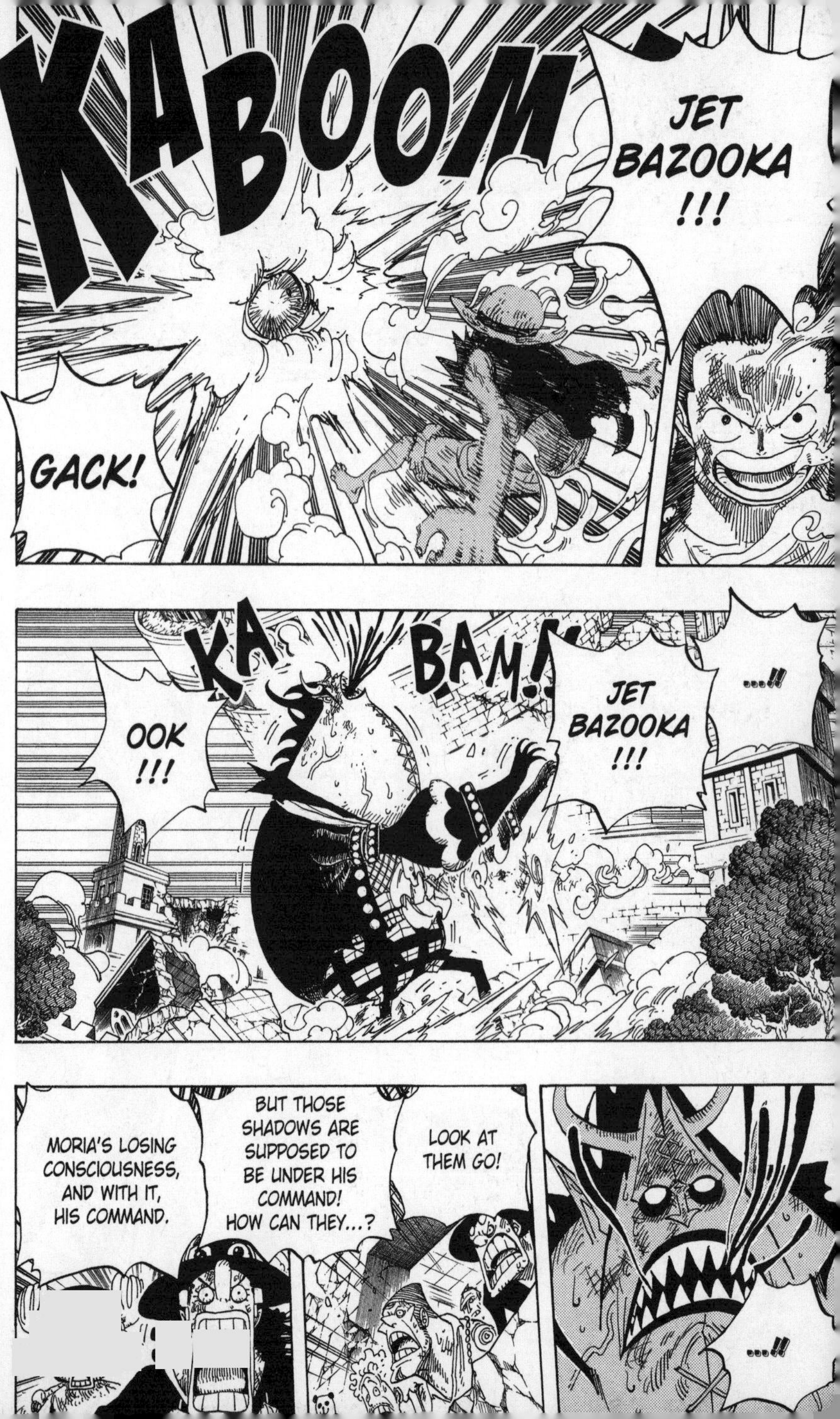
JET BAZOOKA !!!
KABOOM
GACK!
...!!
JET BAZOOKA !!!
KA BAM!!
OOK !!!
...!!
LOOK AT THEM GO!
BUT THOSE SHADOWS ARE SUPPOSED TO BE UNDER HIS COMMAND! HOW CAN THEY...?
MORIA'S LOSING CONSCIOUSNESS, AND WITH IT, HIS COMMAND.

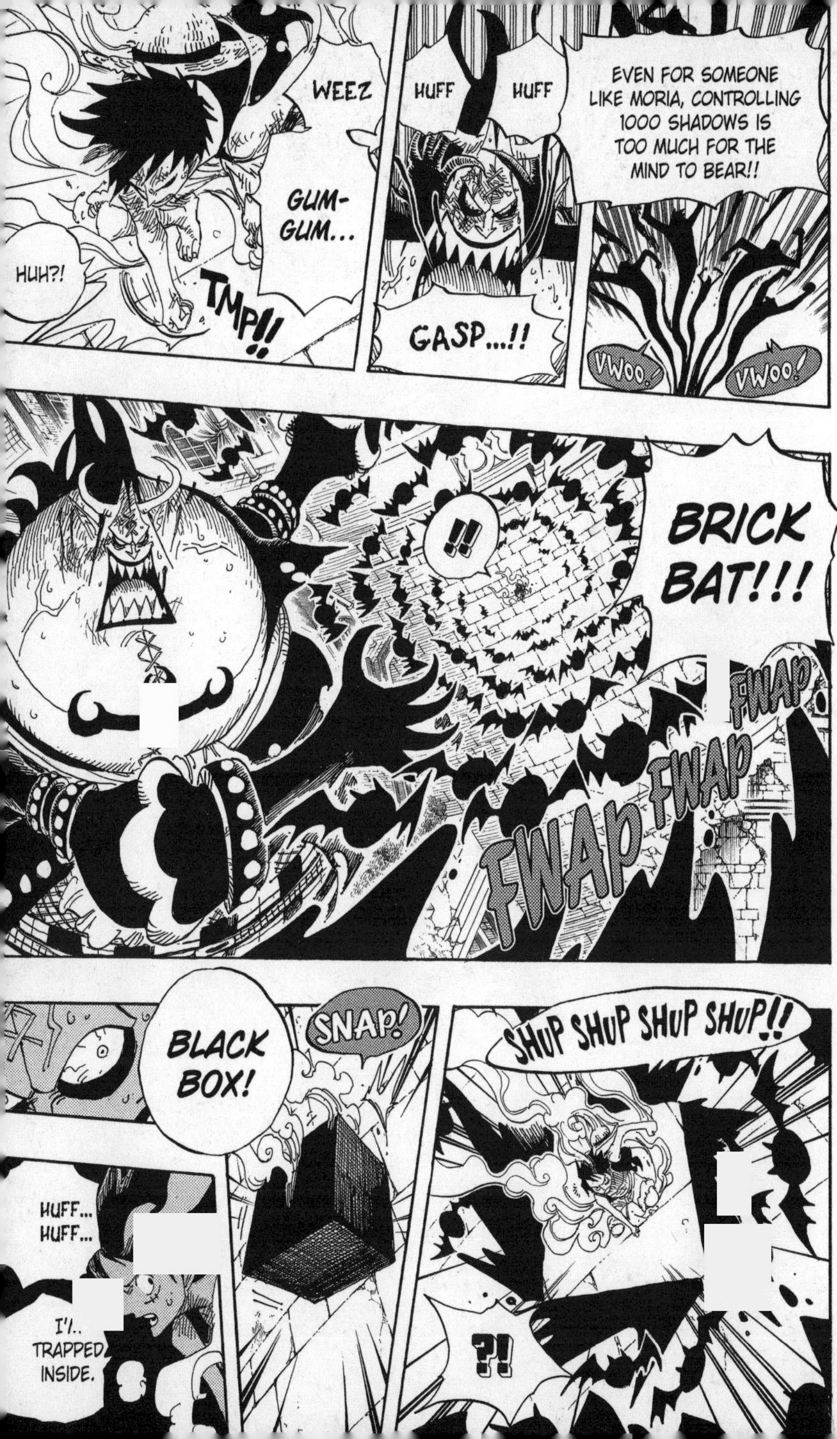
EVEN FOR SOMEONE LIKE MORIA, CONTROLLING 1000 SHADOWS IS TOO MUCH FOR THE MIND TO BEAR!!
VWOO!
VWOO!
HUFF
HUFF
GASP...!!
WEEZ
GUM-GUM...
TMP!!
HUH?!
BRICK BAT!!!
!!
FWAP
FWAP
FWAP
SHUP SHUP SHUP SHUP!!
?!
SNAP!
BLACK BOX!
HUFF... HUFF...
I'.. TRAPPED INSIDE.

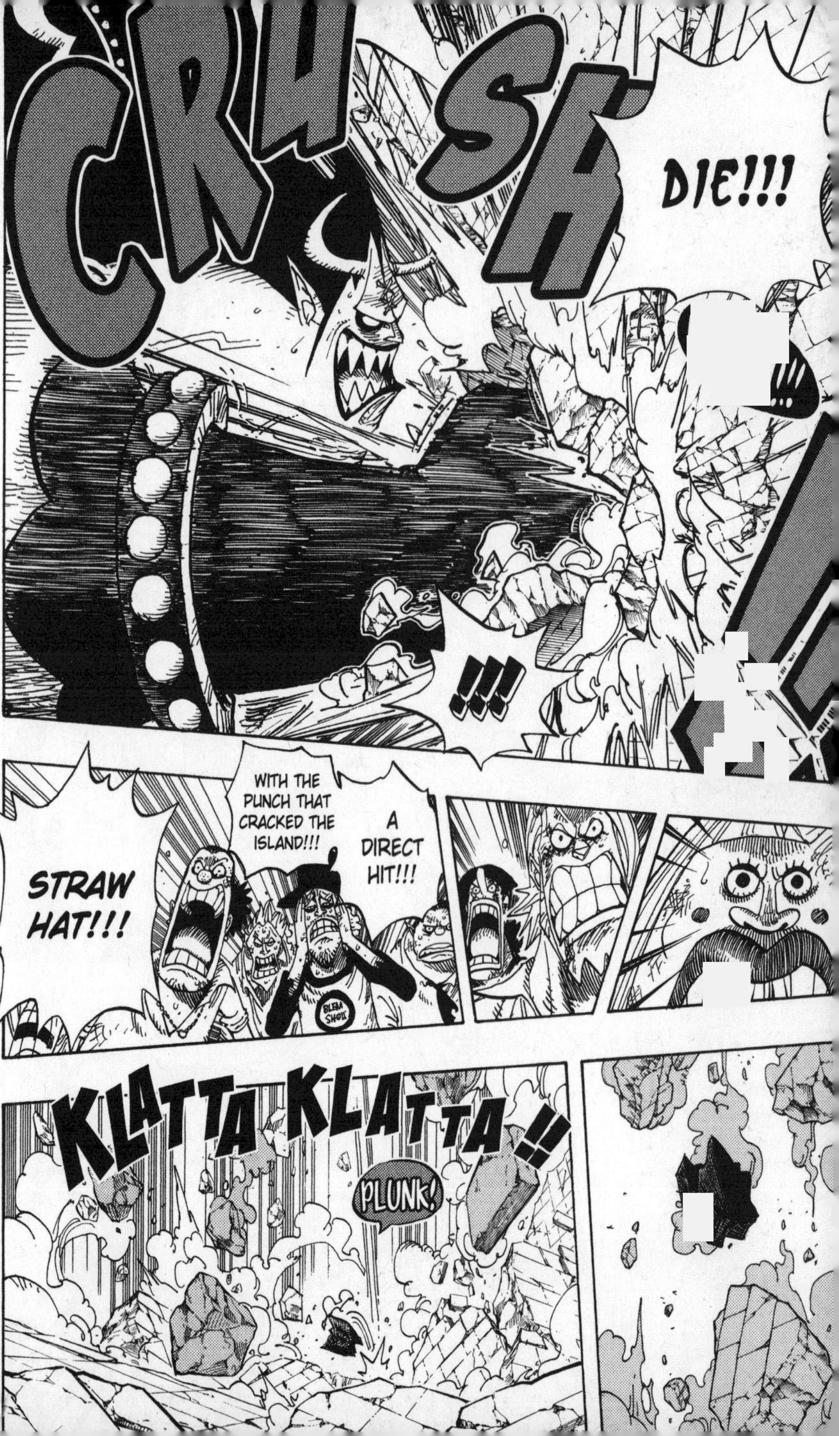
CRUSH
DIE!!!
!!!
A DIRECT HIT!!!
WITH THE PUNCH THAT CRACKED THE ISLAND!!!
STRAW HAT!!!
KLATTA KLATTA!!
PLUNK!

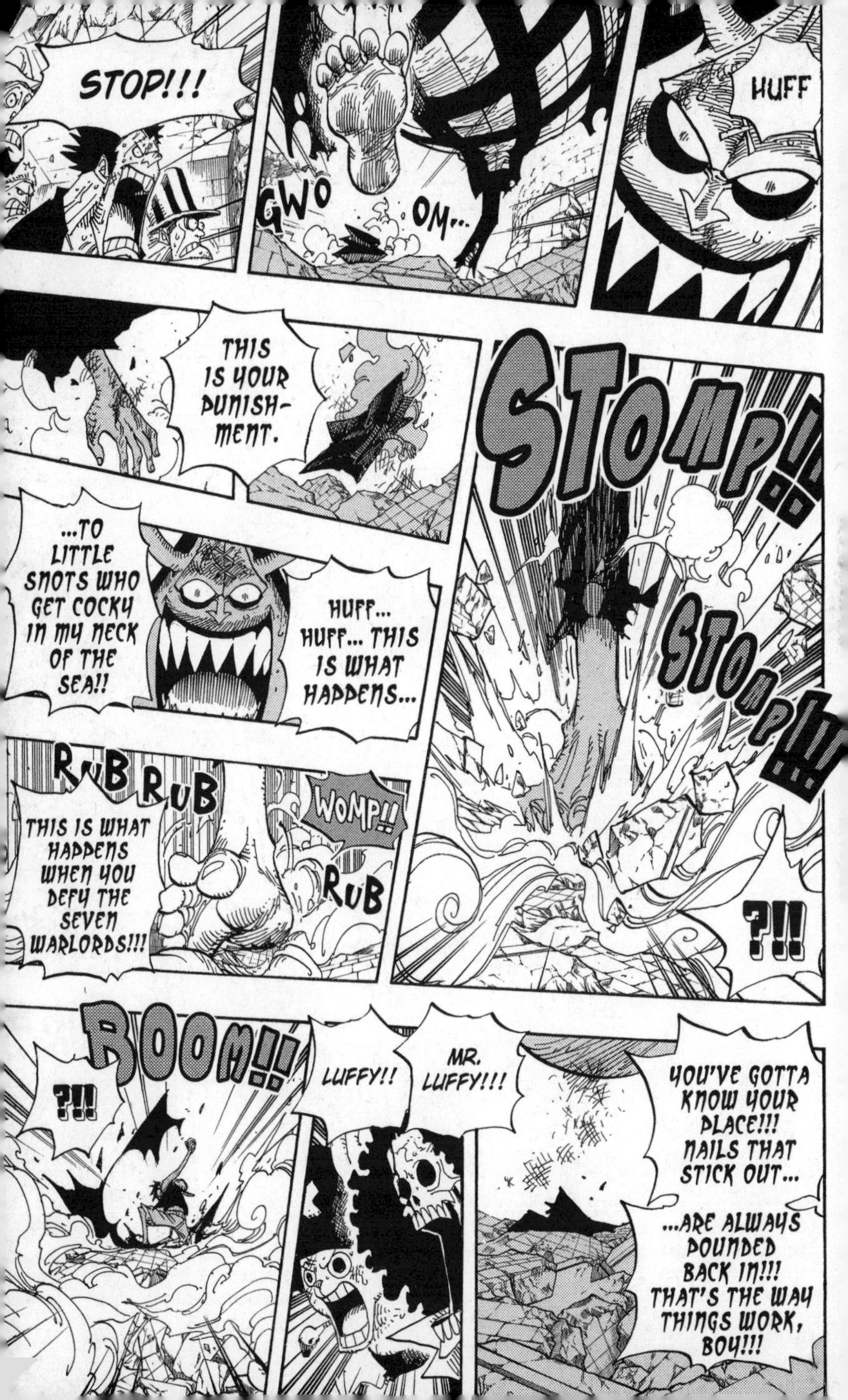
HUFF
GWO OM...
STOP!!!
STOMP!!
STOMP!!!
?!!
THIS IS YOUR PUNISH-MENT.
HUFF... HUFF... THIS IS WHAT HAPPENS...
...TO LITTLE SNOTS WHO GET COCKY IN MY NECK OF THE SEA!!
RUB RUB
WOMP!!
RUB
THIS IS WHAT HAPPENS WHEN YOU DEFY THE SEVEN WARLORDS!!!
YOU'VE GOTTA KNOW YOUR PLACE!!! NAILS THAT STICK OUT...
...ARE ALWAYS POUNDED BACK IN!!! THAT'S THE WAY THINGS WORK, BOY!!!
MR. LUFFY!!!
LUFFY!!
BOOM!!
?!!

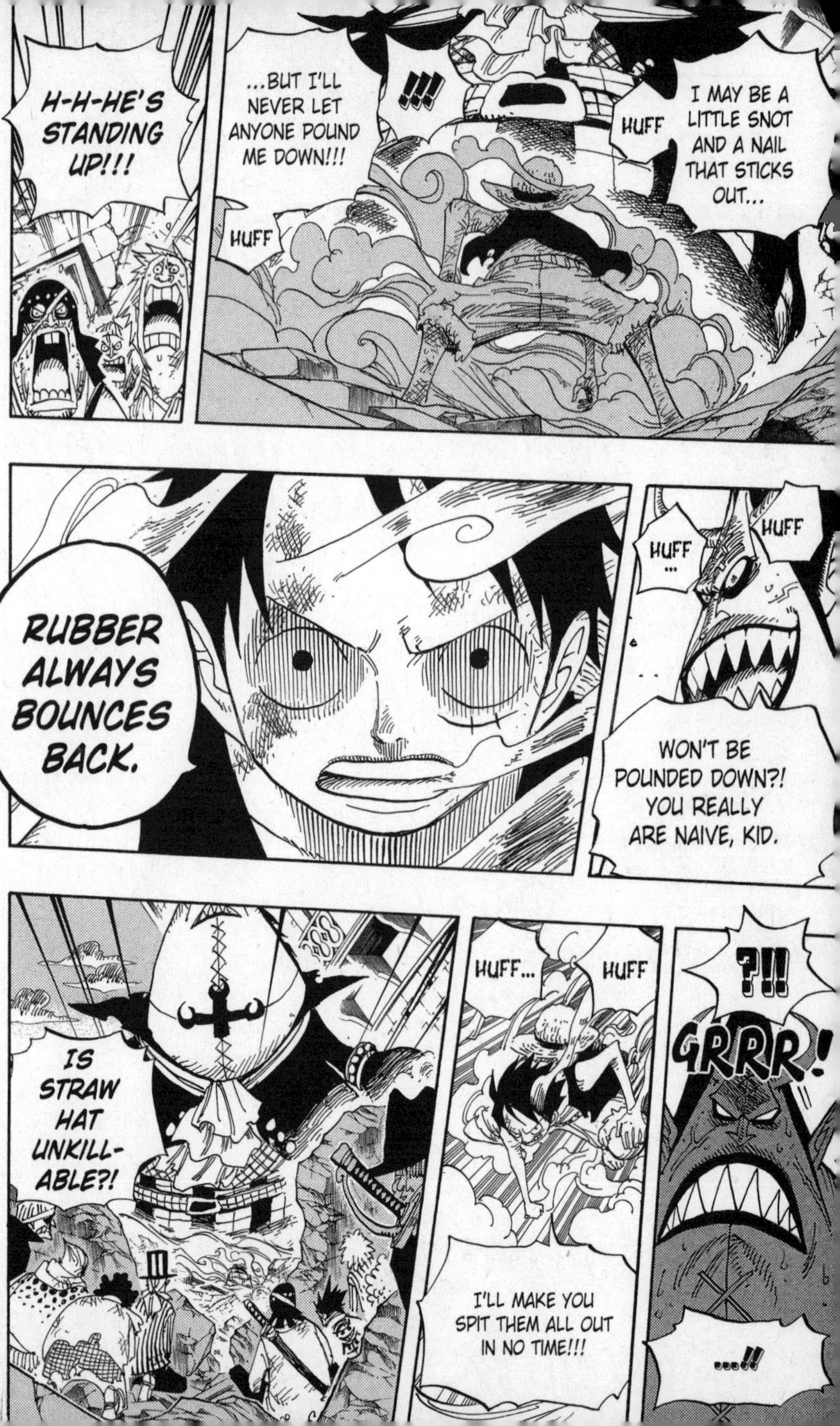
I MAY BE A LITTLE SNOT AND A NAIL THAT STICKS OUT...
HUFF
!!!
...BUT I'LL NEVER LET ANYONE POUND ME DOWN!!!
HUFF
H-H-HE'S STANDING UP!!!
HUFF
HUFF ...
WON'T BE POUNDED DOWN?! YOU REALLY ARE NAIVE, KID.
RUBBER ALWAYS BOUNCES BACK.
?!!
GRRR!
...!!
HUFF
HUFF...
I'LL MAKE YOU SPIT THEM ALL OUT IN NO TIME!!!
IS STRAW HAT UNKILL-ABLE?!

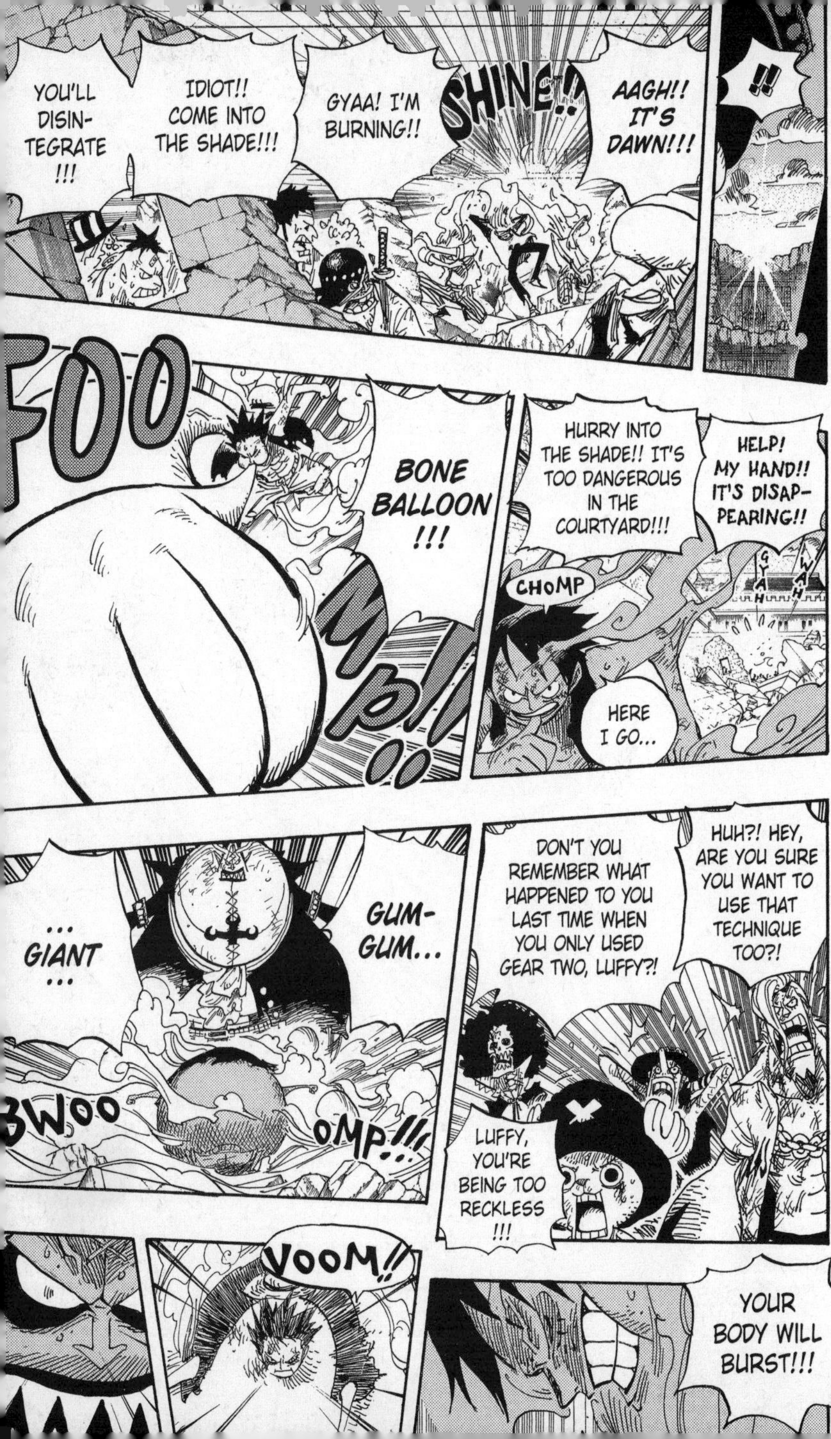
!!
AAGH!! IT'S DAWN!!!
SHINE!!
GYAA! I'M BURNING!!
IDIOT!! COME INTO THE SHADE!!!
YOU'LL DISINTEGRATE!!!
HELP! MY HAND!! IT'S DISAPPEARING!!
HURRY INTO THE SHADE!! IT'S TOO DANGEROUS IN THE COURTYARD!!!
WAAH
GYAAH
CHOMP
HERE I GO...
BONE BALLOON!!!
FOOMP!!
HUH?! HEY, ARE YOU SURE YOU WANT TO USE THAT TECHNIQUE TOO?!
DON'T YOU REMEMBER WHAT HAPPENED TO YOU LAST TIME WHEN YOU ONLY USED GEAR TWO, LUFFY?!
LUFFY, YOU'RE BEING TOO RECKLESS!!!
GUM-GUM...
...GIANT...
BWOOOMP!!!
YOUR BODY WILL BURST!!!
VOOM!!

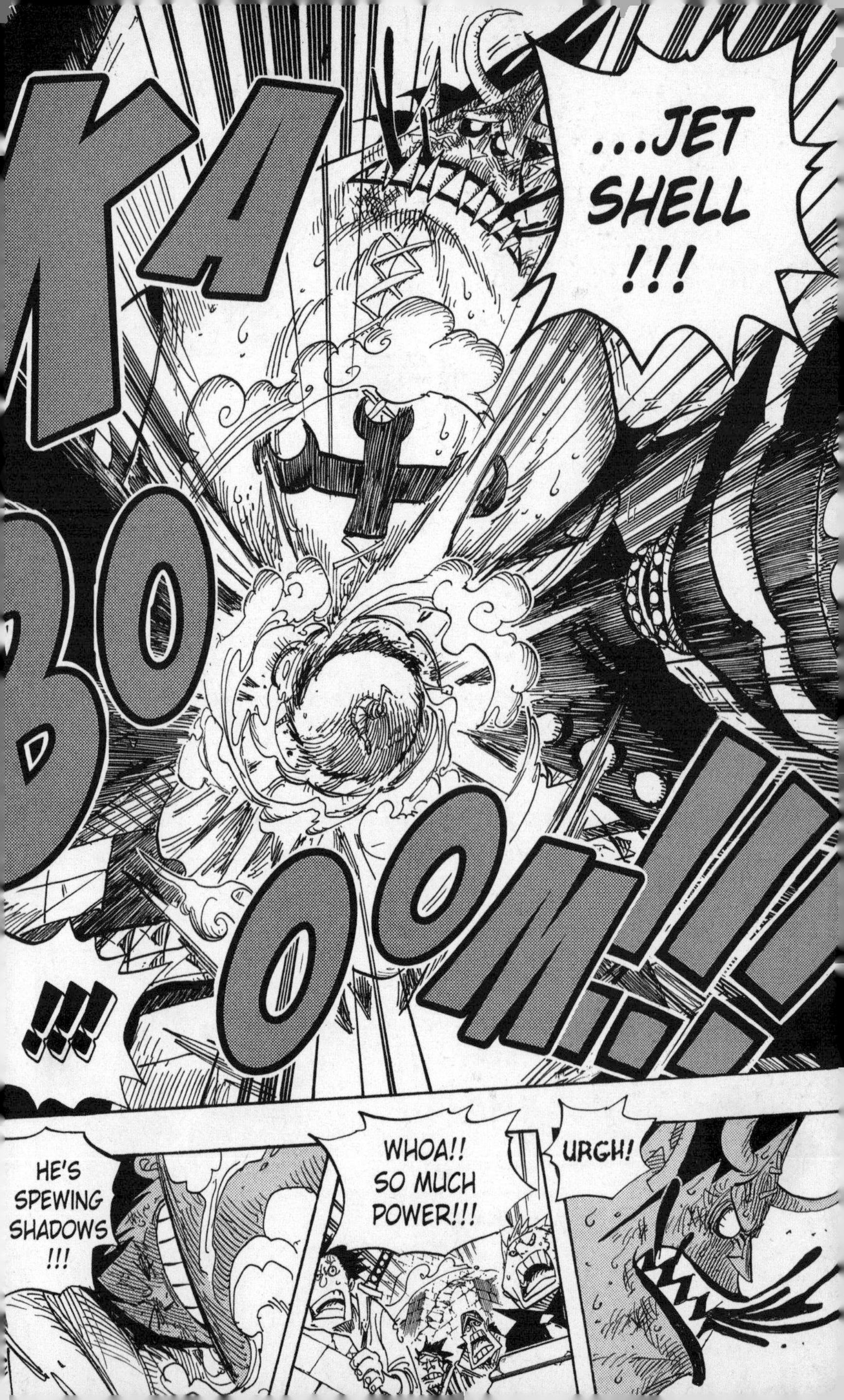
...JET SHELL !!!
KA BOOOOM!!!
URGH!
WHOA!! SO MUCH POWER!!!
HE'S SPEWING SHADOWS !!!

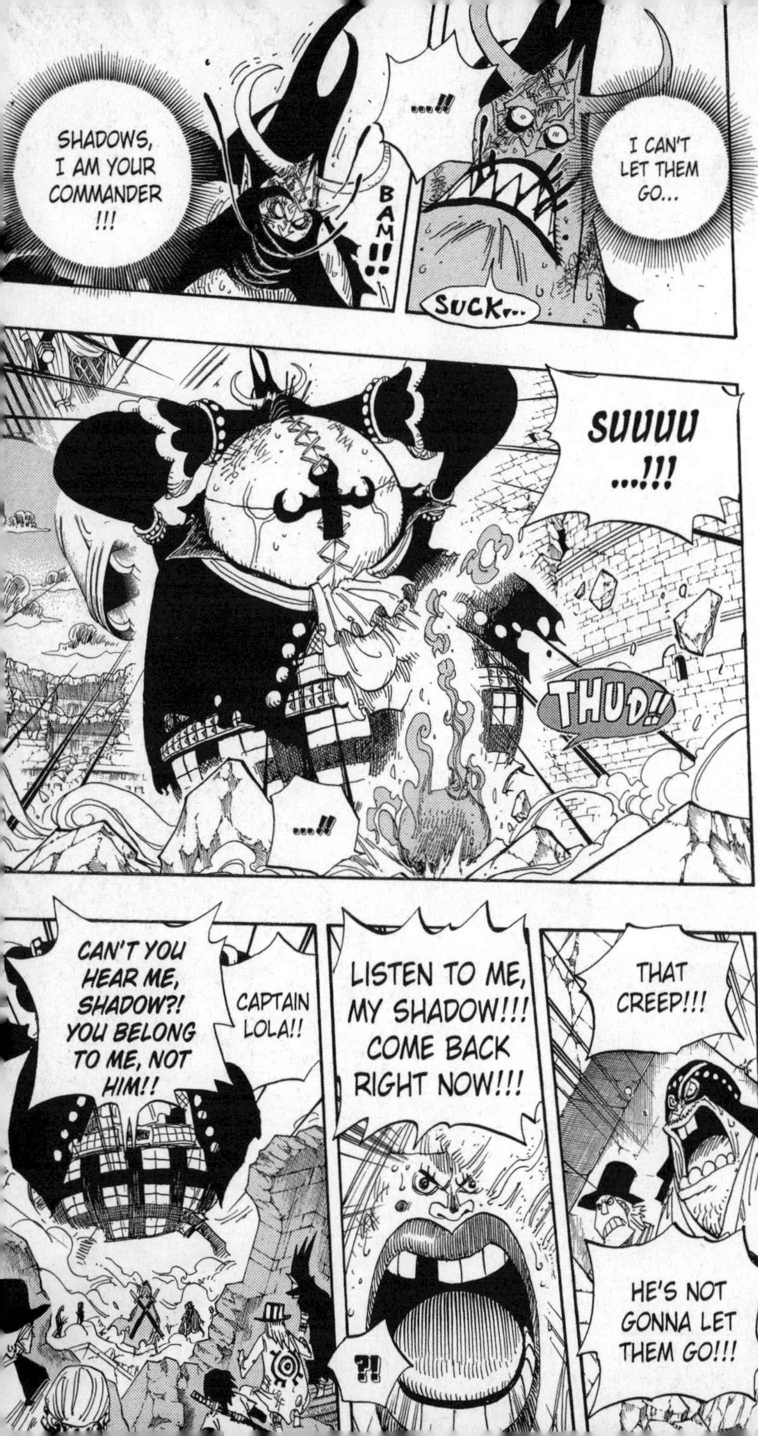
I CAN'T LET THEM GO...
...!!
SUCK...
SHADOWS, I AM YOUR COMMANDER !!!
BAM!!
SUUUU ...!!!
THUD!!
...!!
THAT CREEP!!!
HE'S NOT GONNA LET THEM GO!!!
LISTEN TO ME, MY SHADOW!!! COME BACK RIGHT NOW!!!
?!
CAPTAIN LOLA!!
CAN'T YOU HEAR ME, SHADOW?! YOU BELONG TO ME, NOT HIM!!

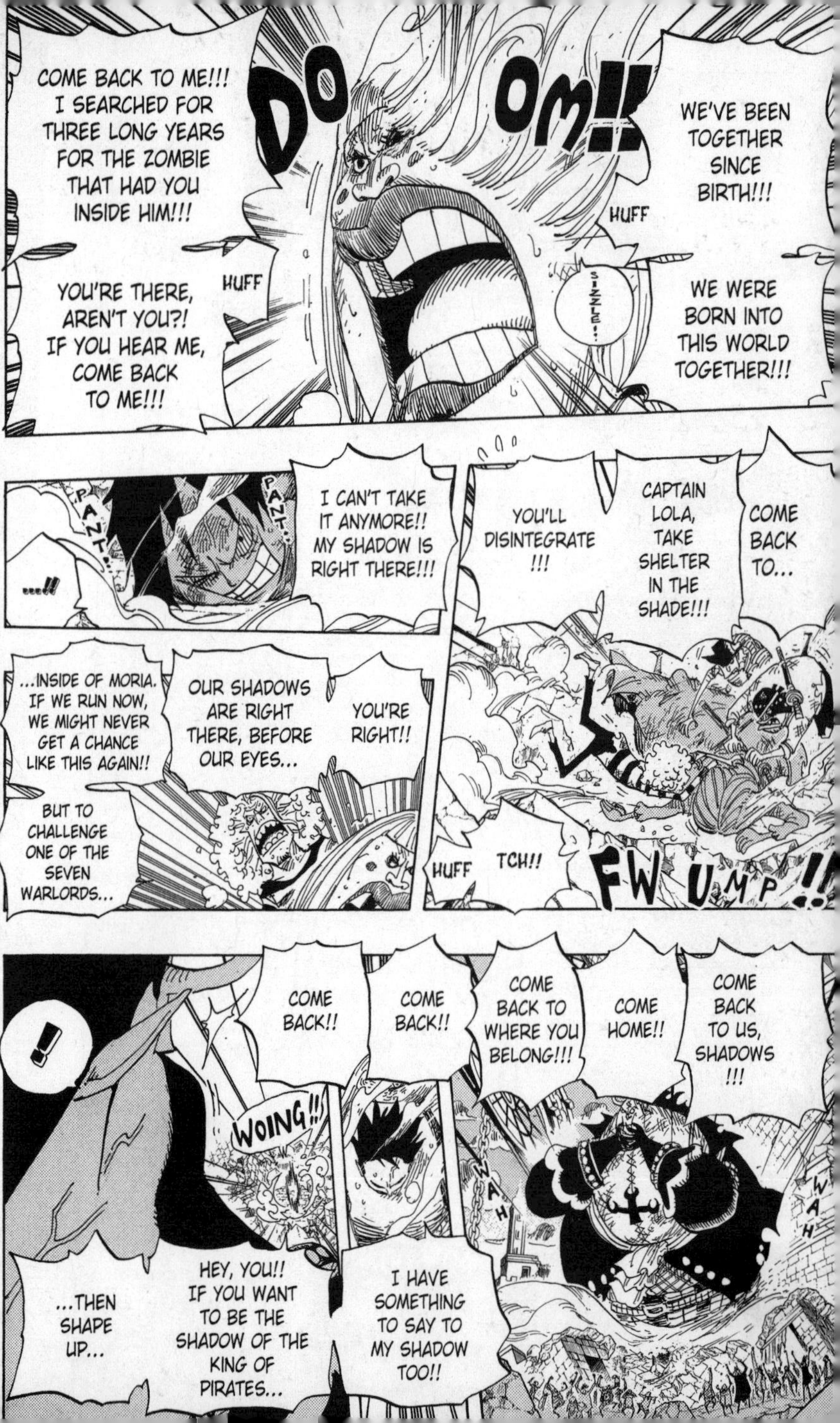
WE'VE BEEN TOGETHER SINCE BIRTH!!!
DOOM!!
HUFF
WE WERE BORN INTO THIS WORLD TOGETHER!!!
SIZZLE...
COME BACK TO ME!!! I SEARCHED FOR THREE LONG YEARS FOR THE ZOMBIE THAT HAD YOU INSIDE HIM!!!
HUFF
YOU'RE THERE, AREN'T YOU?! IF YOU HEAR ME, COME BACK TO ME!!!
COME BACK TO...
CAPTAIN LOLA, TAKE SHELTER IN THE SHADE!!!
YOU'LL DISINTEGRATE!!!
FWUMP!!
TCH!!
HUFF
I CAN'T TAKE IT ANYMORE!! MY SHADOW IS RIGHT THERE!!!
PANT...
PANT...
...!!
YOU'RE RIGHT!!
OUR SHADOWS ARE RIGHT THERE, BEFORE OUR EYES...
...INSIDE OF MORIA. IF WE RUN NOW, WE MIGHT NEVER GET A CHANCE LIKE THIS AGAIN!!
BUT TO CHALLENGE ONE OF THE SEVEN WARLORDS...
COME BACK TO US, SHADOWS!!!
COME HOME!!
COME BACK TO WHERE YOU BELONG!!!
WAH
WAH
COME BACK!!
COME BACK!!
WOING!!
I HAVE SOMETHING TO SAY TO MY SHADOW TOO!!
HEY, YOU!! IF YOU WANT TO BE THE SHADOW OF THE KING OF PIRATES...
!
...THEN SHAPE UP...

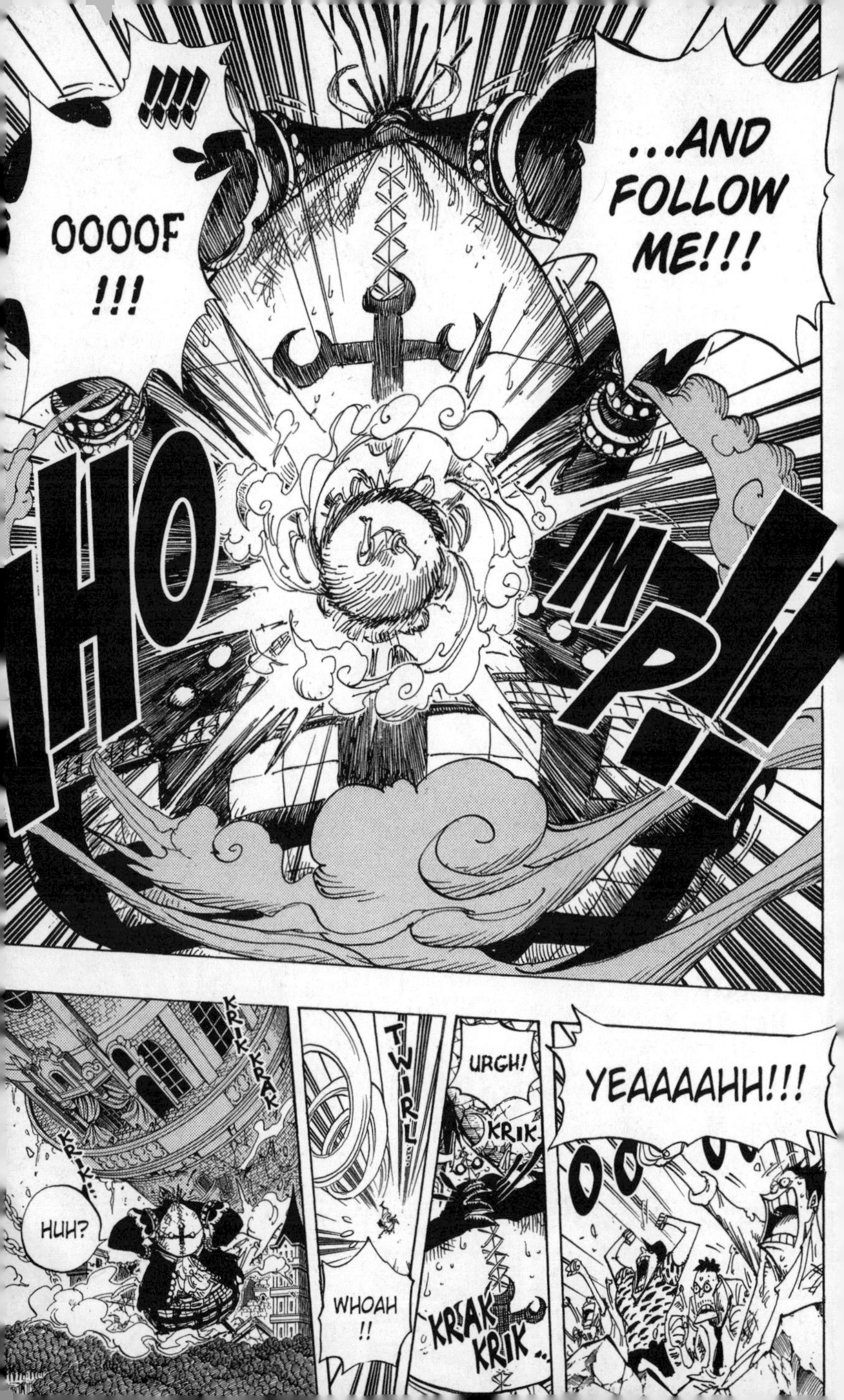
...AND FOLLOW ME!!!
!!!!
OOOOF !!!
WHOMP!!
YEAAAAHH!!!
URGH!
KRIK
KRAK KRIK...
TWIRL
WHOAH !!
KRIK KRAK
KRIK...
HUH?

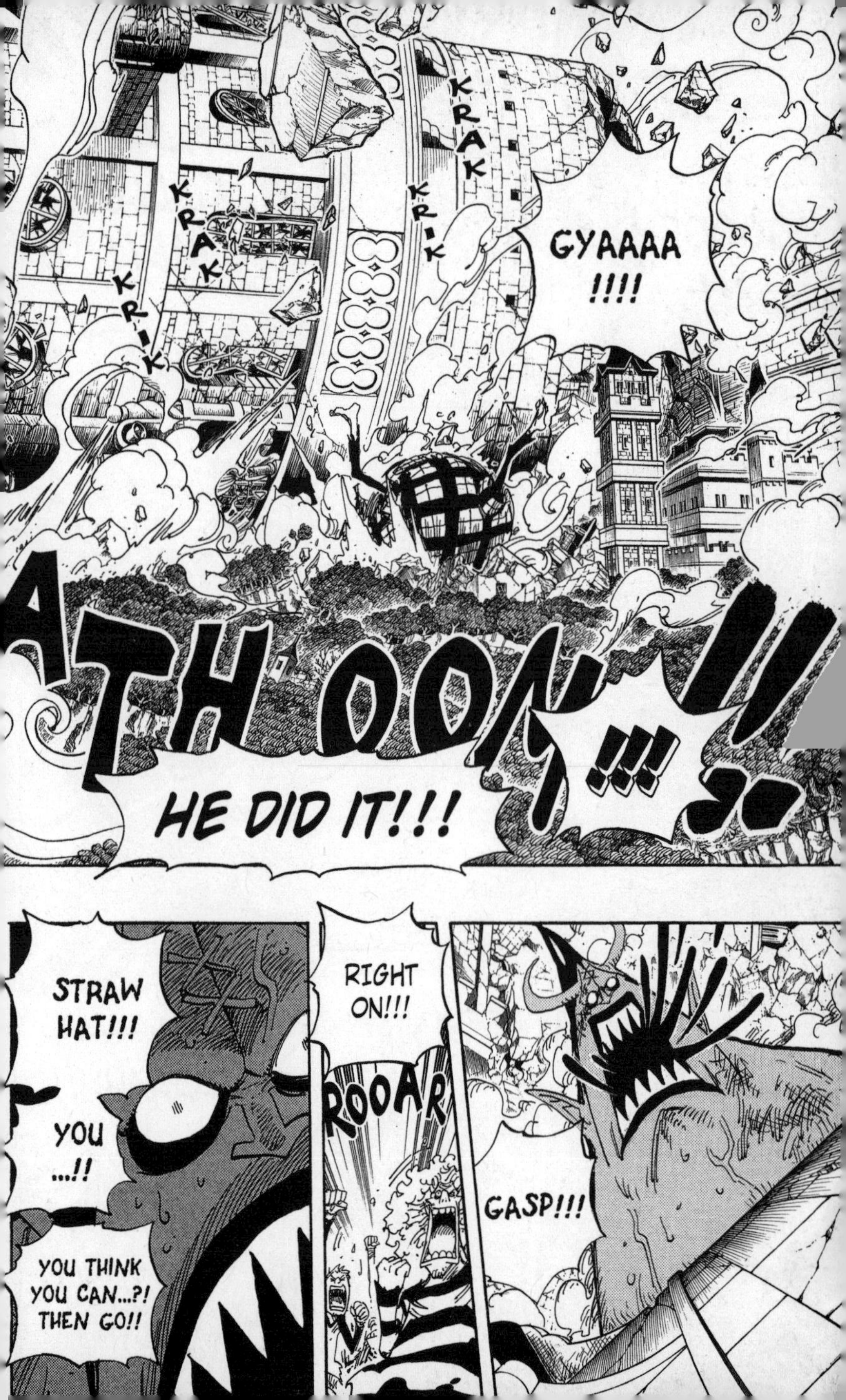
GYAAAA !!!!
KRAK KRIK
KRAK KRIK
ATHOOM!!!
HE DID IT!!!
GASP!!!
RIGHT ON!!!
ROOAR
STRAW HAT!!!
YOU ...!!
YOU THINK YOU CAN...?! THEN GO!!

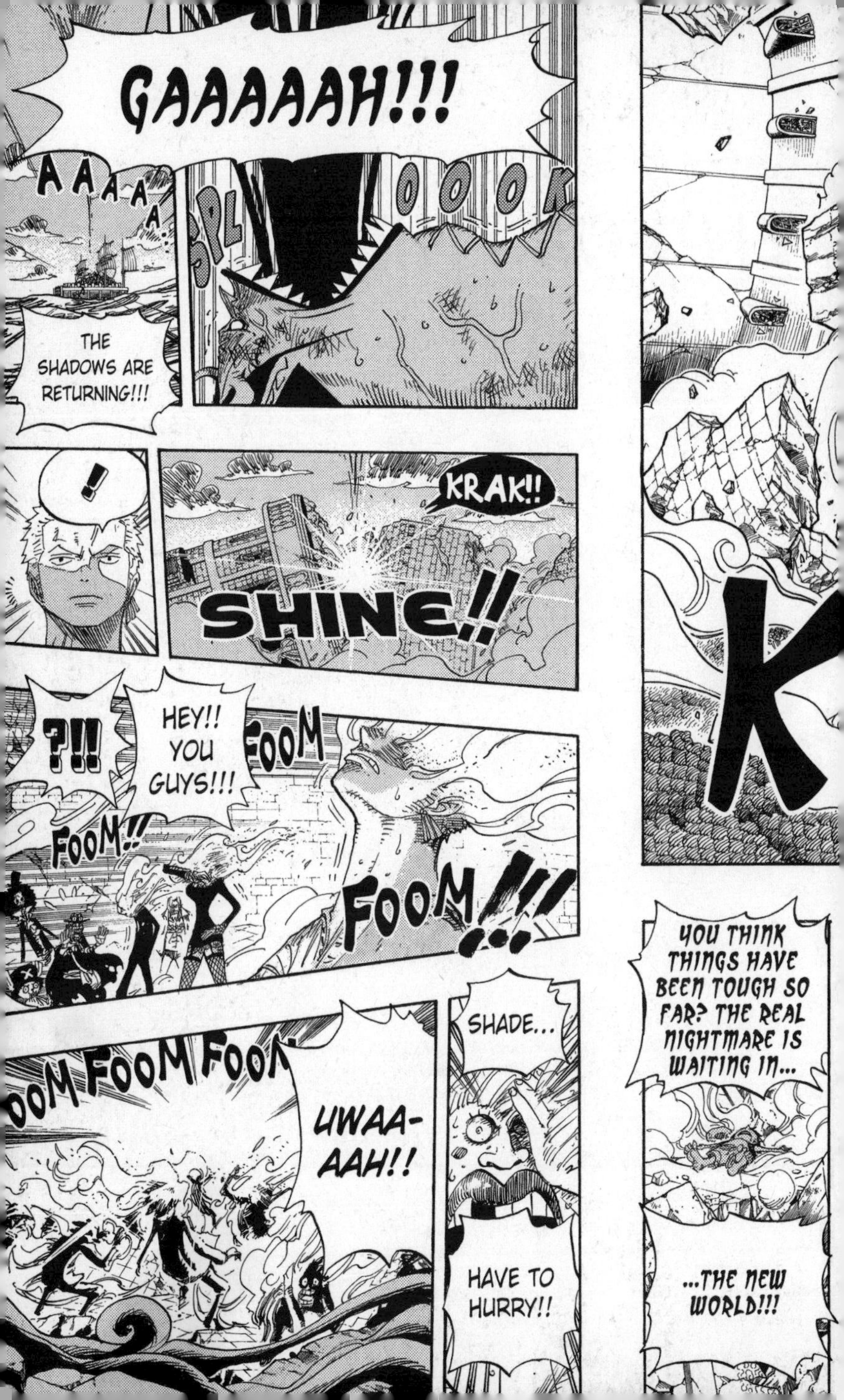
K
YOU THINK THINGS HAVE BEEN TOUGH SO FAR? THE REAL NIGHTMARE IS WAITING IN...
...THE NEW WORLD!!!
GAAAAAH!!!
SPLOOOK
AAAAA
THE SHADOWS ARE RETURNING!!!
KRAK!!
SHINE!!
!
FOOM!!!
FOOM
HEY!! YOU GUYS!!!
?!!
FOOM!!
SHADE...
HAVE TO HURRY!!
FOOM FOOM FOOM
UWAA-AAH!!

END OF THE DREAM

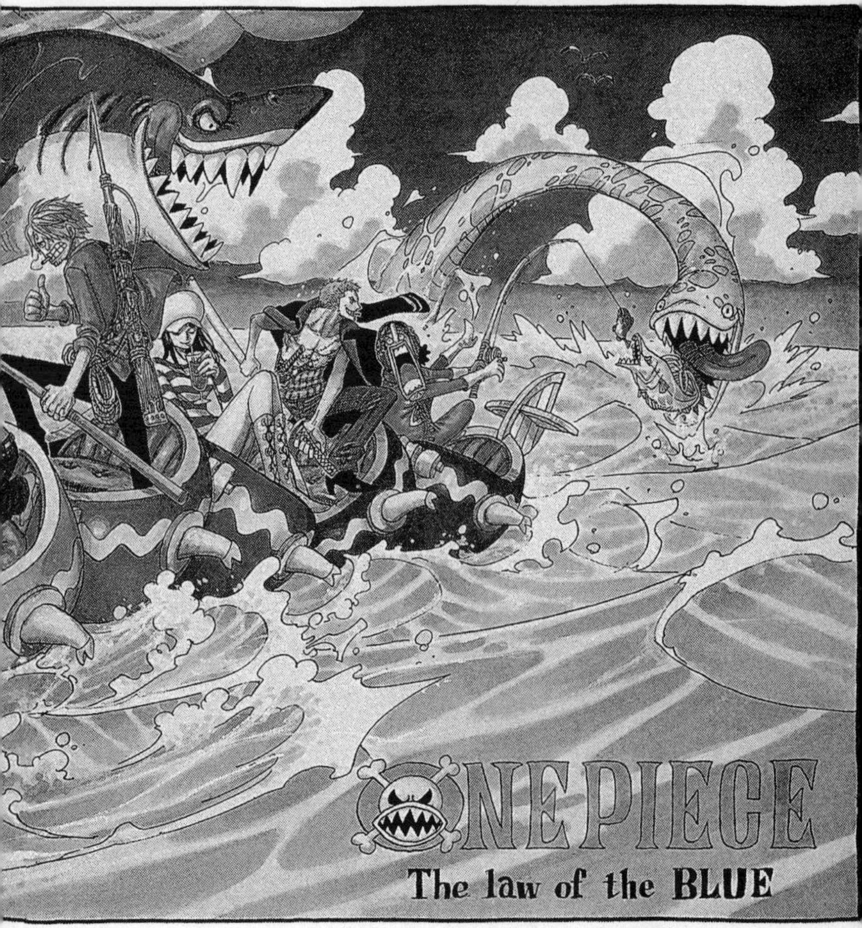
ONE PIECE
The law of the BLUE

Chapter 483: THE

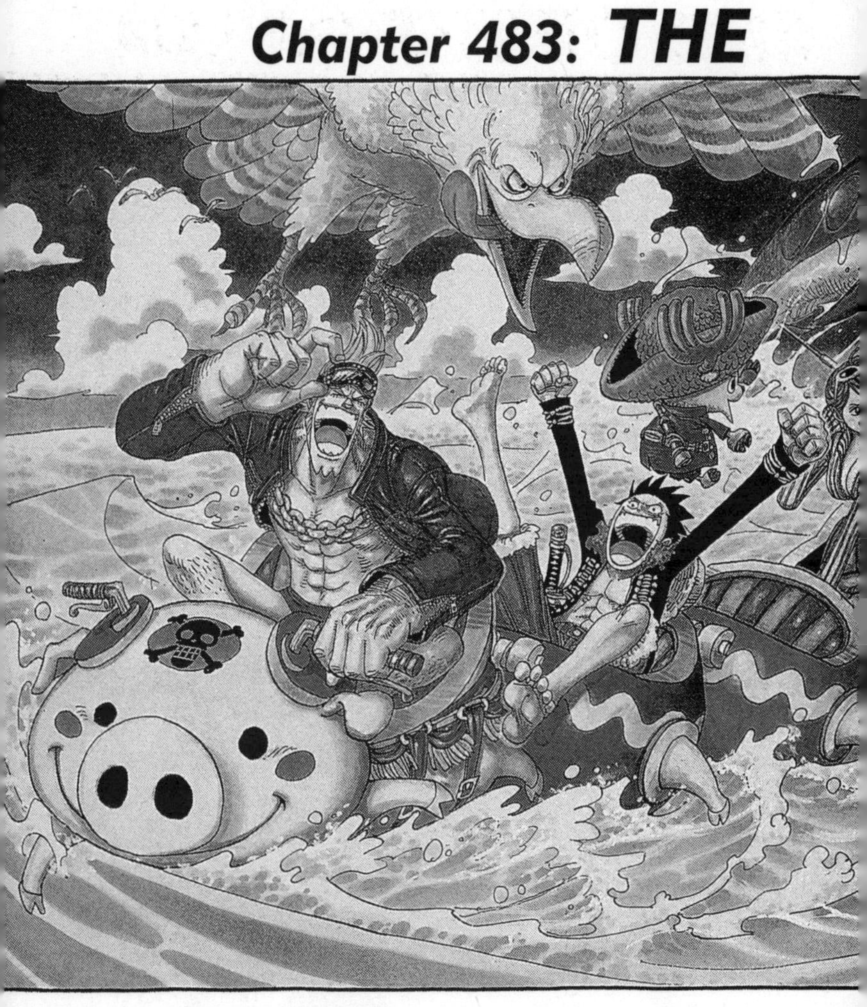

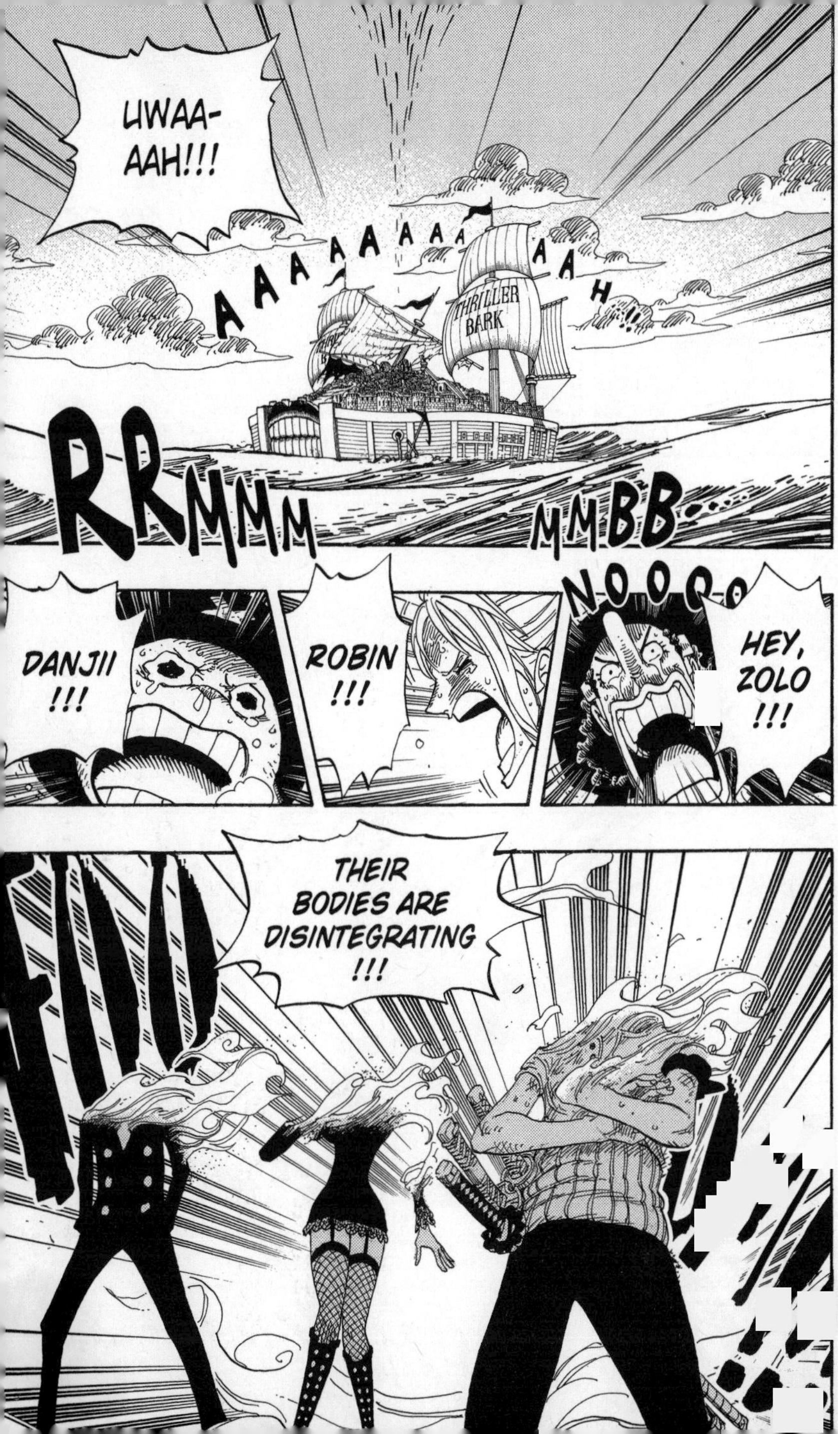

UWAAA-AAH!!!
AAAAAAAAAAH!!
RRMMMM MMBB...
NOOOO
HEY, ZOLO!!!
ROBIN!!!
DANJII!!!
THEIR BODIES ARE DISINTEGRATING!!!

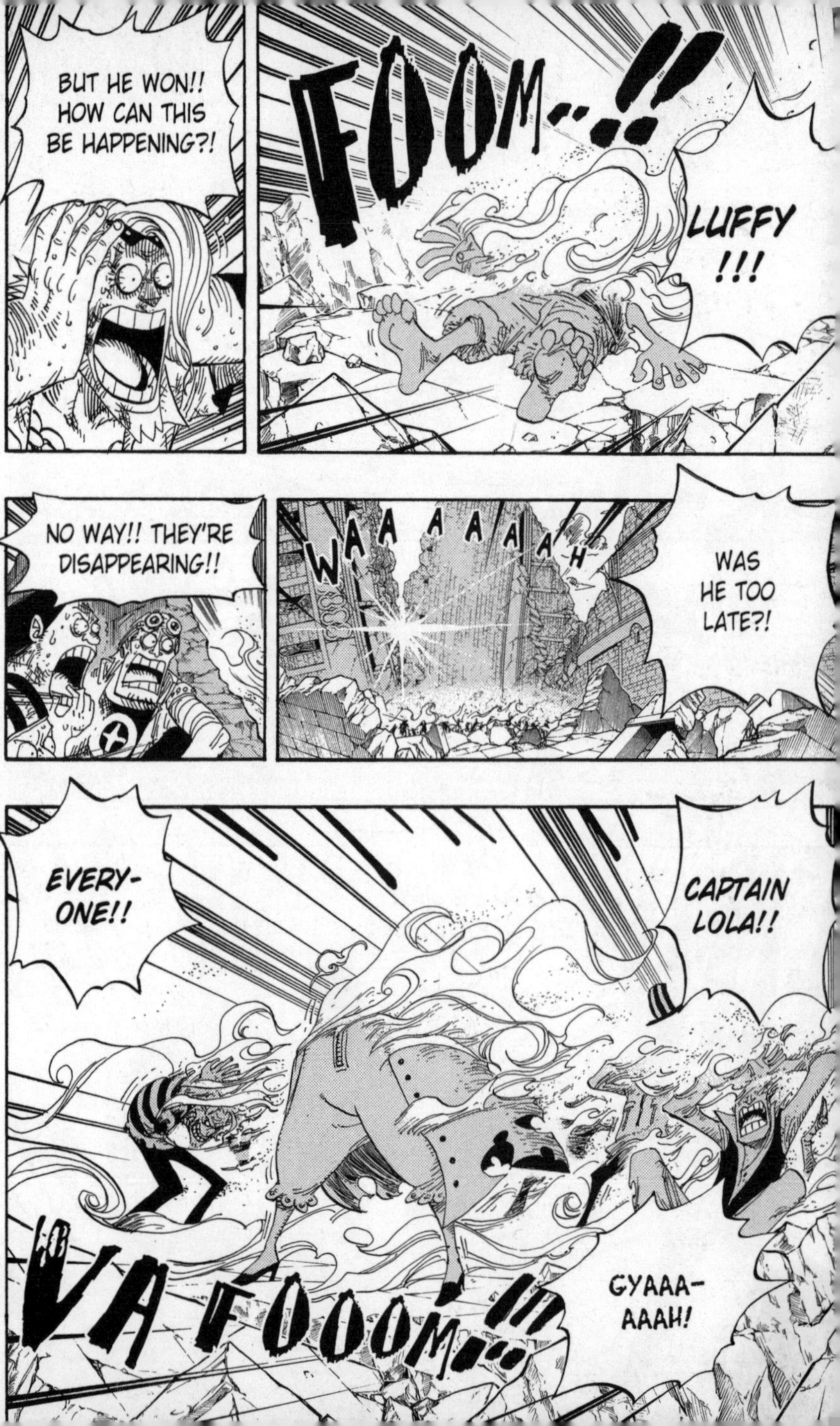
FOOM..!!
LUFFY !!!
BUT HE WON!! HOW CAN THIS BE HAPPENING?!
WAS HE TOO LATE?!
WAAAAAAH
NO WAY!! THEY'RE DISAPPEARING!!
CAPTAIN LOLA!!
EVERY-ONE!!
GYAAA-AAAH!
VA FOOOM..!!

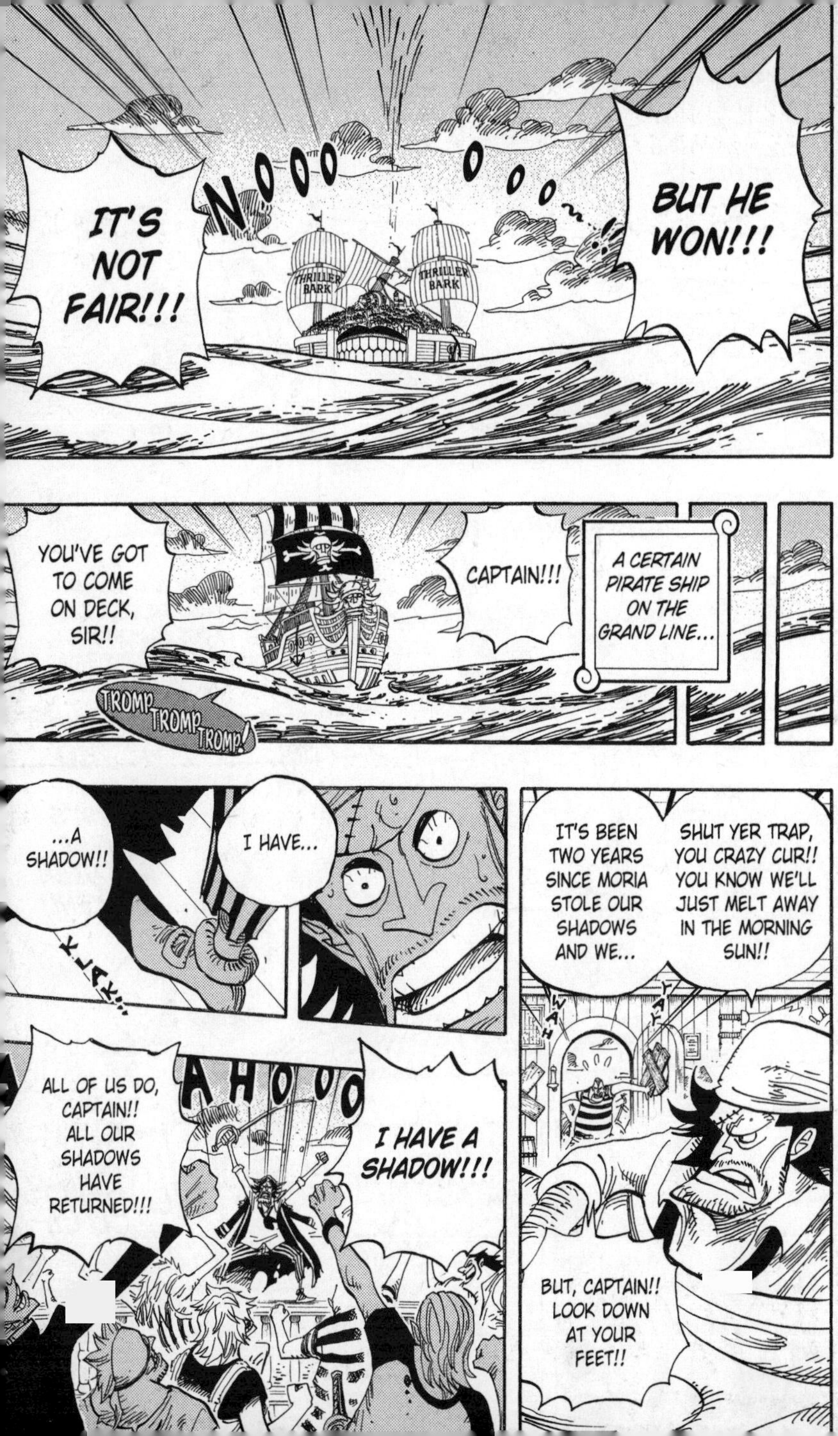
BUT HE WON!!!
NOOOOOOO
IT'S NOT FAIR!!!
A CERTAIN PIRATE SHIP ON THE GRAND LINE...
CAPTAIN!!!
YOU'VE GOT TO COME ON DECK, SIR!!
TROMP TROMP TROMP
SHUT YER TRAP, YOU CRAZY CUR!! YOU KNOW WE'LL JUST MELT AWAY IN THE MORNING SUN!!
IT'S BEEN TWO YEARS SINCE MORIA STOLE OUR SHADOWS AND WE...
BUT, CAPTAIN!! LOOK DOWN AT YOUR FEET!!
I HAVE...
...A SHADOW!!
KLAK
I HAVE A SHADOW!!!
AHOOO
ALL OF US DO, CAPTAIN!! ALL OUR SHADOWS HAVE RETURNED!!!

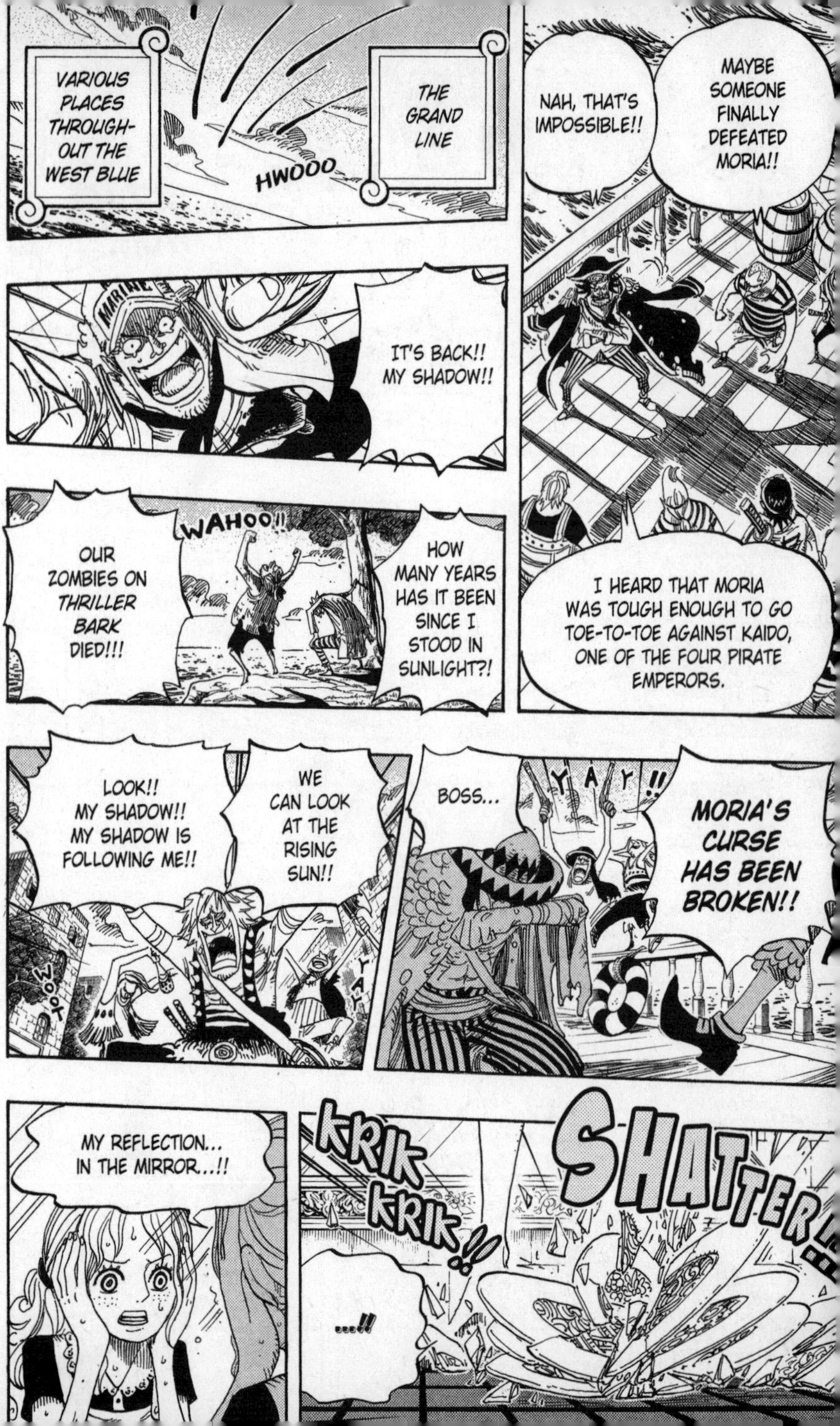
MAYBE SOMEONE FINALLY DEFEATED MORIA!!
NAH, THAT'S IMPOSSIBLE!!
I HEARD THAT MORIA WAS TOUGH ENOUGH TO GO TOE-TO-TOE AGAINST KAIDO, ONE OF THE FOUR PIRATE EMPERORS.
THE GRAND LINE
VARIOUS PLACES THROUGH-OUT THE WEST BLUE
HWOOO
IT'S BACK!! MY SHADOW!!
HOW MANY YEARS HAS IT BEEN SINCE I STOOD IN SUNLIGHT?!
WAHOO!!
OUR ZOMBIES ON THRILLER BARK DIED!!!
MORIA'S CURSE HAS BEEN BROKEN!!
YAY!!
BOSS...
WE CAN LOOK AT THE RISING SUN!!
LOOK!! MY SHADOW!! MY SHADOW IS FOLLOWING ME!!
YAY
WOOT
SHATTER!!
KRIK KRIK!!
...!!
MY REFLECTION... IN THE MIRROR...!!

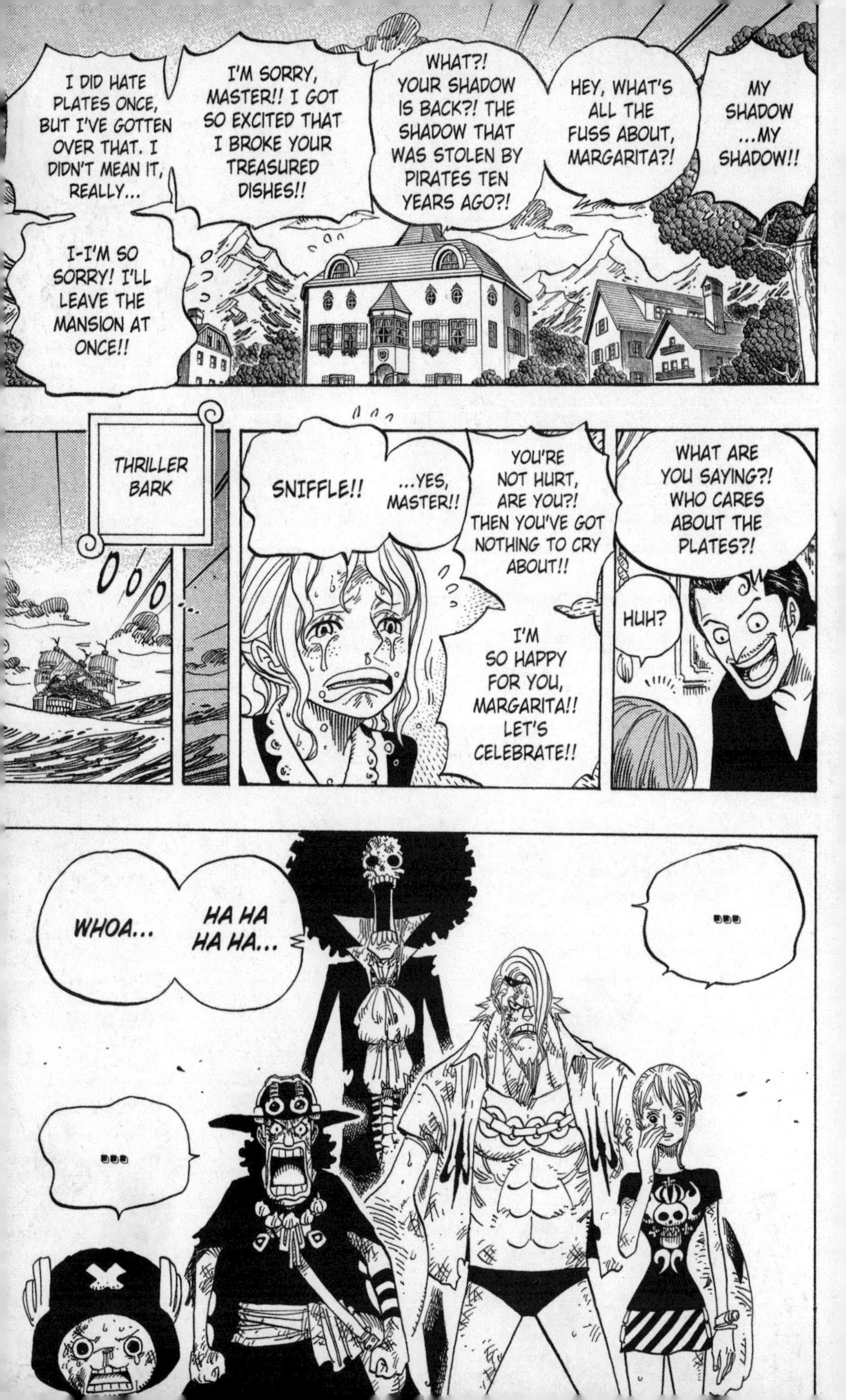
MY SHADOW ...MY SHADOW!!
HEY, WHAT'S ALL THE FUSS ABOUT, MARGARITA?!
WHAT?! YOUR SHADOW IS BACK?! THE SHADOW THAT WAS STOLEN BY PIRATES TEN YEARS AGO?!
I'M SORRY, MASTER!! I GOT SO EXCITED THAT I BROKE YOUR TREASURED DISHES!!
I DID HATE PLATES ONCE, BUT I'VE GOTTEN OVER THAT. I DIDN'T MEAN IT, REALLY...
I-I'M SO SORRY! I'LL LEAVE THE MANSION AT ONCE!!
WHAT ARE YOU SAYING?! WHO CARES ABOUT THE PLATES?!
HUH?
YOU'RE NOT HURT, ARE YOU?! THEN YOU'VE GOT NOTHING TO CRY ABOUT!!
...YES, MASTER!!
SNIFFLE!!
I'M SO HAPPY FOR YOU, MARGARITA!! LET'S CELEBRATE!!
THRILLER BARK
...
WHOA... HA HA HA HA...
...

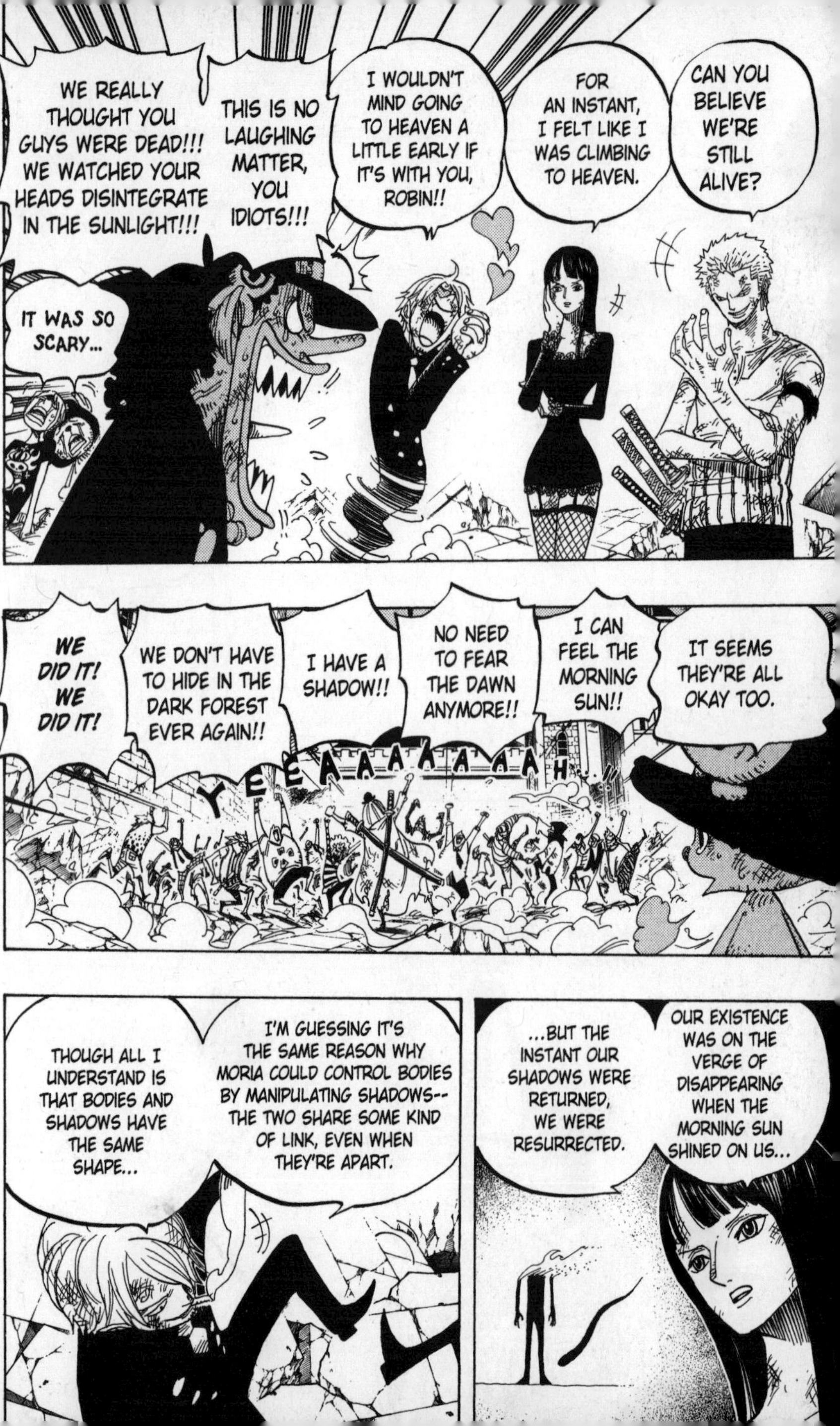
CAN YOU BELIEVE WE'RE STILL ALIVE?
FOR AN INSTANT, I FELT LIKE I WAS CLIMBING TO HEAVEN.
I WOULDN'T MIND GOING TO HEAVEN A LITTLE EARLY IF IT'S WITH YOU, ROBIN!!
THIS IS NO LAUGHING MATTER, YOU IDIOTS!!!
WE REALLY THOUGHT YOU GUYS WERE DEAD!!! WE WATCHED YOUR HEADS DISINTEGRATE IN THE SUNLIGHT!!!
IT WAS SO SCARY...
IT SEEMS THEY'RE ALL OKAY TOO.
I CAN FEEL THE MORNING SUN!!
NO NEED TO FEAR THE DAWN ANYMORE!!
I HAVE A SHADOW!!
WE DON'T HAVE TO HIDE IN THE DARK FOREST EVER AGAIN!!
WE DID IT! WE DID IT!
YEEAAAAAAAAH!!
OUR EXISTENCE WAS ON THE VERGE OF DISAPPEARING WHEN THE MORNING SUN SHINED ON US...
...BUT THE INSTANT OUR SHADOWS WERE RETURNED, WE WERE RESURRECTED.
I'M GUESSING IT'S THE SAME REASON WHY MORIA COULD CONTROL BODIES BY MANIPULATING SHADOWS-- THE TWO SHARE SOME KIND OF LINK, EVEN WHEN THEY'RE APART.
THOUGH ALL I UNDERSTAND IS THAT BODIES AND SHADOWS HAVE THE SAME SHAPE...

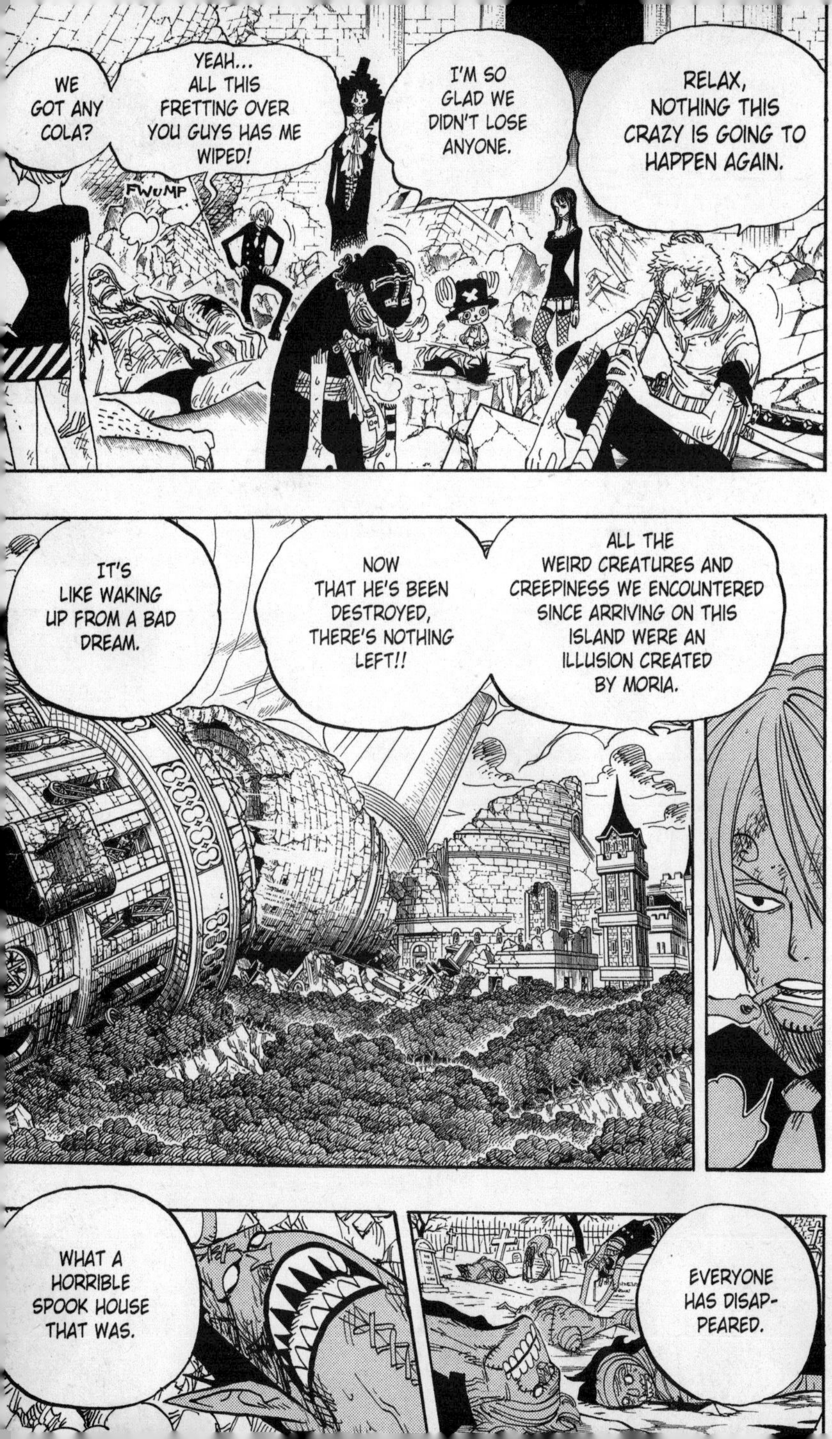
RELAX, NOTHING THIS CRAZY IS GOING TO HAPPEN AGAIN.
I'M SO GLAD WE DIDN'T LOSE ANYONE.
YEAH... ALL THIS FRETTING OVER YOU GUYS HAS ME WIPED!
FWUMP
WE GOT ANY COLA?
ALL THE WEIRD CREATURES AND CREEPINESS WE ENCOUNTERED SINCE ARRIVING ON THIS ISLAND WERE AN ILLUSION CREATED BY MORIA.
NOW THAT HE'S BEEN DESTROYED, THERE'S NOTHING LEFT!!
IT'S LIKE WAKING UP FROM A BAD DREAM.
EVERYONE HAS DISAP-PEARED.
WHAT A HORRIBLE SPOOK HOUSE THAT WAS.

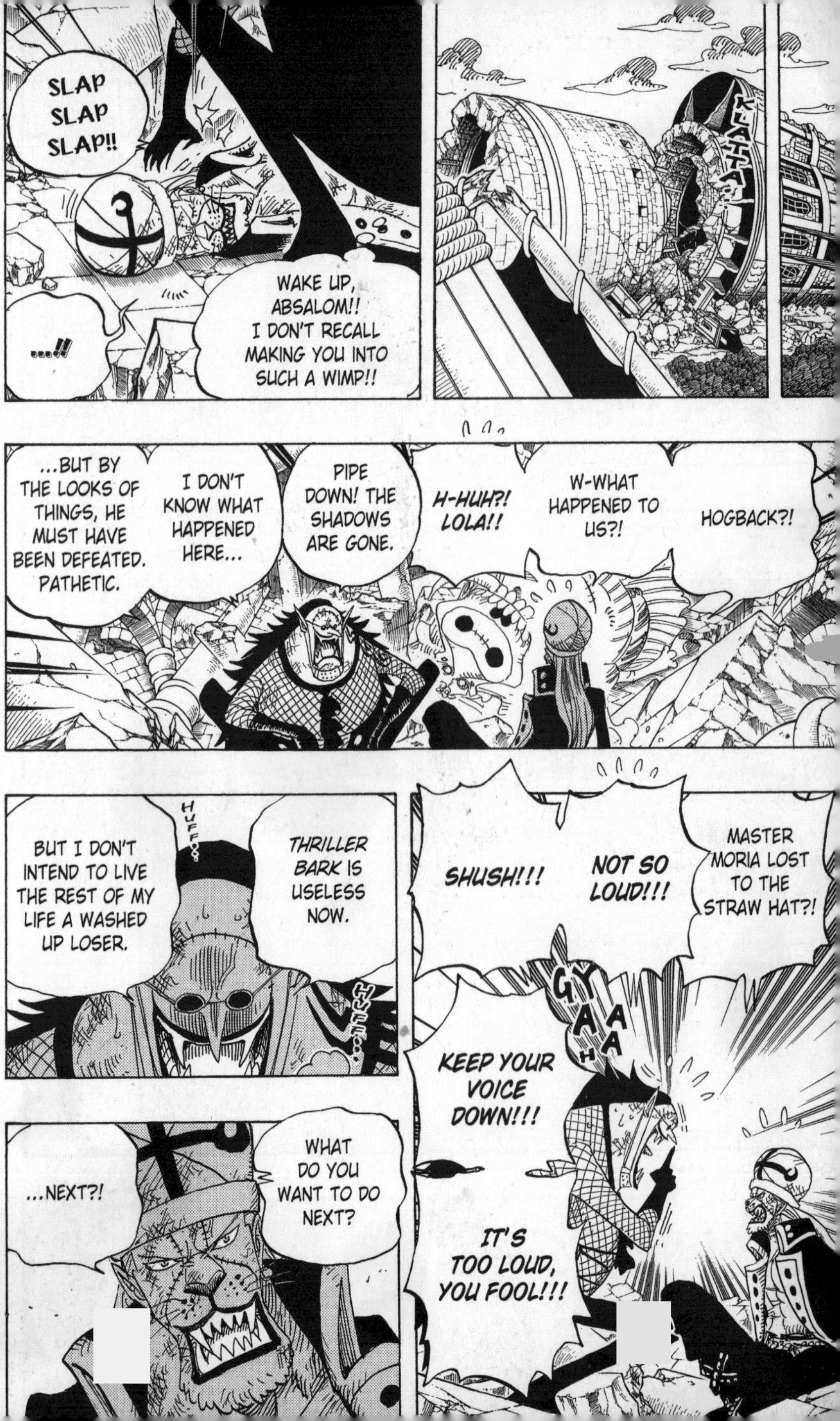
KLATTA
SLAP SLAP SLAP!!
WAKE UP, ABSALOM!! I DON'T RECALL MAKING YOU INTO SUCH A WIMP!!
...!!
HOGBACK?!
W-WHAT HAPPENED TO US?!
H-HUH?! LOLA!!
PIPE DOWN! THE SHADOWS ARE GONE.
I DON'T KNOW WHAT HAPPENED HERE...
...BUT BY THE LOOKS OF THINGS, HE MUST HAVE BEEN DEFEATED. PATHETIC.
MASTER MORIA LOST TO THE STRAW HAT?!
NOT SO LOUD!!!
SHUSH!!!
GYAAAAH
KEEP YOUR VOICE DOWN!!!
IT'S TOO LOUD, YOU FOOL!!!
HUFF
THRILLER BARK IS USELESS NOW.
BUT I DON'T INTEND TO LIVE THE REST OF MY LIFE A WASHED UP LOSER.
HUFF
WHAT DO YOU WANT TO DO NEXT?
...NEXT?!

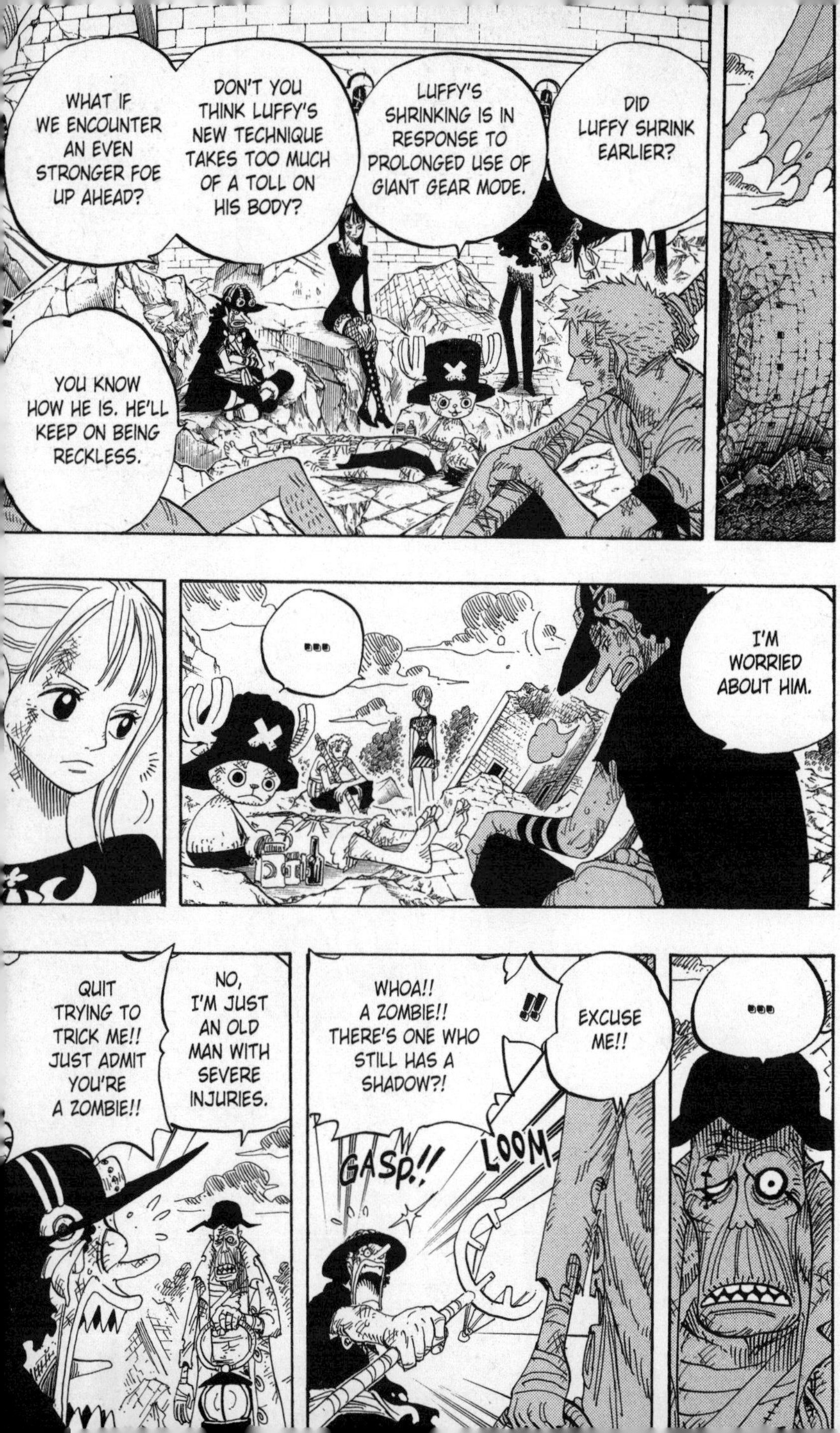
DID LUFFY SHRINK EARLIER?
LUFFY'S SHRINKING IS IN RESPONSE TO PROLONGED USE OF GIANT GEAR MODE.
DON'T YOU THINK LUFFY'S NEW TECHNIQUE TAKES TOO MUCH OF A TOLL ON HIS BODY?
WHAT IF WE ENCOUNTER AN EVEN STRONGER FOE UP AHEAD?
YOU KNOW HOW HE IS. HE'LL KEEP ON BEING RECKLESS.
I'M WORRIED ABOUT HIM.
...
...
EXCUSE ME!!
!!
WHOA!! A ZOMBIE!! THERE'S ONE WHO STILL HAS A SHADOW?!
LOOM
GASP!!
NO, I'M JUST AN OLD MAN WITH SEVERE INJURIES.
QUIT TRYING TO TRICK ME!! JUST ADMIT YOU'RE A ZOMBIE!!

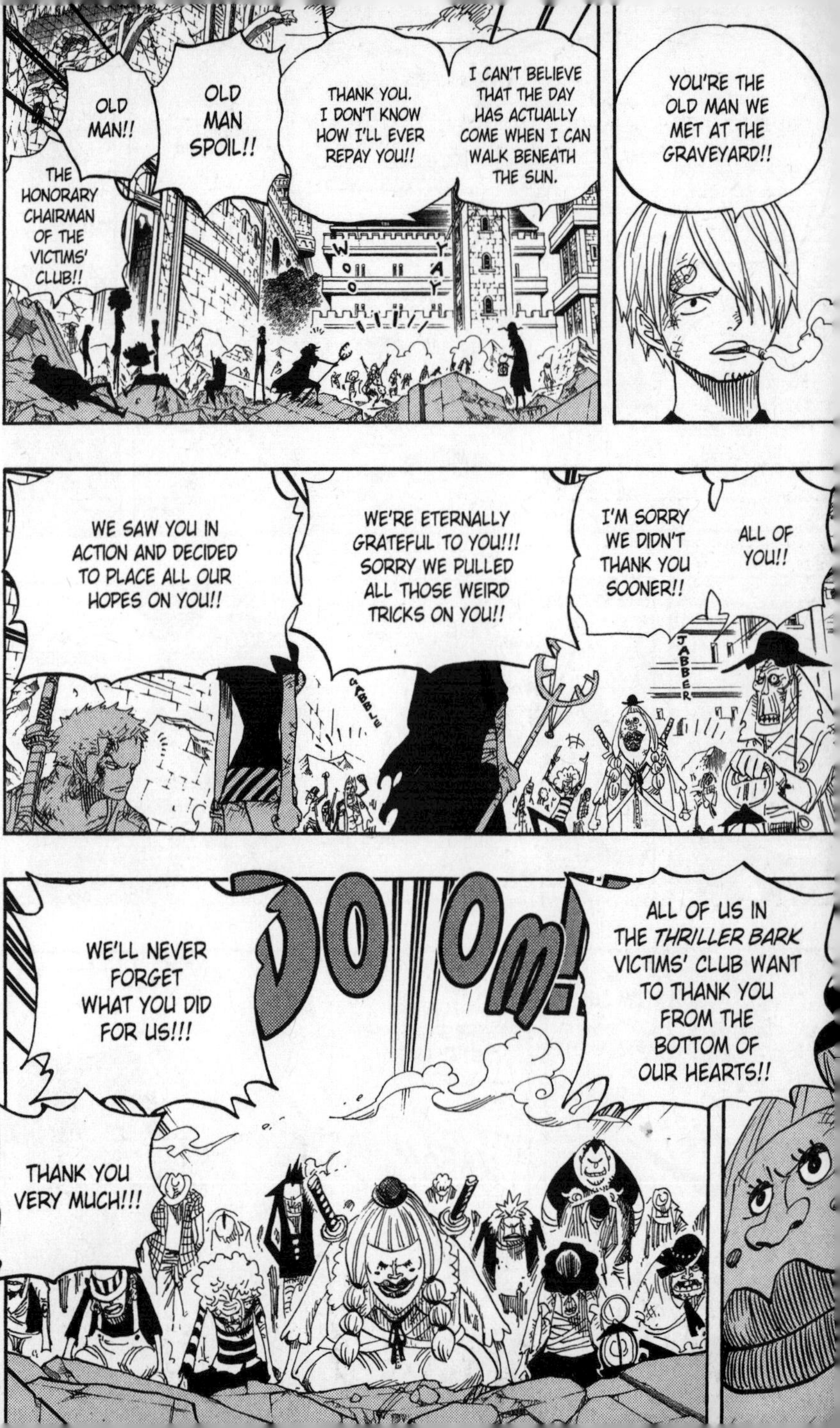
YOU'RE THE OLD MAN WE MET AT THE GRAVEYARD!!
I CAN'T BELIEVE THAT THE DAY HAS ACTUALLY COME WHEN I CAN WALK BENEATH THE SUN.
THANK YOU. I DON'T KNOW HOW I'LL EVER REPAY YOU!!
OLD MAN SPOIL!!
OLD MAN!!
THE HONORARY CHAIRMAN OF THE VICTIMS' CLUB!!
ALL OF YOU!!
I'M SORRY WE DIDN'T THANK YOU SOONER!!
JABBER
WE'RE ETERNALLY GRATEFUL TO YOU!!! SORRY WE PULLED ALL THOSE WEIRD TRICKS ON YOU!!
GABBLE
WE SAW YOU IN ACTION AND DECIDED TO PLACE ALL OUR HOPES ON YOU!!
ALL OF US IN THE *THRILLER BARK* VICTIMS' CLUB WANT TO THANK YOU FROM THE BOTTOM OF OUR HEARTS!!
DOOM!
WE'LL NEVER FORGET WHAT YOU DID FOR US!!!
THANK YOU VERY MUCH!!!

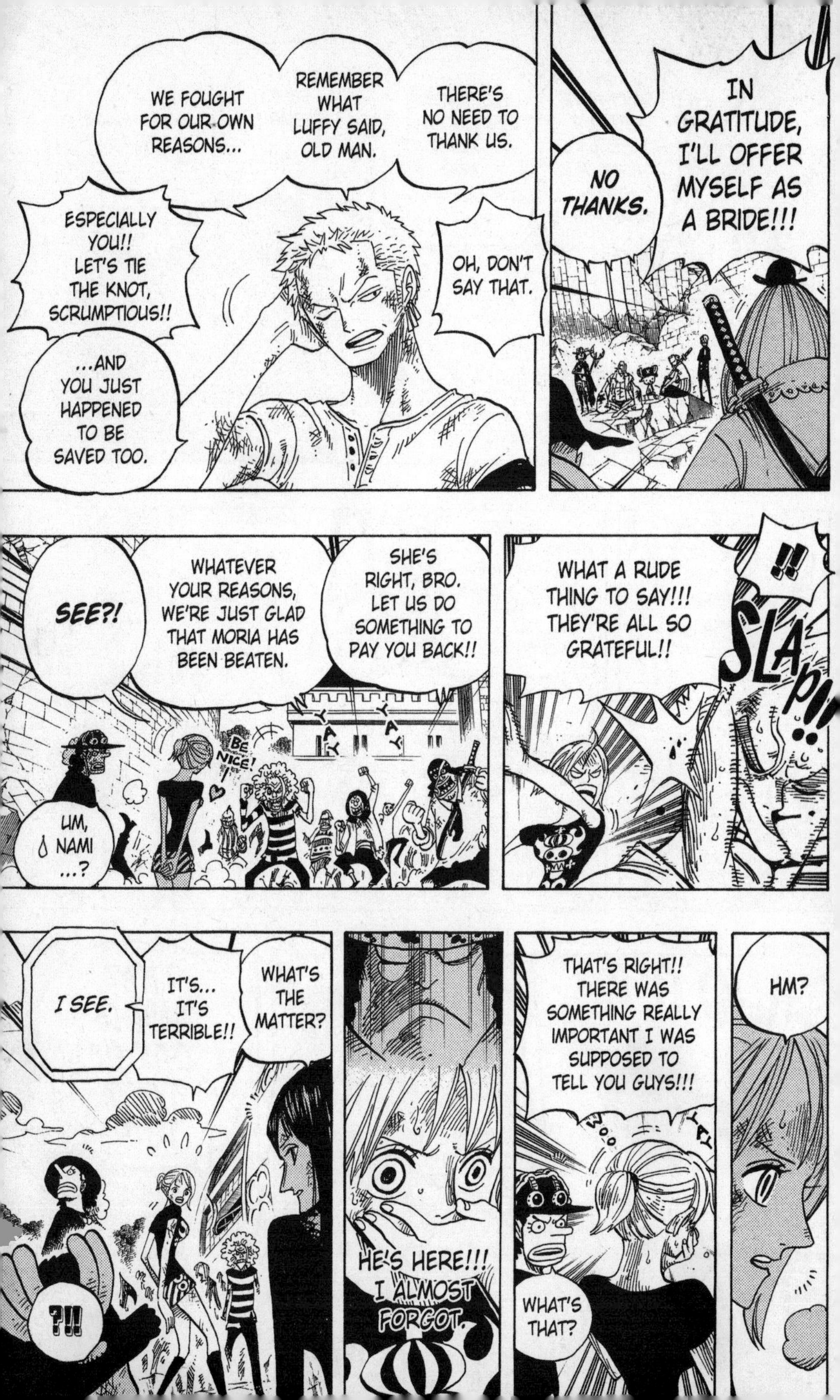
IN GRATITUDE, I'LL OFFER MYSELF AS A BRIDE!!!
NO THANKS.
THERE'S NO NEED TO THANK US.
REMEMBER WHAT LUFFY SAID, OLD MAN.
WE FOUGHT FOR OUR OWN REASONS...
OH, DON'T SAY THAT.
ESPECIALLY YOU!! LET'S TIE THE KNOT, SCRUMPTIOUS!!
...AND YOU JUST HAPPENED TO BE SAVED TOO.
!!
SLAP!!
WHAT A RUDE THING TO SAY!!! THEY'RE ALL SO GRATEFUL!!
SHE'S RIGHT, BRO. LET US DO SOMETHING TO PAY YOU BACK!!
WHATEVER YOUR REASONS, WE'RE JUST GLAD THAT MORIA HAS BEEN BEATEN.
SEE?!
YAY
YAY
BE NICE!
UM, NAMI ...?
HM?
THAT'S RIGHT!! THERE WAS SOMETHING REALLY IMPORTANT I WAS SUPPOSED TO TELL YOU GUYS!!!
YAY
WOO
WHAT'S THAT?
HE'S HERE!!! I ALMOST FORGOT.
WHAT'S THE MATTER?
IT'S... IT'S TERRIBLE!!
I SEE.
?!!

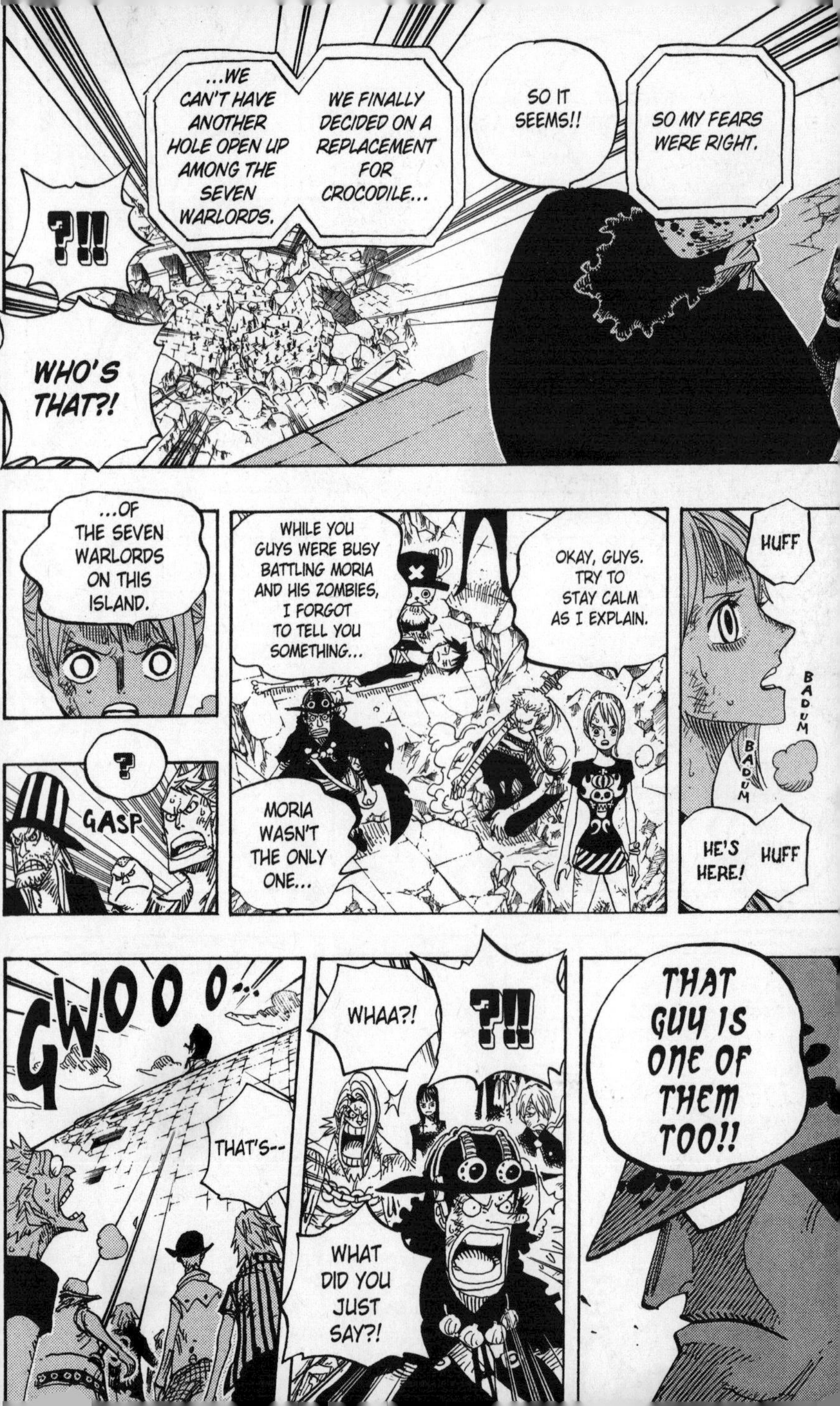
SO MY FEARS WERE RIGHT.
SO IT SEEMS!!
WE FINALLY DECIDED ON A REPLACEMENT FOR CROCODILE...
...WE CAN'T HAVE ANOTHER HOLE OPEN UP AMONG THE SEVEN WARLORDS.
?!!
WHO'S THAT?!
HUFF
BADUM
BADUM
HE'S HERE!
HUFF
OKAY, GUYS. TRY TO STAY CALM AS I EXPLAIN.
WHILE YOU GUYS WERE BUSY BATTLING MORIA AND HIS ZOMBIES, I FORGOT TO TELL YOU SOMETHING...
MORIA WASN'T THE ONLY ONE...
...OF THE SEVEN WARLORDS ON THIS ISLAND.
?
GASP
THAT GUY IS ONE OF THEM TOO!!
?!!
WHAA?!
WHAT DID YOU JUST SAY?!
GWOOO..
THAT'S--

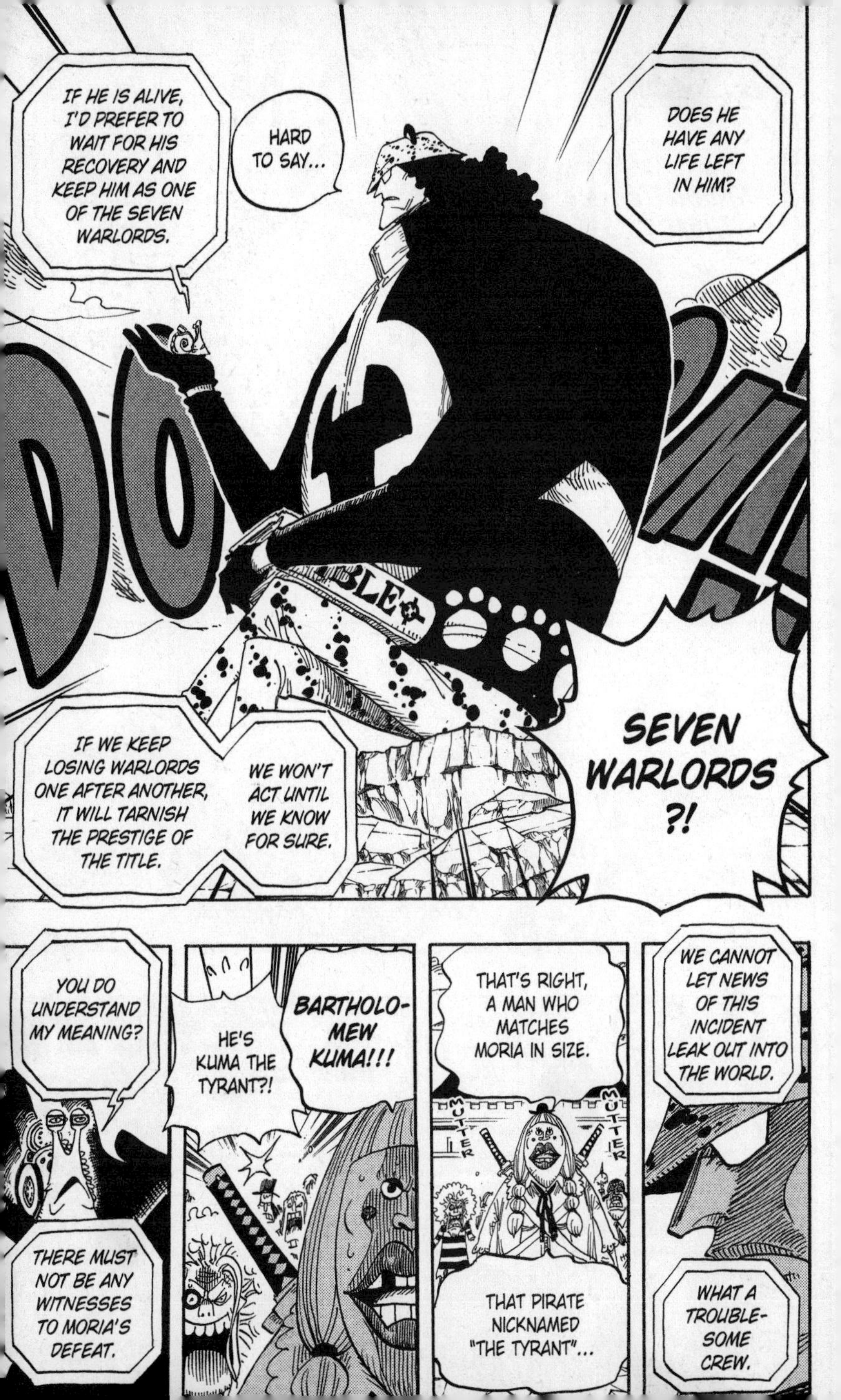

DOES HE HAVE ANY LIFE LEFT IN HIM?
HARD TO SAY...
IF HE IS ALIVE, I'D PREFER TO WAIT FOR HIS RECOVERY AND KEEP HIM AS ONE OF THE SEVEN WARLORDS.
SEVEN WARLORDS ?!
WE WON'T ACT UNTIL WE KNOW FOR SURE.
IF WE KEEP LOSING WARLORDS ONE AFTER ANOTHER, IT WILL TARNISH THE PRESTIGE OF THE TITLE.
WE CANNOT LET NEWS OF THIS INCIDENT LEAK OUT INTO THE WORLD.
WHAT A TROUBLE-SOME CREW.
THAT'S RIGHT, A MAN WHO MATCHES MORIA IN SIZE.
MUTTER
MUTTER
THAT PIRATE NICKNAMED "THE TYRANT"...
BARTHOLO-MEW KUMA!!!
HE'S KUMA THE TYRANT?!
YOU DO UNDERSTAND MY MEANING?
THERE MUST NOT BE ANY WITNESSES TO MORIA'S DEFEAT.

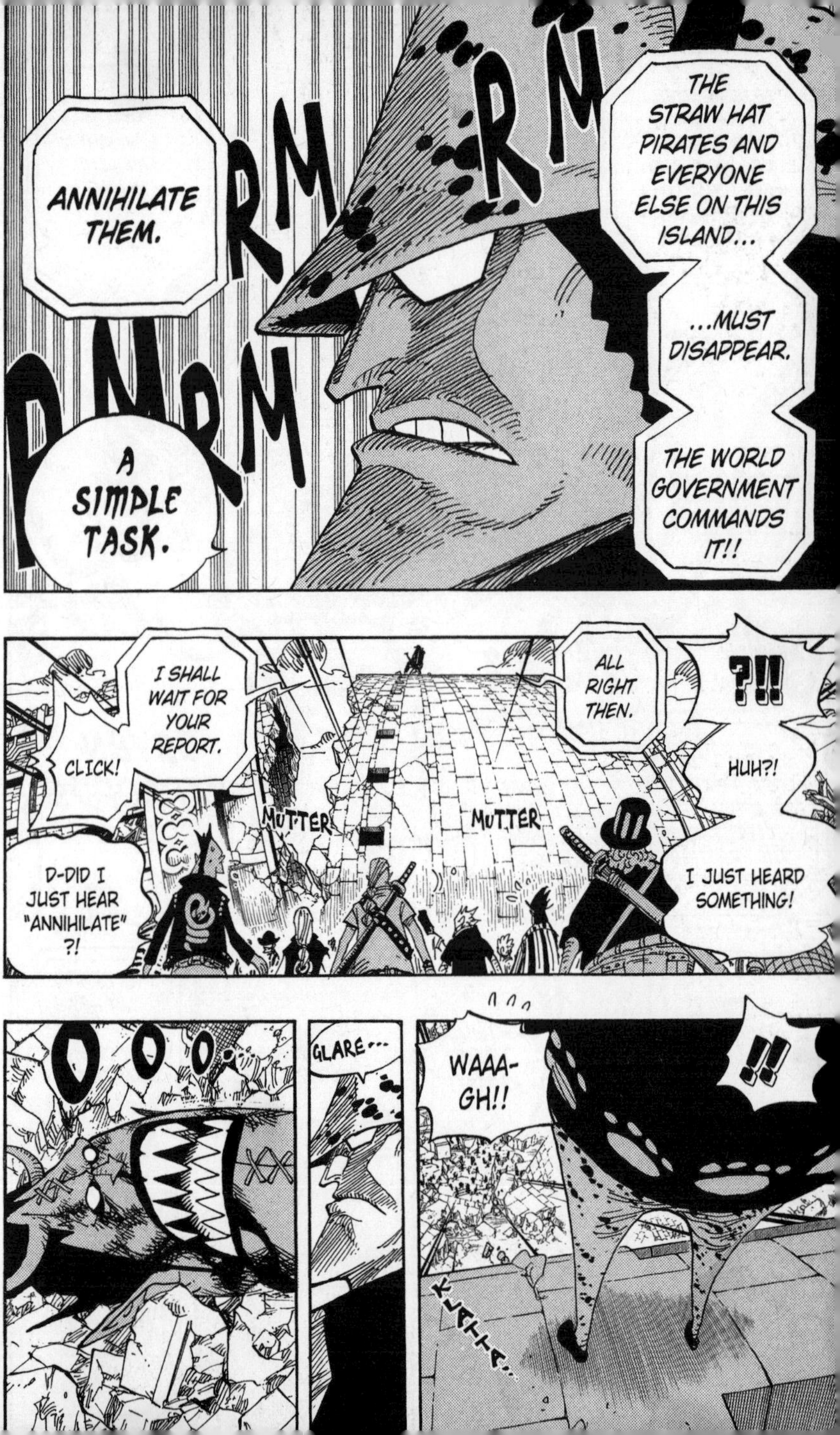
THE STRAW HAT PIRATES AND EVERYONE ELSE ON THIS ISLAND...
...MUST DISAPPEAR.
THE WORLD GOVERNMENT COMMANDS IT!!
ANNIHILATE THEM.
A SIMPLE TASK.
?!!
HUH?!
ALL RIGHT THEN.
I SHALL WAIT FOR YOUR REPORT.
CLICK!
MUTTER
MUTTER
I JUST HEARD SOMETHING!
D-DID I JUST HEAR "ANNIHILATE"?!
!!
WAAA-GH!!
KLATTA...
GLARE...

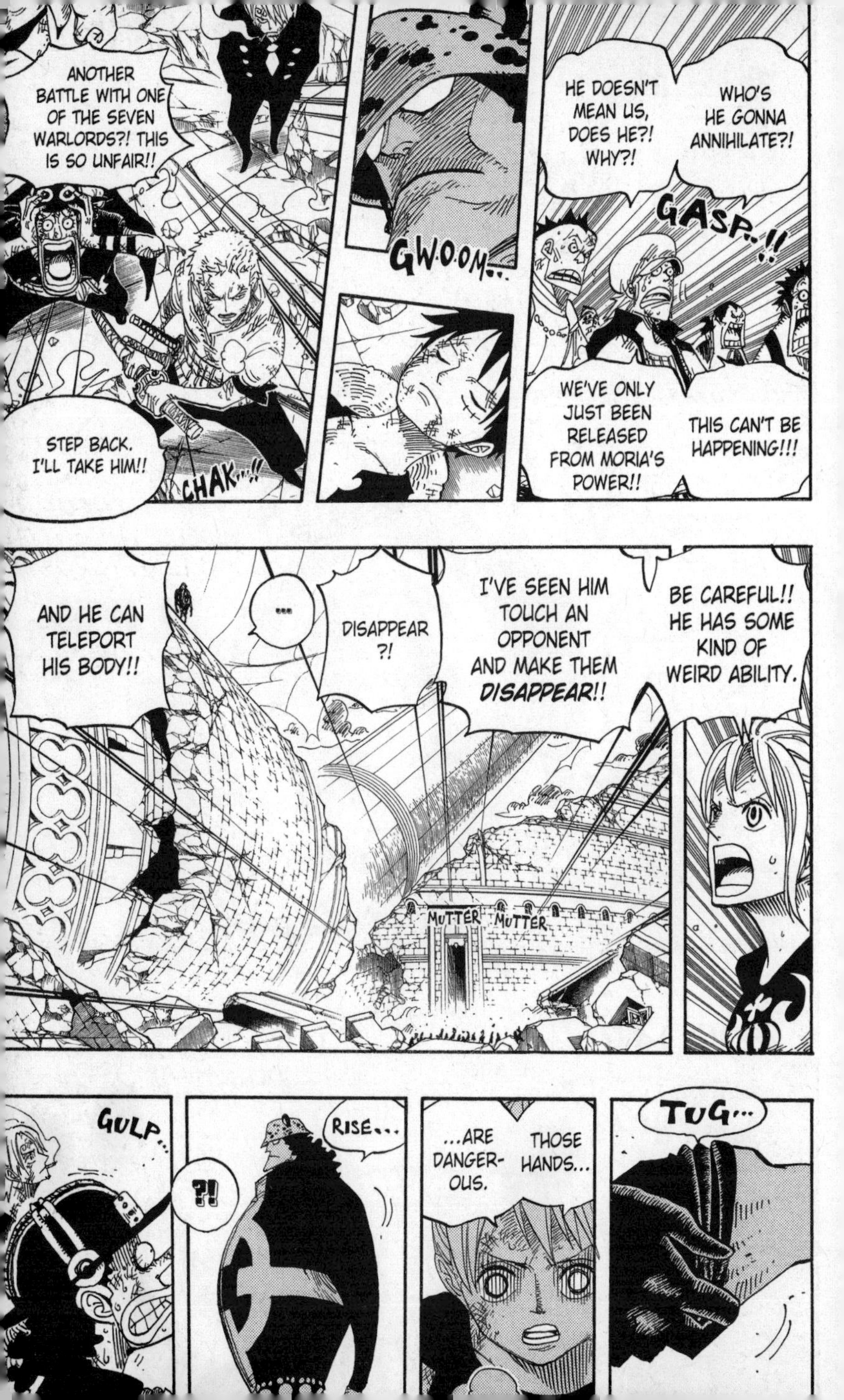
WHO'S HE GONNA ANNIHILATE?!
HE DOESN'T MEAN US, DOES HE?! WHY?!
GASP..!!
THIS CAN'T BE HAPPENING!!!
WE'VE ONLY JUST BEEN RELEASED FROM MORIA'S POWER!!
GWOOM...
ANOTHER BATTLE WITH ONE OF THE SEVEN WARLORDS?! THIS IS SO UNFAIR!!
STEP BACK. I'LL TAKE HIM!!
CHAK..!!
BE CAREFUL!! HE HAS SOME KIND OF WEIRD ABILITY.
I'VE SEEN HIM TOUCH AN OPPONENT AND MAKE THEM DISAPPEAR!!
DISAPPEAR?!
...
AND HE CAN TELEPORT HIS BODY!!
MUTTER MUTTER
TUG...
THOSE HANDS...
...ARE DANGER-OUS.
RISE...
?!
GULP...

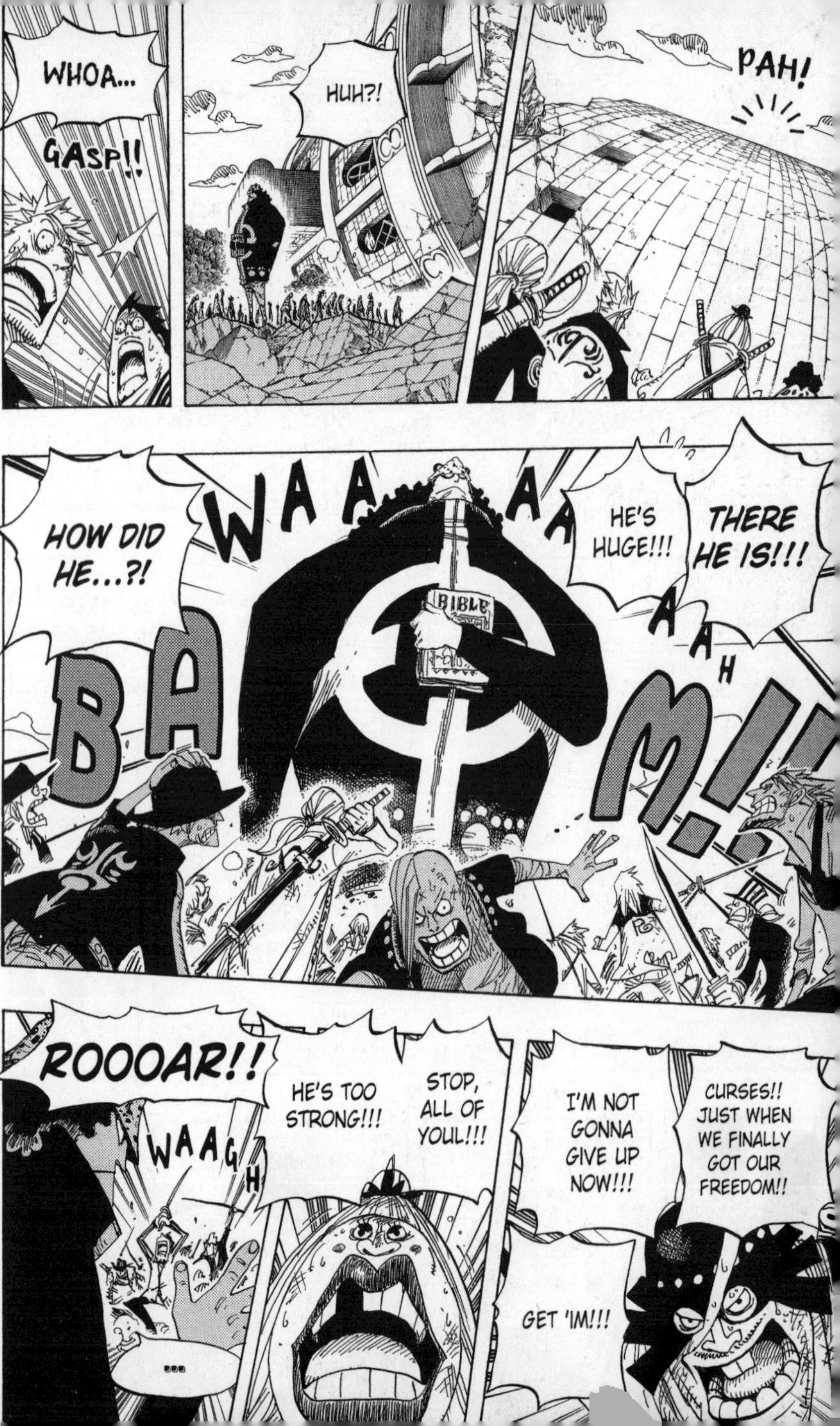

PAH!
HUH?!
WHOA...
GASP!!
THERE HE IS!!!
HE'S HUGE!!!
WAAAAAAH
HOW DID HE...?!
BAM!!
CURSES!! JUST WHEN WE FINALLY GOT OUR FREEDOM!!
I'M NOT GONNA GIVE UP NOW!!!
GET 'IM!!!
STOP, ALL OF YOU!!!
HE'S TOO STRONG!!!
ROOOAR!!
WAAGH
...

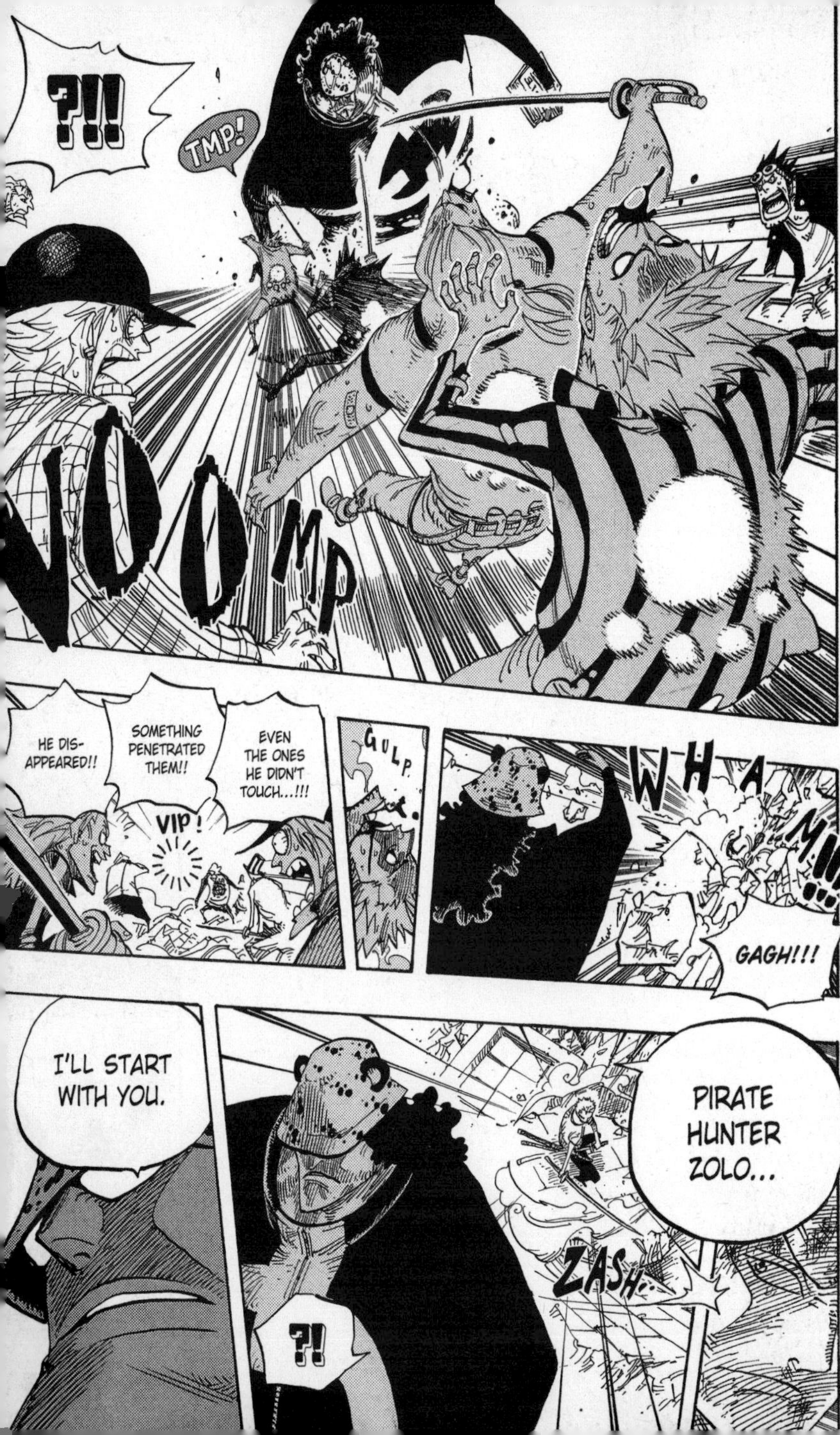
TMP!
?!!
VOOOMP
WHAM!!!
GAGH!!!
GULP
EVEN THE ONES HE DIDN'T TOUCH...!!!
SOMETHING PENETRATED THEM!!
HE DIS-APPEARED!!
VIP!
PIRATE HUNTER ZOLO...
ZASH
?!
I'LL START WITH YOU.

Chapter 484: SQUISH

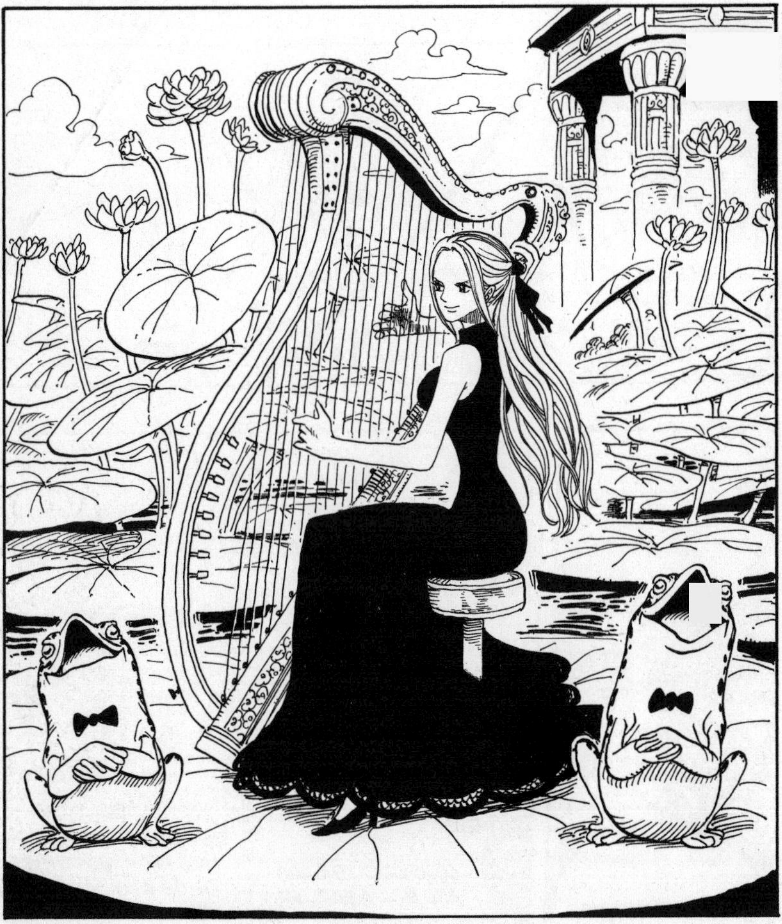

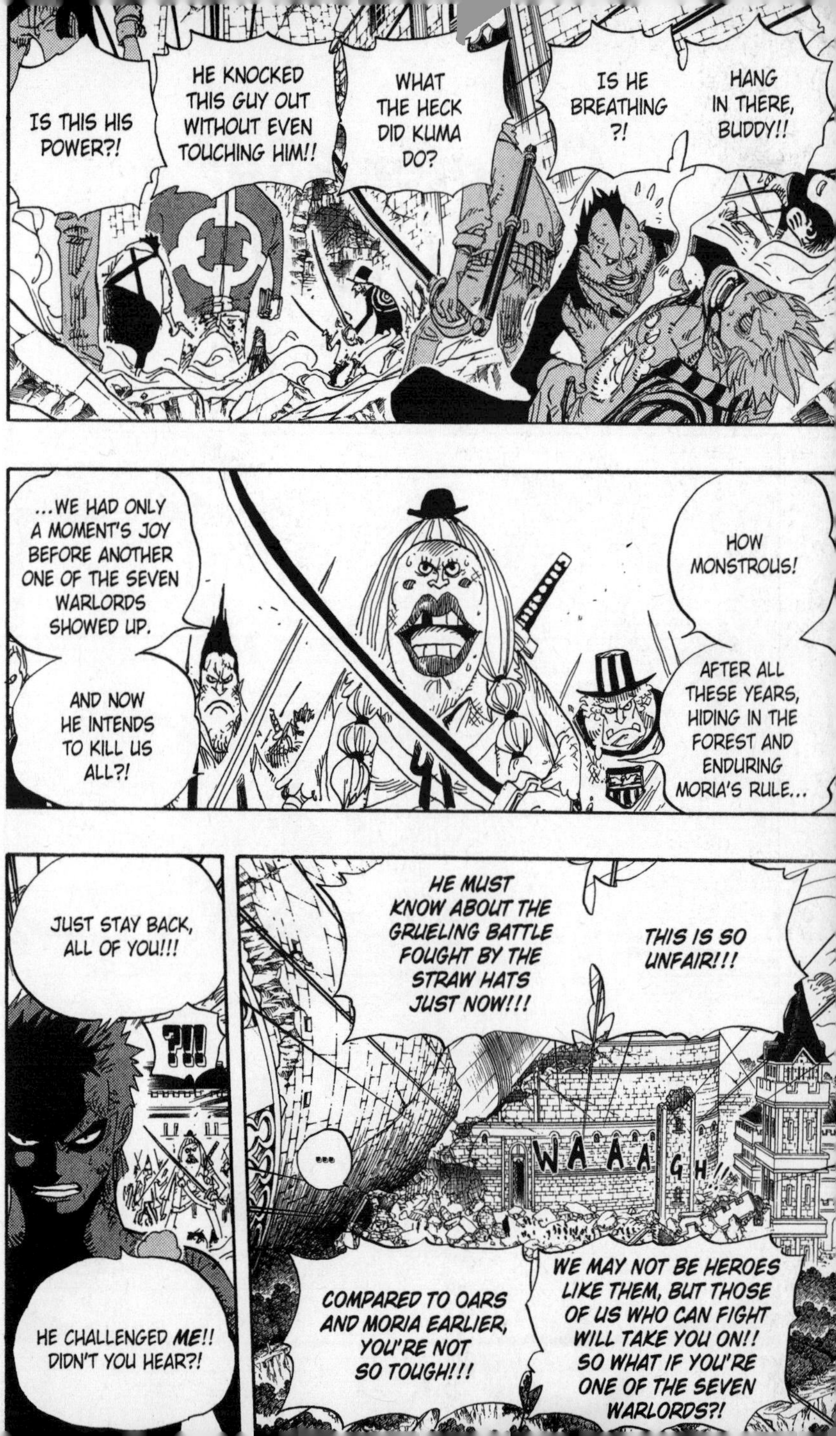
HANG IN THERE, BUDDY!!
IS HE BREATHING?!
WHAT THE HECK DID KUMA DO?
HE KNOCKED THIS GUY OUT WITHOUT EVEN TOUCHING HIM!!
IS THIS HIS POWER?!
HOW MONSTROUS!
AFTER ALL THESE YEARS, HIDING IN THE FOREST AND ENDURING MORIA'S RULE...
...WE HAD ONLY A MOMENT'S JOY BEFORE ANOTHER ONE OF THE SEVEN WARLORDS SHOWED UP.
AND NOW HE INTENDS TO KILL US ALL?!
THIS IS SO UNFAIR!!!
HE MUST KNOW ABOUT THE GRUELING BATTLE FOUGHT BY THE STRAW HATS JUST NOW!!!
...
WAAAGH!!
WE MAY NOT BE HEROES LIKE THEM, BUT THOSE OF US WHO CAN FIGHT WILL TAKE YOU ON!! SO WHAT IF YOU'RE ONE OF THE SEVEN WARLORDS?!
COMPARED TO OARS AND MORIA EARLIER, YOU'RE NOT SO TOUGH!!!
JUST STAY BACK, ALL OF YOU!!!
?!!
HE CHALLENGED ME!! DIDN'T YOU HEAR?!

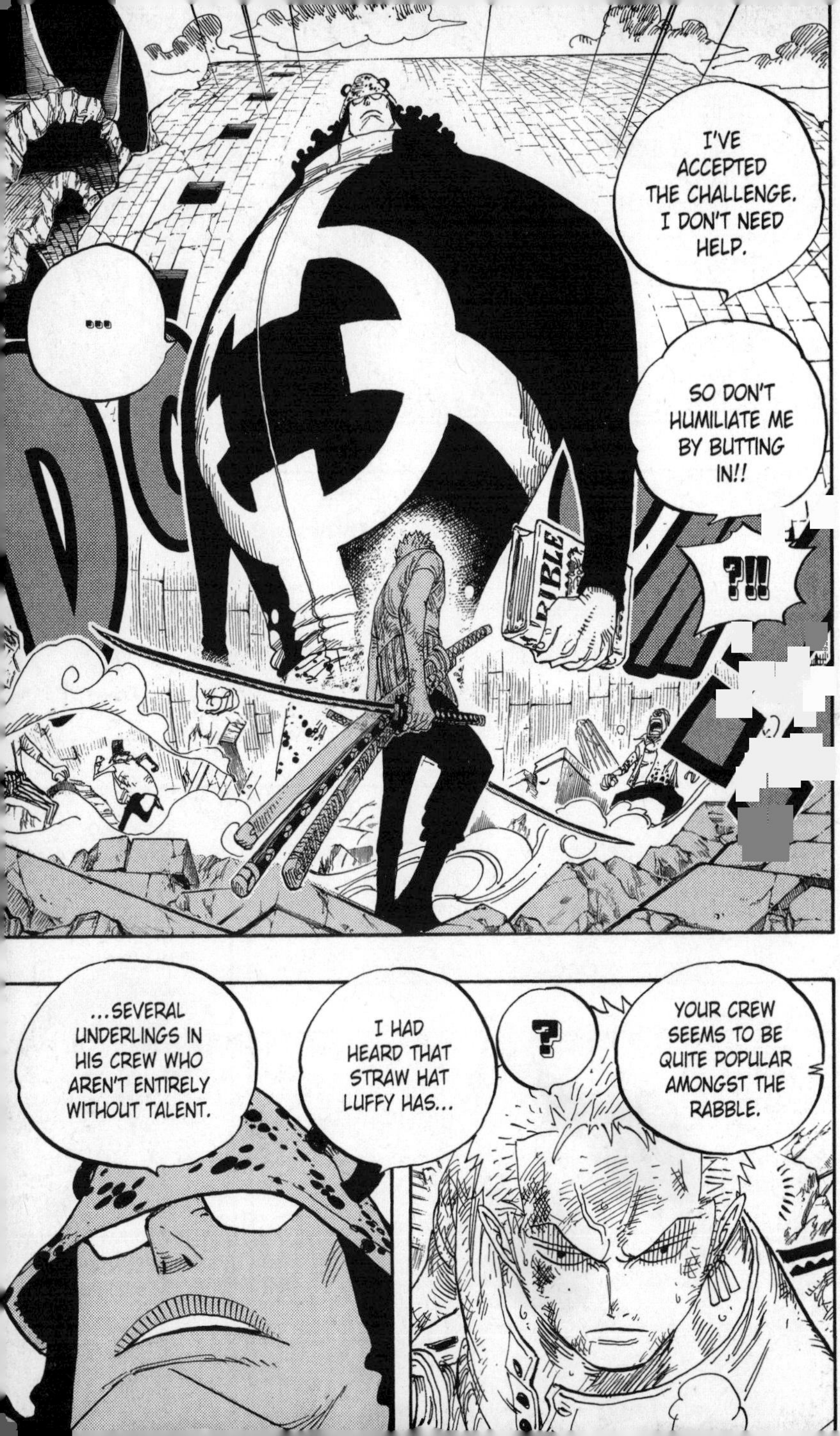
I'VE ACCEPTED THE CHALLENGE. I DON'T NEED HELP.
SO DON'T HUMILIATE ME BY BUTTING IN!!
?!!
...
YOUR CREW SEEMS TO BE QUITE POPULAR AMONGST THE RABBLE.
?
I HAD HEARD THAT STRAW HAT LUFFY HAS...
...SEVERAL UNDERLINGS IN HIS CREW WHO AREN'T ENTIRELY WITHOUT TALENT.
BIBLE

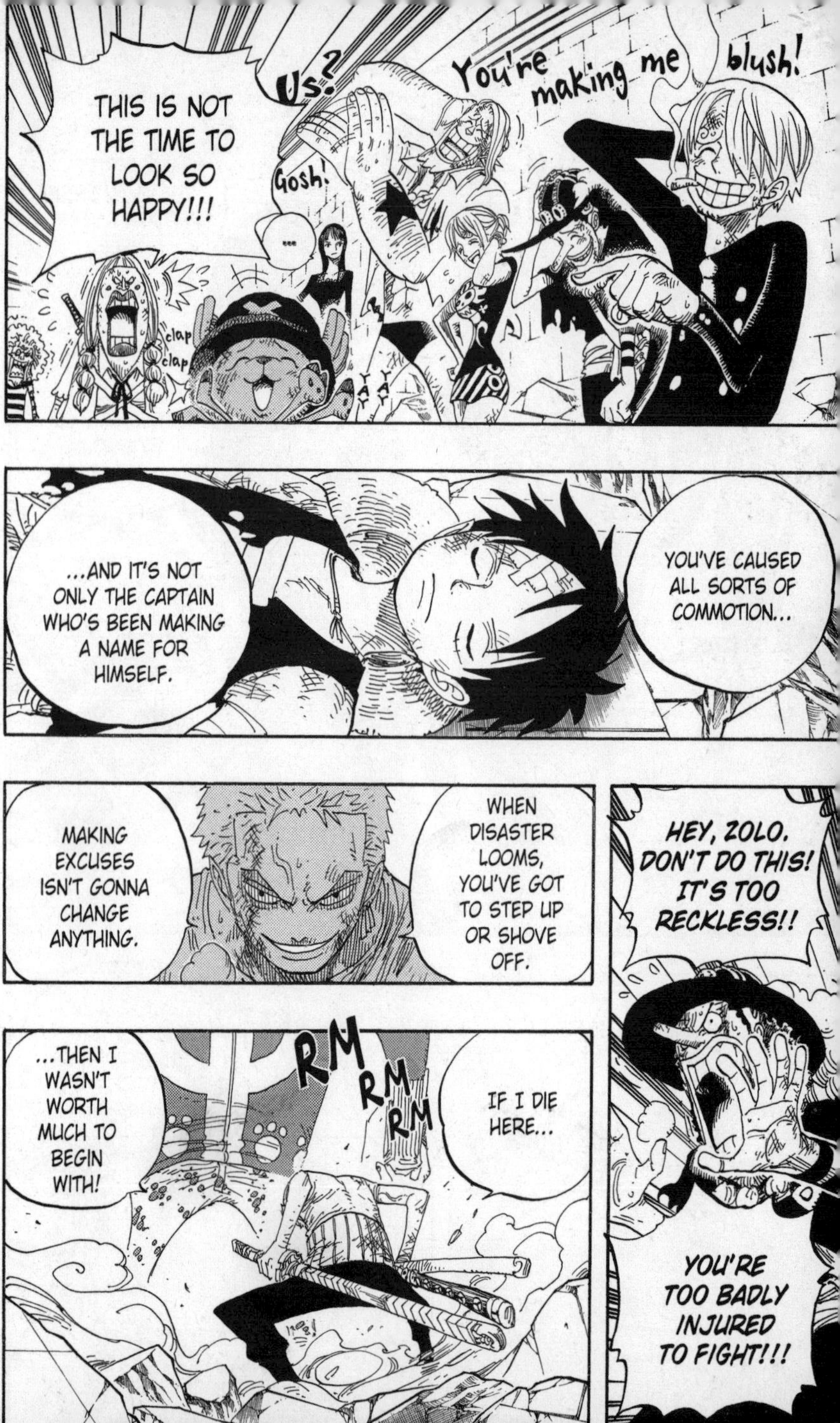
You're making me blush!
Us?
Gosh!
THIS IS NOT THE TIME TO LOOK SO HAPPY!!!
...
YAY YAY
clap clap
YOU'VE CAUSED ALL SORTS OF COMMOTION...
...AND IT'S NOT ONLY THE CAPTAIN WHO'S BEEN MAKING A NAME FOR HIMSELF.
HEY, ZOLO. DON'T DO THIS! IT'S TOO RECKLESS!!
YOU'RE TOO BADLY INJURED TO FIGHT!!!
WHEN DISASTER LOOMS, YOU'VE GOT TO STEP UP OR SHOVE OFF.
MAKING EXCUSES ISN'T GONNA CHANGE ANYTHING.
IF I DIE HERE...
RM RM RM RM
...THEN I WASN'T WORTH MUCH TO BEGIN WITH!

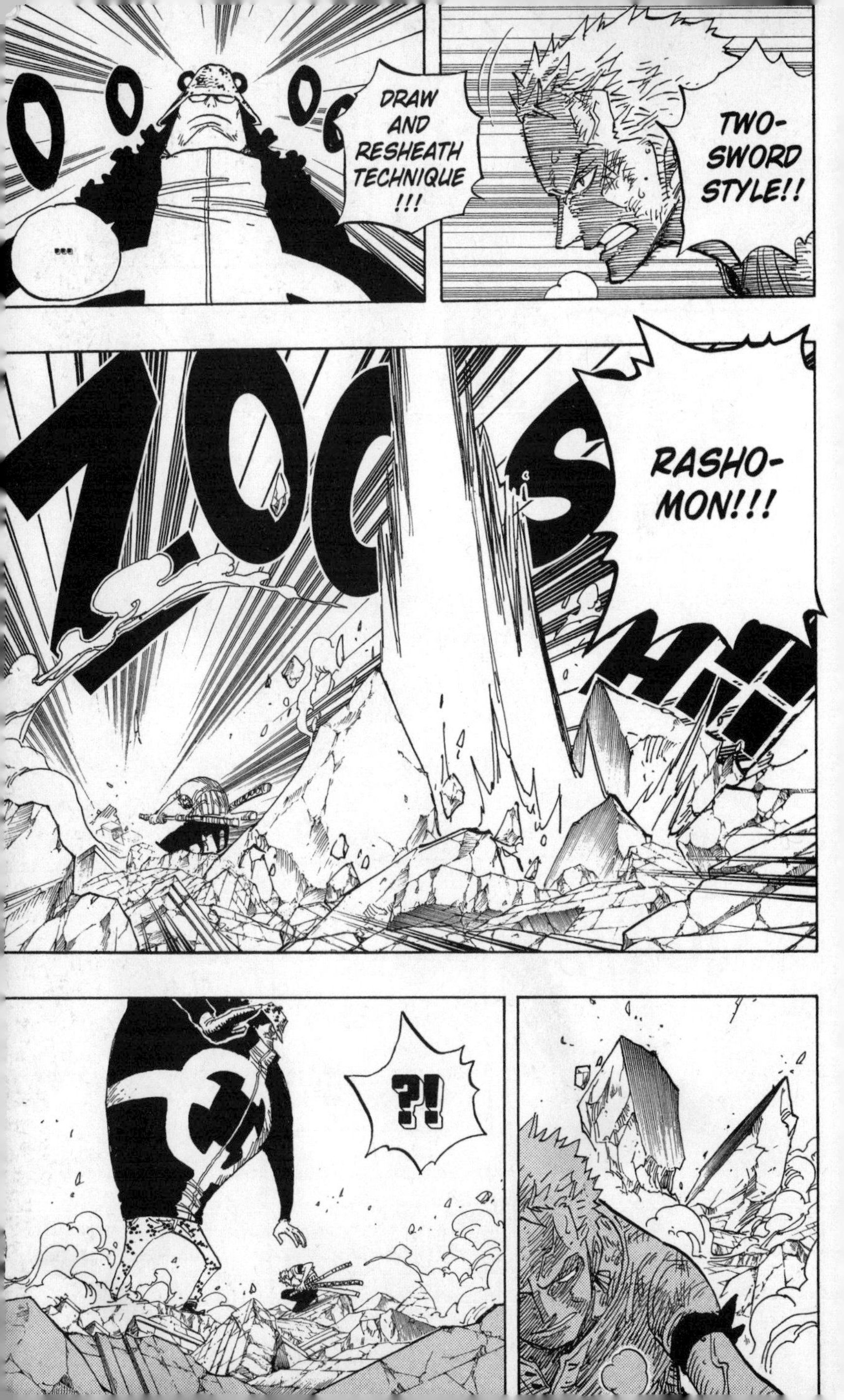
TWO-SWORD STYLE!!
DRAW AND RESHEATH TECHNIQUE!!!
...
RASHOMON!!!
ZOOSH!!
?!

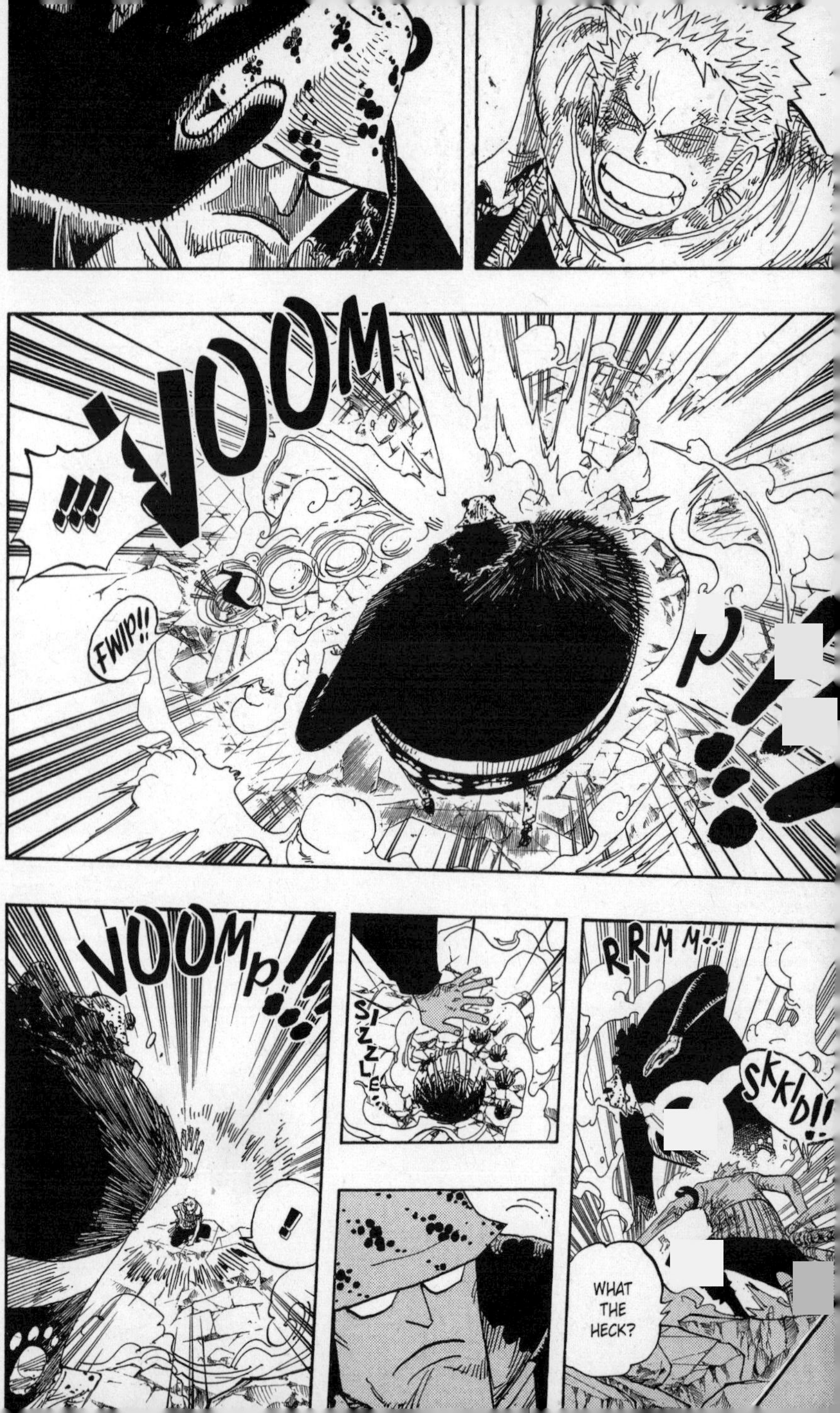
VOOM!!!
FWIP!!
RRMM..
SKKID!!
WHAT THE HECK?
SIZZLE...
VOOMP!!!
!

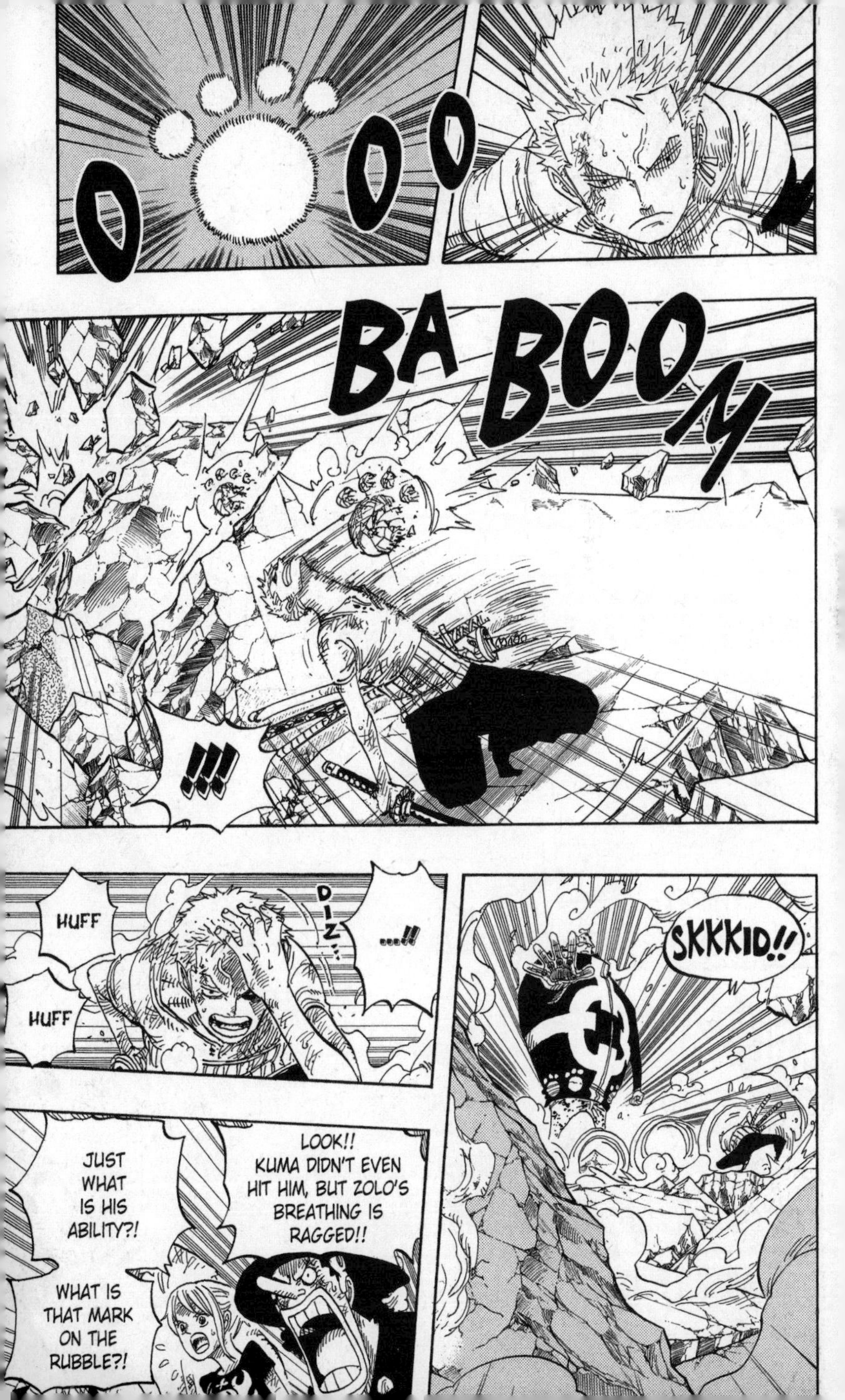

OOOO
BA BOOM
!!!
SKKID!!
...!!
DIZ...
HUFF
HUFF
LOOK!! KUMA DIDN'T EVEN HIT HIM, BUT ZOLO'S BREATHING IS RAGGED!!
JUST WHAT IS HIS ABILITY?!
WHAT IS THAT MARK ON THE RUBBLE?!

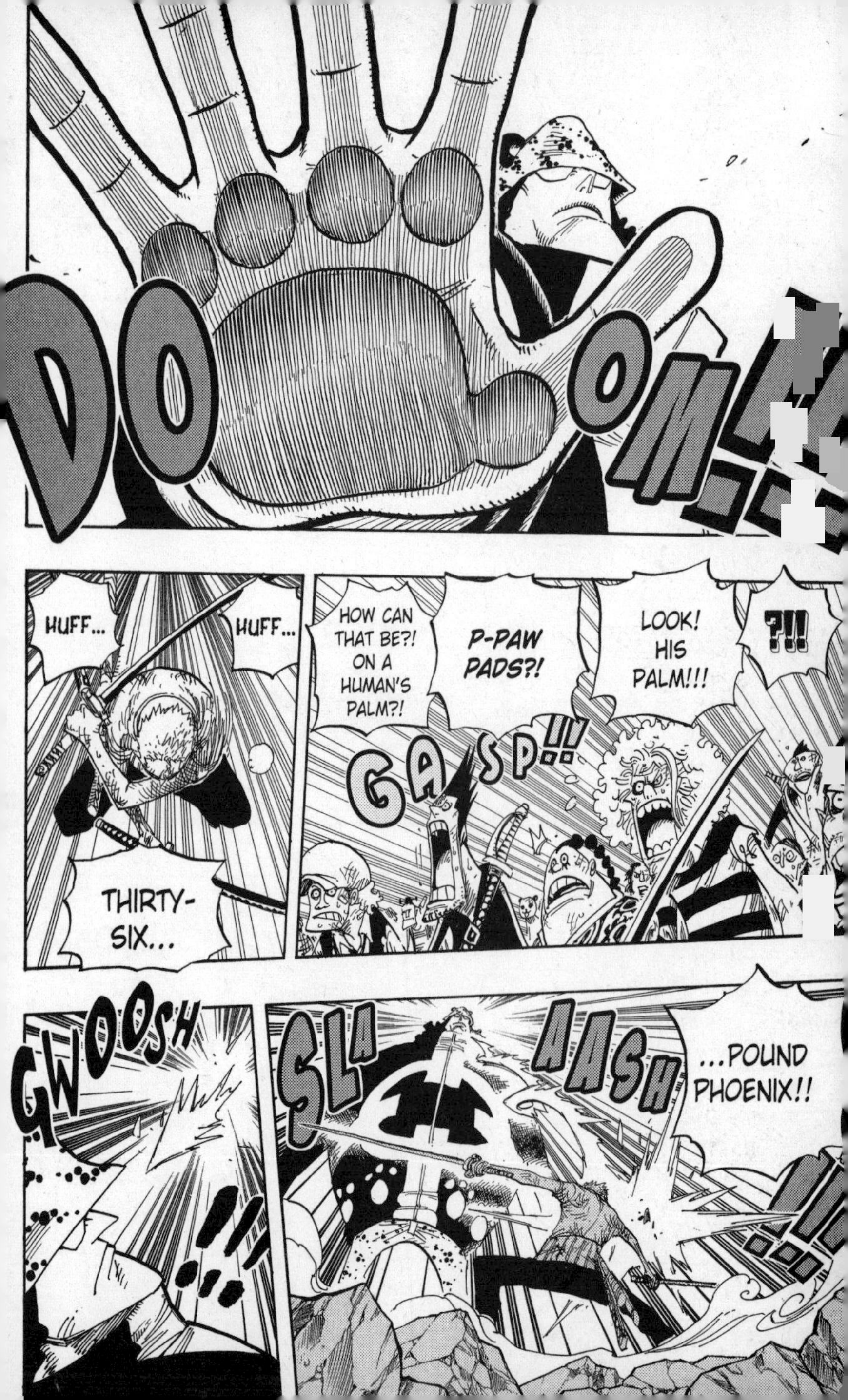
DOON
?!!
LOOK! HIS PALM!!!
P-PAW PADS?!
HOW CAN THAT BE?! ON A HUMAN'S PALM?!
GASP!!
HUFF...
HUFF...
THIRTY-SIX...
...POUND PHOENIX!!
SLAASH
GWOOSH

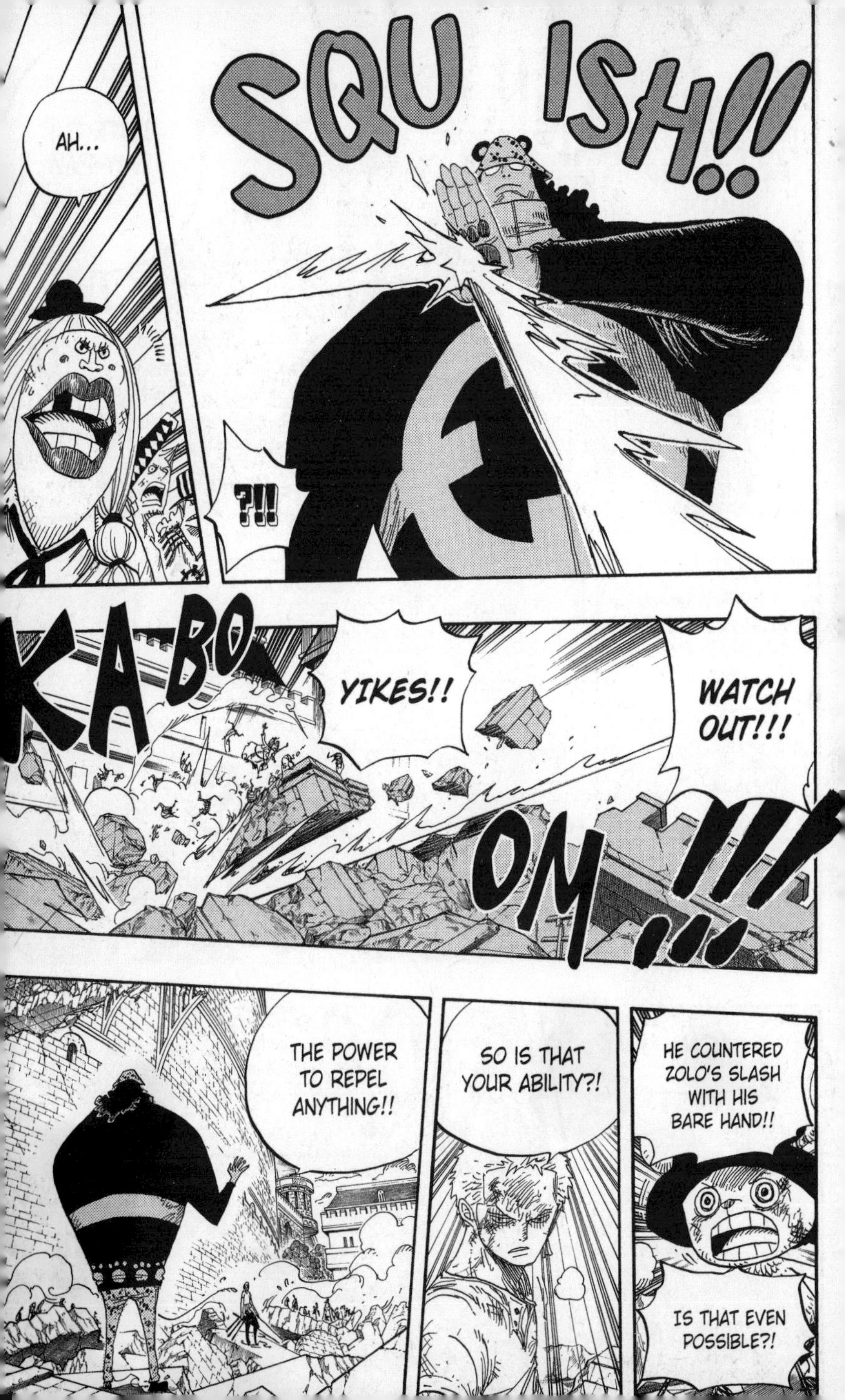
SQUISH!!
?!!
AH...
WATCH OUT!!!
YIKES!!
KABOOM!!!
HE COUNTERED ZOLO'S SLASH WITH HIS BARE HAND!!
IS THAT EVEN POSSIBLE?!
SO IS THAT YOUR ABILITY?!
THE POWER TO REPEL ANYTHING!!

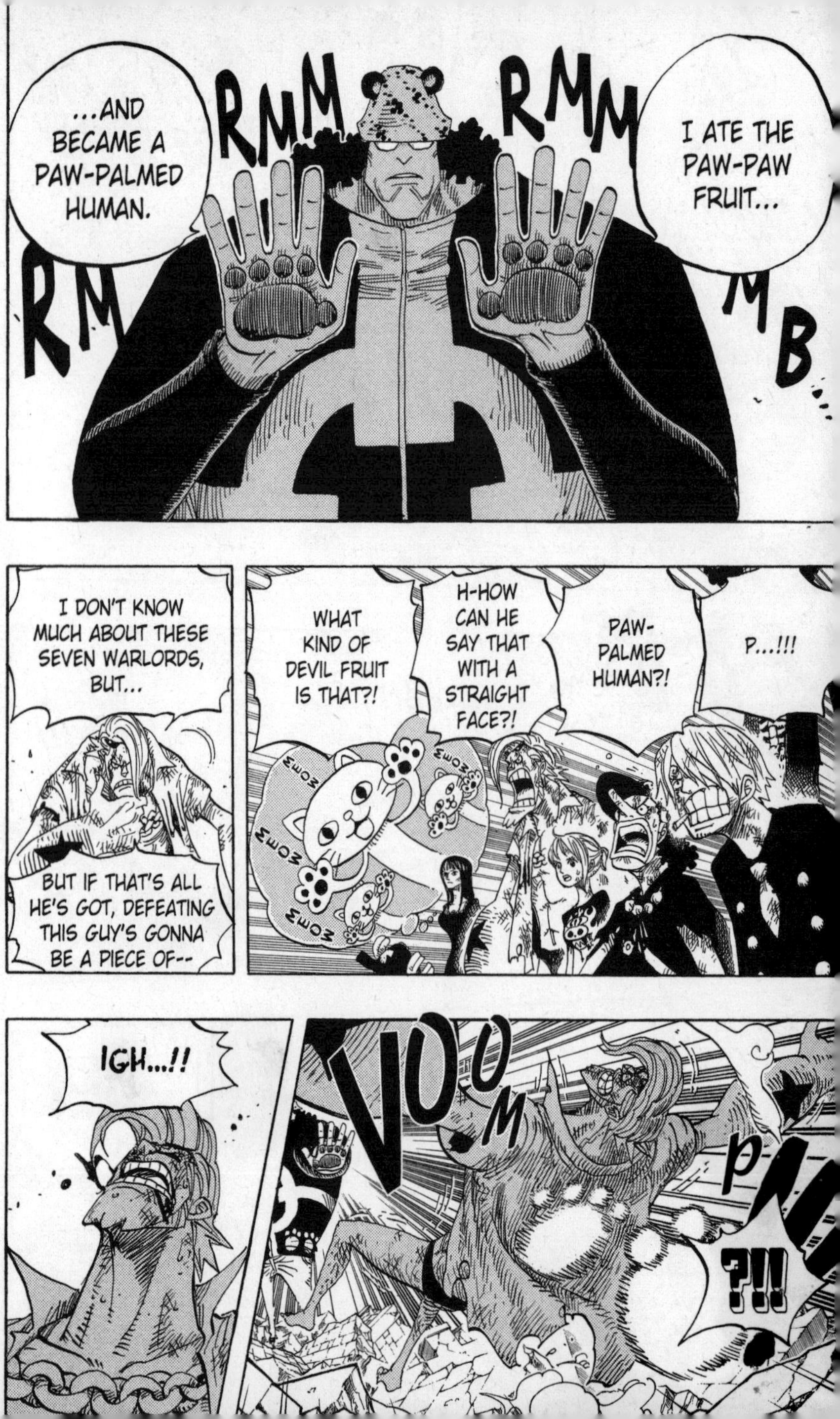
I ATE THE PAW-PAW FRUIT...
...AND BECAME A PAW-PALMED HUMAN.
RMM RMM
RM
MB
P...!!!
PAW-PALMED HUMAN?!
H-HOW CAN HE SAY THAT WITH A STRAIGHT FACE?!
WHAT KIND OF DEVIL FRUIT IS THAT?!
I DON'T KNOW MUCH ABOUT THESE SEVEN WARLORDS, BUT...
BUT IF THAT'S ALL HE'S GOT, DEFEATING THIS GUY'S GONNA BE A PIECE OF--
?!!
VOOM
IGH...!!

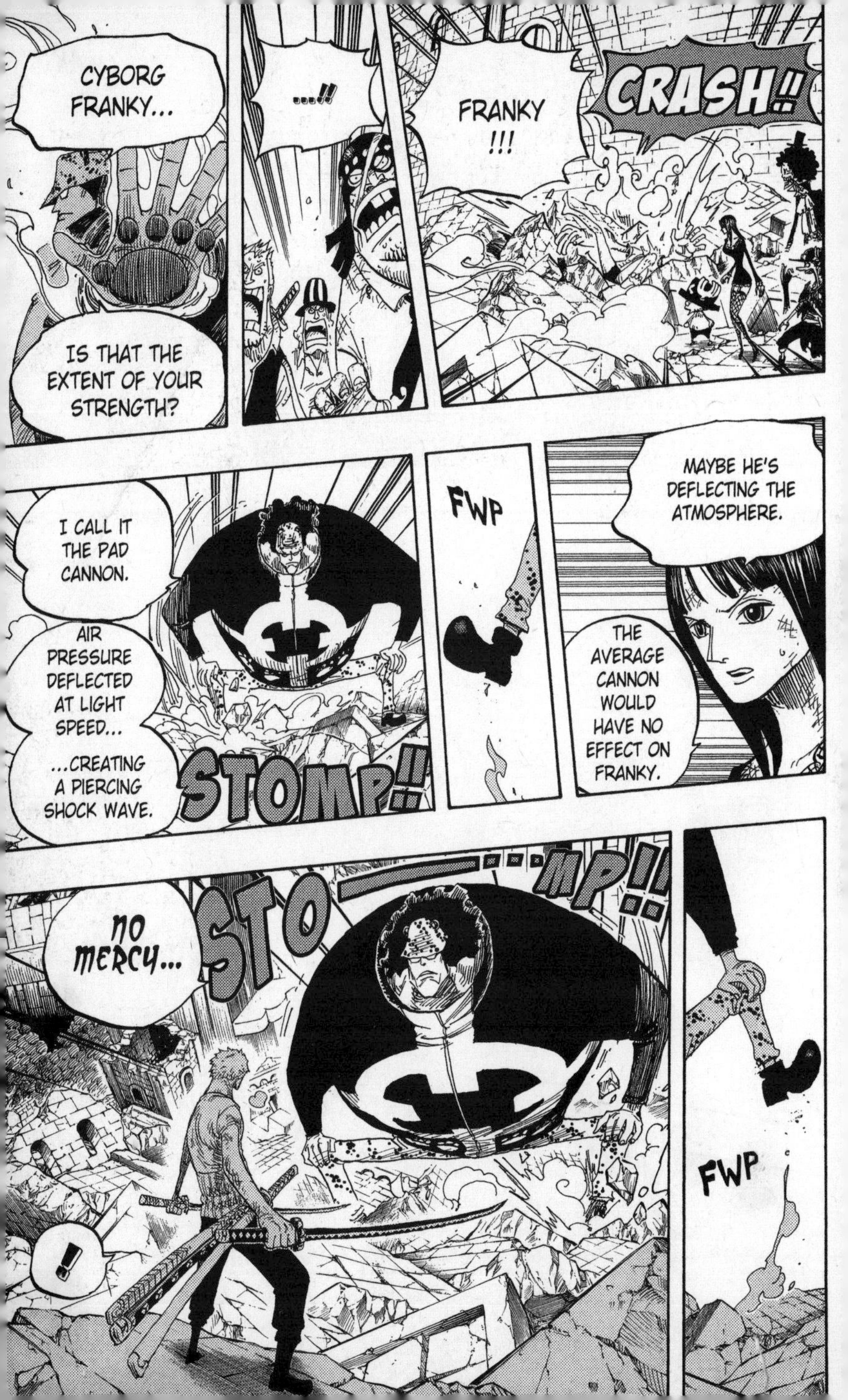
CRASH!!
FRANKY !!!
...!!
CYBORG FRANKY...
IS THAT THE EXTENT OF YOUR STRENGTH?
MAYBE HE'S DEFLECTING THE ATMOSPHERE.
THE AVERAGE CANNON WOULD HAVE NO EFFECT ON FRANKY.
FWP
I CALL IT THE PAD CANNON.
AIR PRESSURE DEFLECTED AT LIGHT SPEED...
...CREATING A PIERCING SHOCK WAVE.
STOMP!!
FWP
STO———MP!!
no mercy...
!

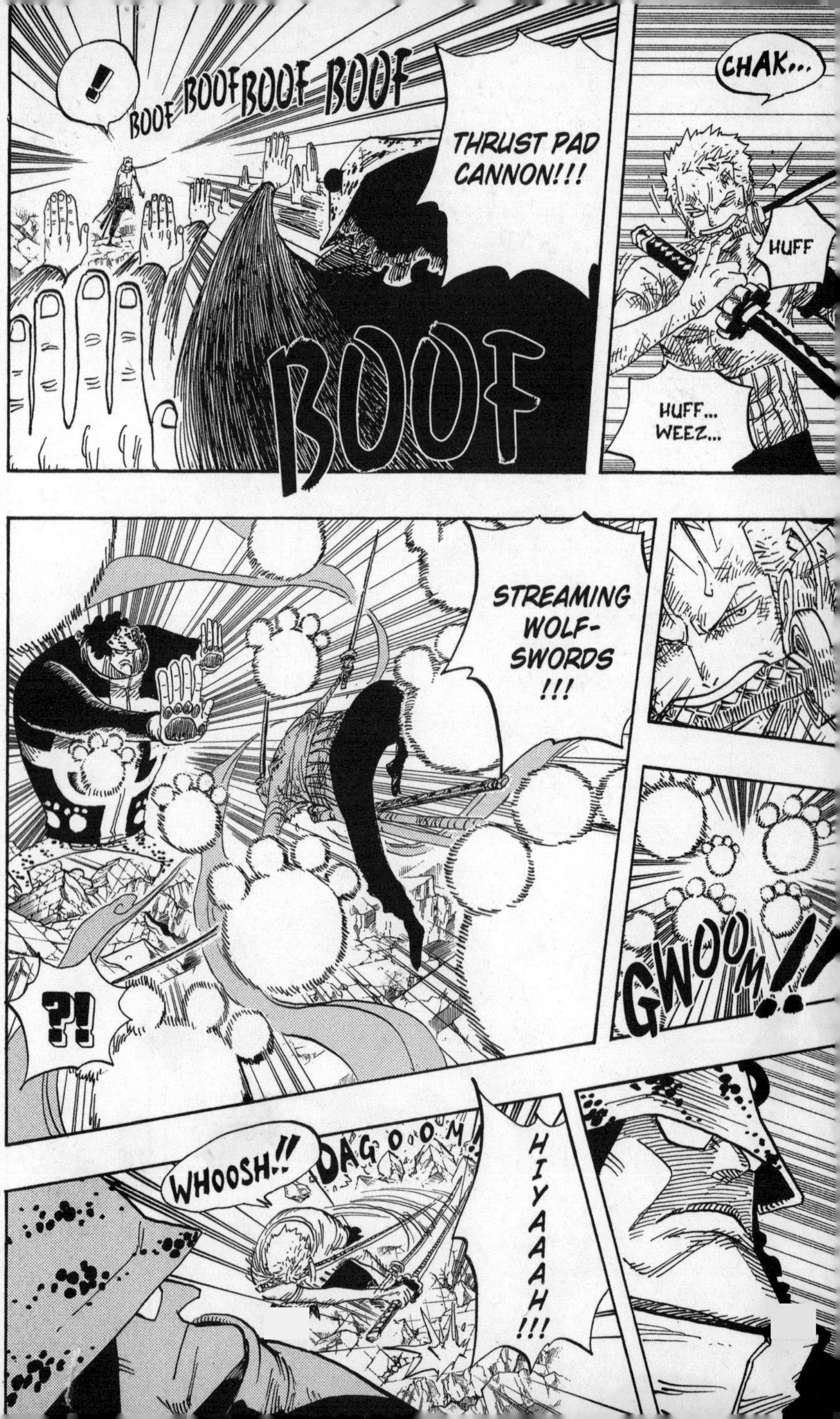
CHAK...
HUFF
HUFF... WEEZ...
!
BOOF BOOF BOOF BOOF
THRUST PAD CANNON!!!
BOOF
GWOOM!!
STREAMING WOLF-SWORDS!!!
?!
HIYAAAAH!!!
DAGOOOM
WHOOSH!!

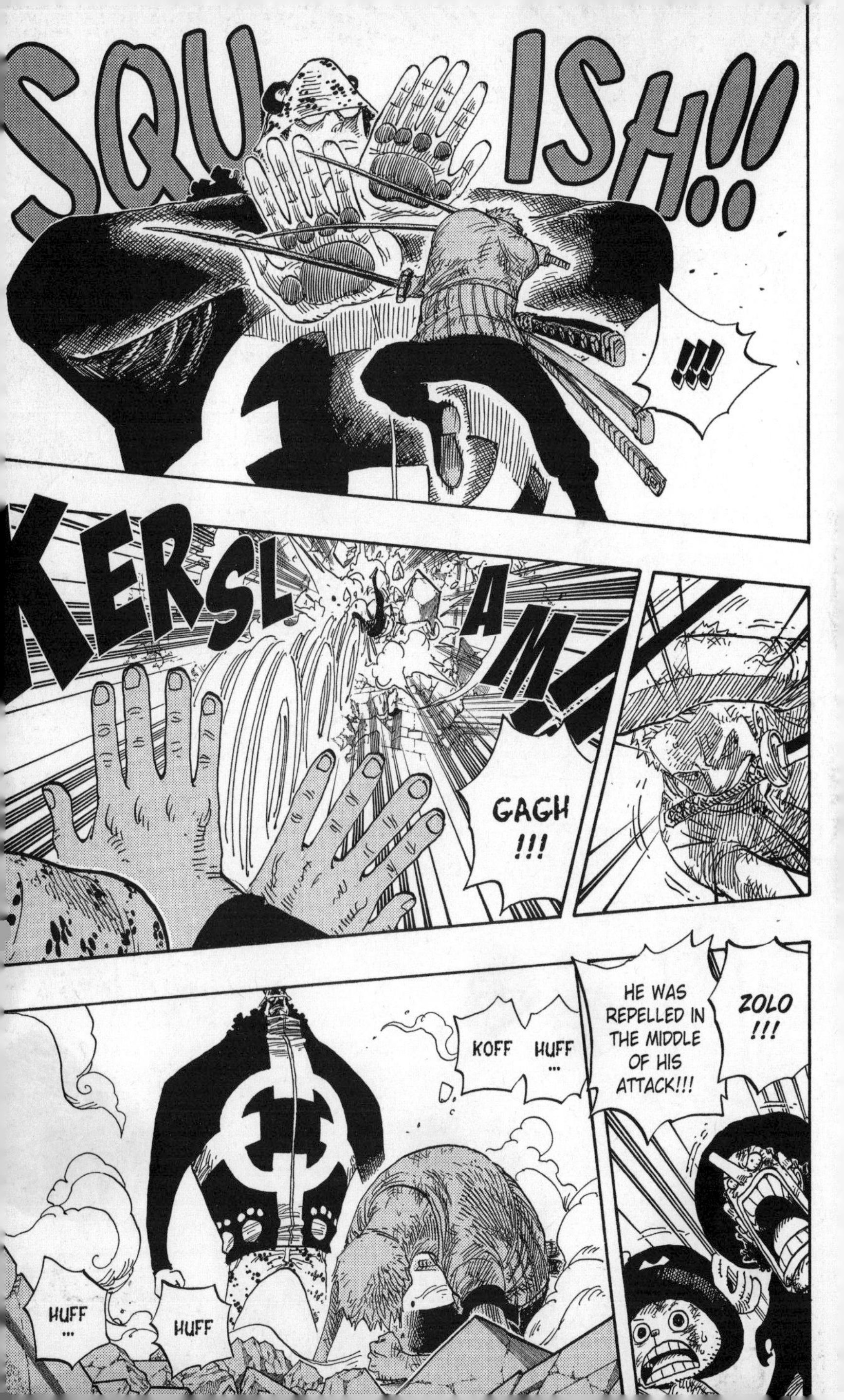
SQU
ISH!!
!!!
KERSLAM
GAGH !!!
ZOLO !!!
HE WAS REPELLED IN THE MIDDLE OF HIS ATTACK!!!
KOFF HUFF ...
HUFF
HUFF ...

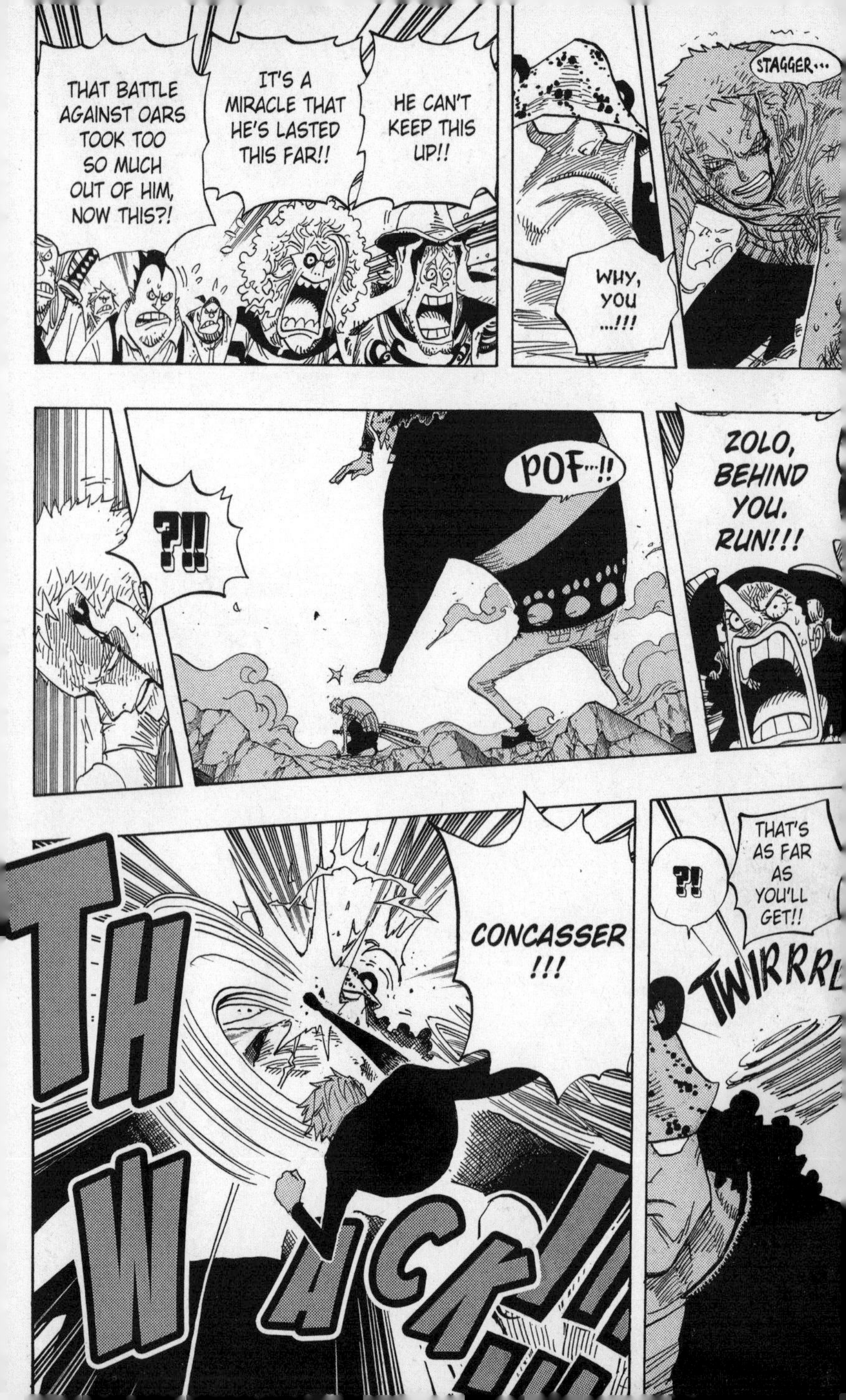
STAGGER...
WHY, YOU ...!!!
HE CAN'T KEEP THIS UP!!
IT'S A MIRACLE THAT HE'S LASTED THIS FAR!!
THAT BATTLE AGAINST OARS TOOK TOO SO MUCH OUT OF HIM, NOW THIS?!
ZOLO, BEHIND YOU. RUN!!!
POF...!!
?!!
THAT'S AS FAR AS YOU'LL GET!!
?!
TWIRRRL
CONCASSER !!!
THWACK

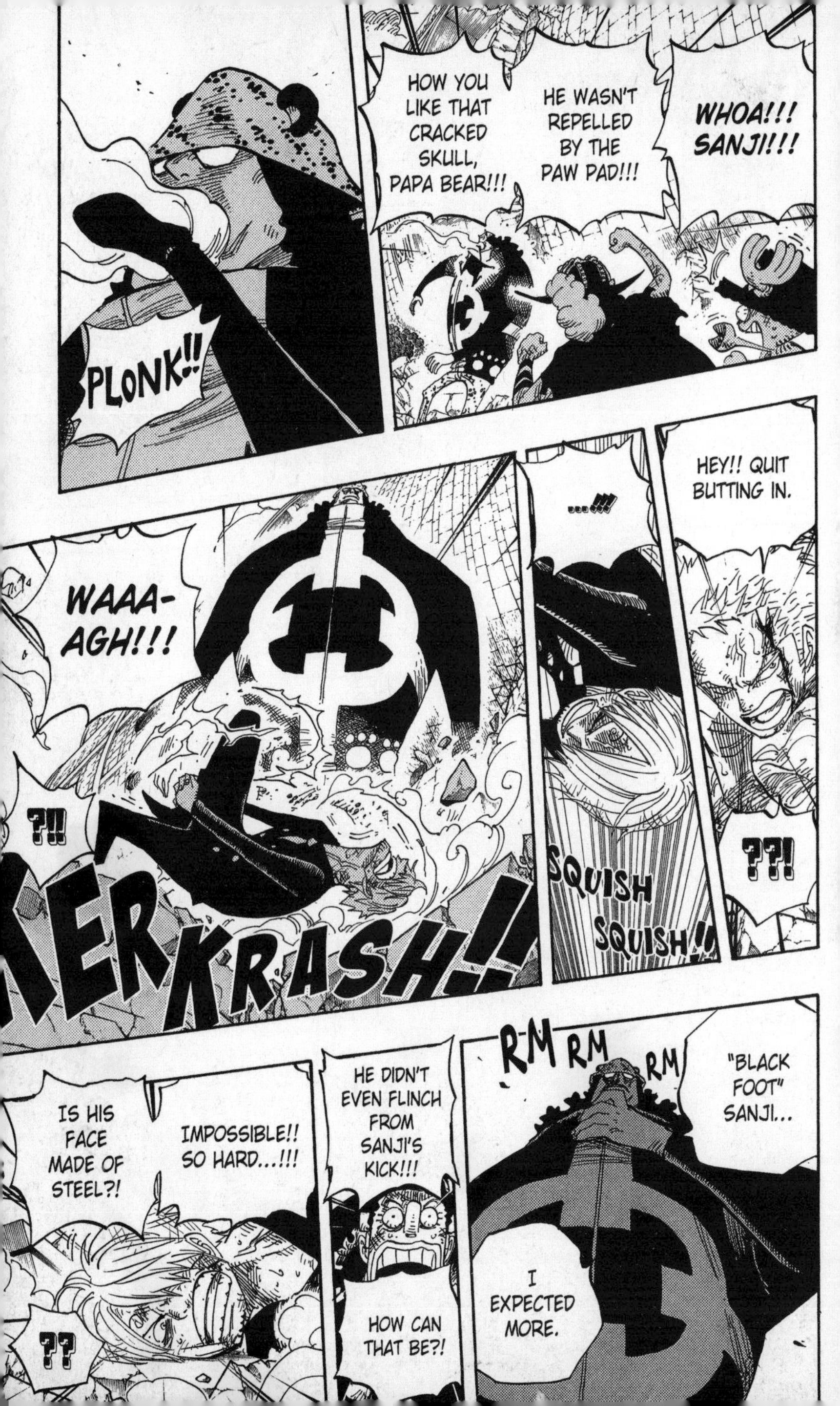
WHOA!!! SANJI!!!!
HE WASN'T REPELLED BY THE PAW PAD!!!
HOW YOU LIKE THAT CRACKED SKULL, PAPA BEAR!!!
PLONK!!
HEY!! QUIT BUTTING IN.
??!
...!!!
SQUISH SQUISH!!
WAAA-AGH!!!
?!!
ERKRASH!!
RM RM RM
"BLACK FOOT" SANJI...
I EXPECTED MORE.
HE DIDN'T EVEN FLINCH FROM SANJI'S KICK!!!
HOW CAN THAT BE?!
IMPOSSIBLE!! SO HARD...!!!
IS HIS FACE MADE OF STEEL?!
??

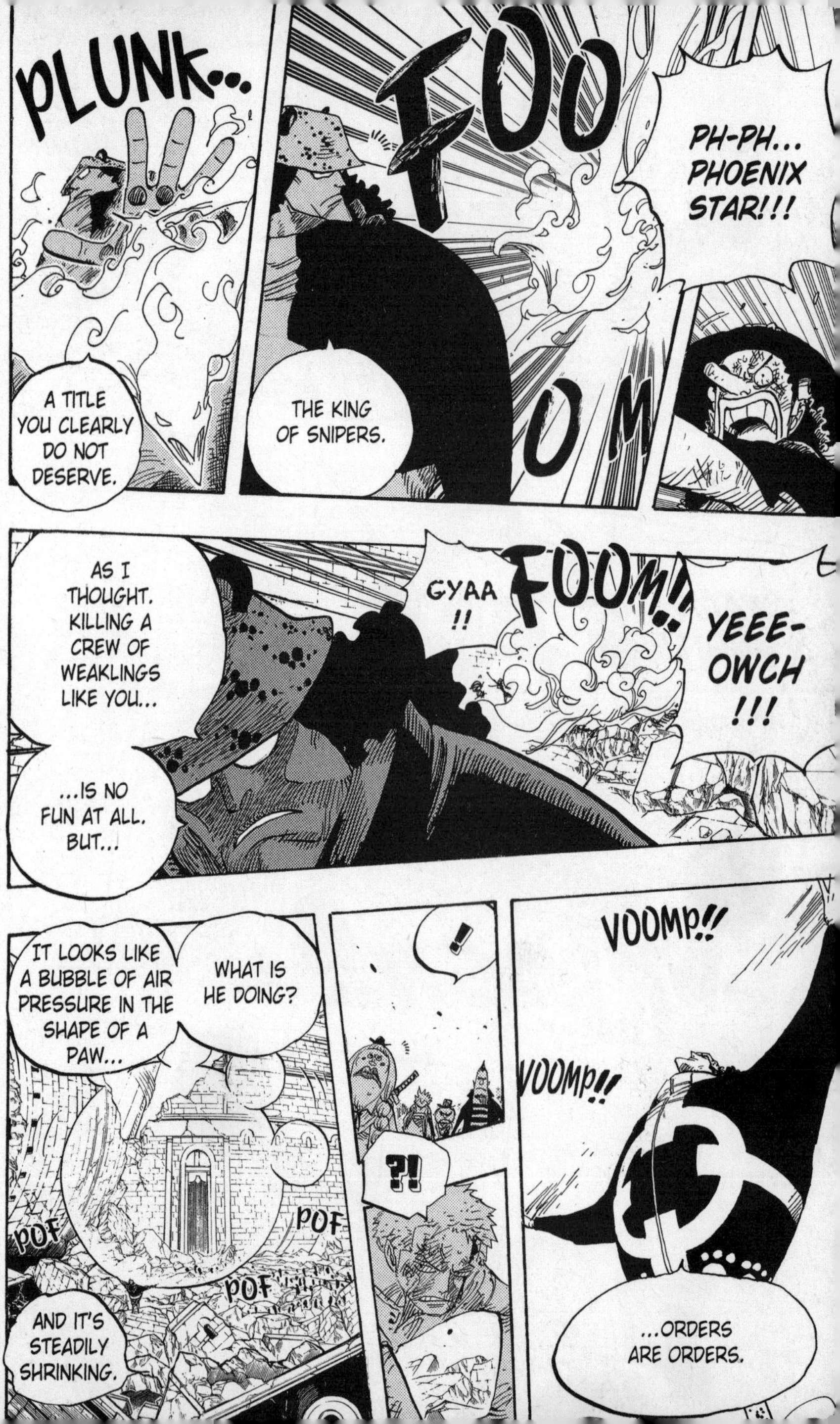
PH-PH... PHOENIX STAR!!!
FOOOM
THE KING OF SNIPERS.
PLUNK...
A TITLE YOU CLEARLY DO NOT DESERVE.
YEEE-OWCH!!!
FOOM!!
GYAA!!
AS I THOUGHT. KILLING A CREW OF WEAKLINGS LIKE YOU...
...IS NO FUN AT ALL. BUT...
VOOMP!!
VOOMP!!
...ORDERS ARE ORDERS.
!
?!
WHAT IS HE DOING?
IT LOOKS LIKE A BUBBLE OF AIR PRESSURE IN THE SHAPE OF A PAW...
POF
POF
POF
AND IT'S STEADILY SHRINKING.

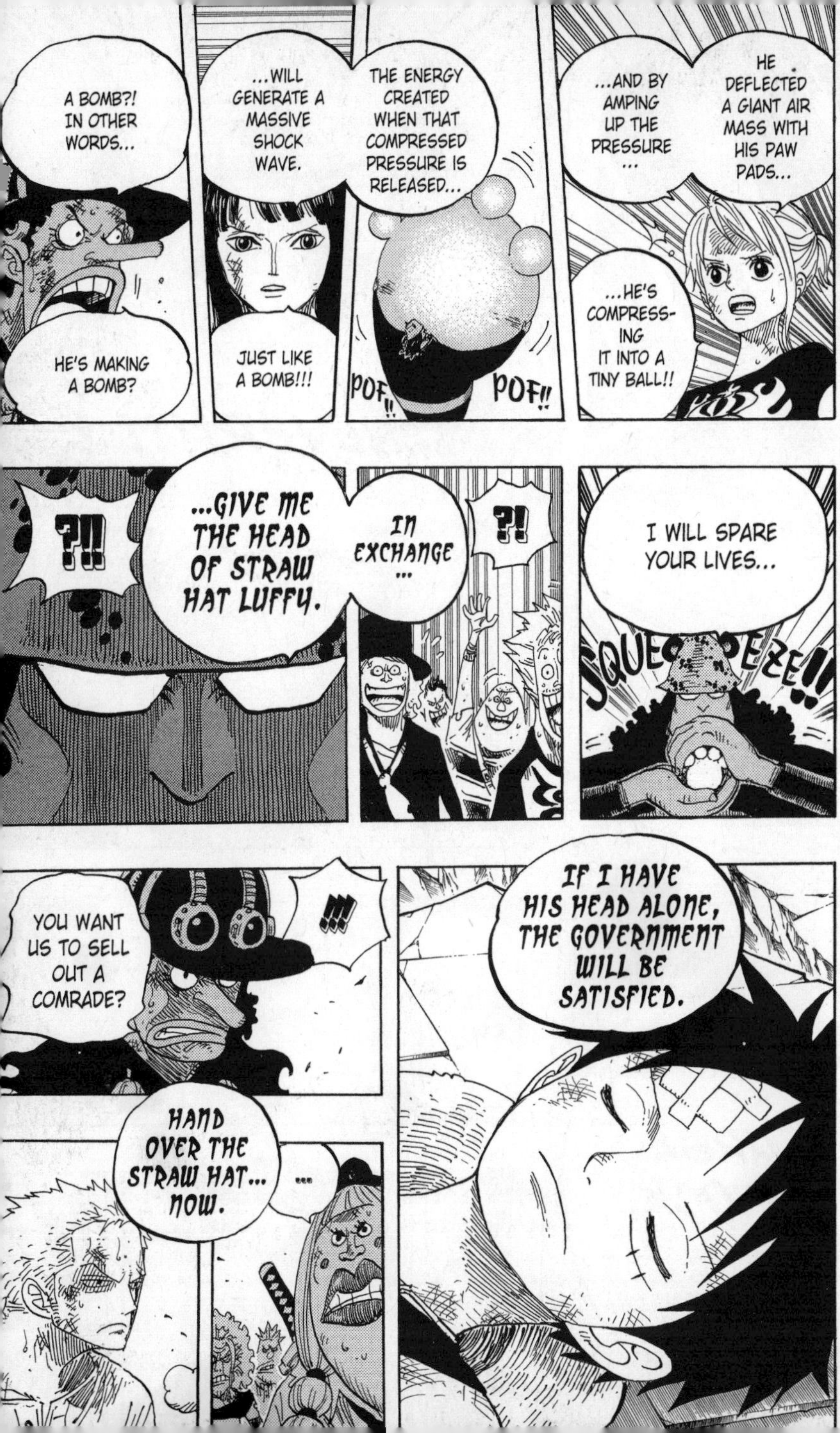
HE DEFLECTED A GIANT AIR MASS WITH HIS PAW PADS...
...AND BY AMPING UP THE PRESSURE ...
...HE'S COMPRESSING IT INTO A TINY BALL!!
THE ENERGY CREATED WHEN THAT COMPRESSED PRESSURE IS RELEASED...
POF!!
POF!!
...WILL GENERATE A MASSIVE SHOCK WAVE.
JUST LIKE A BOMB!!!
A BOMB?! IN OTHER WORDS...
HE'S MAKING A BOMB?
I WILL SPARE YOUR LIVES...
SQUE EZE!!
?!
IN EXCHANGE ...
...GIVE ME THE HEAD OF STRAW HAT LUFFY.
?!!
IF I HAVE HIS HEAD ALONE, THE GOVERNMENT WILL BE SATISFIED.
!!!
YOU WANT US TO SELL OUT A COMRADE?
...
HAND OVER THE STRAW HAT... NOW.

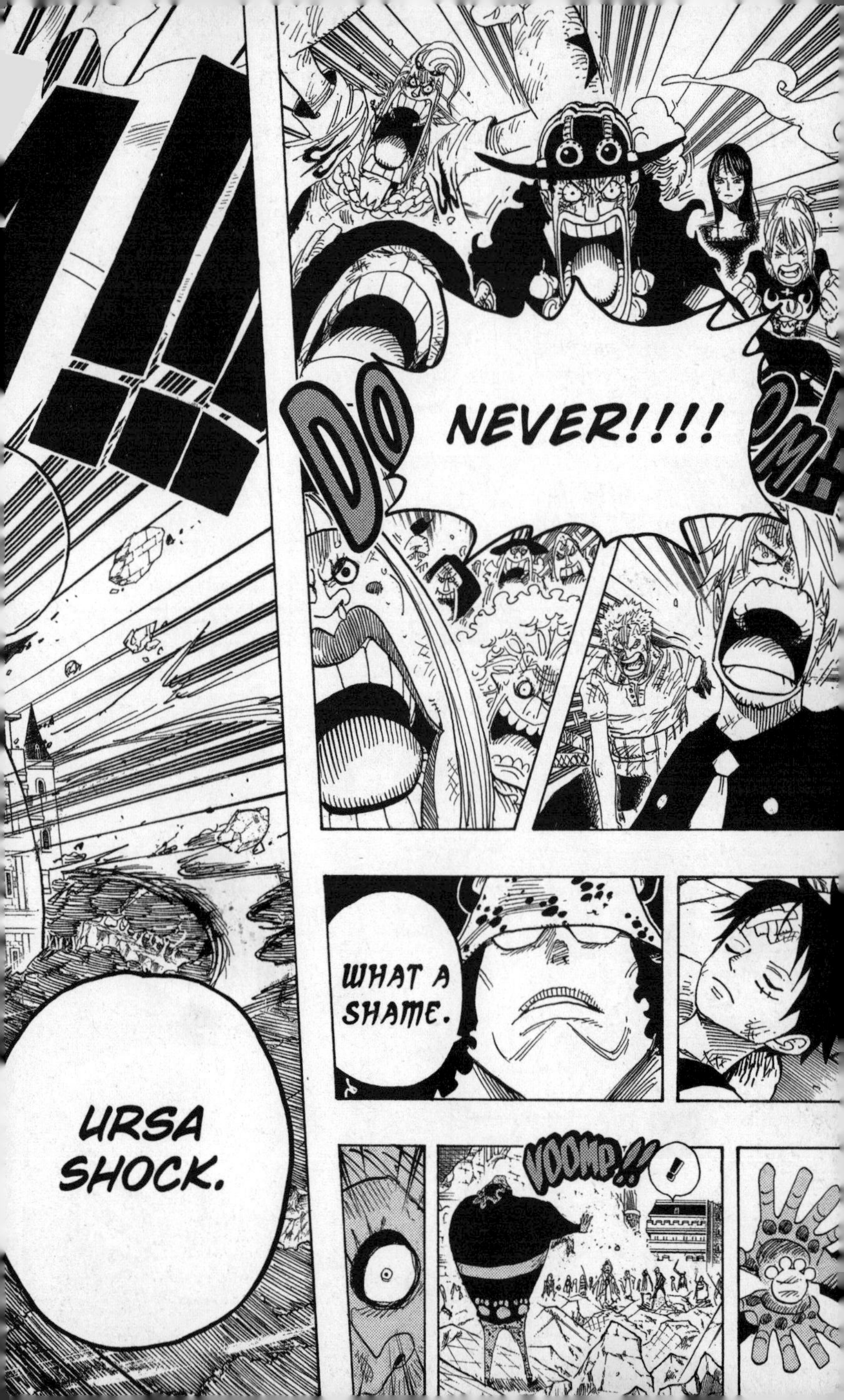
DO
NEVER!!!!
OM!!
WHAT A SHAME.
VOOMP!!
!
URSA SHOCK.

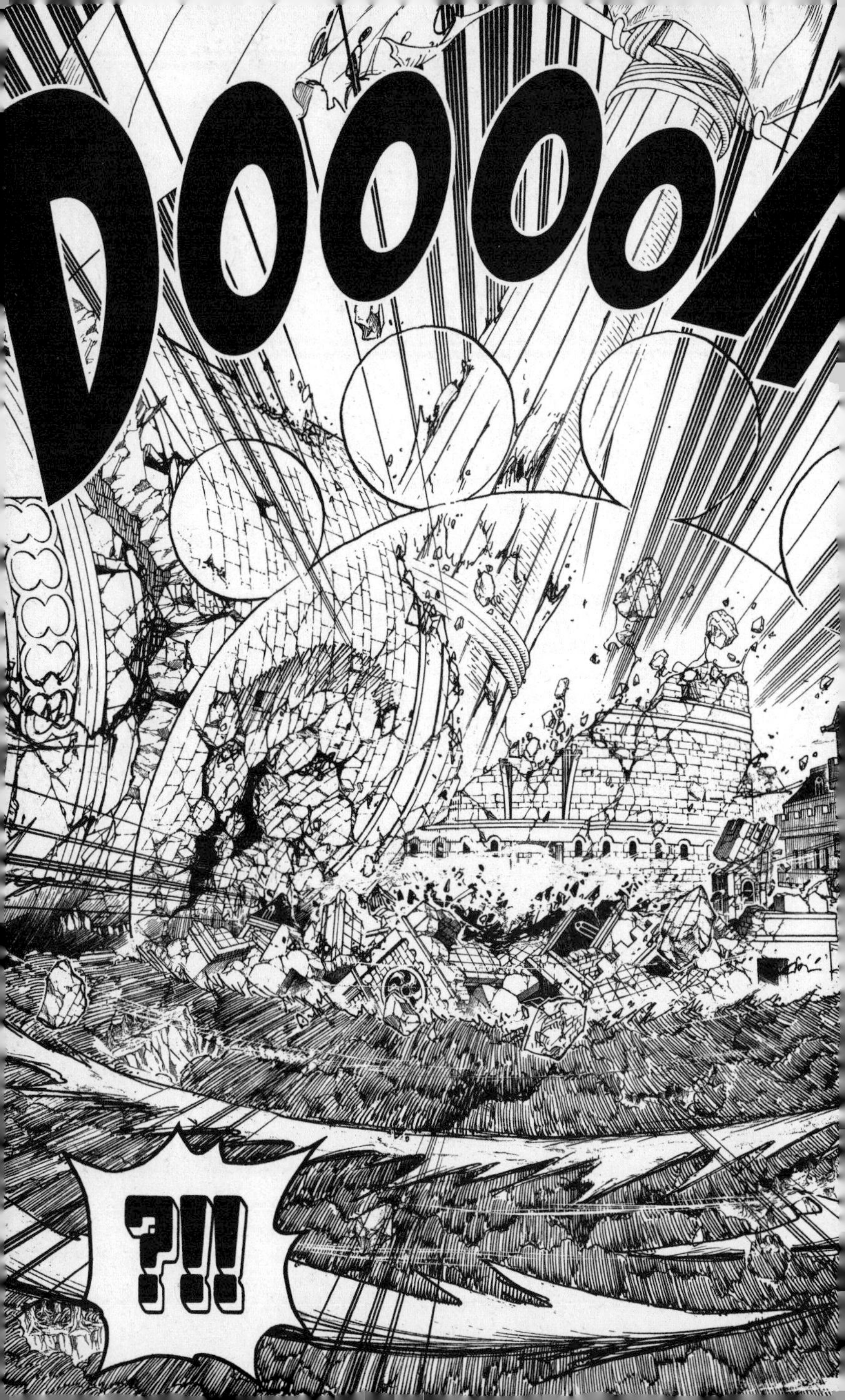
DOOOOM
?!!

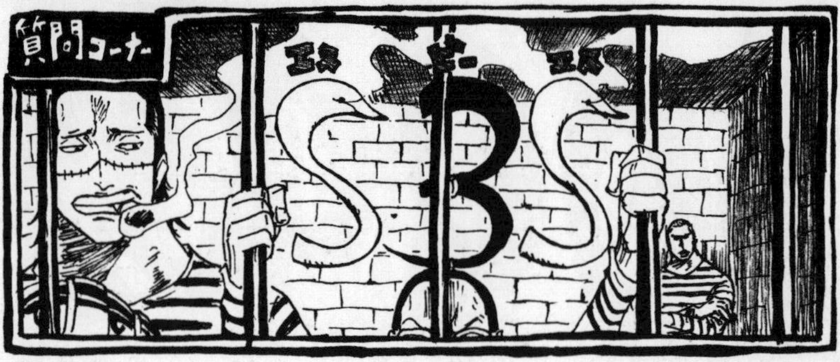
質問コーナー
エス ビー エス
SBS
(Chome, Hyogo)

Reader(Q): "I...will become the king of pirates." --Prince of the Land of Dreams TA5

Oda(A): Okay.

Q: I'm sure today's ships have all the modern conveniences we're used to, but I wonder about the pirate ships of olden days. When the crew had to poop, did they flush? Or did the crew just hold it till they got to land?
--Tamekuchi Suimasenen

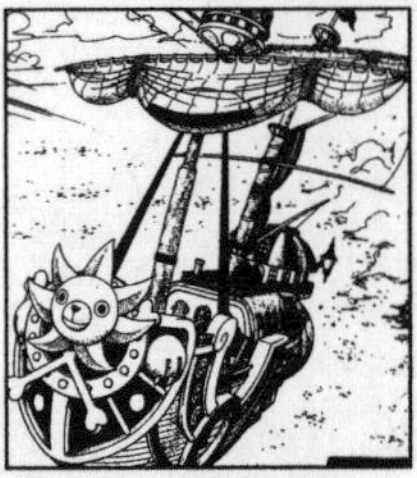

A: Good question. For sailing vessels, a typical "privy" was a hole in the deck that dropped straight into the sea. Even today, there are some sailing vessels that use this old style. Mostly, they have flush toilets now. Just like the toilets on airplanes, they flush quickly with a "VOOSH!!" Please imagine that the Sunny also has toilets like that. However, the men don't worry too much about proper poop etiquette and do it from all sorts of places on the ship where it can flow directly into the sea.

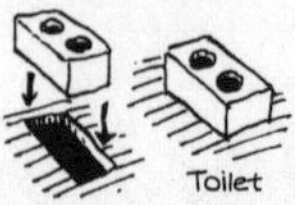
Toilet

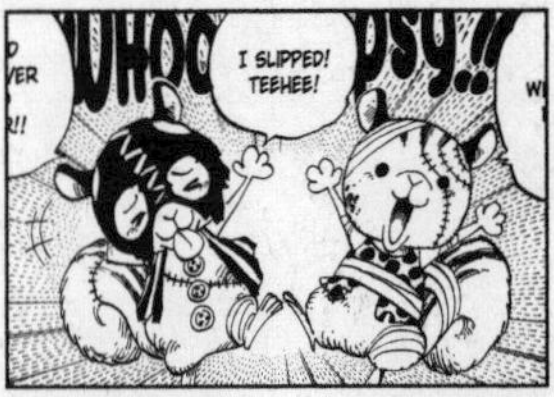
I SLIPPED! TEEHEE!

Q: This is my first postcard to you. In volume 49, chapter 475, "Pirates of the Forest," page 107, panel 3, there are characters named the Risky Brothers! And when Nami is taken to Moria, the zombies (volume 47, chapter 451) are the Risky Brothers too, right?
-- Yoshiki.

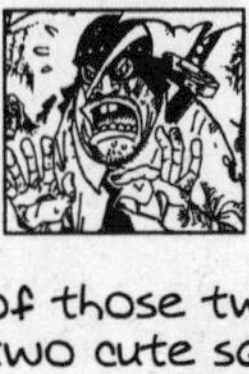

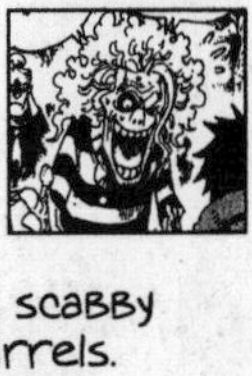

A: Yes, you're right. The shadows of those two scabby sailors were controlled by the two cute squirrels.

Q: Let's end this right here, okay? --Divorce Horror

A: For this installment, okay. But the Question Corner will continue for a long time!

Chapter 485:
STRAW HAT PIRATES--PIRATE HUNTER ZOLO

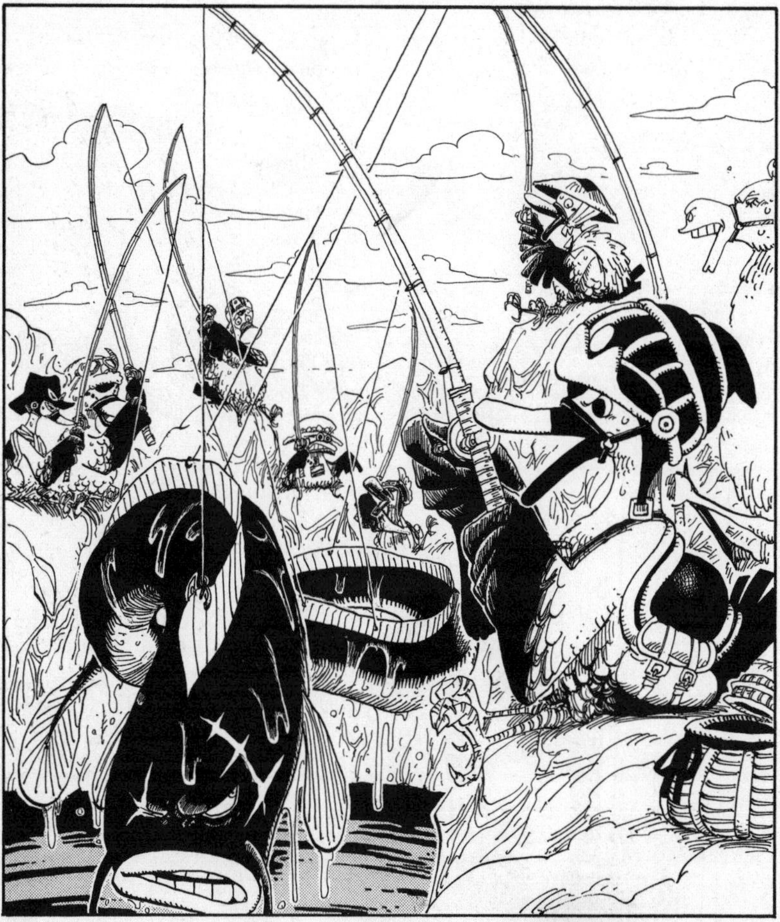

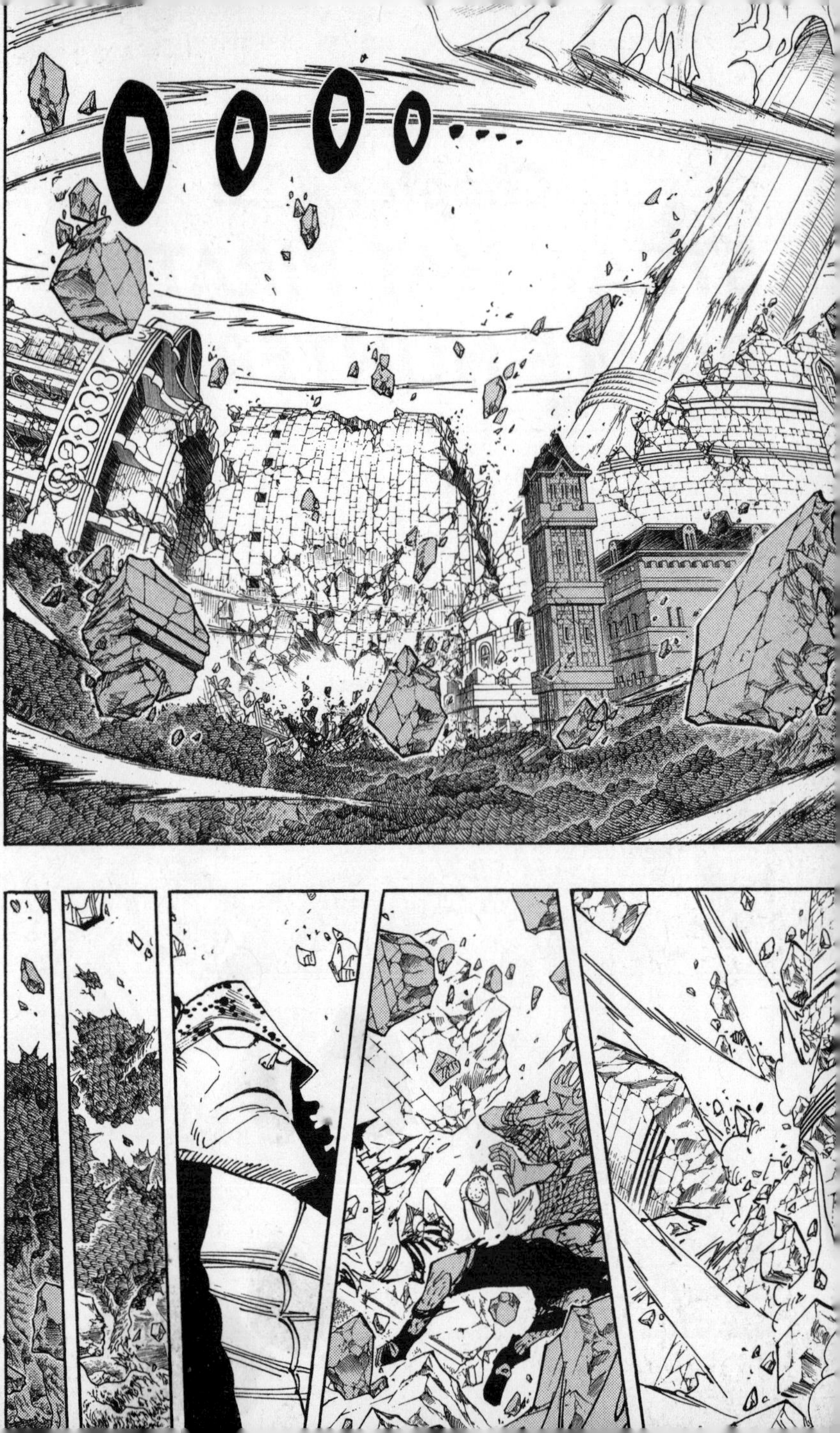
OOOO...

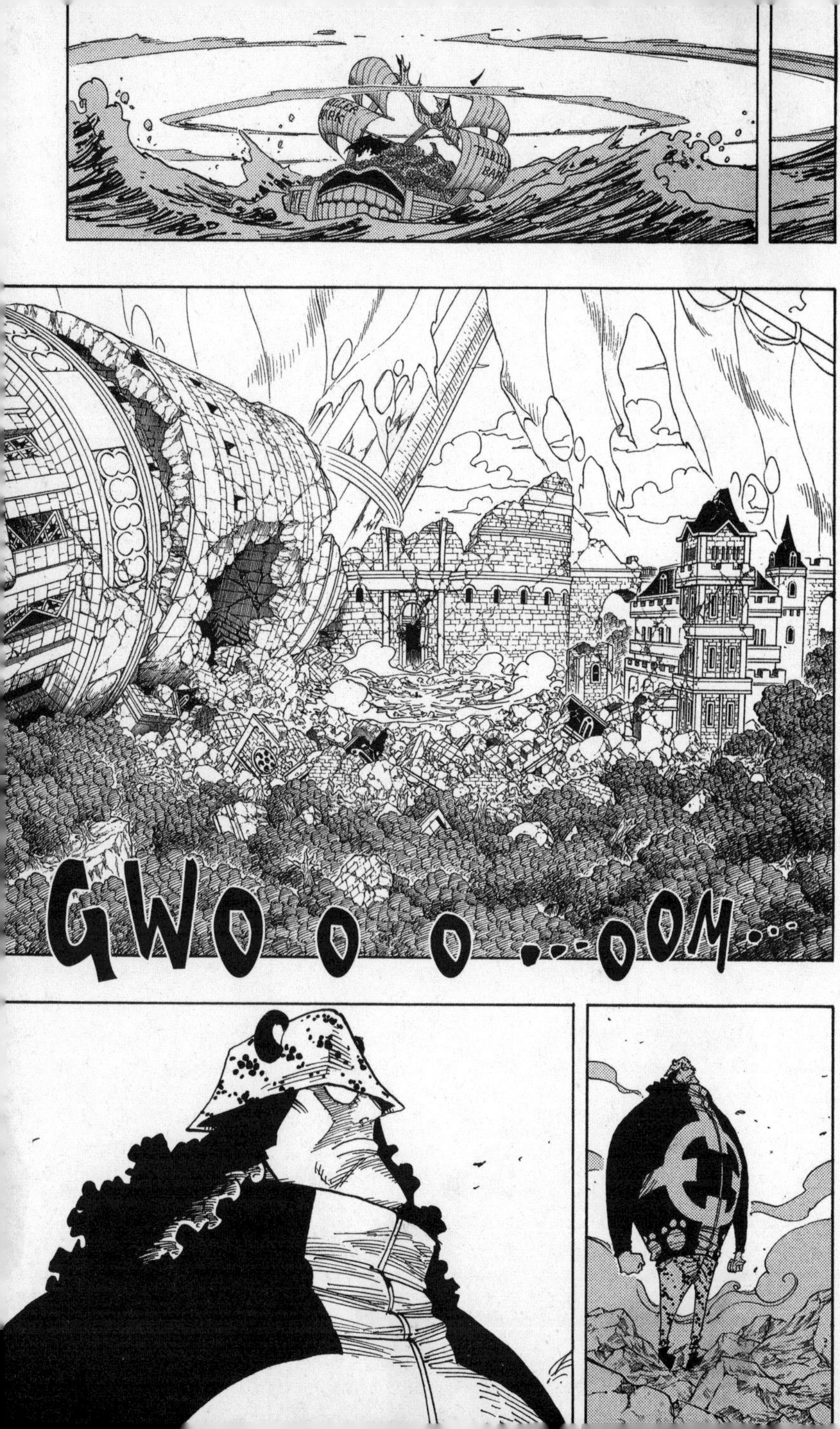
GWOOO...OOM...

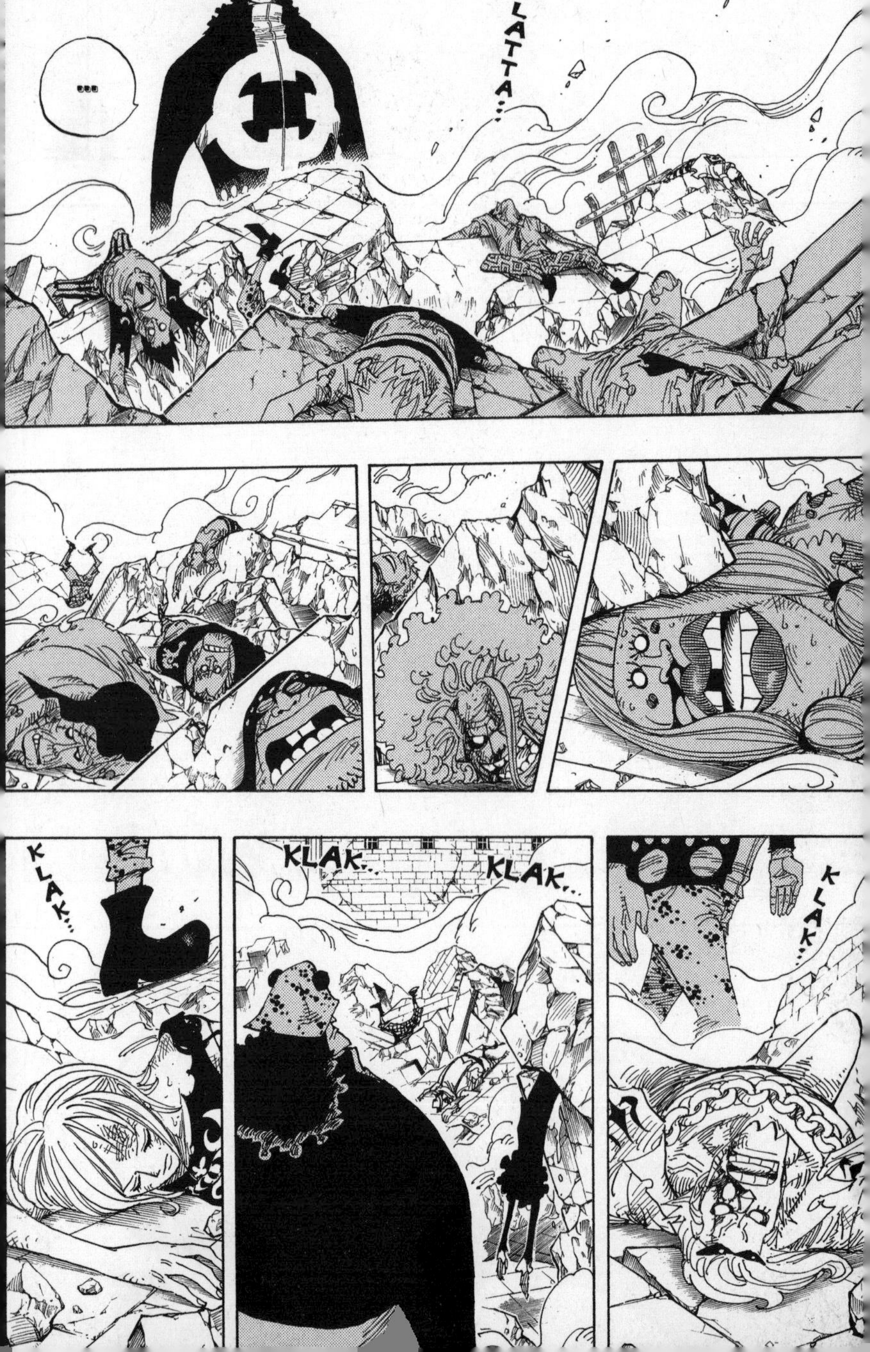
KLATTA...
...
KLAK...
KLAK...
KLAK...
KLAK...

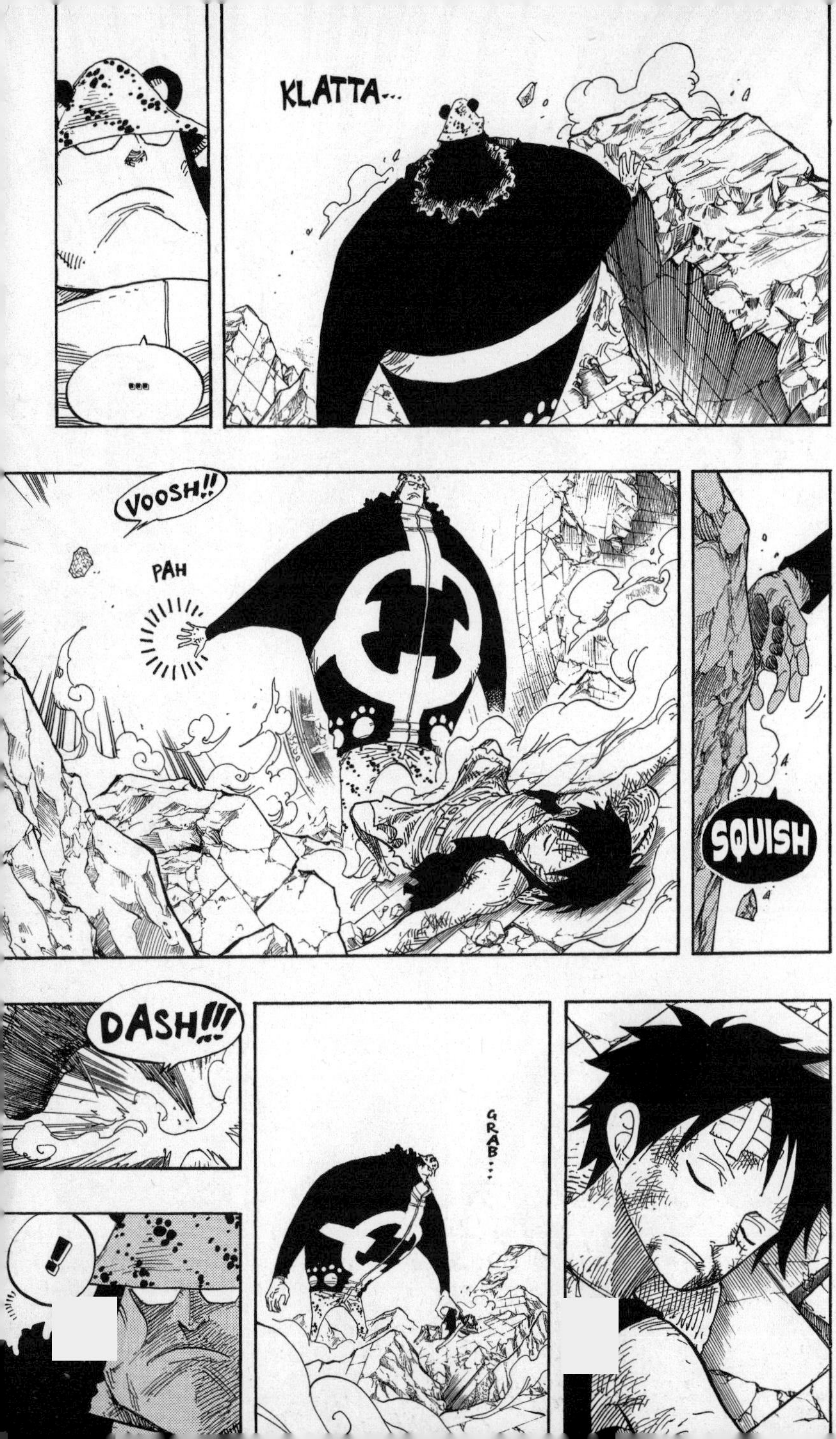
KLATTA...
...
SQUISH
VOOSH!!
PAH
GRAB...
DASH!!!
!

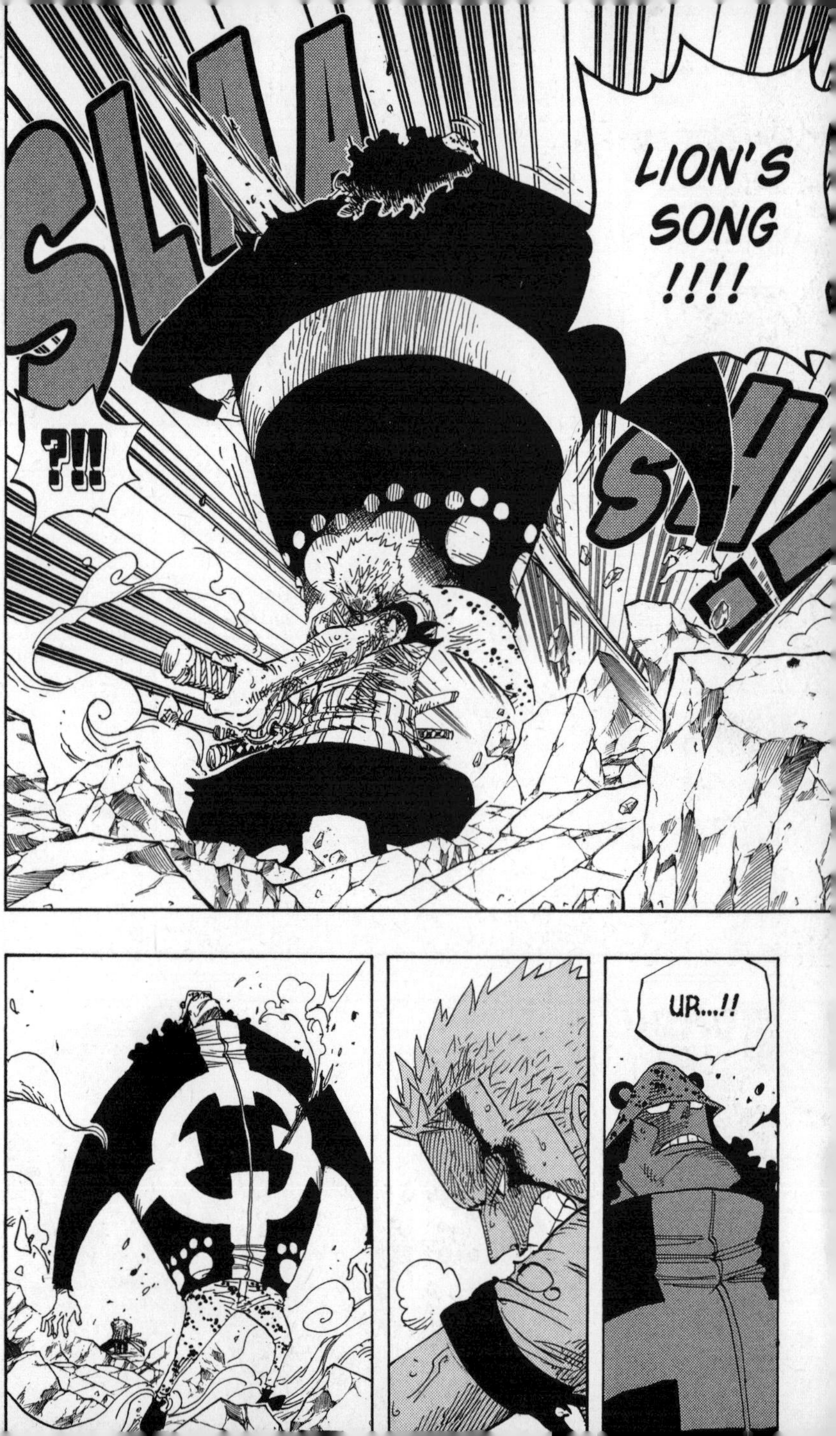
LION'S SONG !!!!
?!!
UR...!!

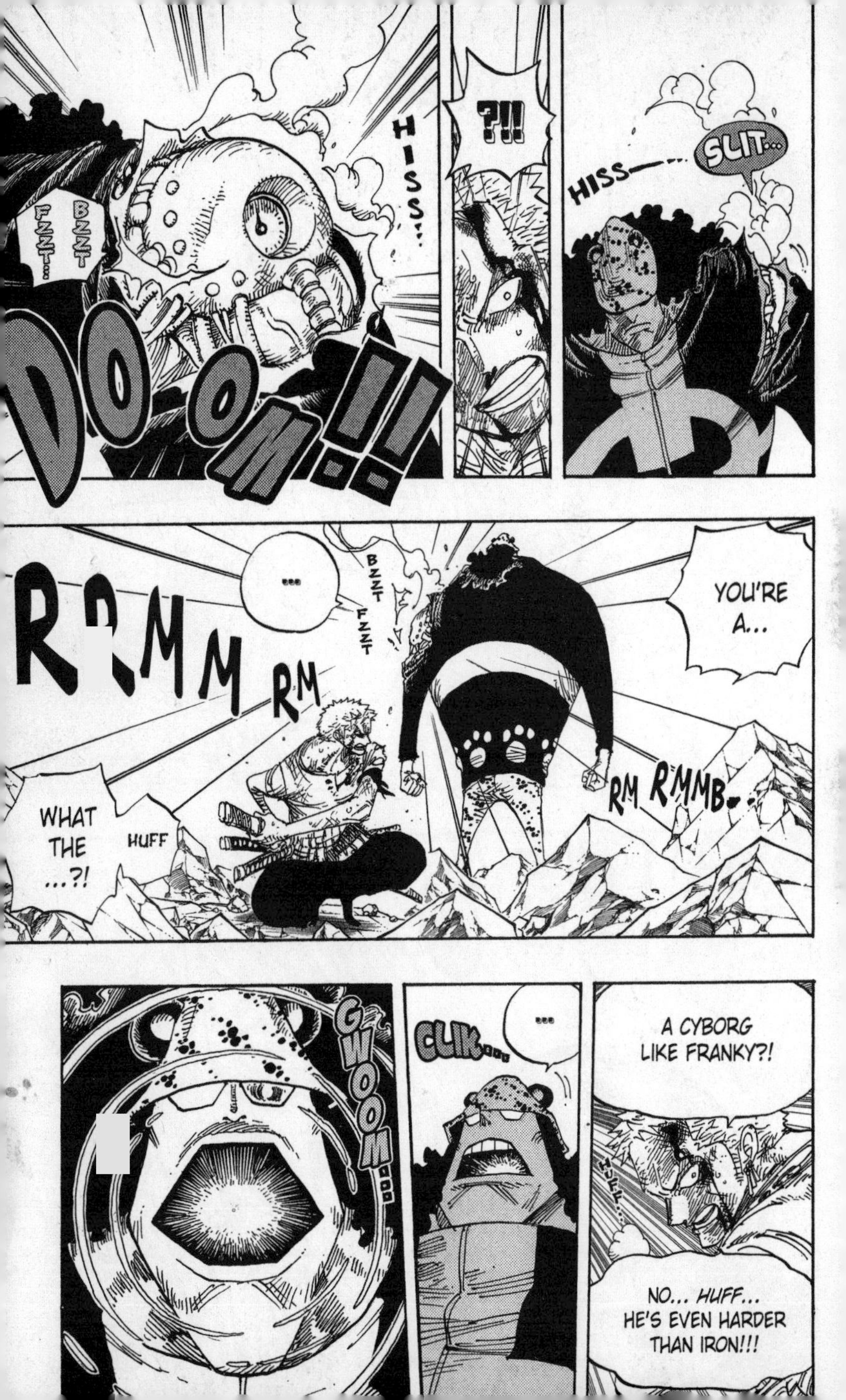
HISS—
SLIT...
?!!
HISS...
BZZT
FZZT...
DOOOM!!
YOU'RE A...
RM RMMB...
BZZT
FZZT
...
RRMM
RM
WHAT THE ...?!
HUFF
A CYBORG LIKE FRANKY?!
HUFF...
NO... *HUFF*... HE'S EVEN HARDER THAN IRON!!!
...
CLIK...
GWOOM...

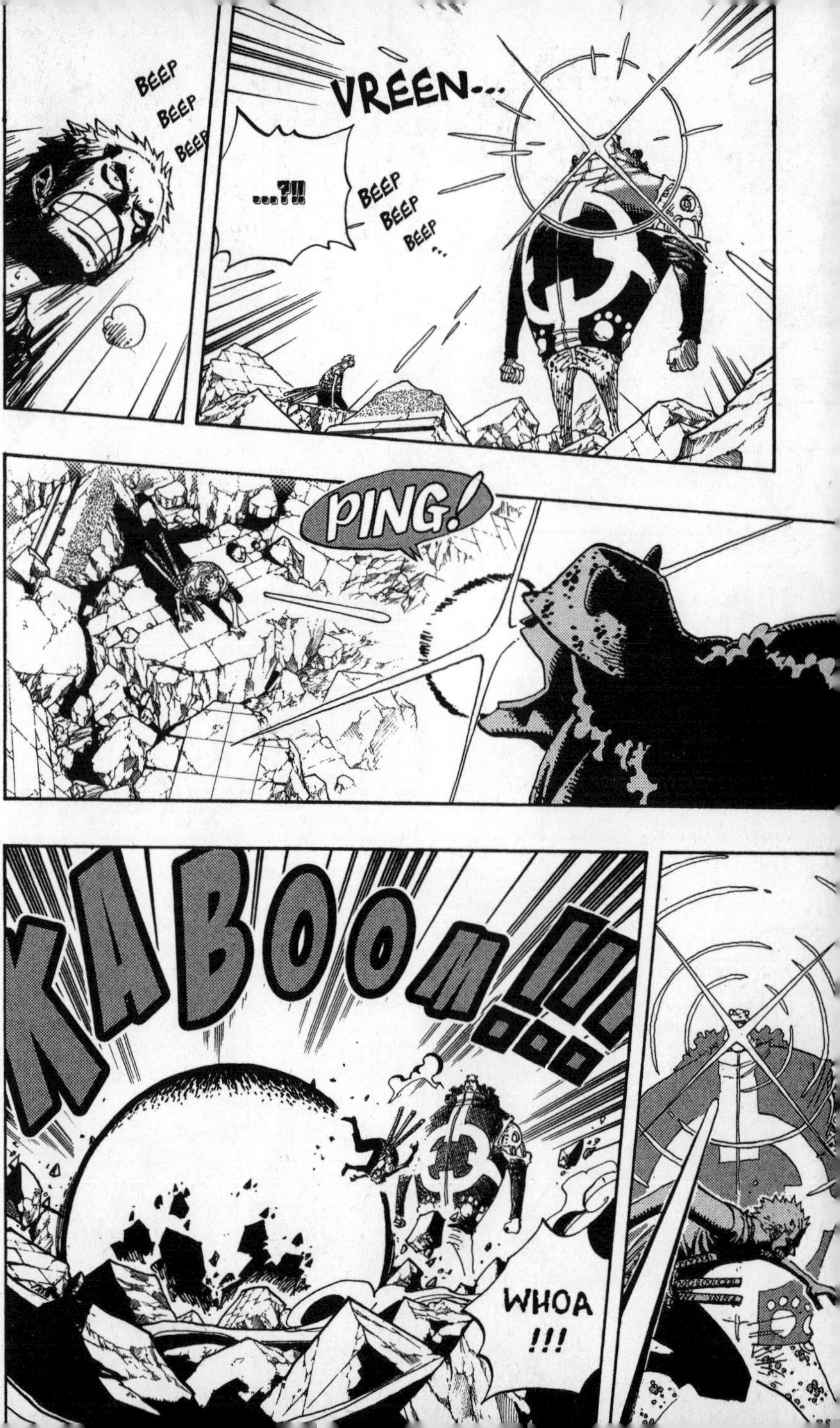
VREEN...
...?!!
BEEP
BEEP
BEEP...
BEEP
BEEP
BEEP
PING!
WHOA
!!!
KABOOM!!!

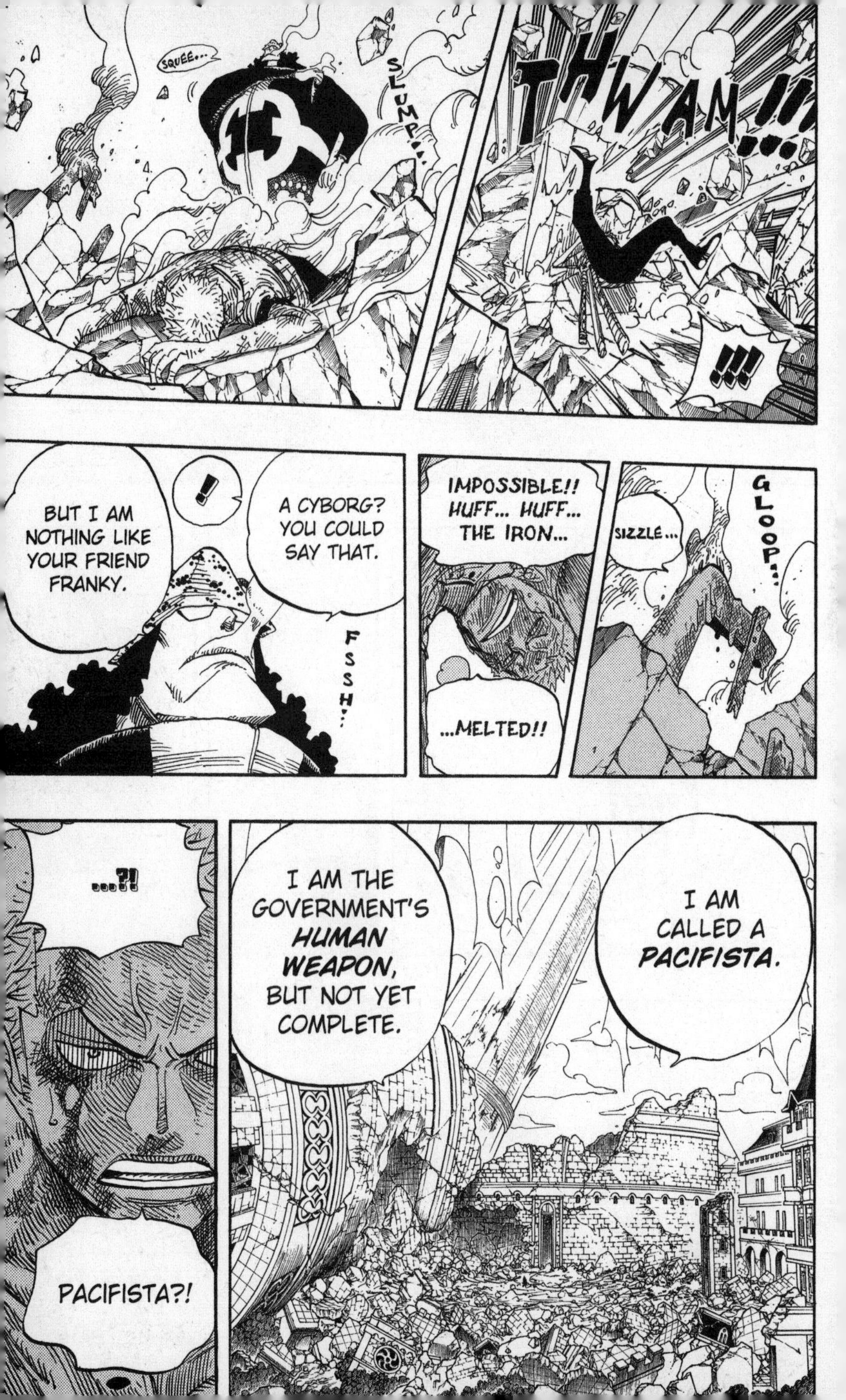
THWAM!!!
!!!
SLUMP...
SQUEE...
GLOOP...
SIZZLE...
IMPOSSIBLE!! HUFF... HUFF... THE IRON...
...MELTED!!
A CYBORG? YOU COULD SAY THAT.
!
BUT I AM NOTHING LIKE YOUR FRIEND FRANKY.
FSSH...
I AM CALLED A PACIFISTA.
I AM THE GOVERNMENT'S HUMAN WEAPON, BUT NOT YET COMPLETE.
...?!
PACIFISTA?!

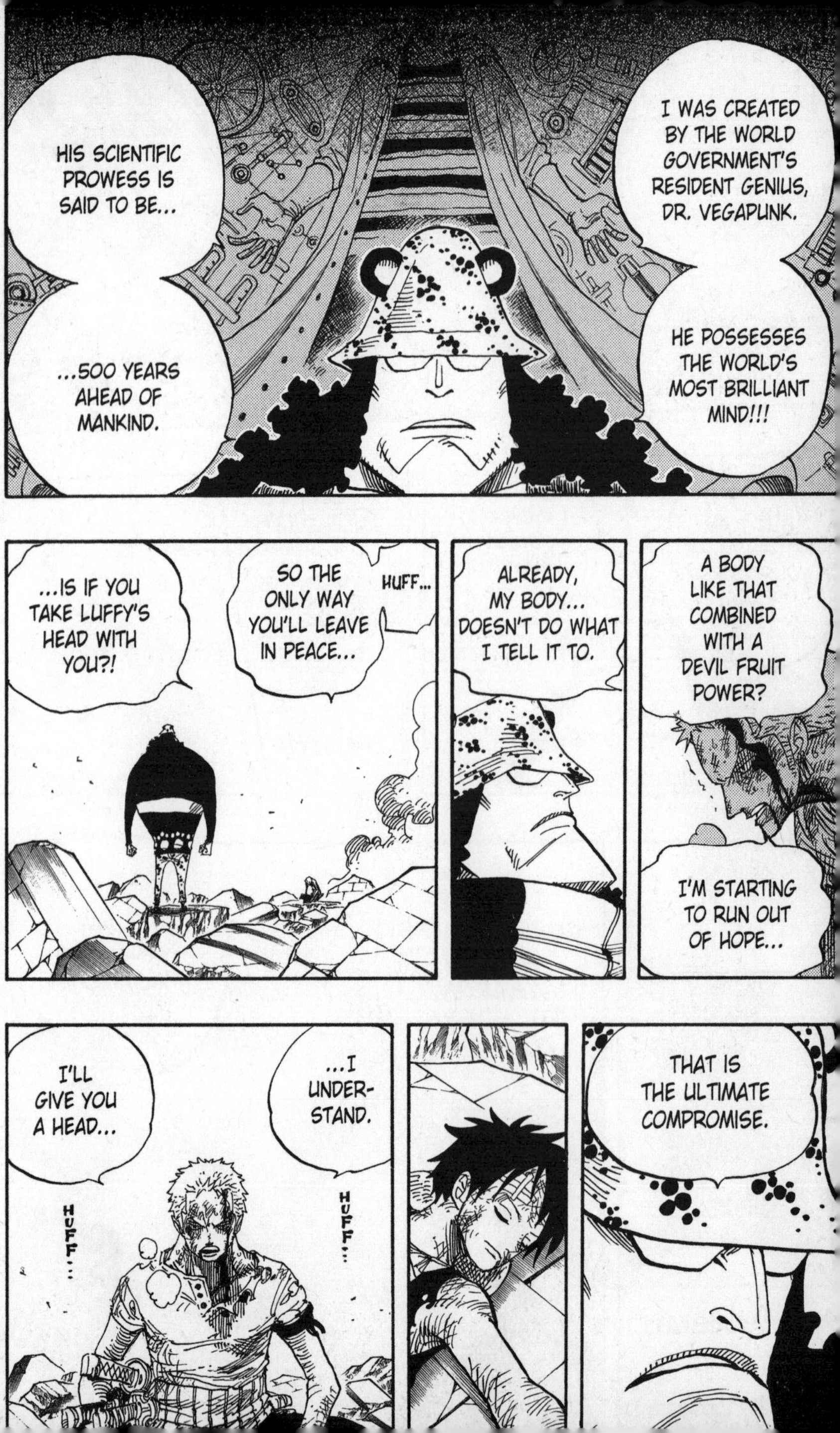
I WAS CREATED BY THE WORLD GOVERNMENT'S RESIDENT GENIUS, DR. VEGAPUNK.
HE POSSESSES THE WORLD'S MOST BRILLIANT MIND!!!
HIS SCIENTIFIC PROWESS IS SAID TO BE...
...500 YEARS AHEAD OF MANKIND.
A BODY LIKE THAT COMBINED WITH A DEVIL FRUIT POWER?
I'M STARTING TO RUN OUT OF HOPE...
ALREADY, MY BODY... DOESN'T DO WHAT I TELL IT TO.
HUFF...
SO THE ONLY WAY YOU'LL LEAVE IN PEACE...
...IS IF YOU TAKE LUFFY'S HEAD WITH YOU?!
THAT IS THE ULTIMATE COMPROMISE.
...I UNDERSTAND.
HUFF...
I'LL GIVE YOU A HEAD...
HUFF...

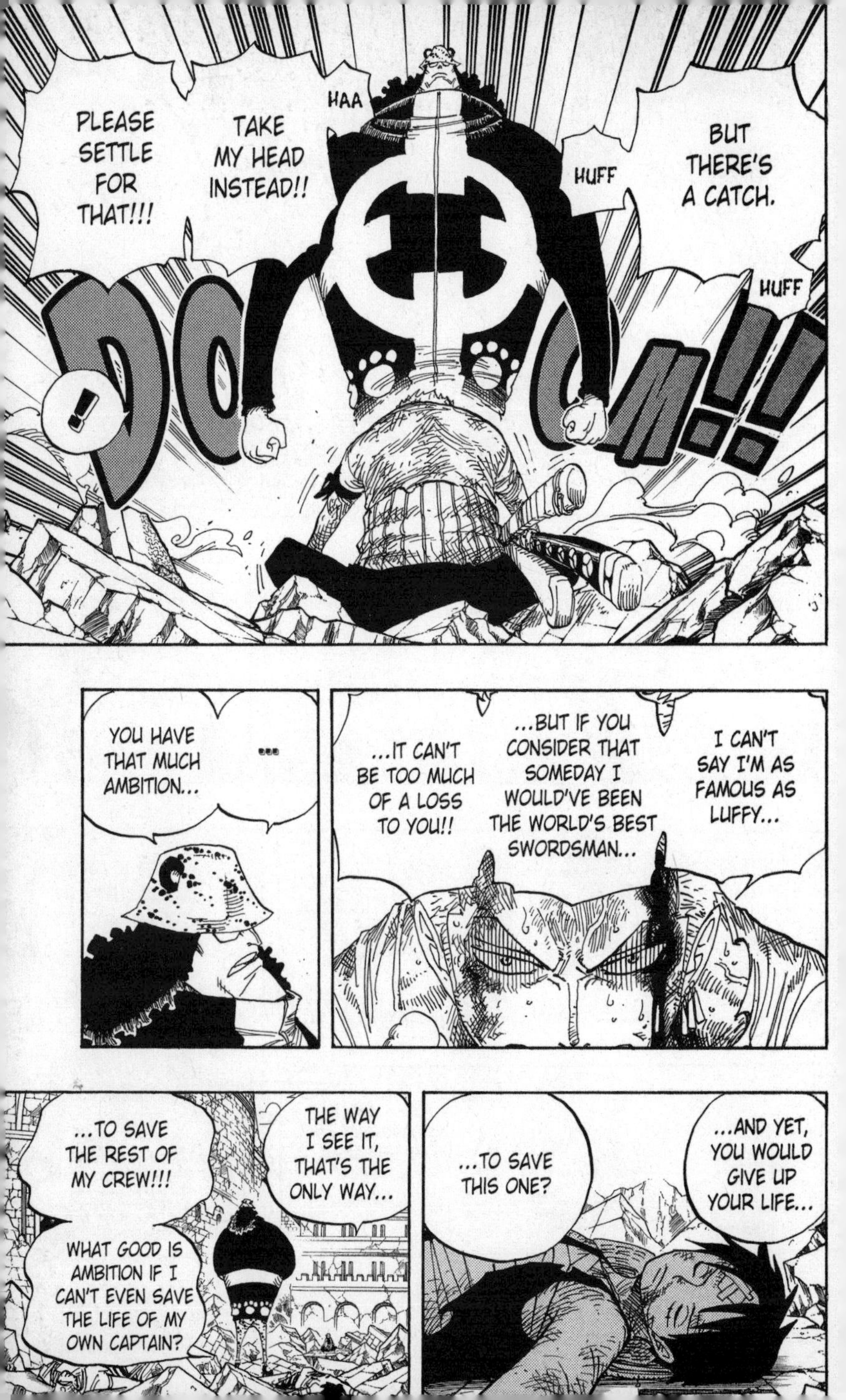
BUT THERE'S A CATCH.
HUFF
HUFF
HAA
TAKE MY HEAD INSTEAD!!
PLEASE SETTLE FOR THAT!!!
DOOM!!
!
I CAN'T SAY I'M AS FAMOUS AS LUFFY...
...BUT IF YOU CONSIDER THAT SOMEDAY I WOULD'VE BEEN THE WORLD'S BEST SWORDSMAN...
...IT CAN'T BE TOO MUCH OF A LOSS TO YOU!!
...
YOU HAVE THAT MUCH AMBITION...
...AND YET, YOU WOULD GIVE UP YOUR LIFE...
...TO SAVE THIS ONE?
THE WAY I SEE IT, THAT'S THE ONLY WAY...
...TO SAVE THE REST OF MY CREW!!!
WHAT GOOD IS AMBITION IF I CAN'T EVEN SAVE THE LIFE OF MY OWN CAPTAIN?

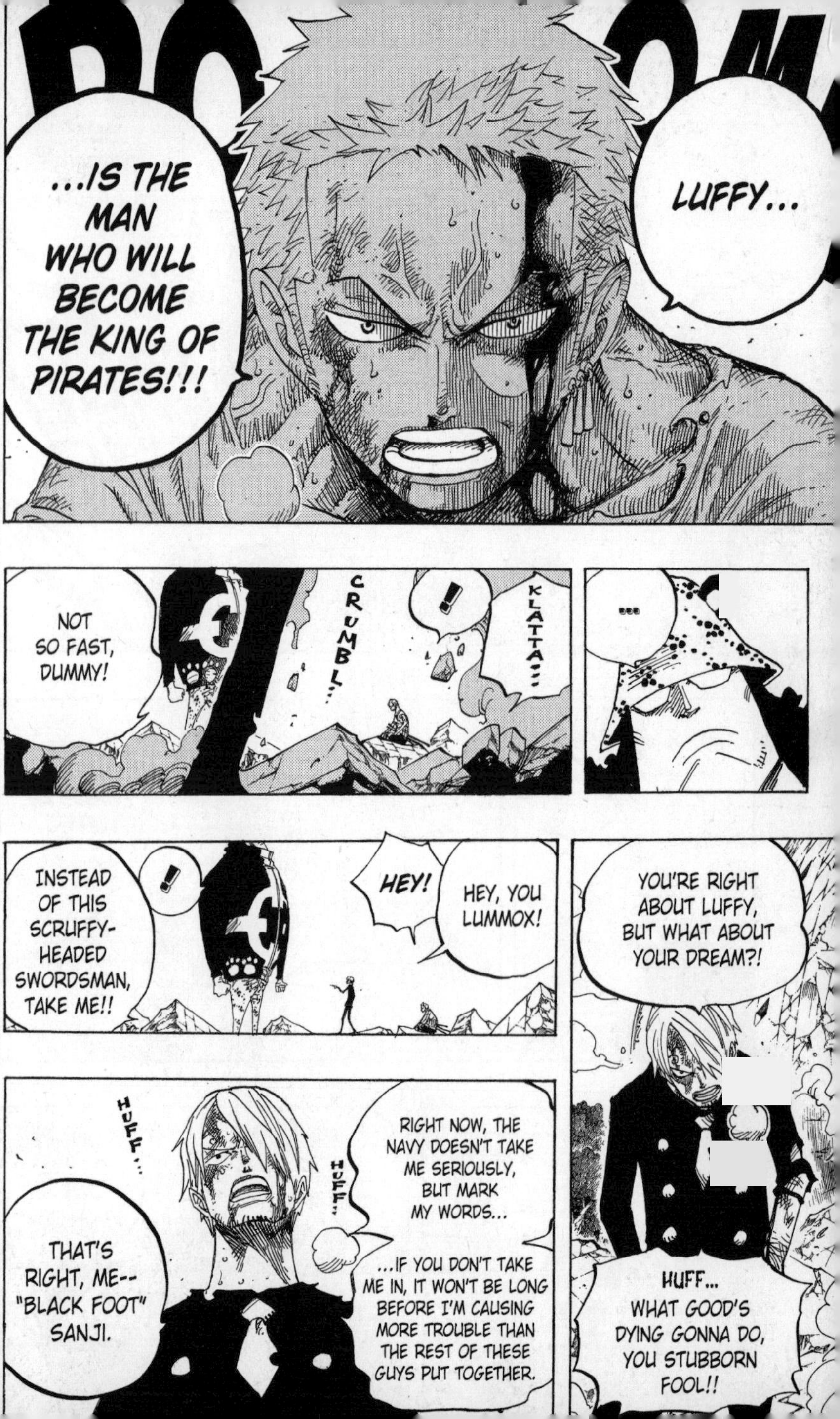
LUFFY...
...IS THE MAN WHO WILL BECOME THE KING OF PIRATES!!!
...
!
KLATTA...
CRUMBL...
NOT SO FAST, DUMMY!
YOU'RE RIGHT ABOUT LUFFY, BUT WHAT ABOUT YOUR DREAM?!
HUFF... WHAT GOOD'S DYING GONNA DO, YOU STUBBORN FOOL!!
HEY, YOU LUMMOX!
HEY!
!
INSTEAD OF THIS SCRUFFY-HEADED SWORDSMAN, TAKE ME!!
RIGHT NOW, THE NAVY DOESN'T TAKE ME SERIOUSLY, BUT MARK MY WORDS...
HUFF...
...IF YOU DON'T TAKE ME IN, IT WON'T BE LONG BEFORE I'M CAUSING MORE TROUBLE THAN THE REST OF THESE GUYS PUT TOGETHER.
HUFF...
THAT'S RIGHT, ME-- "BLACK FOOT" SANJI.

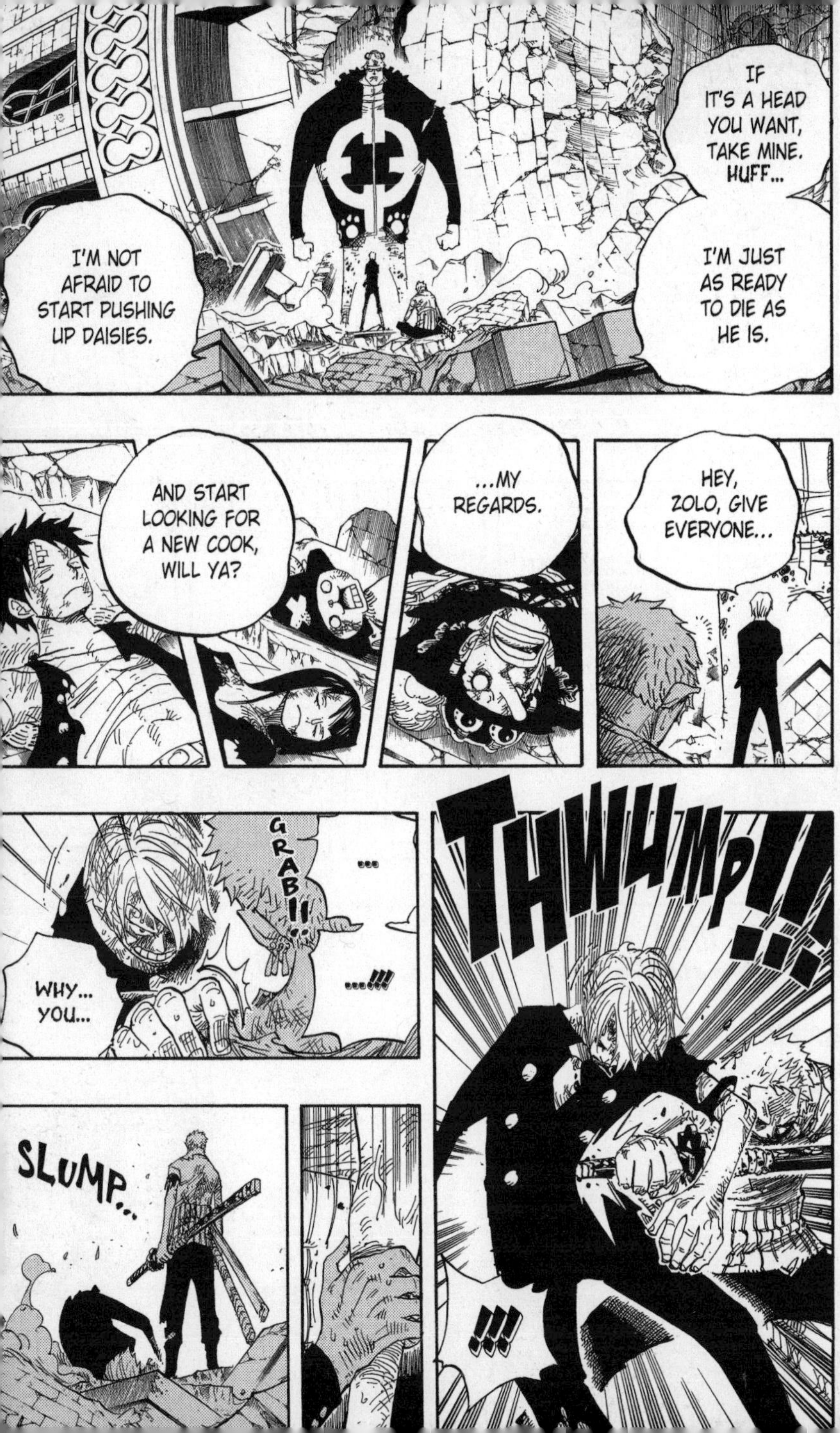
IF IT'S A HEAD YOU WANT, TAKE MINE. HUFF...
I'M JUST AS READY TO DIE AS HE IS.
I'M NOT AFRAID TO START PUSHING UP DAISIES.
HEY, ZOLO, GIVE EVERYONE...
...MY REGARDS.
AND START LOOKING FOR A NEW COOK, WILL YA?
THWUMP!!
!!!
GRAB!!
...
...!!!
WHY... YOU...
SLUMP...

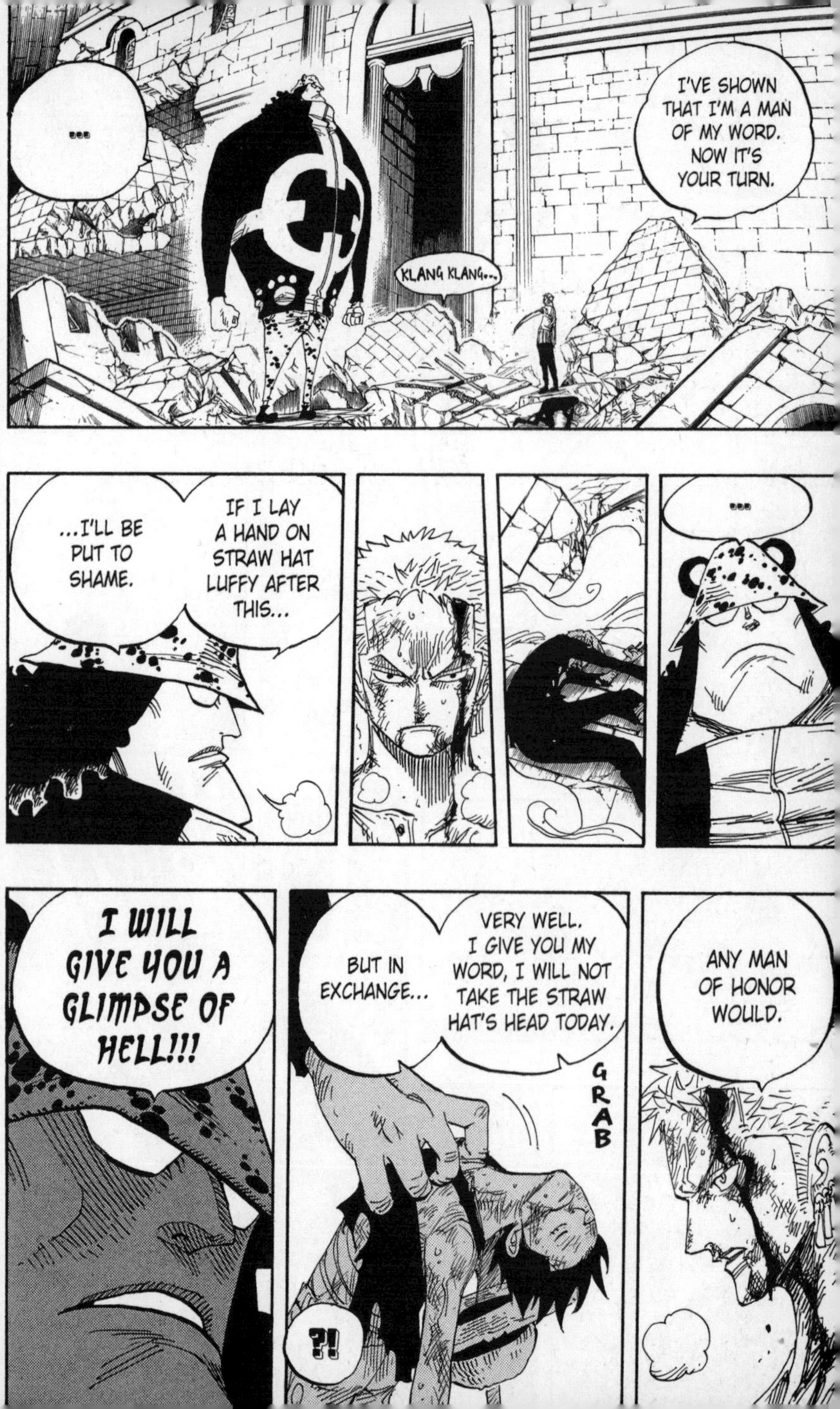
I'VE SHOWN THAT I'M A MAN OF MY WORD. NOW IT'S YOUR TURN.
KLANG KLANG...
...
...
IF I LAY A HAND ON STRAW HAT LUFFY AFTER THIS...
...I'LL BE PUT TO SHAME.
ANY MAN OF HONOR WOULD.
VERY WELL. I GIVE YOU MY WORD, I WILL NOT TAKE THE STRAW HAT'S HEAD TODAY.
BUT IN EXCHANGE...
GRAB
?!
I WILL GIVE YOU A GLIMPSE OF HELL!!!

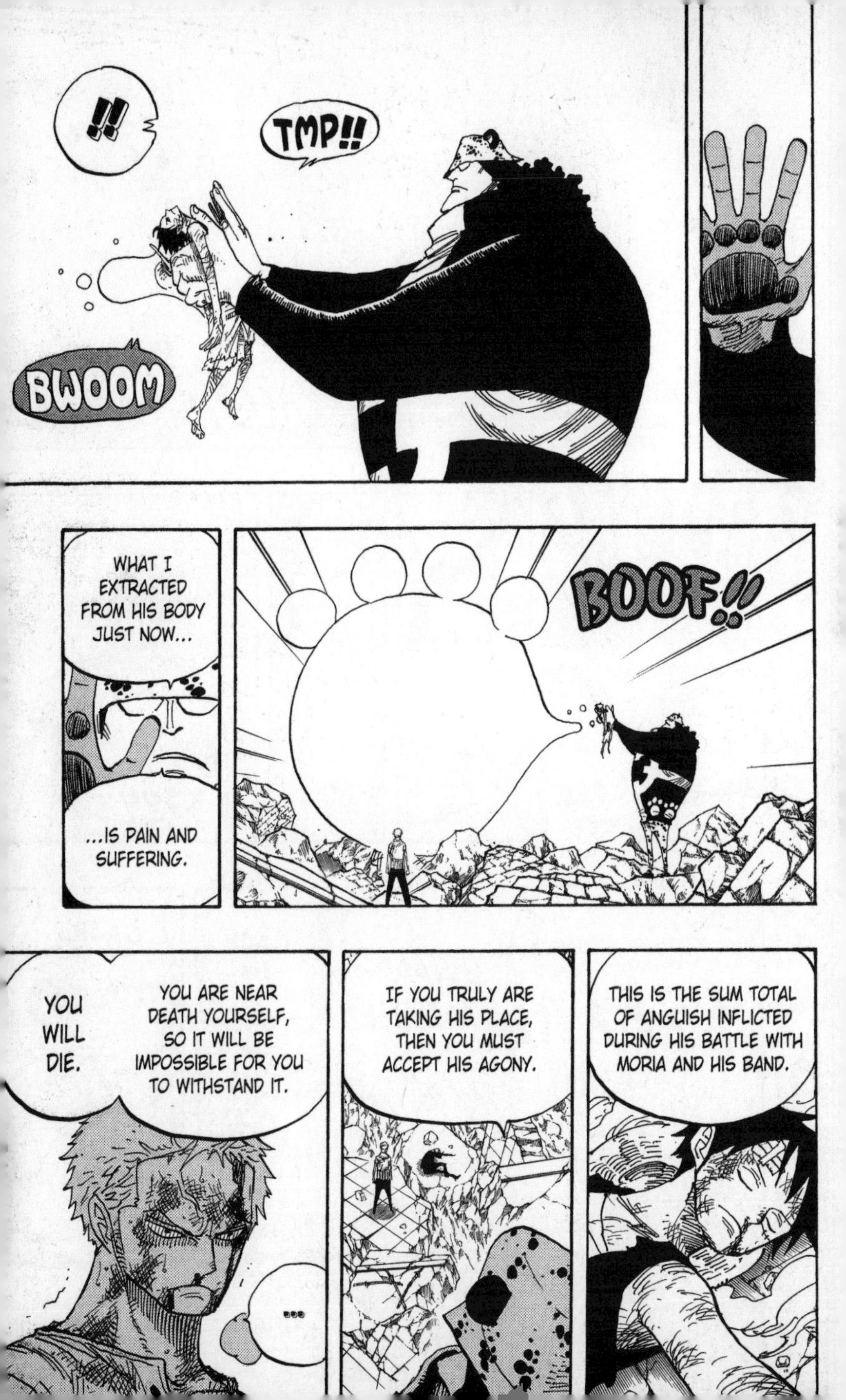
TMP!!
!!
BWOOM
BOOF!!
WHAT I EXTRACTED FROM HIS BODY JUST NOW...
...IS PAIN AND SUFFERING.
THIS IS THE SUM TOTAL OF ANGUISH INFLICTED DURING HIS BATTLE WITH MORIA AND HIS BAND.
IF YOU TRULY ARE TAKING HIS PLACE, THEN YOU MUST ACCEPT HIS AGONY.
YOU ARE NEAR DEATH YOURSELF, SO IT WILL BE IMPOSSIBLE FOR YOU TO WITHSTAND IT.
YOU WILL DIE.
...

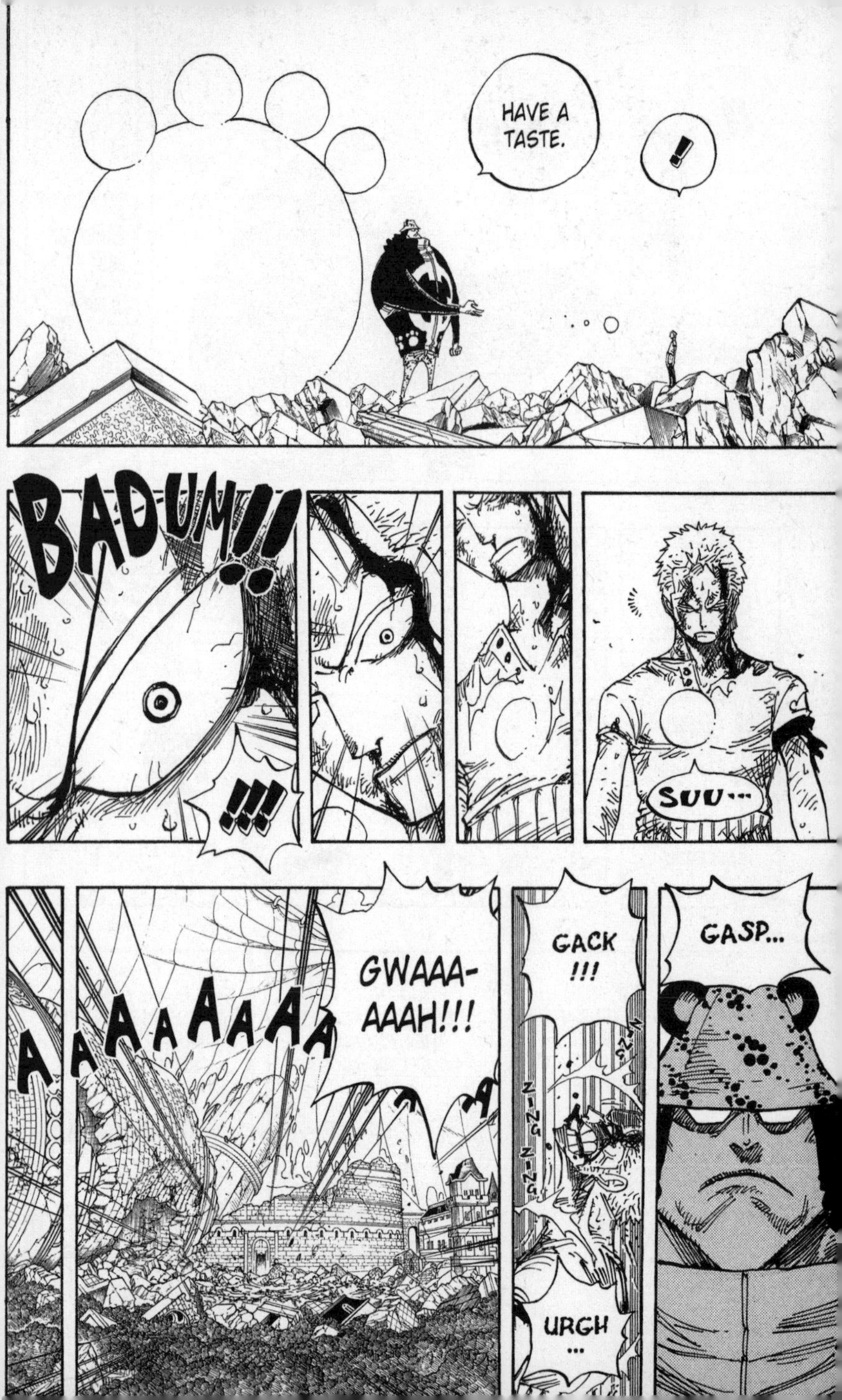
HAVE A TASTE.
!
SUU...
BADUM!!
!!!
GASP...
GACK !!!
ZING
ZING
ZING
URGH ...
GWAAA-AAAH!!!
AAAAAAAAA

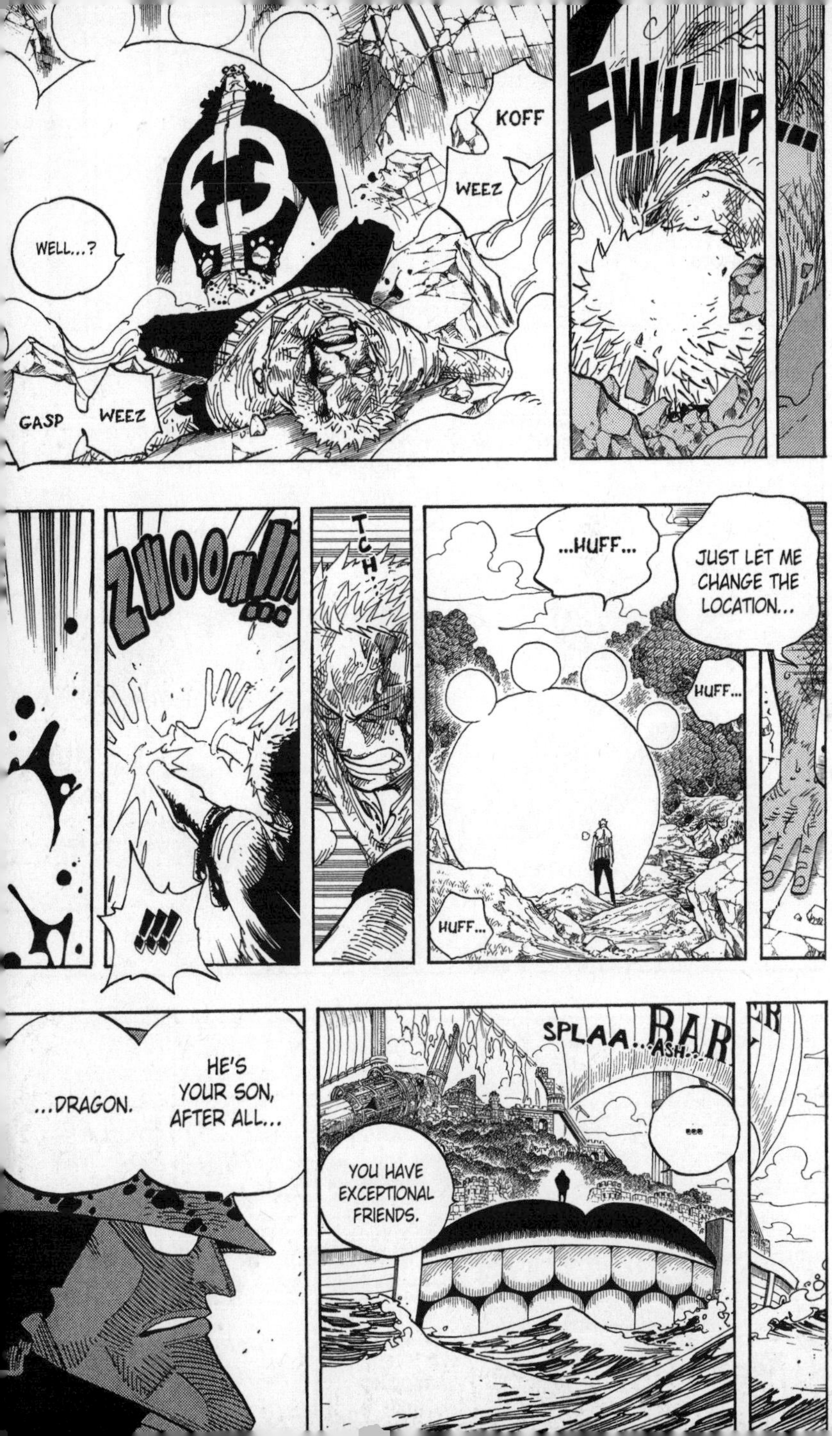
FWUMP...
KOFF
WEEZ
WELL...?
WEEZ
GASP
JUST LET ME CHANGE THE LOCATION...
...HUFF...
HUFF...
HUFF...
TCH
ZWOOM!!!...
!!!
SPLAA...ASH...
...
YOU HAVE EXCEPTIONAL FRIENDS.
HE'S YOUR SON, AFTER ALL...
...DRAGON.

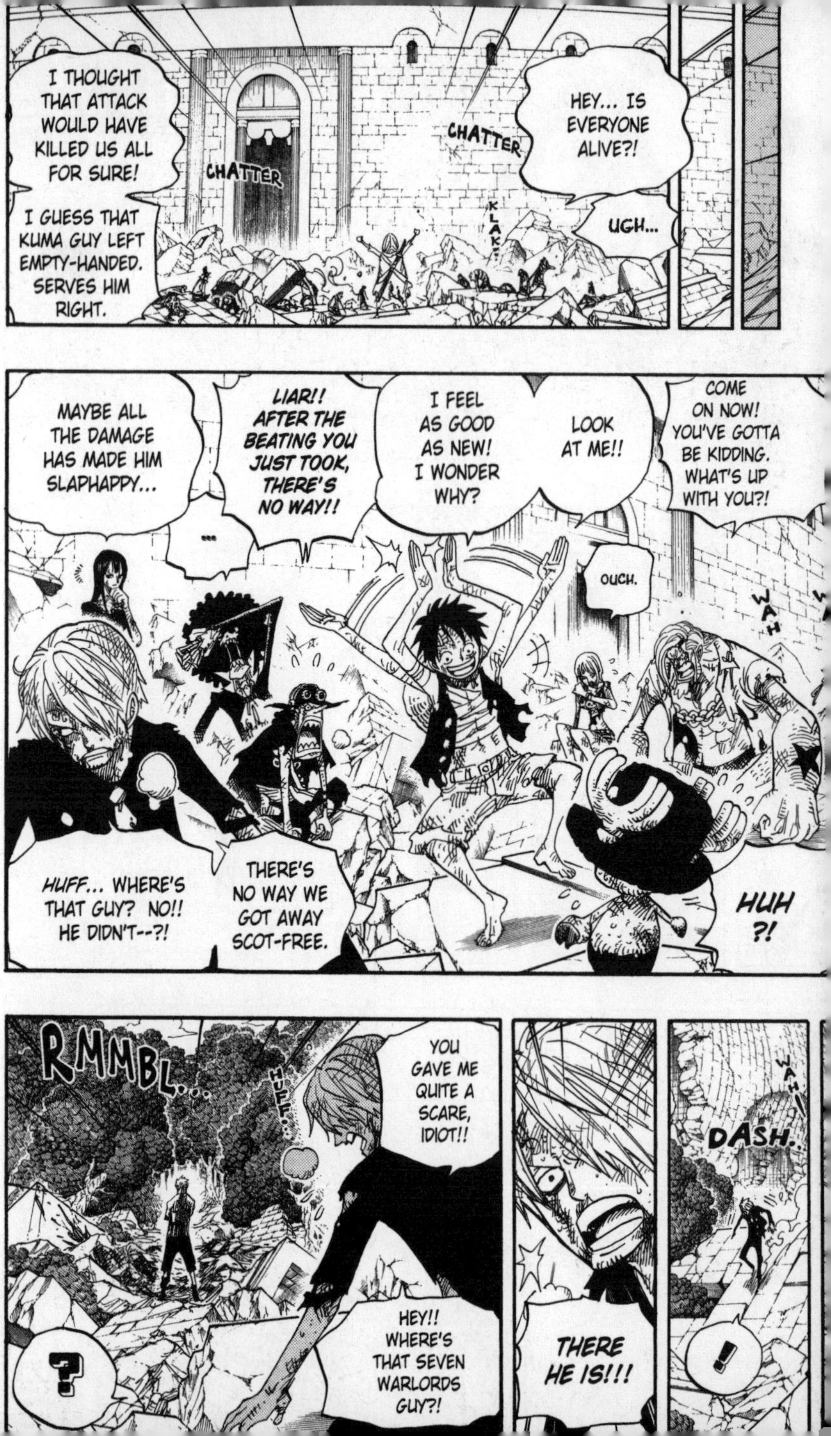
HEY... IS EVERYONE ALIVE?!
CHATTER
UGH...
KLAK
I THOUGHT THAT ATTACK WOULD HAVE KILLED US ALL FOR SURE!
CHATTER
I GUESS THAT KUMA GUY LEFT EMPTY-HANDED. SERVES HIM RIGHT.
COME ON NOW! YOU'VE GOTTA BE KIDDING. WHAT'S UP WITH YOU?!
LOOK AT ME!!
I FEEL AS GOOD AS NEW! I WONDER WHY?
LIAR!! AFTER THE BEATING YOU JUST TOOK, THERE'S NO WAY!!
MAYBE ALL THE DAMAGE HAS MADE HIM SLAPHAPPY...
...
WAH
OUCH.
HUH ?!
THERE'S NO WAY WE GOT AWAY SCOT-FREE.
HUFF... WHERE'S THAT GUY? NO!! HE DIDN'T--?!
WAH!
DASH.
!
THERE HE IS!!!
YOU GAVE ME QUITE A SCARE, IDIOT!!
RMMBL...
HUFF...
HEY!! WHERE'S THAT SEVEN WARLORDS GUY?!
?

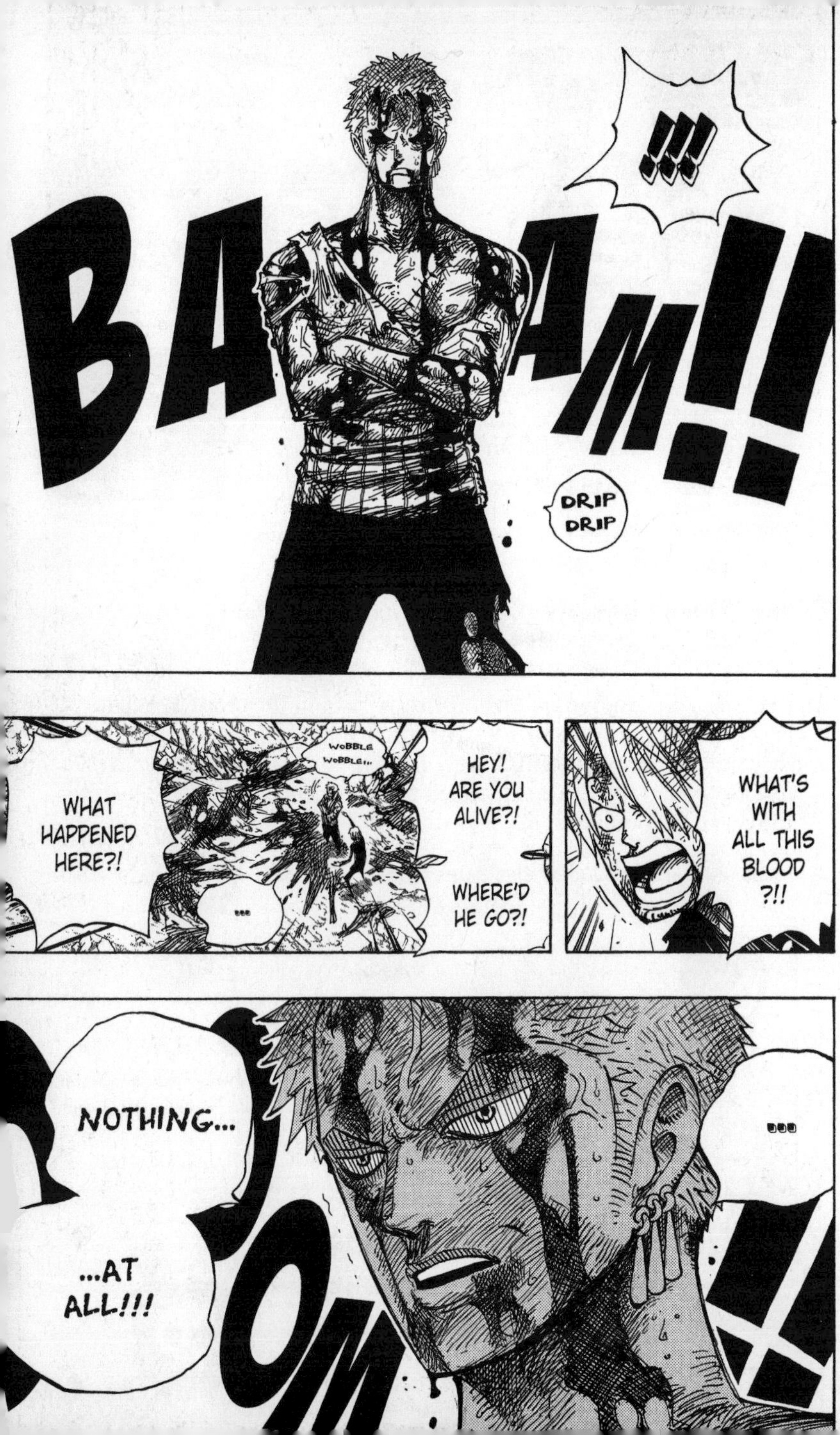
!!!!
BAM!!
DRIP DRIP
WHAT'S WITH ALL THIS BLOOD ?!!
HEY! ARE YOU ALIVE?!
WHERE'D HE GO?!
WOBBLE WOBBLE...
WHAT HAPPENED HERE?!
...
...
NOTHING...
...AT ALL!!!

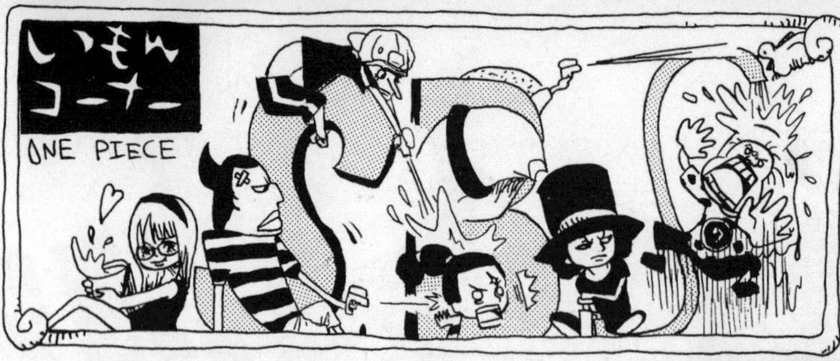
しつもんコーナー
ONE PIECE

(Misakis, Osaka)

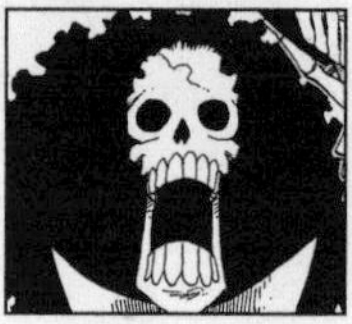

Q: Oda Sensei!! Hello♡ Regarding Brook's birthday, since he ate the Revive-Revive (Yomi-Yomi) Fruit, I think April 3 would be nice because four and three can be read as "Yo" and "Mi" in Japanese.

--Lala

A: Okay, that's settled. April 3 it is.

Q: Oda Sensei♡ Turn this way♡ Boob attack! Boing.

--Kachiko and Chika's giant jugs

A: Yay! ♡ I'm in heaven... ♡ Are you crazy?! Cripes!! Cut that out!! Don't drag the Question Corner into the gutter! *Huff... Huff...*

Q: Oda Sensei! Congratulations on Brook joining the crew! I'm like jelly when it comes to Brook! My bones turn to flesh!! Anyway, now that the eighth member has been chosen, can you answer some questions that we've already asked for previous members? Please answer quickly!

--Getchu Inazuma

A: I see. And you included the questions. Thanks! That makes it easier.

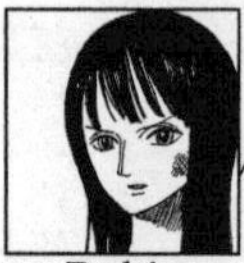

Robin

- If she were an animal, what animal would she be? -Crane

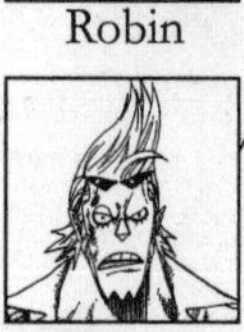

Franky

- If he were an animal? -Fighting Bull
- Lucky number? -08
- Favorite color? -Light Blue
- His smell? -Cola
- Favorite island? -Spring Island in summer

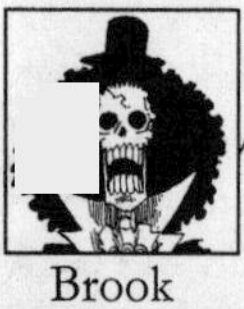

Brook

- If he were an animal? -Horse
- Lucky number? -09
- His smell? -Black tea
- Favorite color? -White and Black
- Favorite island? -Spring Island in fall
- If the Straw Hats were literally a family, what family member would Brook be? -Grandfather
- Brook's pirate flag?↓

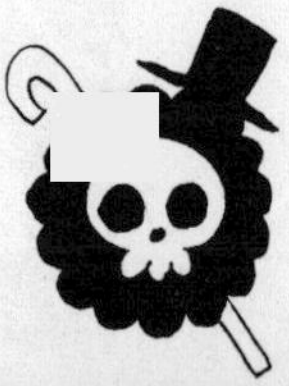

Chapter 486:
PIANO

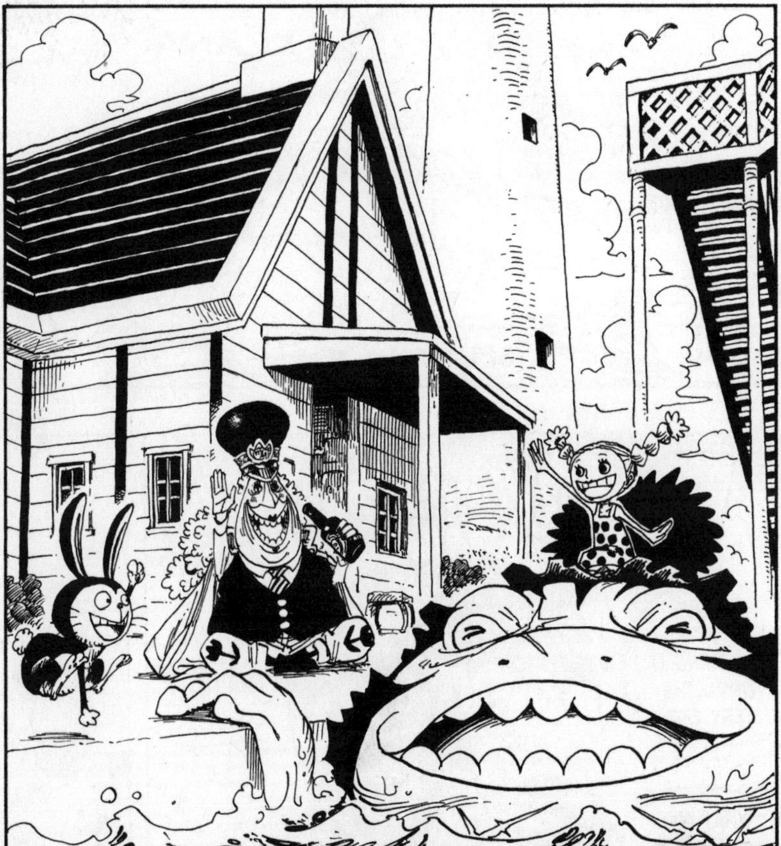

WHERE ARE THEY NOW? SHOT 4: "YOKOZUNA NO LONGER CHALLENGES THE SEA TRAIN"

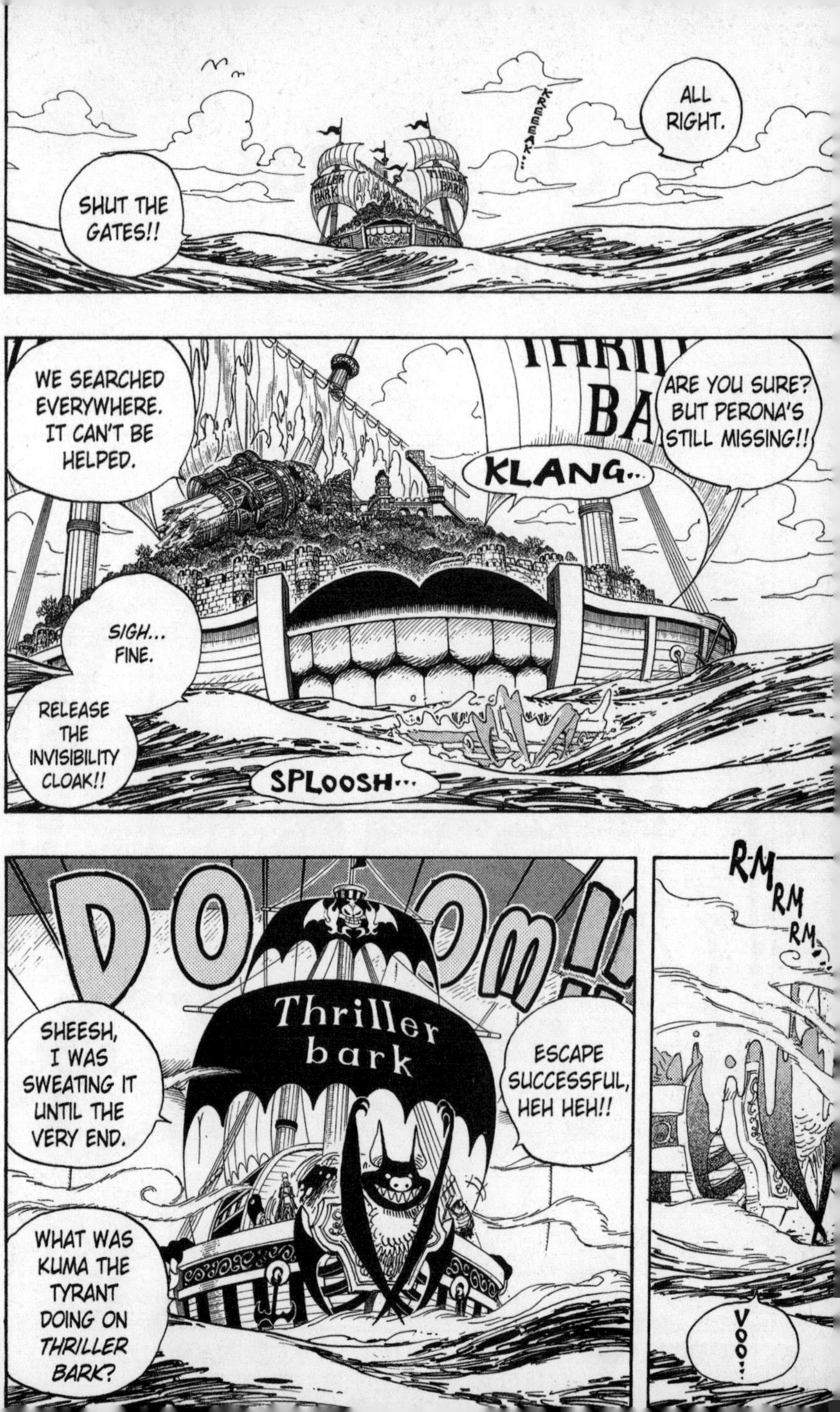
ALL RIGHT.
KREEEAK...
SHUT THE GATES!!
ARE YOU SURE? BUT PERONA'S STILL MISSING!!
WE SEARCHED EVERYWHERE. IT CAN'T BE HELPED.
KLANG..
SIGH... FINE.
RELEASE THE INVISIBILITY CLOAK!!
SPLOOSH...
R-M RM RM
VOO...
DOOM!!
Thriller bark
ESCAPE SUCCESSFUL, HEH HEH!!
SHEESH, I WAS SWEATING IT UNTIL THE VERY END.
WHAT WAS KUMA THE TYRANT DOING ON THRILLER BARK?

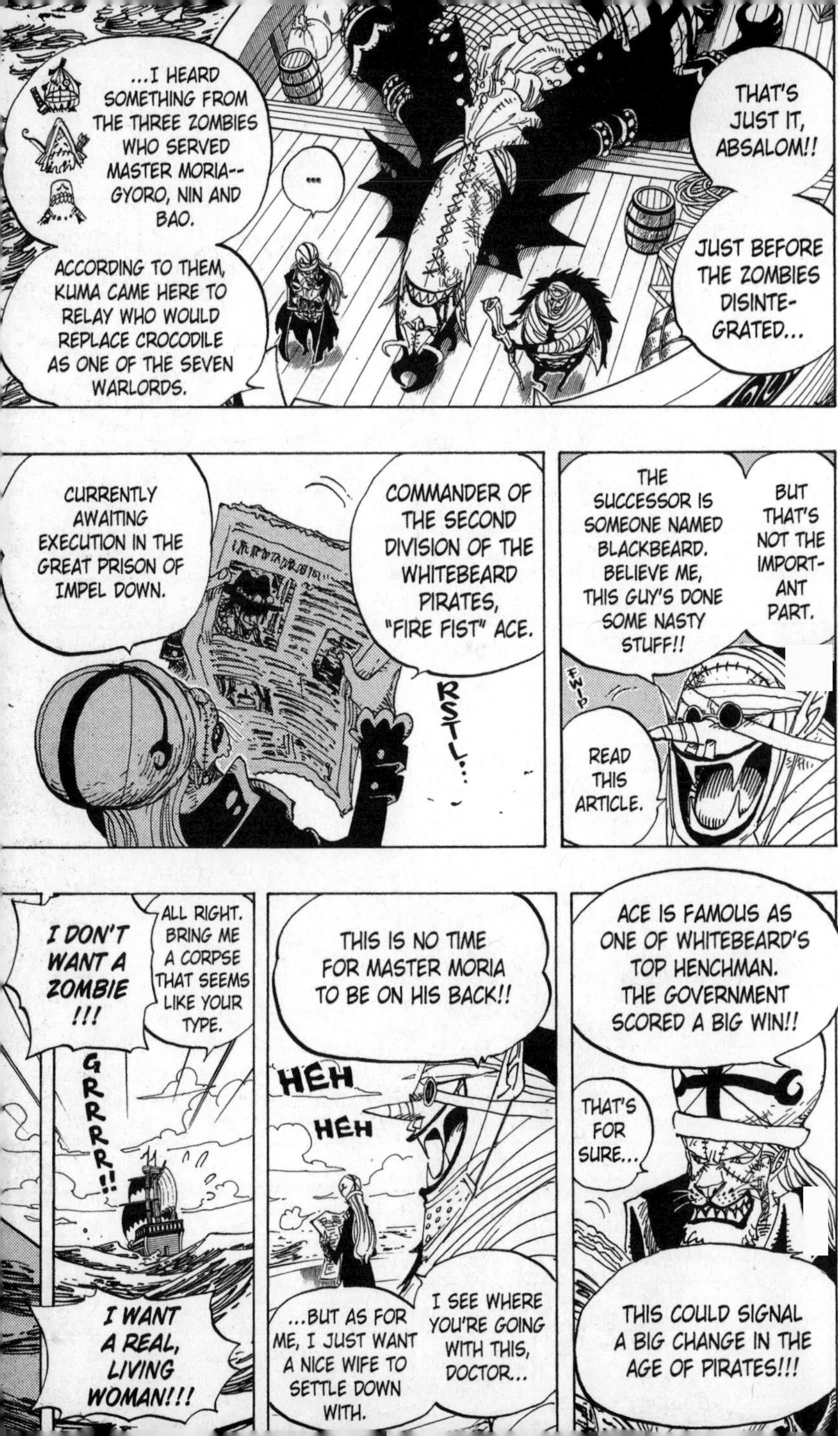
THAT'S JUST IT, ABSALOM!!
JUST BEFORE THE ZOMBIES DISINTE-GRATED...
...
...I HEARD SOMETHING FROM THE THREE ZOMBIES WHO SERVED MASTER MORIA-- GYORO, NIN AND BAO.
ACCORDING TO THEM, KUMA CAME HERE TO RELAY WHO WOULD REPLACE CROCODILE AS ONE OF THE SEVEN WARLORDS.
THE SUCCESSOR IS SOMEONE NAMED BLACKBEARD. BELIEVE ME, THIS GUY'S DONE SOME NASTY STUFF!!
BUT THAT'S NOT THE IMPORT-ANT PART.
FWIP
READ THIS ARTICLE.
COMMANDER OF THE SECOND DIVISION OF THE WHITEBEARD PIRATES, "FIRE FIST" ACE.
RSTL...
CURRENTLY AWAITING EXECUTION IN THE GREAT PRISON OF IMPEL DOWN.
ACE IS FAMOUS AS ONE OF WHITEBEARD'S TOP HENCHMAN. THE GOVERNMENT SCORED A BIG WIN!!
THAT'S FOR SURE...
THIS COULD SIGNAL A BIG CHANGE IN THE AGE OF PIRATES!!!
THIS IS NO TIME FOR MASTER MORIA TO BE ON HIS BACK!!
HEH
HEH
I SEE WHERE YOU'RE GOING WITH THIS, DOCTOR...
...BUT AS FOR ME, I JUST WANT A NICE WIFE TO SETTLE DOWN WITH.
ALL RIGHT. BRING ME A CORPSE THAT SEEMS LIKE YOUR TYPE.
I DON'T WANT A ZOMBIE!!!
GRRRR!!
I WANT A REAL, LIVING WOMAN!!!

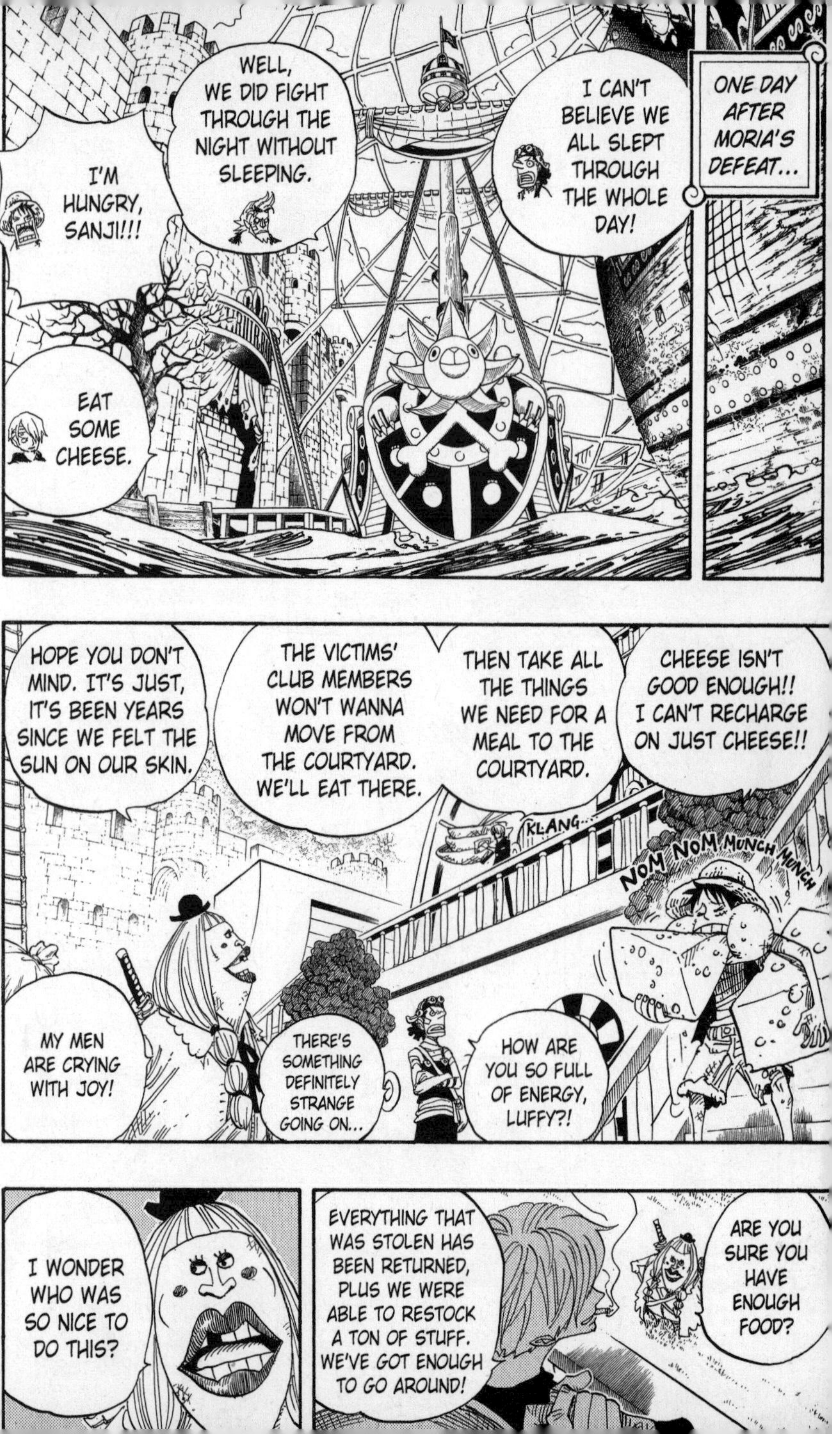
ONE DAY AFTER MORIA'S DEFEAT...
I CAN'T BELIEVE WE ALL SLEPT THROUGH THE WHOLE DAY!
WELL, WE DID FIGHT THROUGH THE NIGHT WITHOUT SLEEPING.
I'M HUNGRY, SANJI!!!
EAT SOME CHEESE.
CHEESE ISN'T GOOD ENOUGH!! I CAN'T RECHARGE ON JUST CHEESE!!
THEN TAKE ALL THE THINGS WE NEED FOR A MEAL TO THE COURTYARD.
THE VICTIMS' CLUB MEMBERS WON'T WANNA MOVE FROM THE COURTYARD. WE'LL EAT THERE.
HOPE YOU DON'T MIND. IT'S JUST, IT'S BEEN YEARS SINCE WE FELT THE SUN ON OUR SKIN.
KLANG...
NOM NOM MUNCH MUNCH
HOW ARE YOU SO FULL OF ENERGY, LUFFY?!
THERE'S SOMETHING DEFINITELY STRANGE GOING ON...
MY MEN ARE CRYING WITH JOY!
ARE YOU SURE YOU HAVE ENOUGH FOOD?
EVERYTHING THAT WAS STOLEN HAS BEEN RETURNED, PLUS WE WERE ABLE TO RESTOCK A TON OF STUFF. WE'VE GOT ENOUGH TO GO AROUND!
I WONDER WHO WAS SO NICE TO DO THIS?

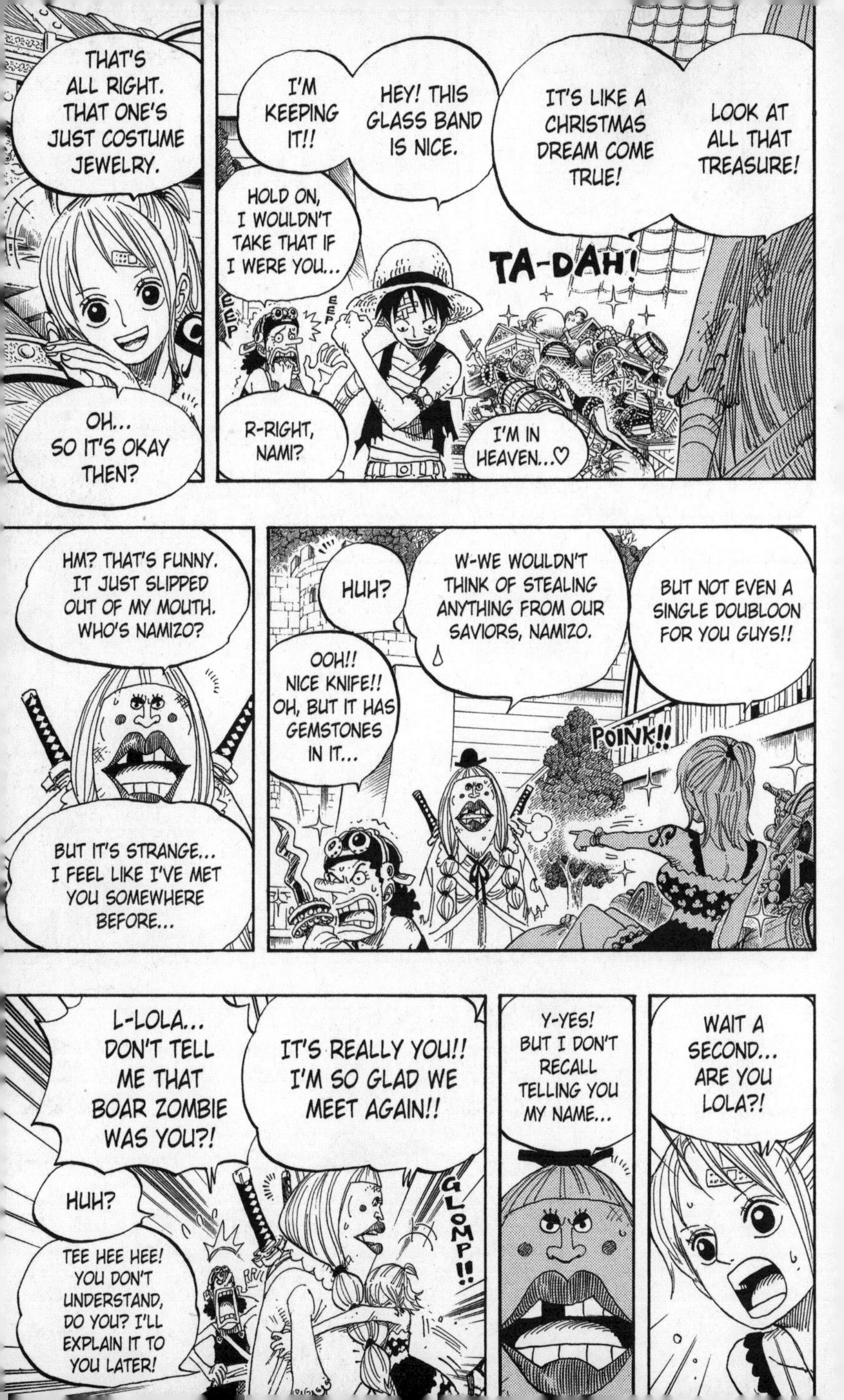
LOOK AT ALL THAT TREASURE!
IT'S LIKE A CHRISTMAS DREAM COME TRUE!
TA-DAH!
HEY! THIS GLASS BAND IS NICE.
I'M KEEPING IT!!
HOLD ON, I WOULDN'T TAKE THAT IF I WERE YOU...
EEP
EEP
I'M IN HEAVEN...♡
R-RIGHT, NAMI?
THAT'S ALL RIGHT. THAT ONE'S JUST COSTUME JEWELRY.
OH... SO IT'S OKAY THEN?
BUT NOT EVEN A SINGLE DOUBLOON FOR YOU GUYS!!
W-WE WOULDN'T THINK OF STEALING ANYTHING FROM OUR SAVIORS, NAMIZO.
HUH?
OOH!! NICE KNIFE!! OH, BUT IT HAS GEMSTONES IN IT...
POINK!!
HM? THAT'S FUNNY. IT JUST SLIPPED OUT OF MY MOUTH. WHO'S NAMIZO?
BUT IT'S STRANGE... I FEEL LIKE I'VE MET YOU SOMEWHERE BEFORE...
WAIT A SECOND... ARE YOU LOLA?!
Y-YES! BUT I DON'T RECALL TELLING YOU MY NAME...
IT'S REALLY YOU!! I'M SO GLAD WE MEET AGAIN!!
L-LOLA... DON'T TELL ME THAT BOAR ZOMBIE WAS YOU?!
GLOMP!!
HUH?
TEE HEE HEE! YOU DON'T UNDERSTAND, DO YOU? I'LL EXPLAIN IT TO YOU LATER!

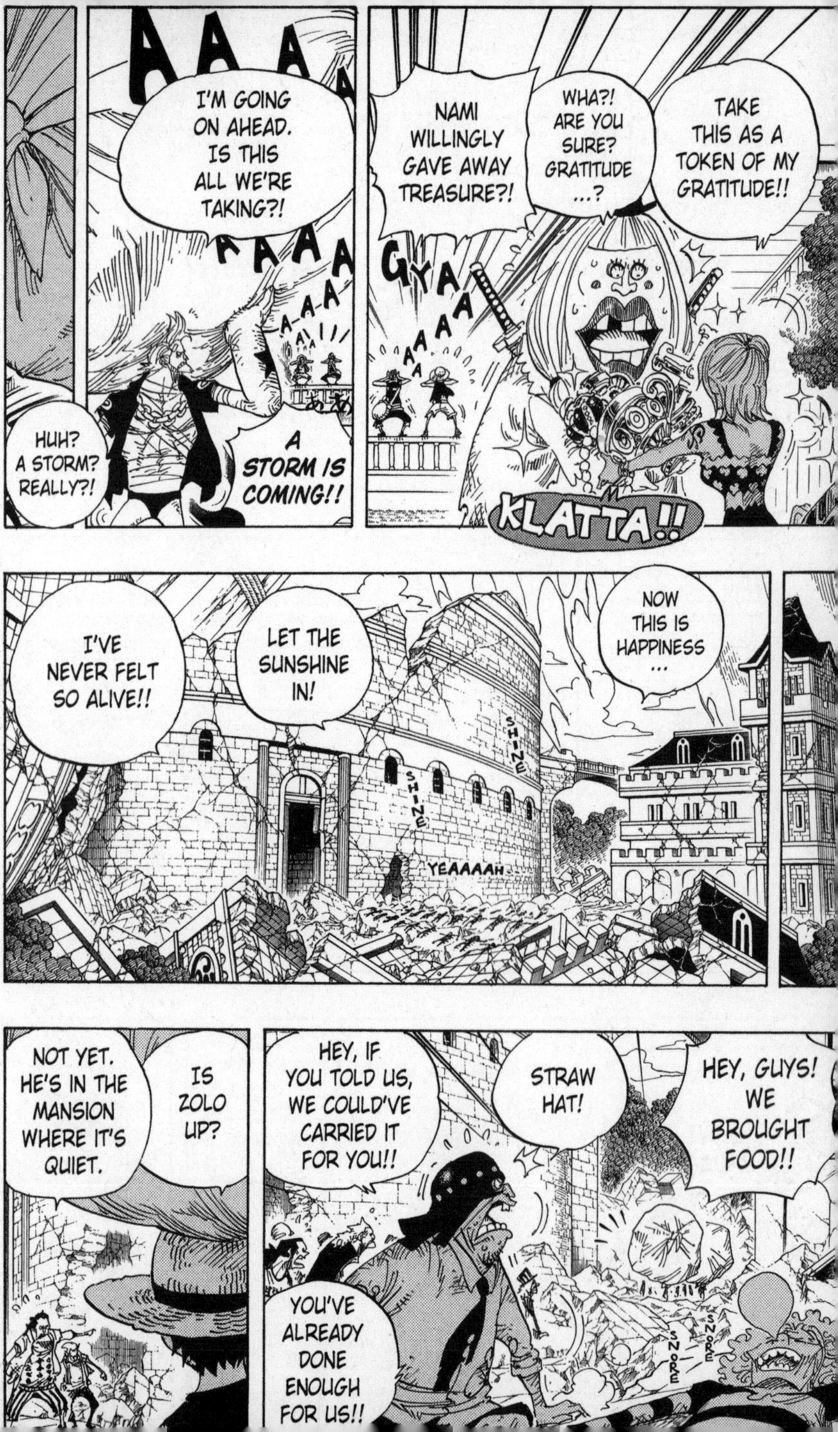
TAKE THIS AS A TOKEN OF MY GRATITUDE!!
WHA?! ARE YOU SURE? GRATITUDE ...?
KLATTA!!
NAMI WILLINGLY GAVE AWAY TREASURE?!
GYAAAA
I'M GOING ON AHEAD. IS THIS ALL WE'RE TAKING?!
A STORM IS COMING!!
HUH? A STORM? REALLY?!
NOW THIS IS HAPPINESS ...
SHINE
LET THE SUNSHINE IN!
SHINE
I'VE NEVER FELT SO ALIVE!!
YEAAAAH
HEY, GUYS! WE BROUGHT FOOD!!
STRAW HAT!
HEY, IF YOU TOLD US, WE COULD'VE CARRIED IT FOR YOU!!
YOU'VE ALREADY DONE ENOUGH FOR US!!
SNORE
SNORE
IS ZOLO UP?
NOT YET. HE'S IN THE MANSION WHERE IT'S QUIET.

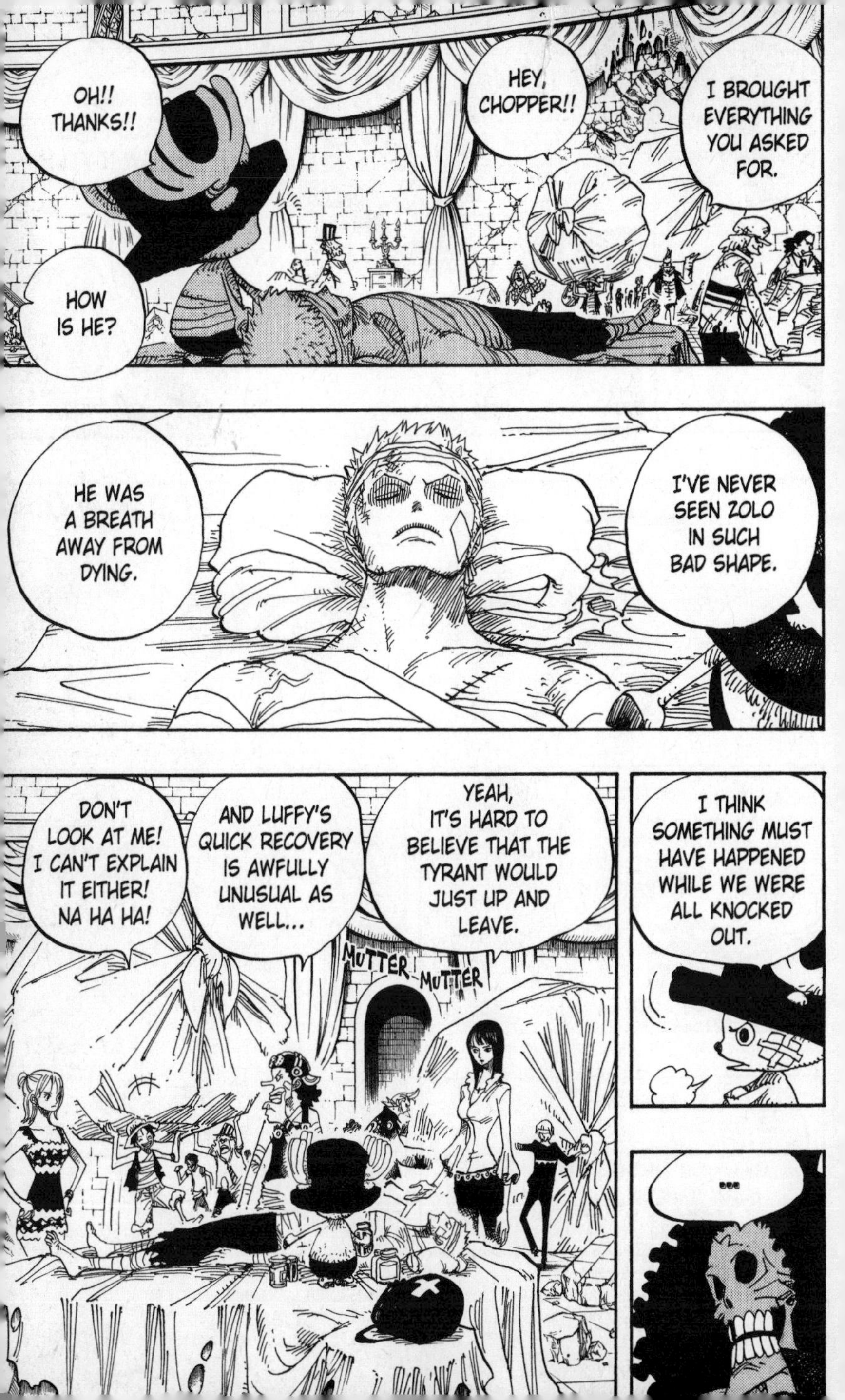
I BROUGHT EVERYTHING YOU ASKED FOR.
HEY, CHOPPER!!
OH!! THANKS!!
HOW IS HE?
I'VE NEVER SEEN ZOLO IN SUCH BAD SHAPE.
HE WAS A BREATH AWAY FROM DYING.
I THINK SOMETHING MUST HAVE HAPPENED WHILE WE WERE ALL KNOCKED OUT.
...
YEAH, IT'S HARD TO BELIEVE THAT THE TYRANT WOULD JUST UP AND LEAVE.
AND LUFFY'S QUICK RECOVERY IS AWFULLY UNUSUAL AS WELL...
DON'T LOOK AT ME! I CAN'T EXPLAIN IT EITHER! NA HA HA!
MUTTER MUTTER

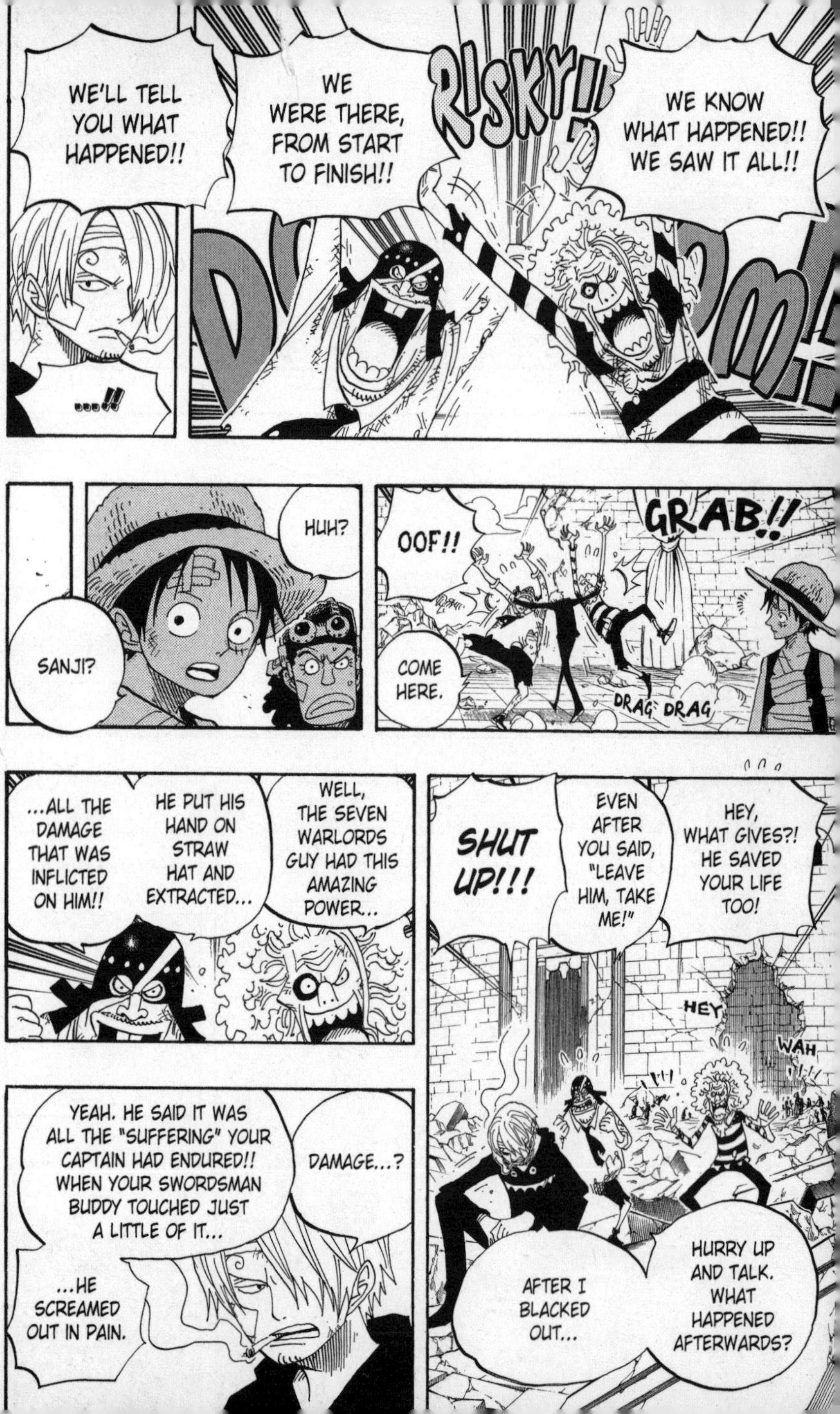
WE KNOW WHAT HAPPENED!! WE SAW IT ALL!!
RISKY!!
WE WERE THERE, FROM START TO FINISH!!
WE'LL TELL YOU WHAT HAPPENED!!
...!!
GRAB!!
OOF!!
COME HERE.
DRAG DRAG
HUH?
SANJI?
HEY, WHAT GIVES?! HE SAVED YOUR LIFE TOO!
EVEN AFTER YOU SAID, "LEAVE HIM, TAKE ME!"
SHUT UP!!!
HEY
WAH
WELL, THE SEVEN WARLORDS GUY HAD THIS AMAZING POWER...
HE PUT HIS HAND ON STRAW HAT AND EXTRACTED...
...ALL THE DAMAGE THAT WAS INFLICTED ON HIM!!
HURRY UP AND TALK. WHAT HAPPENED AFTERWARDS?
AFTER I BLACKED OUT...
DAMAGE...?
YEAH. HE SAID IT WAS ALL THE "SUFFERING" YOUR CAPTAIN HAD ENDURED!! WHEN YOUR SWORDSMAN BUDDY TOUCHED JUST A LITTLE OF IT...
...HE SCREAMED OUT IN PAIN.

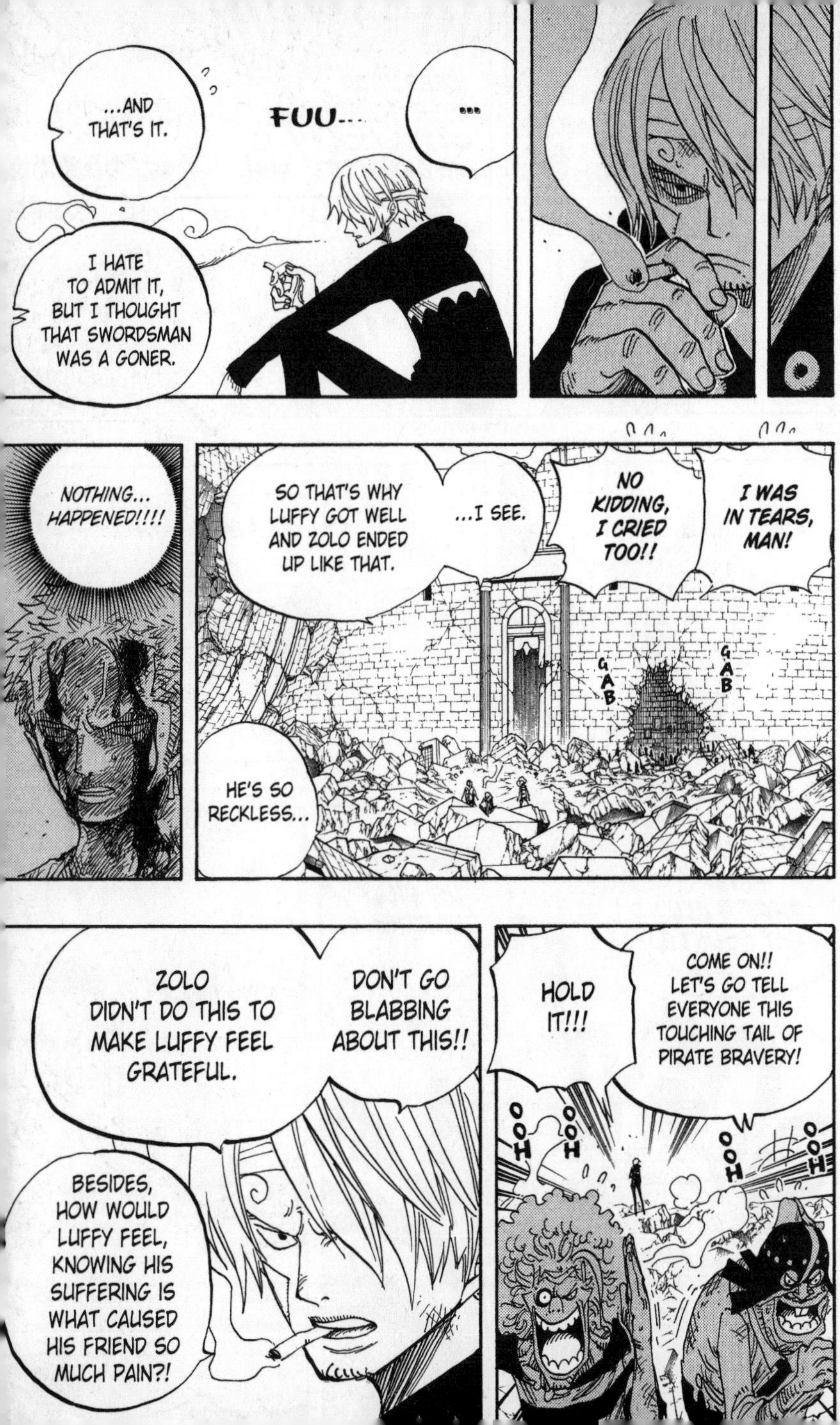
...
FUU...
...AND THAT'S IT.
I HATE TO ADMIT IT, BUT I THOUGHT THAT SWORDSMAN WAS A GONER.
I WAS IN TEARS, MAN!
NO KIDDING, I CRIED TOO!!
...I SEE.
SO THAT'S WHY LUFFY GOT WELL AND ZOLO ENDED UP LIKE THAT.
GAB
GAB
HE'S SO RECKLESS...
NOTHING... HAPPENED!!!!
COME ON!! LET'S GO TELL EVERYONE THIS TOUCHING TAIL OF PIRATE BRAVERY!
HOLD IT!!!
OOH
OOH
OOH
OOH
DON'T GO BLABBING ABOUT THIS!!
ZOLO DIDN'T DO THIS TO MAKE LUFFY FEEL GRATEFUL.
BESIDES, HOW WOULD LUFFY FEEL, KNOWING HIS SUFFERING IS WHAT CAUSED HIS FRIEND SO MUCH PAIN?!

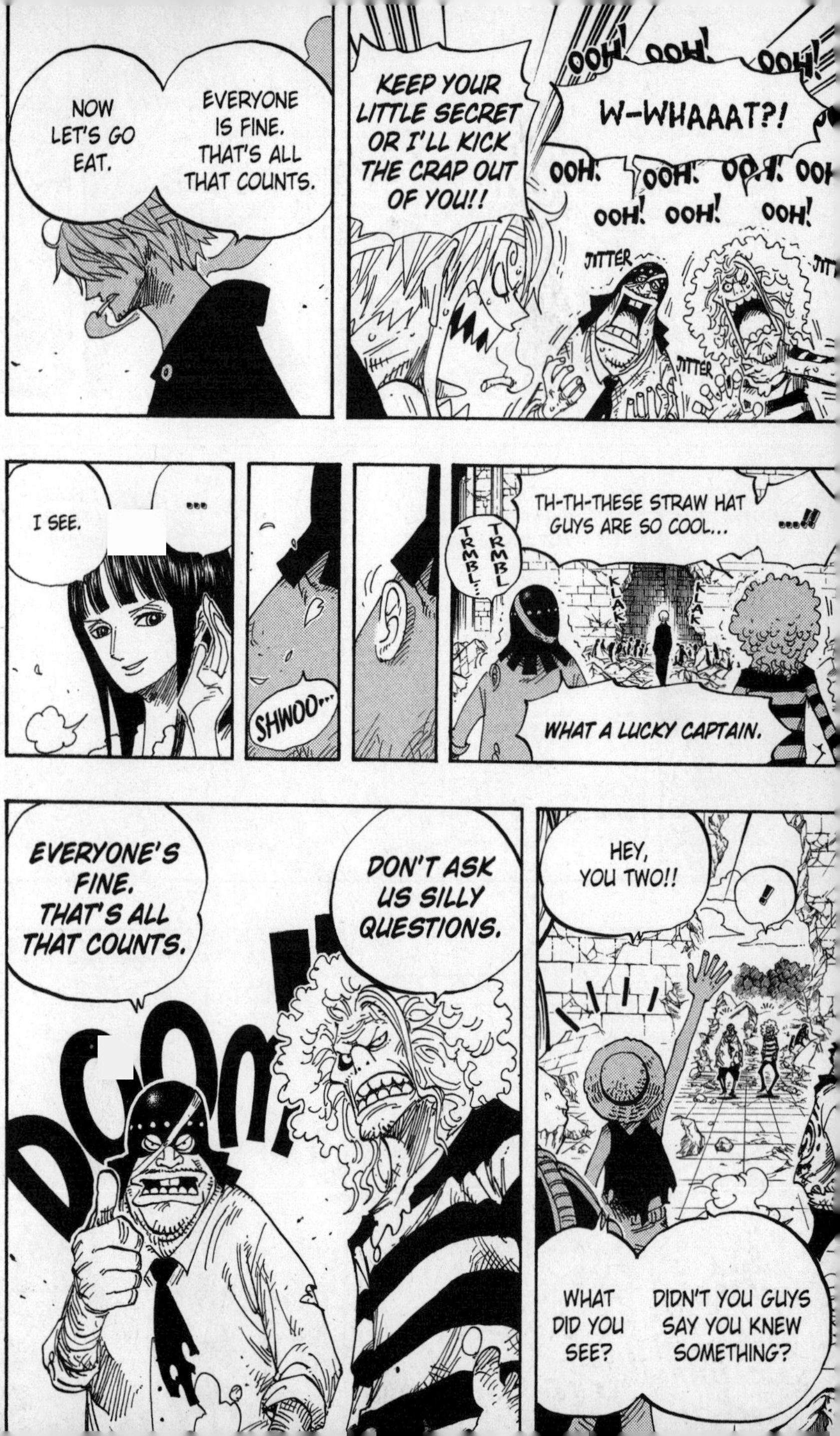
OOH! OOH! OOH!
W-WHAAAT?!
OOH! OOH! OOH! OOH!
OOH! OOH! OOH!
JITTER
JITTER
KEEP YOUR LITTLE SECRET OR I'LL KICK THE CRAP OUT OF YOU!!
EVERYONE IS FINE. THAT'S ALL THAT COUNTS.
NOW LET'S GO EAT.
...!!
TH-TH-THESE STRAW HAT GUYS ARE SO COOL...
TRMBL
TRMBL...
KLAK
KLAK
WHAT A LUCKY CAPTAIN.
SHWOO...
...
I SEE.
HEY, YOU TWO!!
!
DIDN'T YOU GUYS SAY YOU KNEW SOMETHING?
WHAT DID YOU SEE?
DON'T ASK US SILLY QUESTIONS.
EVERYONE'S FINE. THAT'S ALL THAT COUNTS.

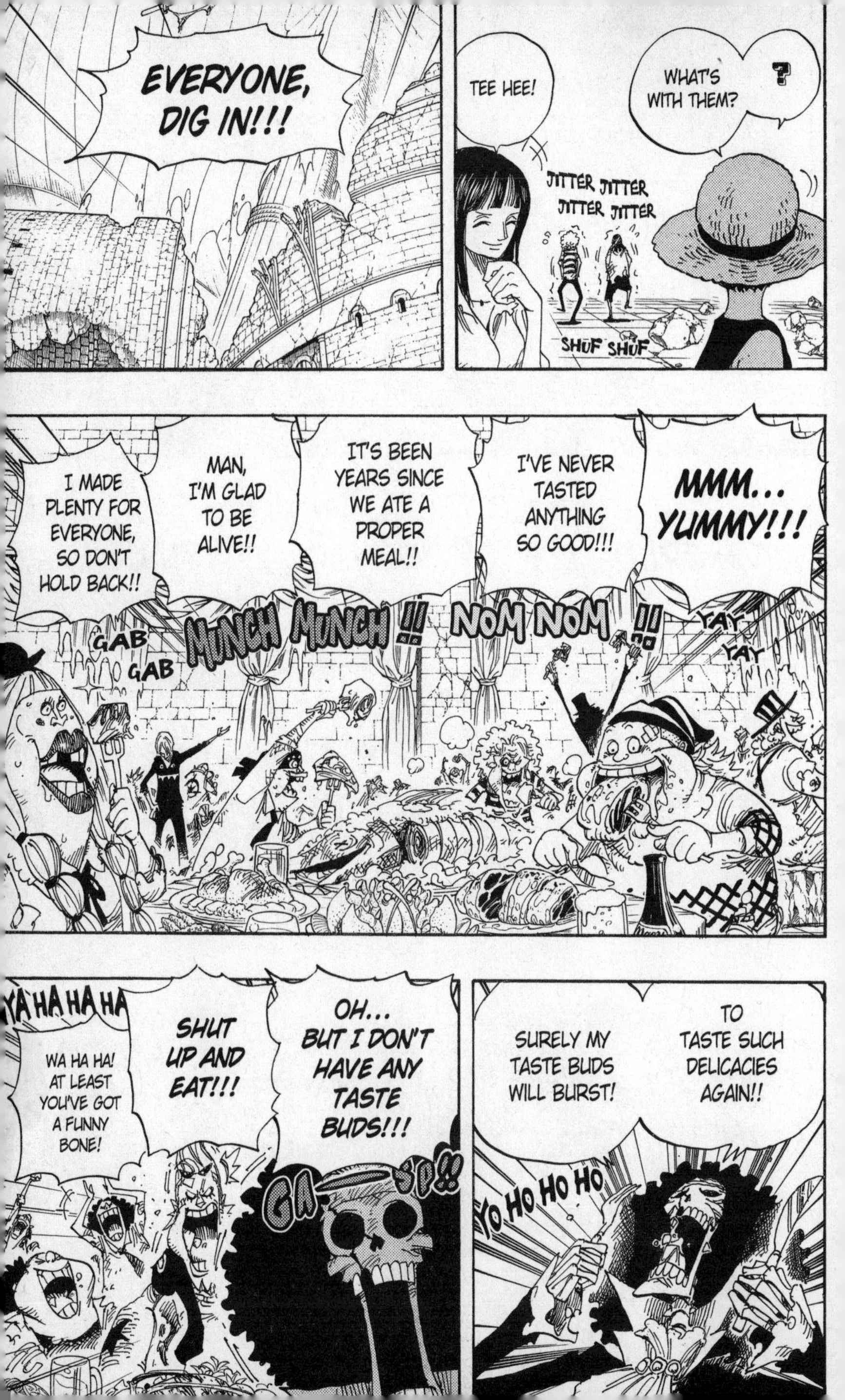

WHAT'S WITH THEM?
?
TEE HEE!
JITTER JITTER
JITTER JITTER
SHUF SHUF
EVERYONE, DIG IN!!!
MMM... YUMMY!!!
I'VE NEVER TASTED ANYTHING SO GOOD!!!
IT'S BEEN YEARS SINCE WE ATE A PROPER MEAL!!
MAN, I'M GLAD TO BE ALIVE!!
I MADE PLENTY FOR EVERYONE, SO DON'T HOLD BACK!!
YAY YAY
NOM NOM!!
MUNCH MUNCH!!
GAB GAB
TO TASTE SUCH DELICACIES AGAIN!!
SURELY MY TASTE BUDS WILL BURST!
YO HO HO HO
OH... BUT I DON'T HAVE ANY TASTE BUDS!!!
GA SP!!
SHUT UP AND EAT!!!
WA HA HA! AT LEAST YOU'VE GOT A FUNNY BONE!
YA HA HA HA

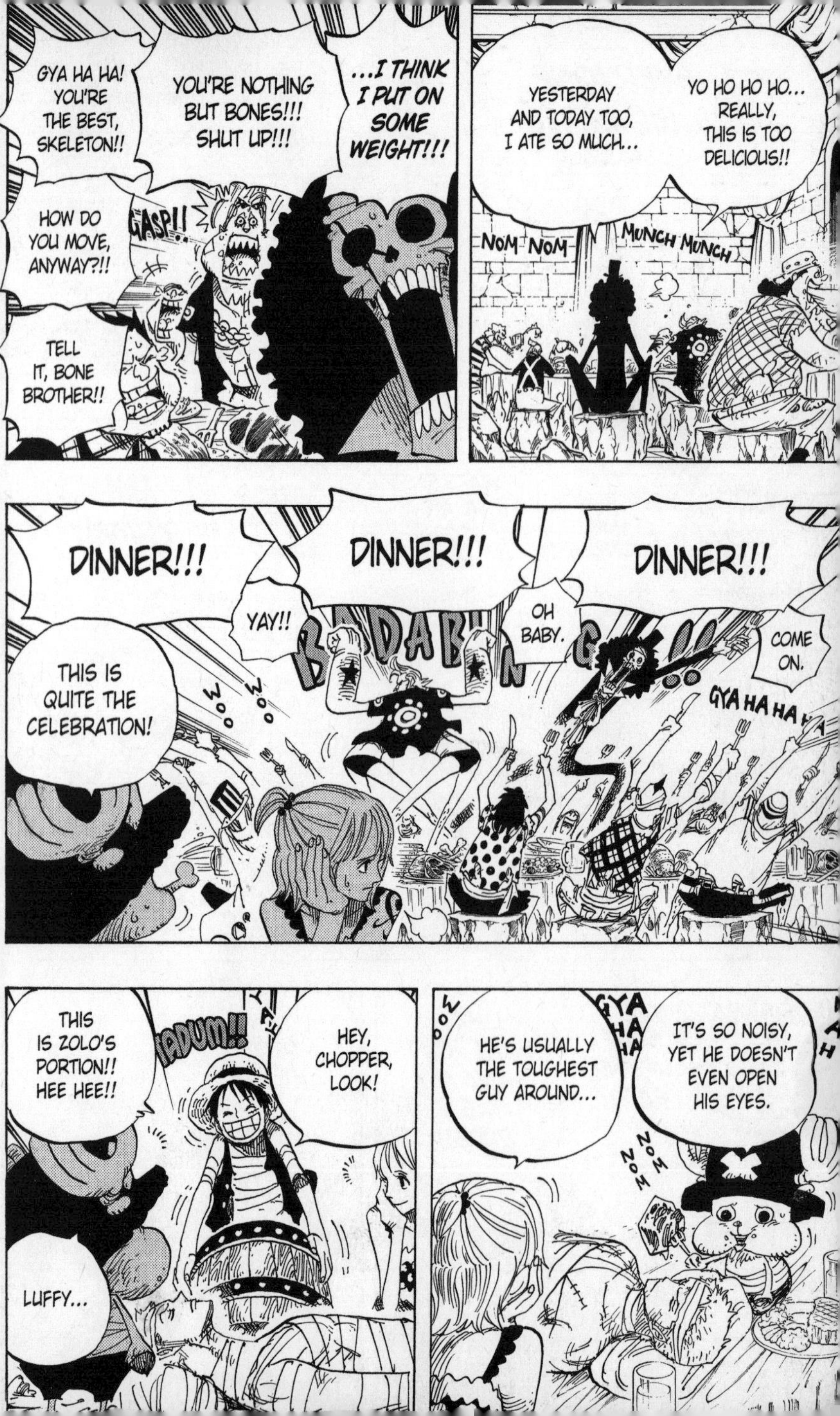

YO HO HO HO... REALLY, THIS IS TOO DELICIOUS!!
YESTERDAY AND TODAY TOO, I ATE SO MUCH...
MUNCH MUNCH
NOM NOM
...I THINK I PUT ON SOME WEIGHT!!!
YOU'RE NOTHING BUT BONES!!! SHUT UP!!!
GYA HA HA! YOU'RE THE BEST, SKELETON!!
GASP!!
HOW DO YOU MOVE, ANYWAY?!!
TELL IT, BONE BROTHER!!
DINNER!!!
DINNER!!!
DINNER!!!
COME ON.
GYA HA HA
OH BABY.
YAY!!
WOO
WOO
THIS IS QUITE THE CELEBRATION!
IT'S SO NOISY, YET HE DOESN'T EVEN OPEN HIS EYES.
GYA HA HA
HE'S USUALLY THE TOUGHEST GUY AROUND...
NOM NOM NOM
HEY, CHOPPER, LOOK!
THIS IS ZOLO'S PORTION!! HEE HEE!!
LUFFY...

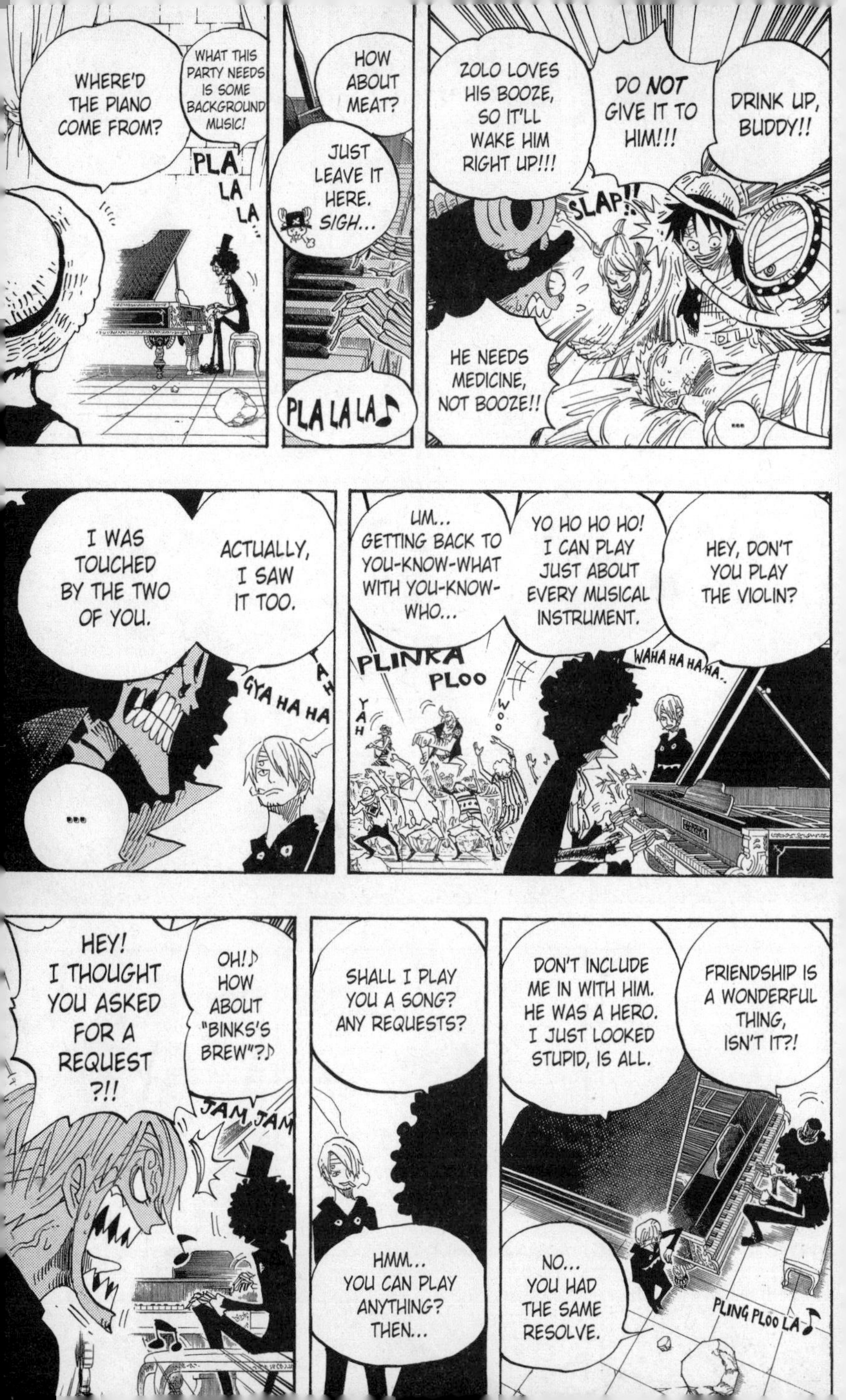
DRINK UP, BUDDY!!
DO NOT GIVE IT TO HIM!!!
ZOLO LOVES HIS BOOZE, SO IT'LL WAKE HIM RIGHT UP!!!
SLAP!!
HE NEEDS MEDICINE, NOT BOOZE!!
...
HOW ABOUT MEAT?
JUST LEAVE IT HERE. SIGH...
PLA LA LA♪
WHAT THIS PARTY NEEDS IS SOME BACKGROUND MUSIC!
WHERE'D THE PIANO COME FROM?
PLA LA LA...
HEY, DON'T YOU PLAY THE VIOLIN?
YO HO HO HO! I CAN PLAY JUST ABOUT EVERY MUSICAL INSTRUMENT.
UM... GETTING BACK TO YOU-KNOW-WHAT WITH YOU-KNOW-WHO...
WAHA HA HA HA..
WOO
PLINKA PLOO
YAH
ACTUALLY, I SAW IT TOO.
I WAS TOUCHED BY THE TWO OF YOU.
YAH
GYA HA HA
...
FRIENDSHIP IS A WONDERFUL THING, ISN'T IT?!
DON'T INCLUDE ME IN WITH HIM. HE WAS A HERO. I JUST LOOKED STUPID, IS ALL.
NO... YOU HAD THE SAME RESOLVE.
PLING PLOO LA♪
SHALL I PLAY YOU A SONG? ANY REQUESTS?
HMM... YOU CAN PLAY ANYTHING? THEN...
OH!♪ HOW ABOUT "BINKS'S BREW"?♪
HEY! I THOUGHT YOU ASKED FOR A REQUEST?!!
JAM JAM

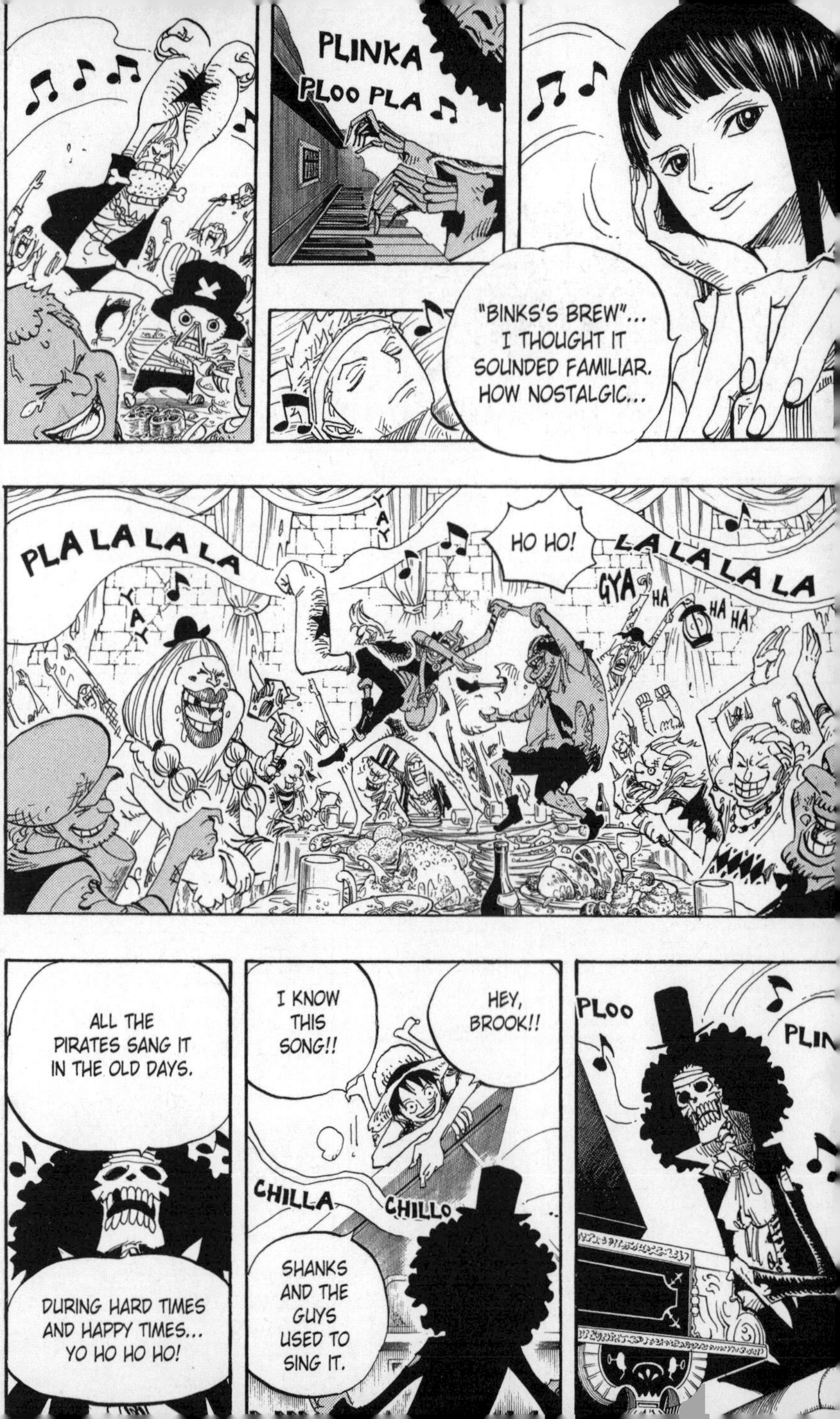
"BINKS'S BREW"... I THOUGHT IT SOUNDED FAMILIAR. HOW NOSTALGIC...
PLINKA
PLOO PLA
LA LA LA LA LA
HA HA
GYA HA
HO HO!
YAY
YAY
PLA LA LA LA
PLIN
PLOO
HEY, BROOK!!
I KNOW THIS SONG!!
CHILLO
CHILLA
SHANKS AND THE GUYS USED TO SING IT.
ALL THE PIRATES SANG IT IN THE OLD DAYS.
DURING HARD TIMES AND HAPPY TIMES... YO HO HO HO!

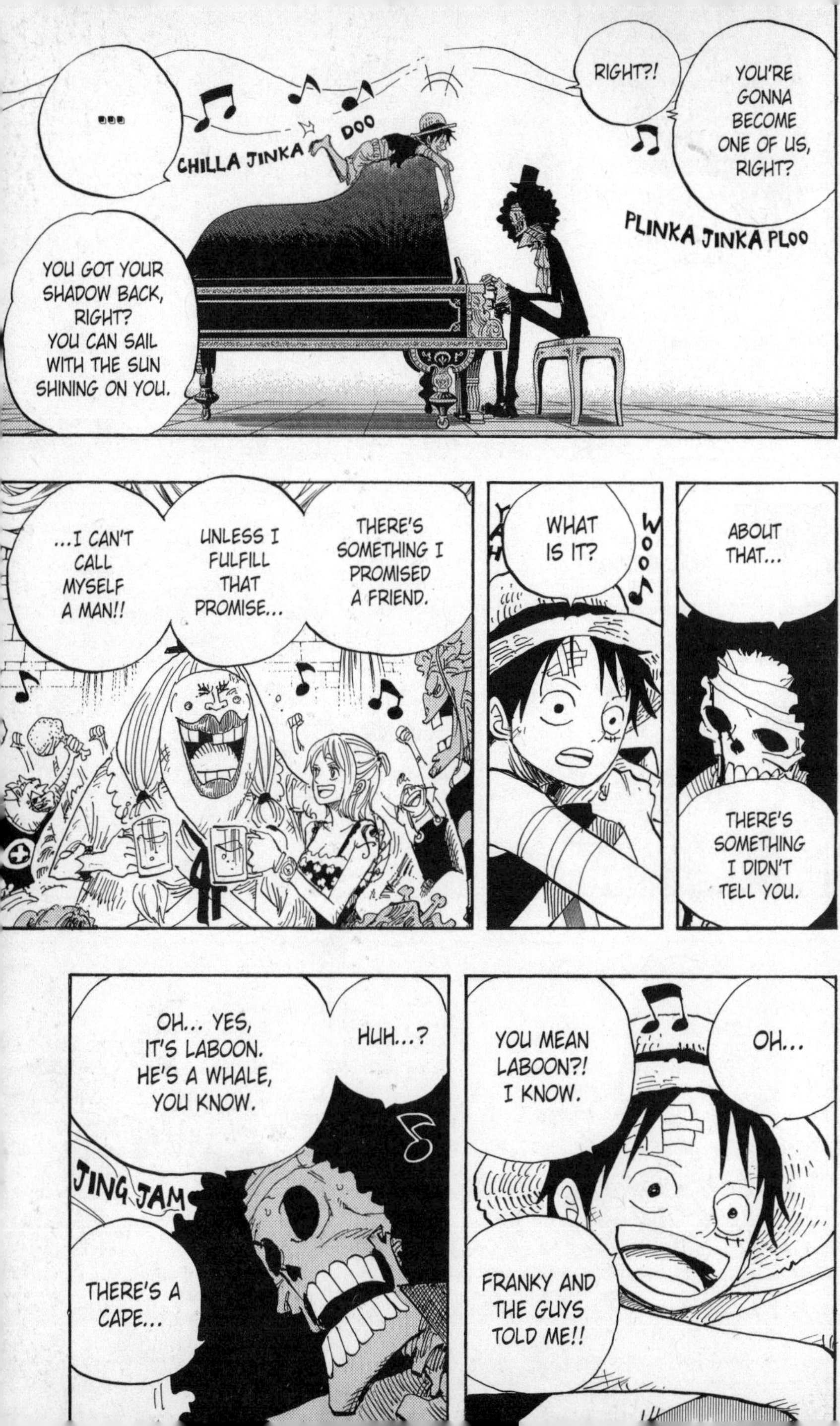
YOU'RE GONNA BECOME ONE OF US, RIGHT?
RIGHT?!
PLINKA JINKA PLOO
CHILLA JINKA DOO
...
YOU GOT YOUR SHADOW BACK, RIGHT? YOU CAN SAIL WITH THE SUN SHINING ON YOU.
ABOUT THAT...
THERE'S SOMETHING I DIDN'T TELL YOU.
WHAT IS IT?
WOO
THERE'S SOMETHING I PROMISED A FRIEND.
UNLESS I FULFILL THAT PROMISE...
...I CAN'T CALL MYSELF A MAN!!
OH...
YOU MEAN LABOON?! I KNOW.
FRANKY AND THE GUYS TOLD ME!!
HUH...?
OH... YES, IT'S LABOON. HE'S A WHALE, YOU KNOW.
JING JAM
THERE'S A CAPE...

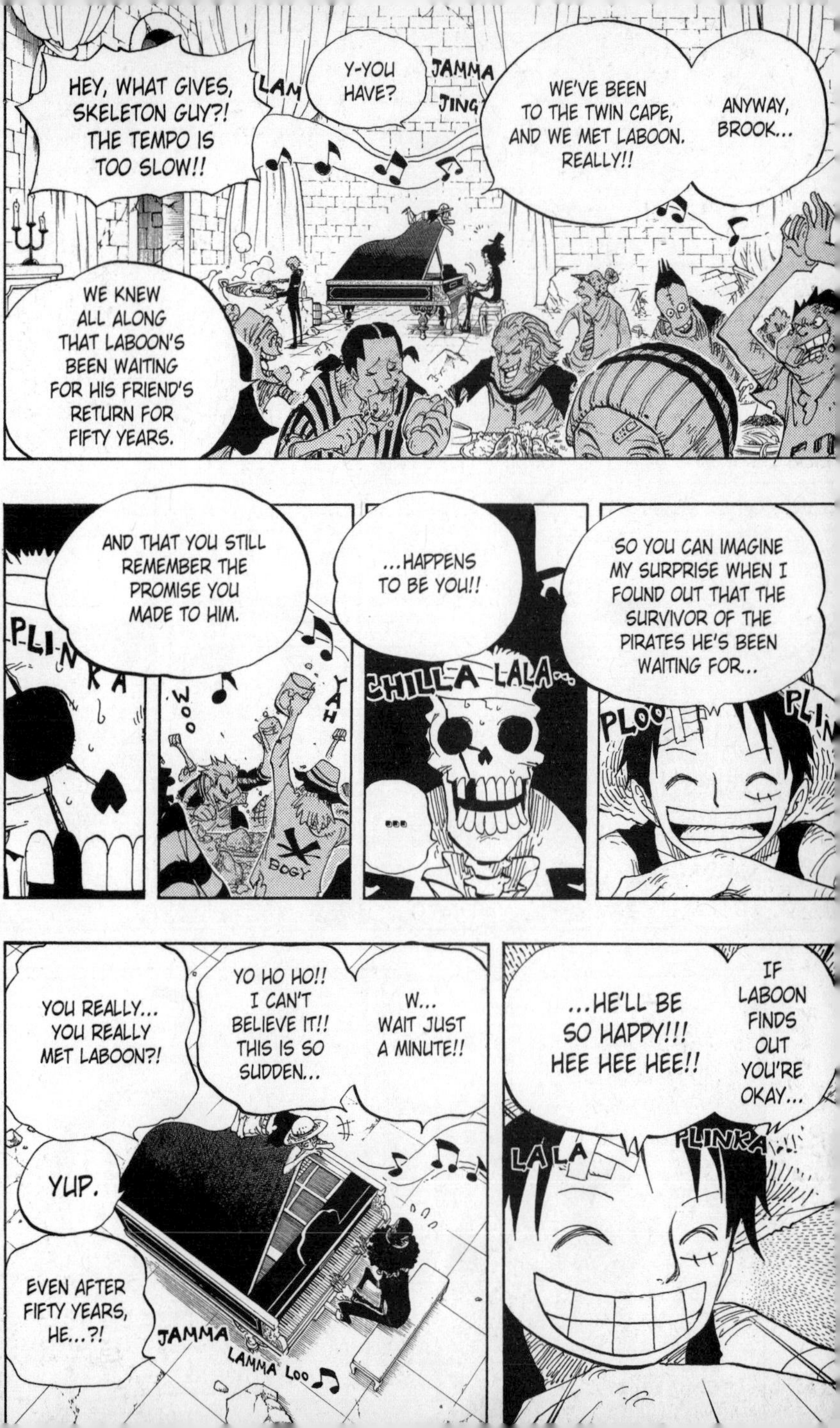
ANYWAY, BROOK...
WE'VE BEEN TO THE TWIN CAPE, AND WE MET LABOON. REALLY!!
JAMMA
JING
Y-YOU HAVE?
LAM
HEY, WHAT GIVES, SKELETON GUY?! THE TEMPO IS TOO SLOW!!
WE KNEW ALL ALONG THAT LABOON'S BEEN WAITING FOR HIS FRIEND'S RETURN FOR FIFTY YEARS.
SO YOU CAN IMAGINE MY SURPRISE WHEN I FOUND OUT THAT THE SURVIVOR OF THE PIRATES HE'S BEEN WAITING FOR...
PLIN
PLOO
...HAPPENS TO BE YOU!!
CHILLA LALA...
...
YAH
WOO
BOGY
AND THAT YOU STILL REMEMBER THE PROMISE YOU MADE TO HIM.
PLI-N-KA
IF LABOON FINDS OUT YOU'RE OKAY...
...HE'LL BE SO HAPPY!!! HEE HEE HEE!!
PLINKA...
LA LA
W... WAIT JUST A MINUTE!!
YO HO HO!! I CAN'T BELIEVE IT!! THIS IS SO SUDDEN...
YOU REALLY... YOU REALLY MET LABOON?!
YUP.
EVEN AFTER FIFTY YEARS, HE...?!
JAMMA
LAMMA LOO

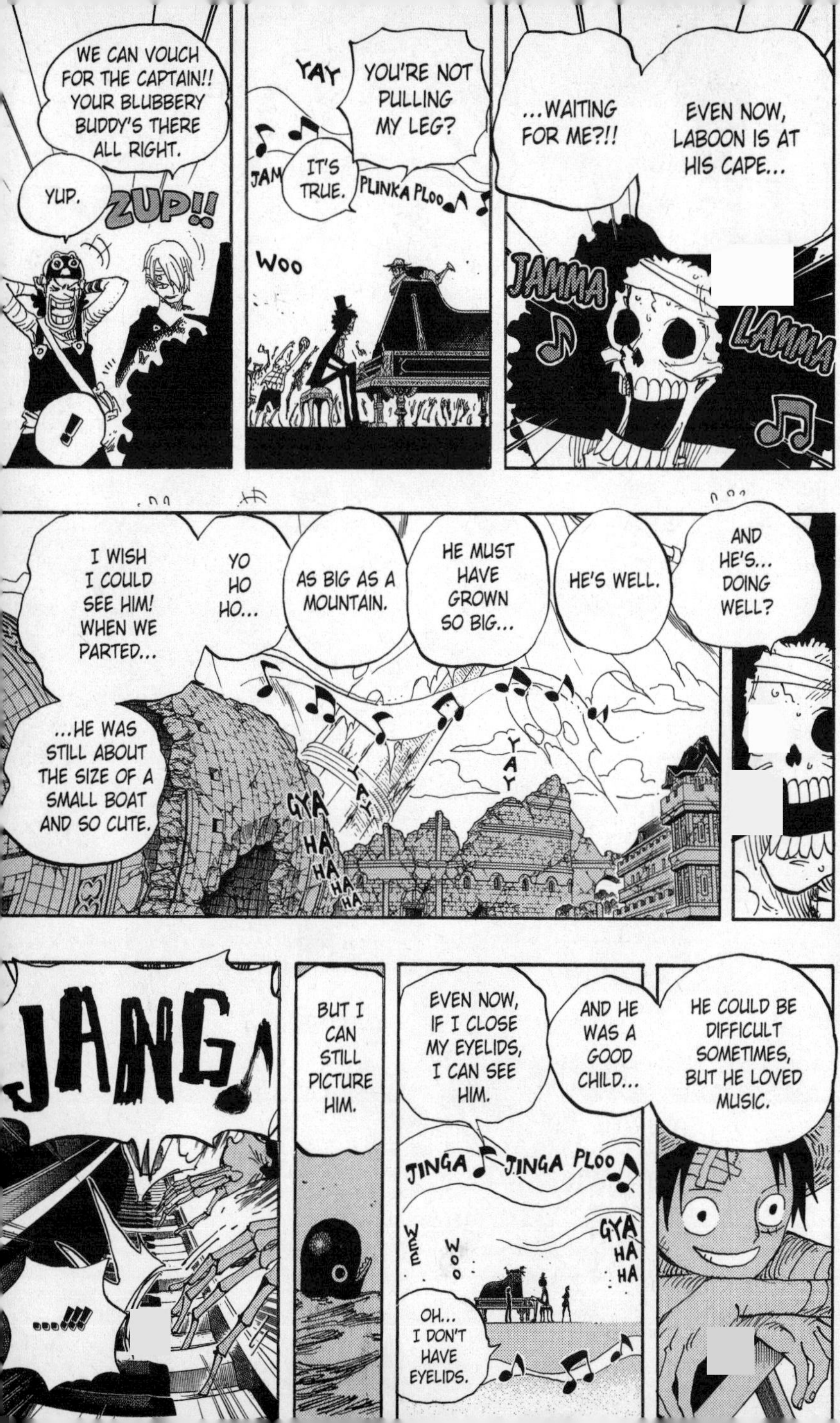
EVEN NOW, LABOON IS AT HIS CAPE...
...WAITING FOR ME?!!
JAMMA
LAMMA
YOU'RE NOT PULLING MY LEG?
YAY
IT'S TRUE.
JAM
PLINKA PLOO
WOO
WE CAN VOUCH FOR THE CAPTAIN!! YOUR BLUBBERY BUDDY'S THERE ALL RIGHT.
YUP.
ZUP!!
AND HE'S... DOING WELL?
HE'S WELL.
HE MUST HAVE GROWN SO BIG...
AS BIG AS A MOUNTAIN.
YO HO HO...
I WISH I COULD SEE HIM! WHEN WE PARTED...
...HE WAS STILL ABOUT THE SIZE OF A SMALL BOAT AND SO CUTE.
YAY
YAY
GYA HA HA HA HA HA
HE COULD BE DIFFICULT SOMETIMES, BUT HE LOVED MUSIC.
AND HE WAS A GOOD CHILD...
EVEN NOW, IF I CLOSE MY EYELIDS, I CAN SEE HIM.
JINGA JINGA PLOO
GYA HA HA
WOO
WEE
OH... I DON'T HAVE EYELIDS.
BUT I CAN STILL PICTURE HIM.
JANG
...!!!

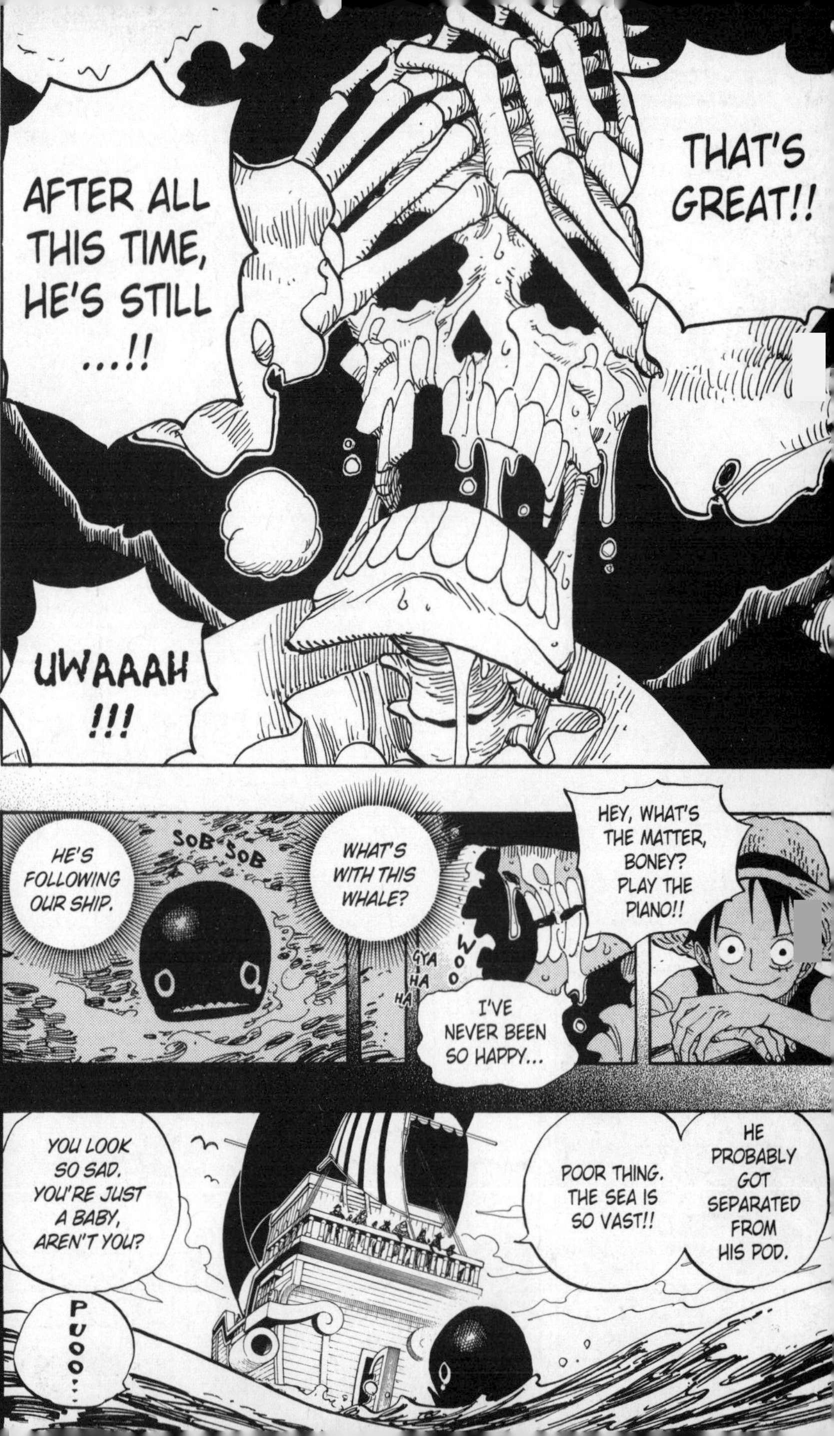
THAT'S GREAT!!
AFTER ALL THIS TIME, HE'S STILL ...!!
UWAAAH !!!
HEY, WHAT'S THE MATTER, BONEY? PLAY THE PIANO!!
WOOO
I'VE NEVER BEEN SO HAPPY...
GYA HA HA
WHAT'S WITH THIS WHALE?
SOB SOB
HE'S FOLLOWING OUR SHIP.
HE PROBABLY GOT SEPARATED FROM HIS POD.
POOR THING. THE SEA IS SO VAST!!
YOU LOOK SO SAD. YOU'RE JUST A BABY, AREN'T YOU?
PUOOO...

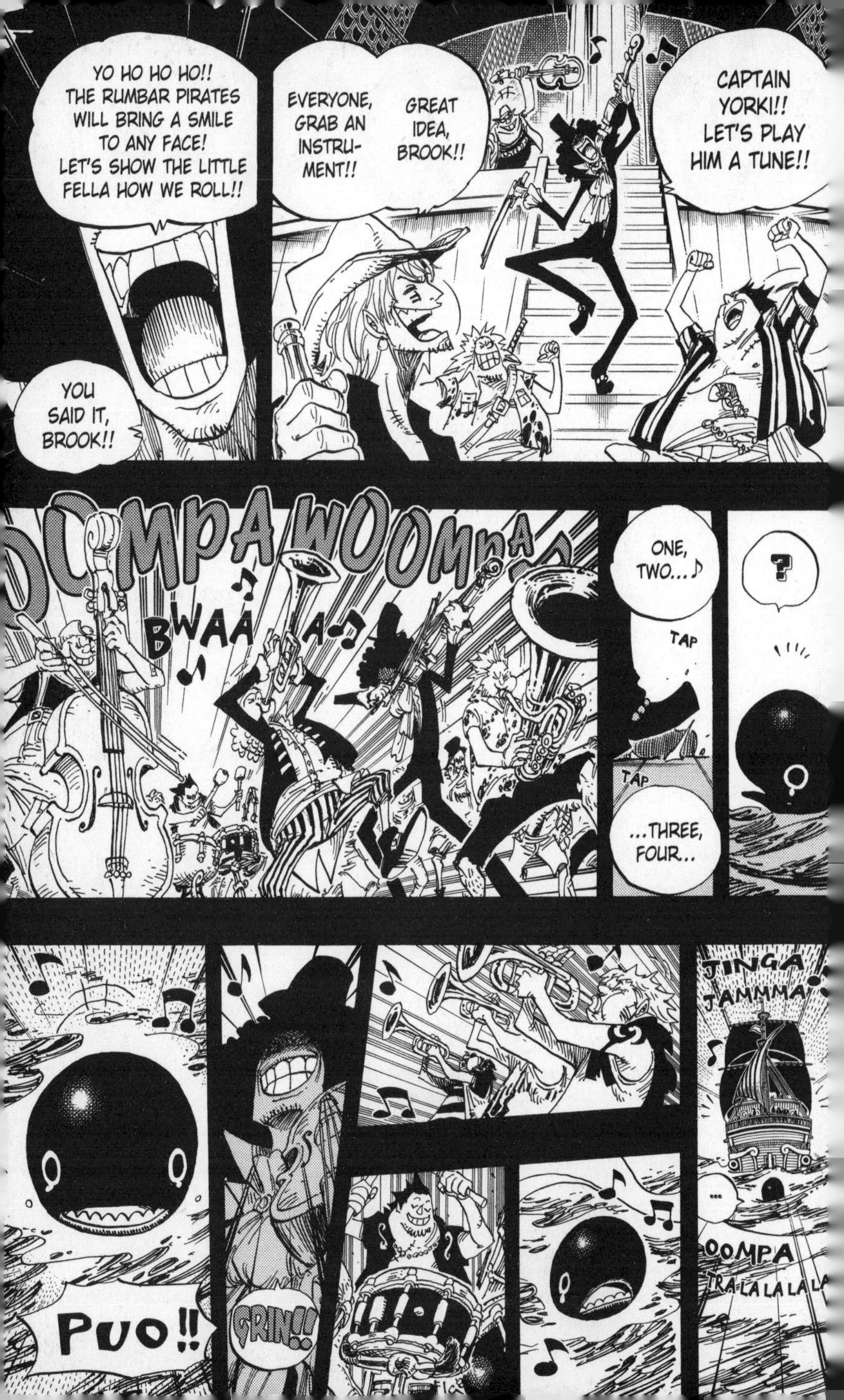

CAPTAIN YORKI!! LET'S PLAY HIM A TUNE!!
GREAT IDEA, BROOK!!
EVERYONE, GRAB AN INSTRU-MENT!!
YO HO HO HO!! THE RUMBAR PIRATES WILL BRING A SMILE TO ANY FACE! LET'S SHOW THE LITTLE FELLA HOW WE ROLL!!
YOU SAID IT, BROOK!!
?
ONE, TWO...♪
TAP
TAP
...THREE, FOUR...
OOMPA WOOMPA
BWAA A
JINGA JAMMA
...
OOMPA
TRA-LA LA LA LA
GRIN!!
PUO!!

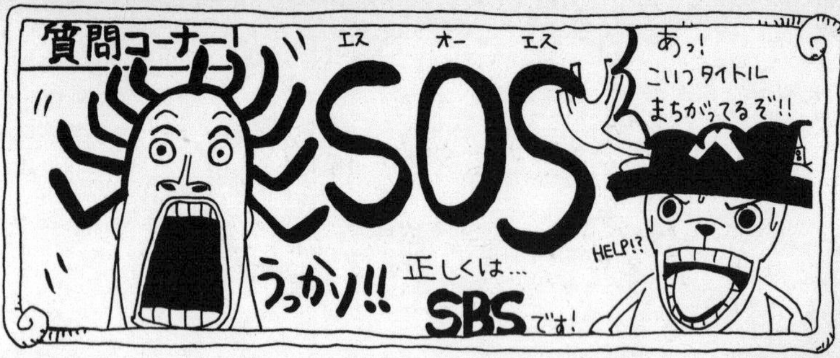
質問コーナー!
エス オー エス
SOS
あっ!
こいつタイトル
まちがってるぞ!!
HELP!?
正しくは…
SBSです!
うっかり!!
(Mikan, Oita)

Q: Oda Sensei, you're always dodging the Finger Pistols from your readers--it's like you have special powers!! Did you once belong to CP9? Please tell me. I'm so concerned, I haven't been able to spend my allowance!

--Female CP9 Research Assistant

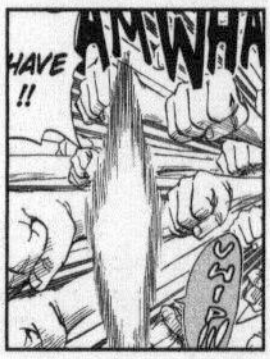
HAVE !!
AMWHA

A: Have I been discovered? I see... Then I might as well fess up. It's true, long ago, I belonged to CP9. But while Lucci and the rest belong to CP9, which stands for "Cipher Pol No. 9," the CP9 I belonged to stood for "Cool Pants 9."

Q: In volumes 47–48, who was it that changed Nami into a wedding dress? It's not that old zombie who was holding a measuring tape in chapter 485, is it? If so, this is a major problem. It means he saw her naked while changing her. That's the pits. What a pervert!!

--Yuka-san

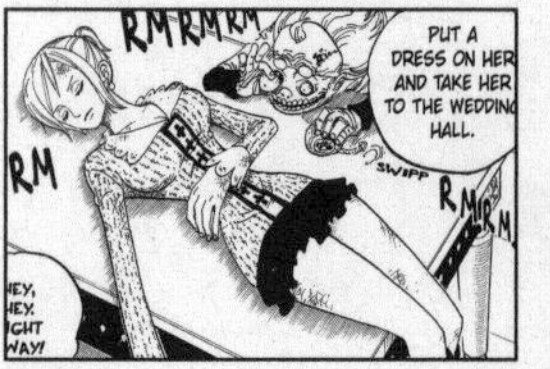
PUT A DRESS ON HER AND TAKE HER TO THE WEDDING HALL.
RMRMRM
RM
SWIFF
RMRM

A: Uhhhhhhh... Oh!!
Sorry! I was stuck in fantasy world there. (Blush♡)
No really, was it him?! That's terrible!! Uhhh...

Q: I have a question. In volume 42, page 80, Sanji says that he doesn't kick women because it was drummed into him as a kid. So the one who drummed that into him was Zeff? Does that mean Zeff was kind to women too? Please tell me.

--Yuka-san

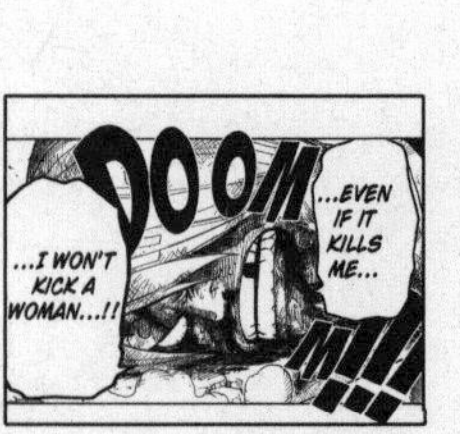
DOOM
...EVEN IF IT KILLS ME...
...I WON'T KICK A WOMAN...!!

A: Two postcards from the same person! But this is a good question, so I'll answer it. When I worked on Sanji vs. Kalifa (chapter 403), some cheered for Sanji and some criticized him as being pathetic. Actually, I didn't want to write any dialogue for that section. It's not that Sanji is against women being kicked--it's just that he personally "can't kick women." That's just his gentlemanly pride talking. I think he was really frustrated. And Nami realized that and broke her resolve to praise Sanji that one time. I'm sure a lot of guy readers can sympathize with Sanji in that scene, but it all depends on how you interpret it. Of course, Zeff was a gentleman too.

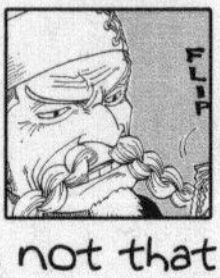
FLIP

Chapter 487:
THAT SONG

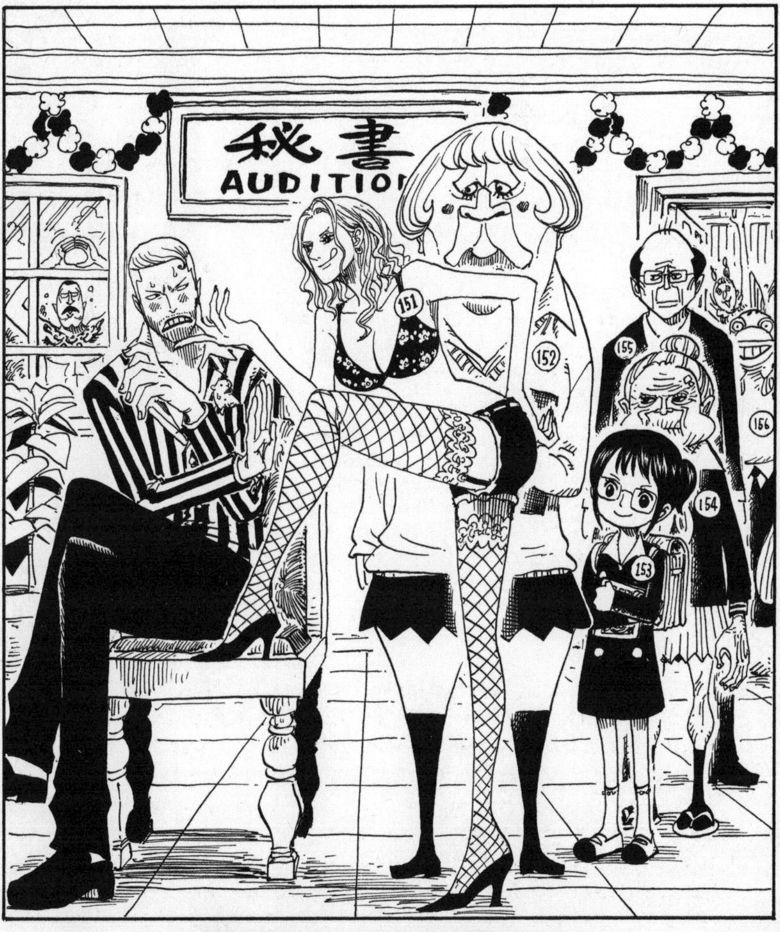
秘書
AUDITIO
151
152
153
154
155
156
WHERE ARE THEY NOW? SHOT 5:
"AUDITIONS FOR ICEBERG'S SECRETARY"

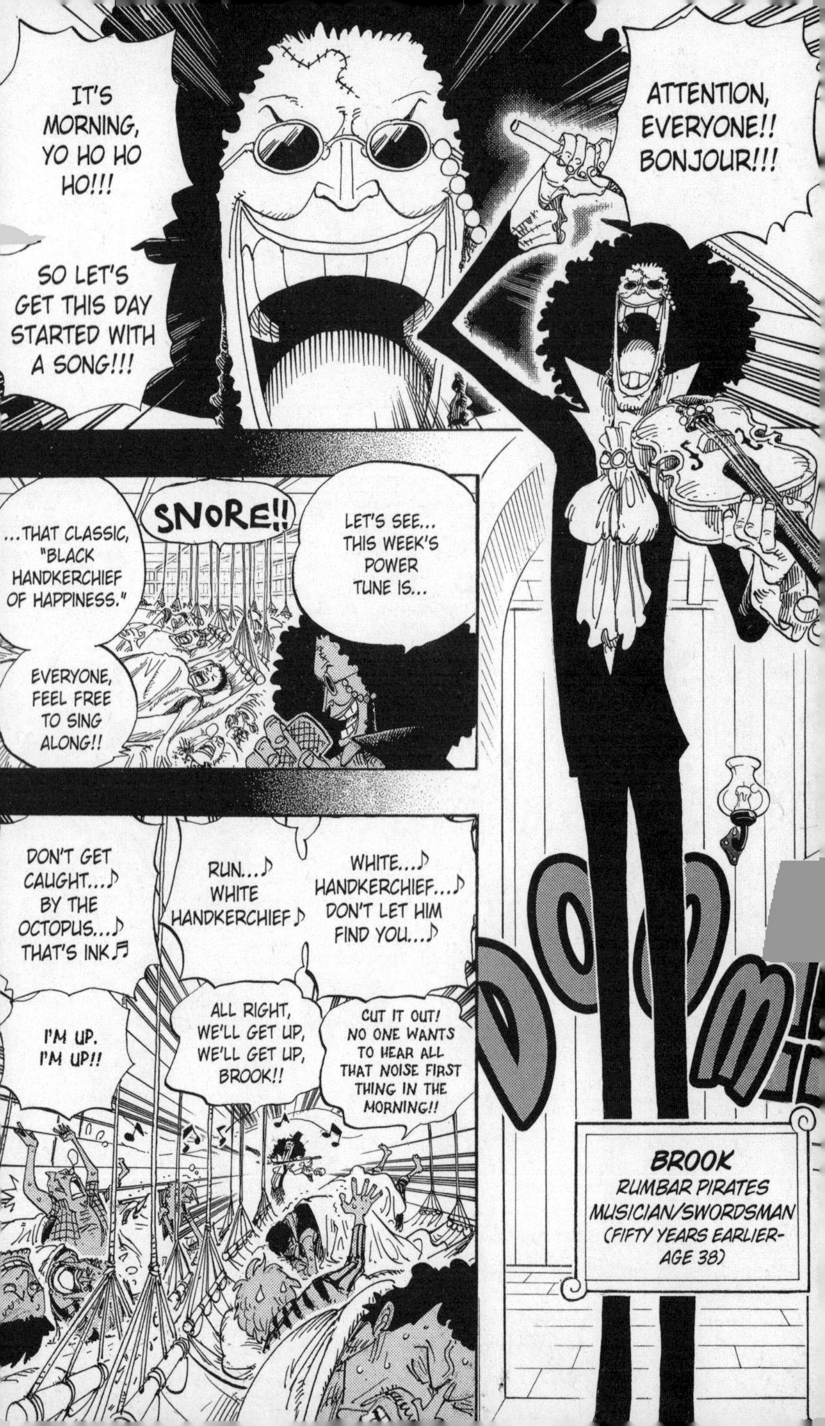
ATTENTION, EVERYONE!! BONJOUR!!!
DOOM
BROOK
RUMBAR PIRATES MUSICIAN/SWORDSMAN (FIFTY YEARS EARLIER-AGE 38)
IT'S MORNING, YO HO HO HO!!!
SO LET'S GET THIS DAY STARTED WITH A SONG!!!
LET'S SEE... THIS WEEK'S POWER TUNE IS...
SNORE!!
...THAT CLASSIC, "BLACK HANDKERCHIEF OF HAPPINESS."
EVERYONE, FEEL FREE TO SING ALONG!!
WHITE...♪ HANDKERCHIEF...♪ DON'T LET HIM FIND YOU...♪
RUN...♪ WHITE HANDKERCHIEF♪
DON'T GET CAUGHT...♪ BY THE OCTOPUS...♪ THAT'S INK♬
CUT IT OUT! NO ONE WANTS TO HEAR ALL THAT NOISE FIRST THING IN THE MORNING!!
ALL RIGHT, WE'LL GET UP, WE'LL GET UP, BROOK!!
I'M UP. I'M UP!!

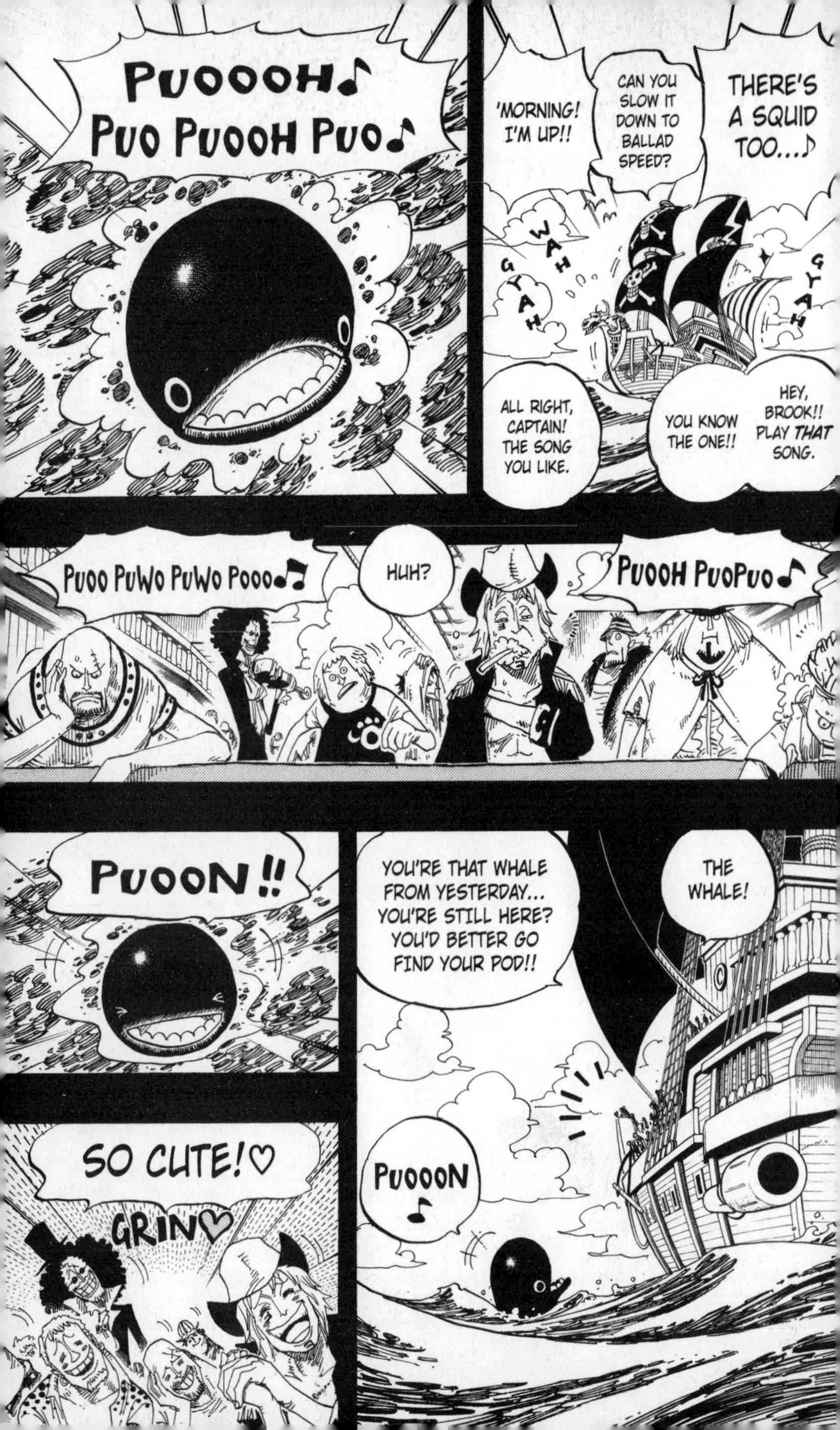
THERE'S A SQUID TOO...♪
CAN YOU SLOW IT DOWN TO BALLAD SPEED?
'MORNING! I'M UP!!
GYAH
WAH
GYAH
HEY, BROOK!! PLAY *THAT* SONG.
YOU KNOW THE ONE!!
ALL RIGHT, CAPTAIN! THE SONG YOU LIKE.
PUOOOH♪ PUO PUOOH PUO♪
PUOOH PUOPUO♪
HUH?
PUOO PUWO PUWO POOO♪♫
THE WHALE!
YOU'RE THAT WHALE FROM YESTERDAY... YOU'RE STILL HERE? YOU'D BETTER GO FIND YOUR POD!!
PUOOON ♪
PUOON!!
SO CUTE!♡
GRIN♡

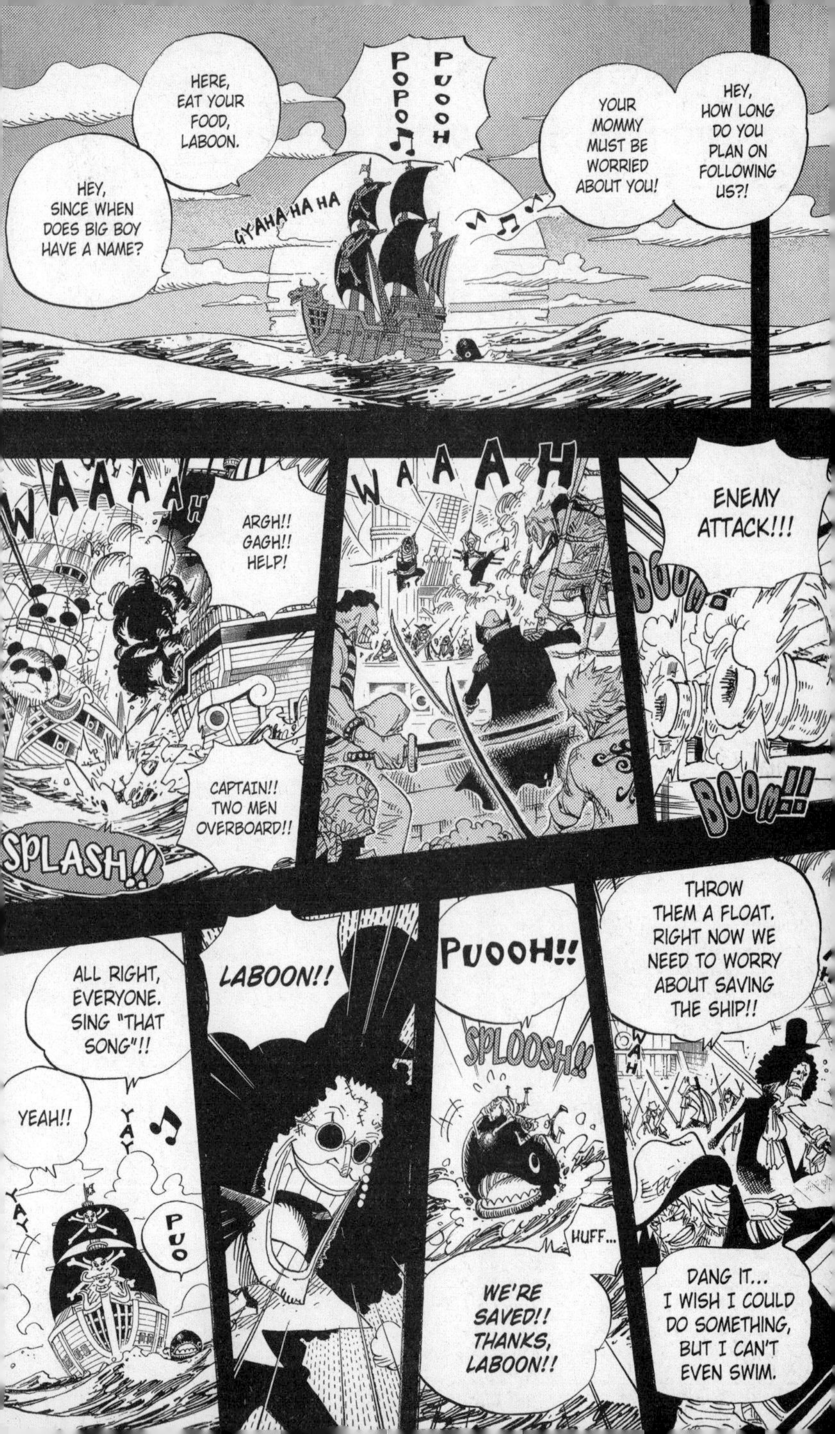
HEY, HOW LONG DO YOU PLAN ON FOLLOWING US?!
YOUR MOMMY MUST BE WORRIED ABOUT YOU!
PUOOH
POPO♪
HERE, EAT YOUR FOOD, LABOON.
HEY, SINCE WHEN DOES BIG BOY HAVE A NAME?
GYAHAHAHA
ENEMY ATTACK!!!
BOOM
BOOM!!
WAAAH
WAAAAH
ARGH!! GAGH!! HELP!
CAPTAIN!! TWO MEN OVERBOARD!!
SPLASH!!
THROW THEM A FLOAT. RIGHT NOW WE NEED TO WORRY ABOUT SAVING THE SHIP!!
WAH
DANG IT... I WISH I COULD DO SOMETHING, BUT I CAN'T EVEN SWIM.
PUOOH!!
SPLOOSH!!
HUFF...
WE'RE SAVED!! THANKS, LABOON!!
LABOON!!
ALL RIGHT, EVERYONE. SING "THAT SONG"!!
YEAH!!
YAY
YAY
PUO

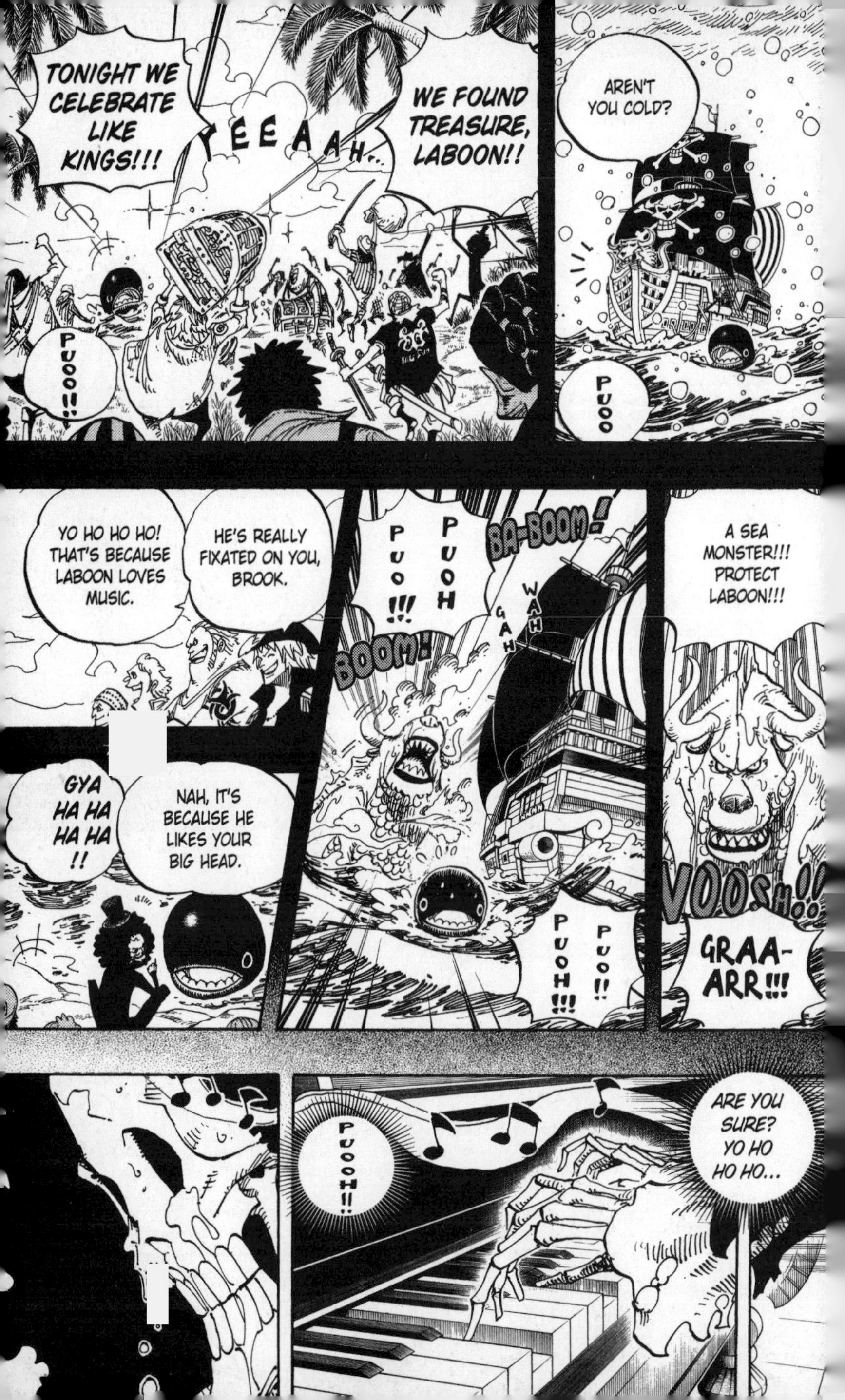
AREN'T YOU COLD?
PUOO
WE FOUND TREASURE, LABOON!!
YEEAAH...
TONIGHT WE CELEBRATE LIKE KINGS!!!
PUOO!!
A SEA MONSTER!!! PROTECT LABOON!!!
VOOSH!!
GRAA-ARR!!!
BA-BOOM!
PUOH
PUO!!!
WAH
GAH
BOOM!
PUO!!
PUOH!!!
HE'S REALLY FIXATED ON YOU, BROOK.
YO HO HO HO! THAT'S BECAUSE LABOON LOVES MUSIC.
NAH, IT'S BECAUSE HE LIKES YOUR BIG HEAD.
GYA HA HA HA HA!!
ARE YOU SURE? YO HO HO HO...
PUOOOH!!

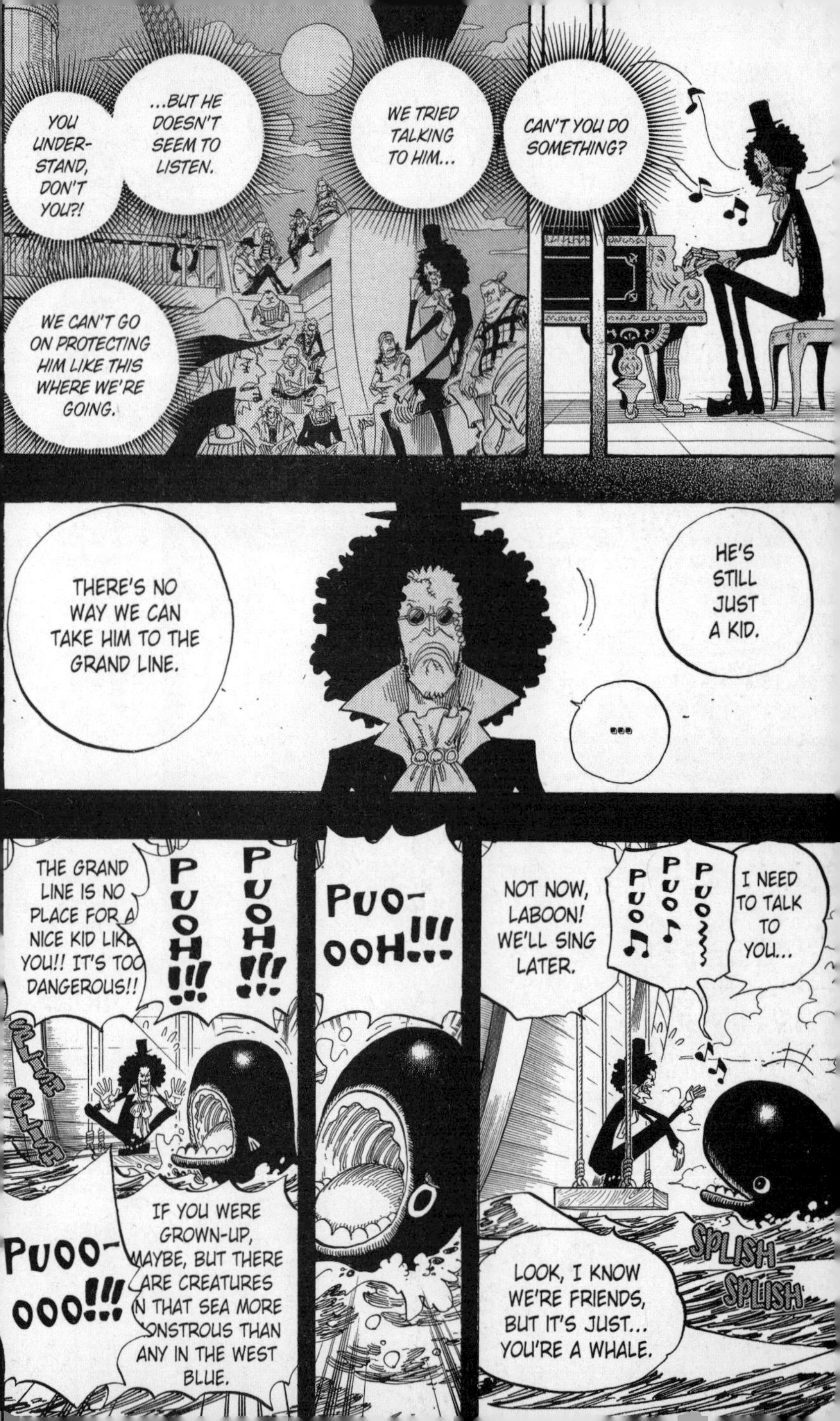
CAN'T YOU DO SOMETHING?
WE TRIED TALKING TO HIM...
...BUT HE DOESN'T SEEM TO LISTEN.
YOU UNDERSTAND, DON'T YOU?!
WE CAN'T GO ON PROTECTING HIM LIKE THIS WHERE WE'RE GOING.
HE'S STILL JUST A KID.
...
THERE'S NO WAY WE CAN TAKE HIM TO THE GRAND LINE.
I NEED TO TALK TO YOU...
PUO~
PUO♪
PUO♫
NOT NOW, LABOON! WE'LL SING LATER.
SPLISH
SPLISH
LOOK, I KNOW WE'RE FRIENDS, BUT IT'S JUST... YOU'RE A WHALE.
PUO-OOH!!!
PUOH!!!
PUOH!!!
THE GRAND LINE IS NO PLACE FOR A NICE KID LIKE YOU!! IT'S TOO DANGEROUS!!
SPLISH
SPLISH
IF YOU WERE GROWN-UP, MAYBE, BUT THERE ARE CREATURES IN THAT SEA MORE MONSTROUS THAN ANY IN THE WEST BLUE.
PUOO-OOO!!!

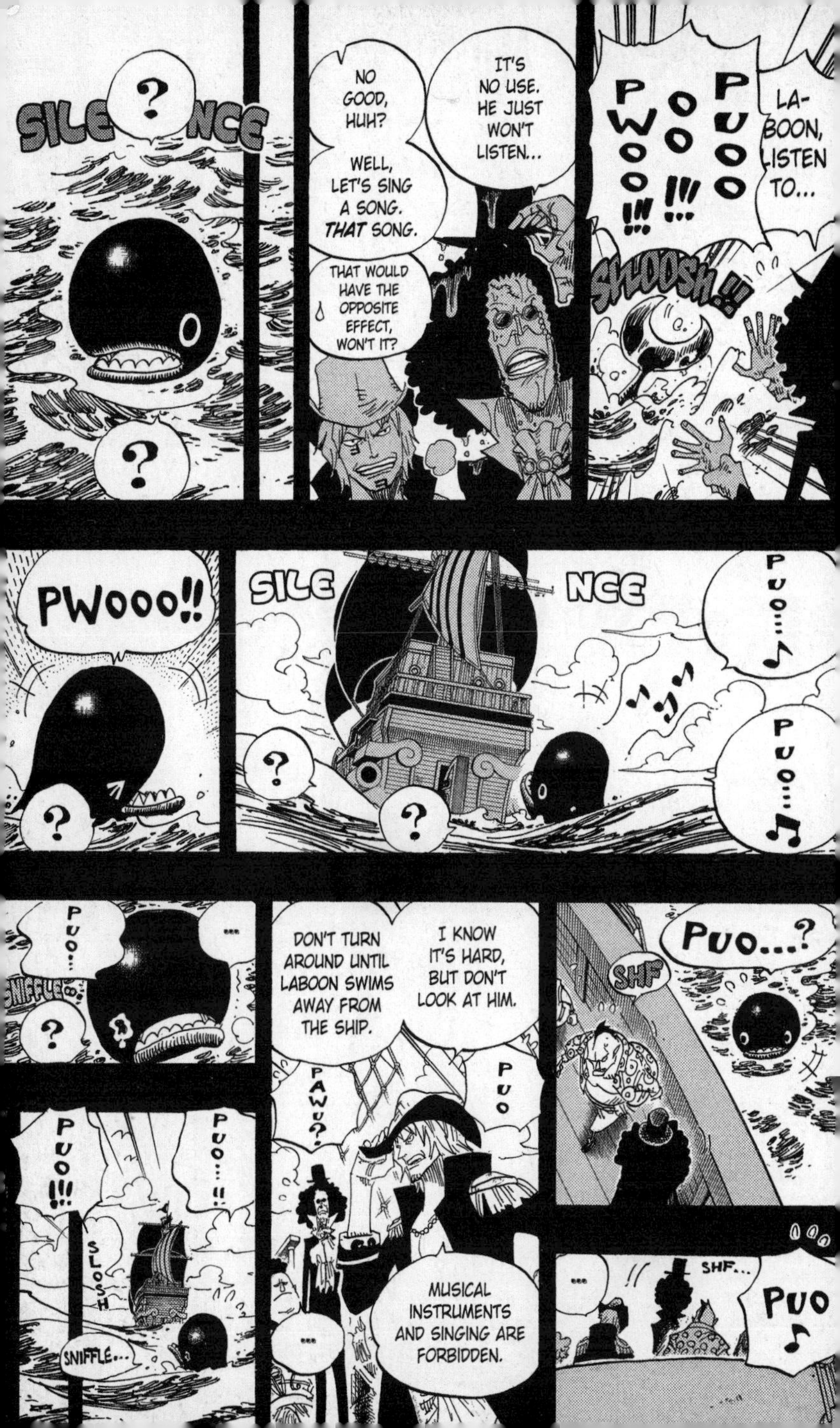

LA-BOON, LISTEN TO...
PUOO
POOO!!!
PWOOO!!!
SWOOSH!!
IT'S NO USE. HE JUST WON'T LISTEN...
NO GOOD, HUH?
WELL, LET'S SING A SONG. *THAT* SONG.
THAT WOULD HAVE THE OPPOSITE EFFECT, WON'T IT?
SILENCE
?
?
PUO...♪
PUO...♪
SILENCE
?
?
PWOOO!!
?
PUO...?
SHF
PUO♪
SHF...
...
I KNOW IT'S HARD, BUT DON'T LOOK AT HIM.
DON'T TURN AROUND UNTIL LABOON SWIMS AWAY FROM THE SHIP.
PUO
PAWU?
MUSICAL INSTRUMENTS AND SINGING ARE FORBIDDEN.
...
...
PUO...
SNIFFLE
?
PUO...!!
PUO!!!
SLOSH
SNIFFLE...

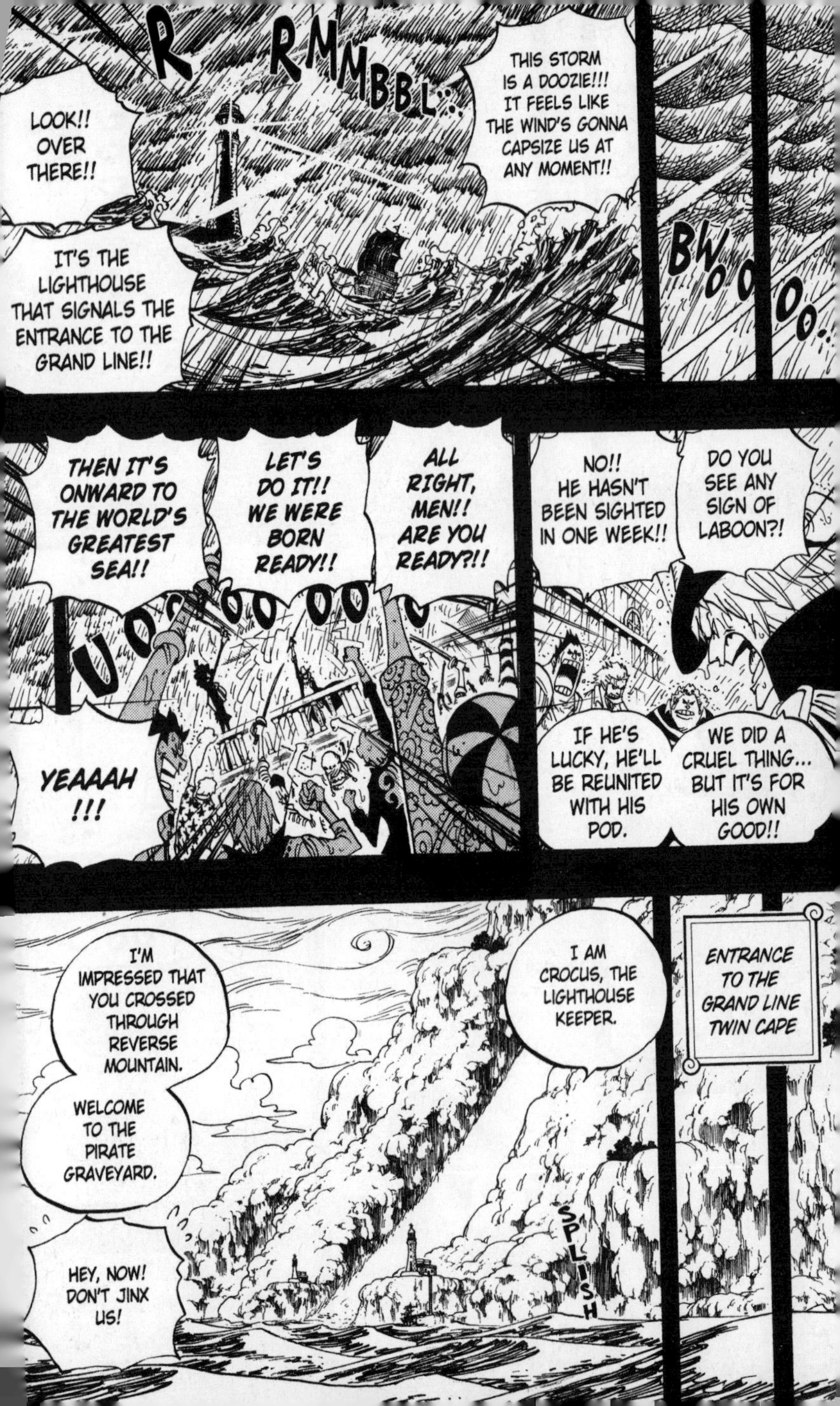
BWOOOOO...
R RMMBBL
THIS STORM IS A DOOZIE!!! IT FEELS LIKE THE WIND'S GONNA CAPSIZE US AT ANY MOMENT!!
LOOK!! OVER THERE!!
IT'S THE LIGHTHOUSE THAT SIGNALS THE ENTRANCE TO THE GRAND LINE!!
DO YOU SEE ANY SIGN OF LABOON?!
NO!! HE HASN'T BEEN SIGHTED IN ONE WEEK!!
WE DID A CRUEL THING... BUT IT'S FOR HIS OWN GOOD!!
IF HE'S LUCKY, HE'LL BE REUNITED WITH HIS POD.
ALL RIGHT, MEN!! ARE YOU READY?!!
LET'S DO IT!! WE WERE BORN READY!!
THEN IT'S ONWARD TO THE WORLD'S GREATEST SEA!!
UOOOOOO
YEAAAH !!!
ENTRANCE TO THE GRAND LINE TWIN CAPE
I AM CROCUS, THE LIGHTHOUSE KEEPER.
I'M IMPRESSED THAT YOU CROSSED THROUGH REVERSE MOUNTAIN.
WELCOME TO THE PIRATE GRAVEYARD.
SPLISH
HEY, NOW! DON'T JINX US!

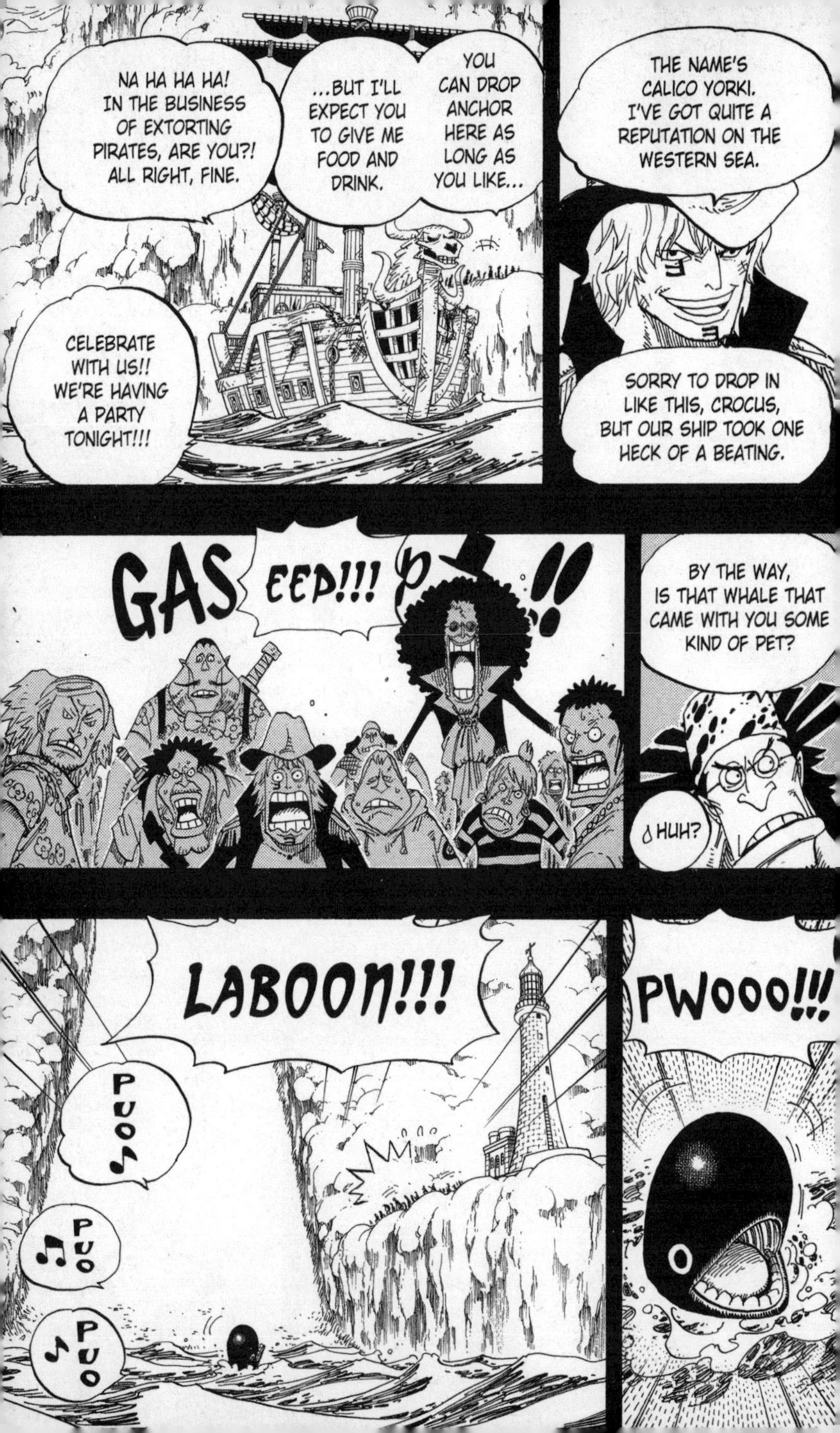
THE NAME'S CALICO YORKI. I'VE GOT QUITE A REPUTATION ON THE WESTERN SEA.
SORRY TO DROP IN LIKE THIS, CROCUS, BUT OUR SHIP TOOK ONE HECK OF A BEATING.
YOU CAN DROP ANCHOR HERE AS LONG AS YOU LIKE...
...BUT I'LL EXPECT YOU TO GIVE ME FOOD AND DRINK.
NA HA HA HA! IN THE BUSINESS OF EXTORTING PIRATES, ARE YOU?! ALL RIGHT, FINE.
CELEBRATE WITH US!! WE'RE HAVING A PARTY TONIGHT!!!
BY THE WAY, IS THAT WHALE THAT CAME WITH YOU SOME KIND OF PET?
HUH?
GASEEP!!!
PWOOO!!!
LABOON!!!
PUO
PUO
PUO

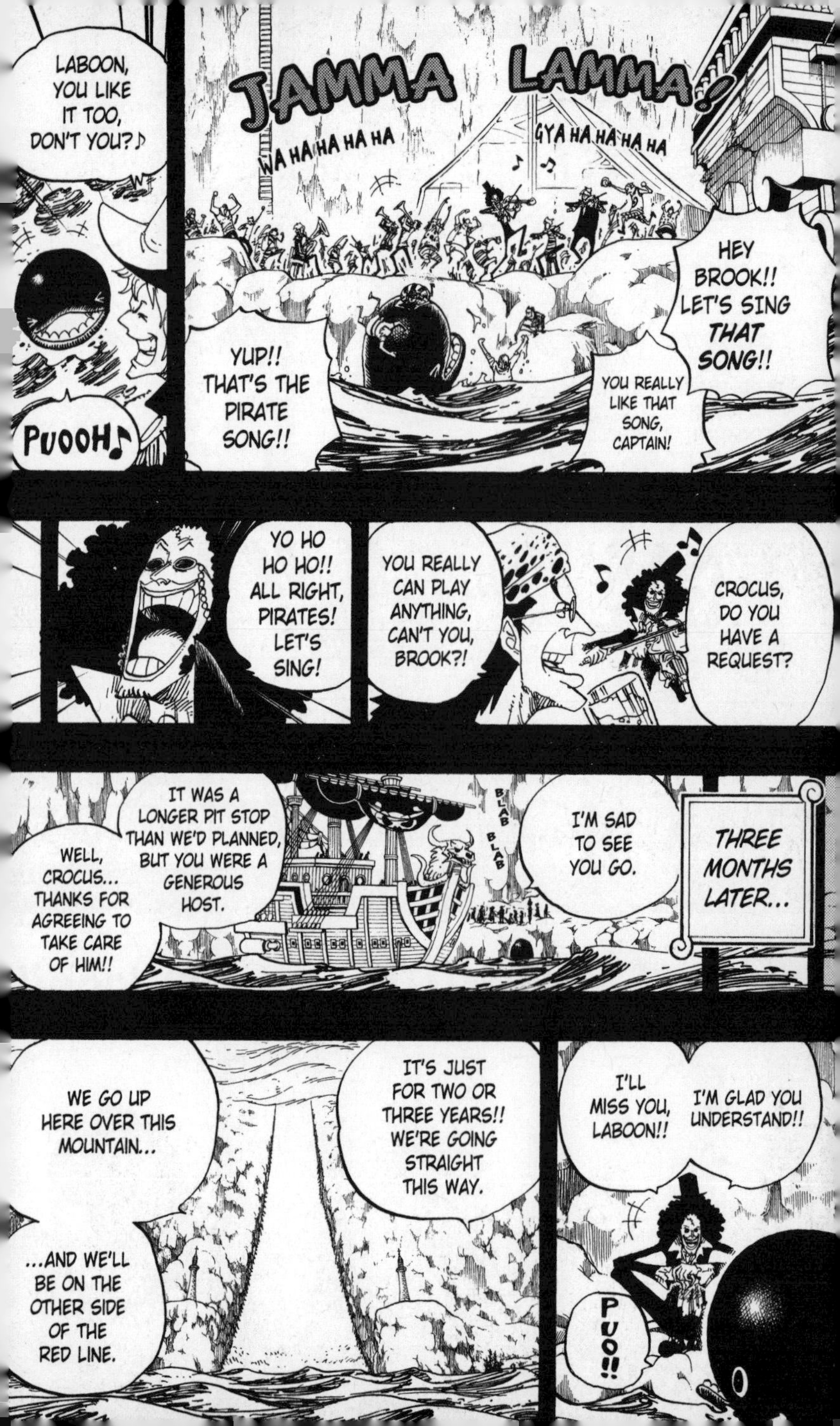
JAMMA LAMMA!
GYA HA HA HA HA
WA HA HA HA HA
HEY BROOK!! LET'S SING THAT SONG!!
YOU REALLY LIKE THAT SONG, CAPTAIN!
YUP!! THAT'S THE PIRATE SONG!!
LABOON, YOU LIKE IT TOO, DON'T YOU?♪
PUOOH♪
CROCUS, DO YOU HAVE A REQUEST?
YOU REALLY CAN PLAY ANYTHING, CAN'T YOU, BROOK?!
YO HO HO HO!! ALL RIGHT, PIRATES! LET'S SING!
THREE MONTHS LATER...
I'M SAD TO SEE YOU GO.
BLAB BLAB
IT WAS A LONGER PIT STOP THAN WE'D PLANNED, BUT YOU WERE A GENEROUS HOST.
WELL, CROCUS... THANKS FOR AGREEING TO TAKE CARE OF HIM!!
I'M GLAD YOU UNDERSTAND!!
I'LL MISS YOU, LABOON!!
PUO!!
IT'S JUST FOR TWO OR THREE YEARS!! WE'RE GOING STRAIGHT THIS WAY.
WE GO UP HERE OVER THIS MOUNTAIN...
...AND WE'LL BE ON THE OTHER SIDE OF THE RED LINE.

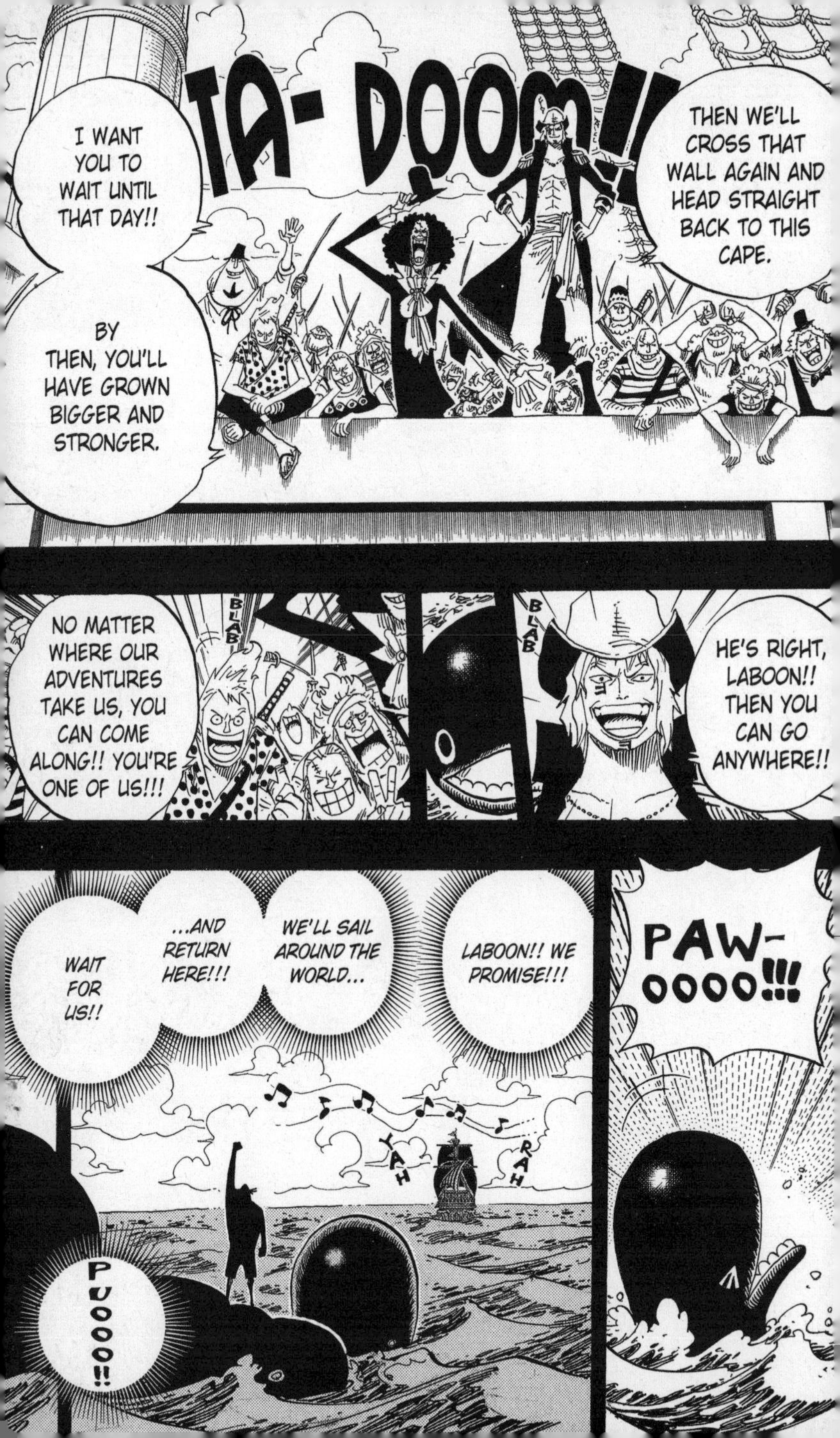
THEN WE'LL CROSS THAT WALL AGAIN AND HEAD STRAIGHT BACK TO THIS CAPE.
TA-DOOM!!
I WANT YOU TO WAIT UNTIL THAT DAY!!
BY THEN, YOU'LL HAVE GROWN BIGGER AND STRONGER.
BLAB
HE'S RIGHT, LABOON!! THEN YOU CAN GO ANYWHERE!!
BLAB
NO MATTER WHERE OUR ADVENTURES TAKE US, YOU CAN COME ALONG!! YOU'RE ONE OF US!!!
PAW-OOOO!!!
LABOON!! WE PROMISE!!!
WE'LL SAIL AROUND THE WORLD...
...AND RETURN HERE!!!
WAIT FOR US!!
RAH
YAH
PUOOOO!!

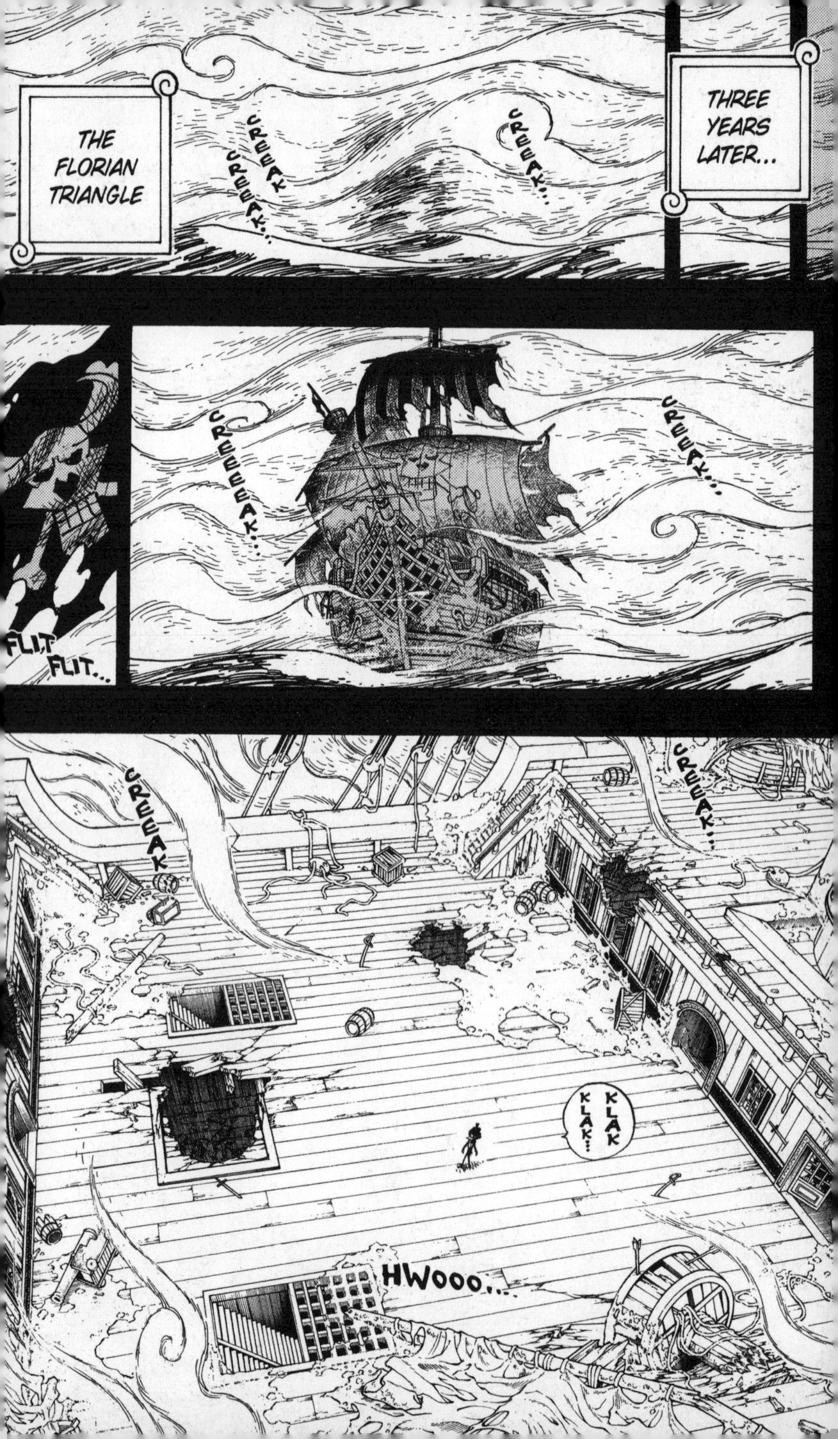
THREE YEARS LATER...
CREEEAK...
CREEAK
CREEEAK...
THE FLORIAN TRIANGLE
CREEAK...
CREEEEEAK...
FLIT FLIT...
CREEEAK...
CREEEAK
KLAK KLAK
HWOOO...

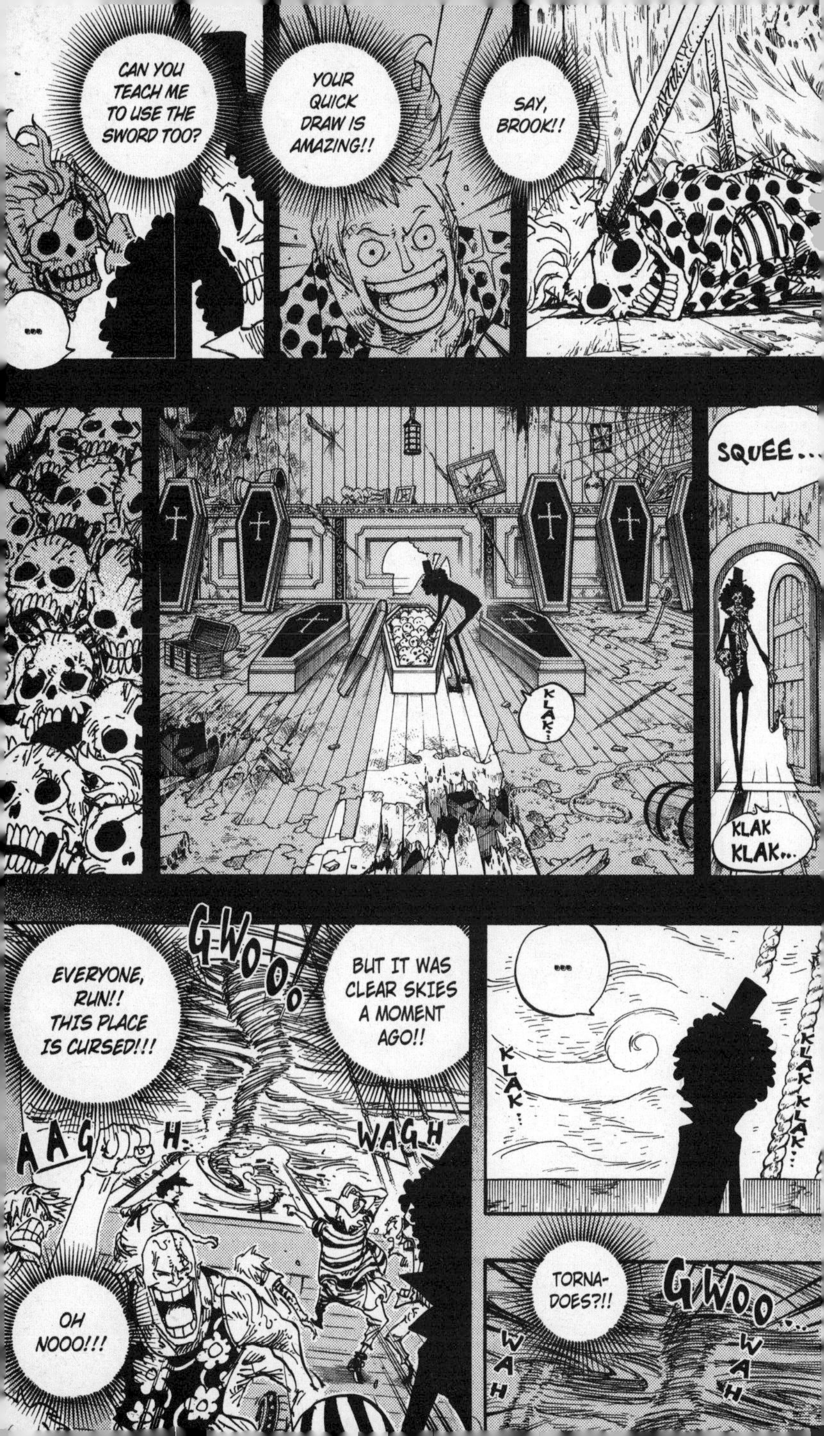
SAY, BROOK!!
YOUR QUICK DRAW IS AMAZING!!
CAN YOU TEACH ME TO USE THE SWORD TOO?
...
SQUEE...
KLAK KLAK...
KLAK...
...
KLAK KLAK KLAK...
KLAK...
TORNA-DOES?!!
GWOO...
WAH
WAH
BUT IT WAS CLEAR SKIES A MOMENT AGO!!
GWOOO
EVERYONE, RUN!! THIS PLACE IS CURSED!!!
WAGH
AAGH
OH NOOO!!!

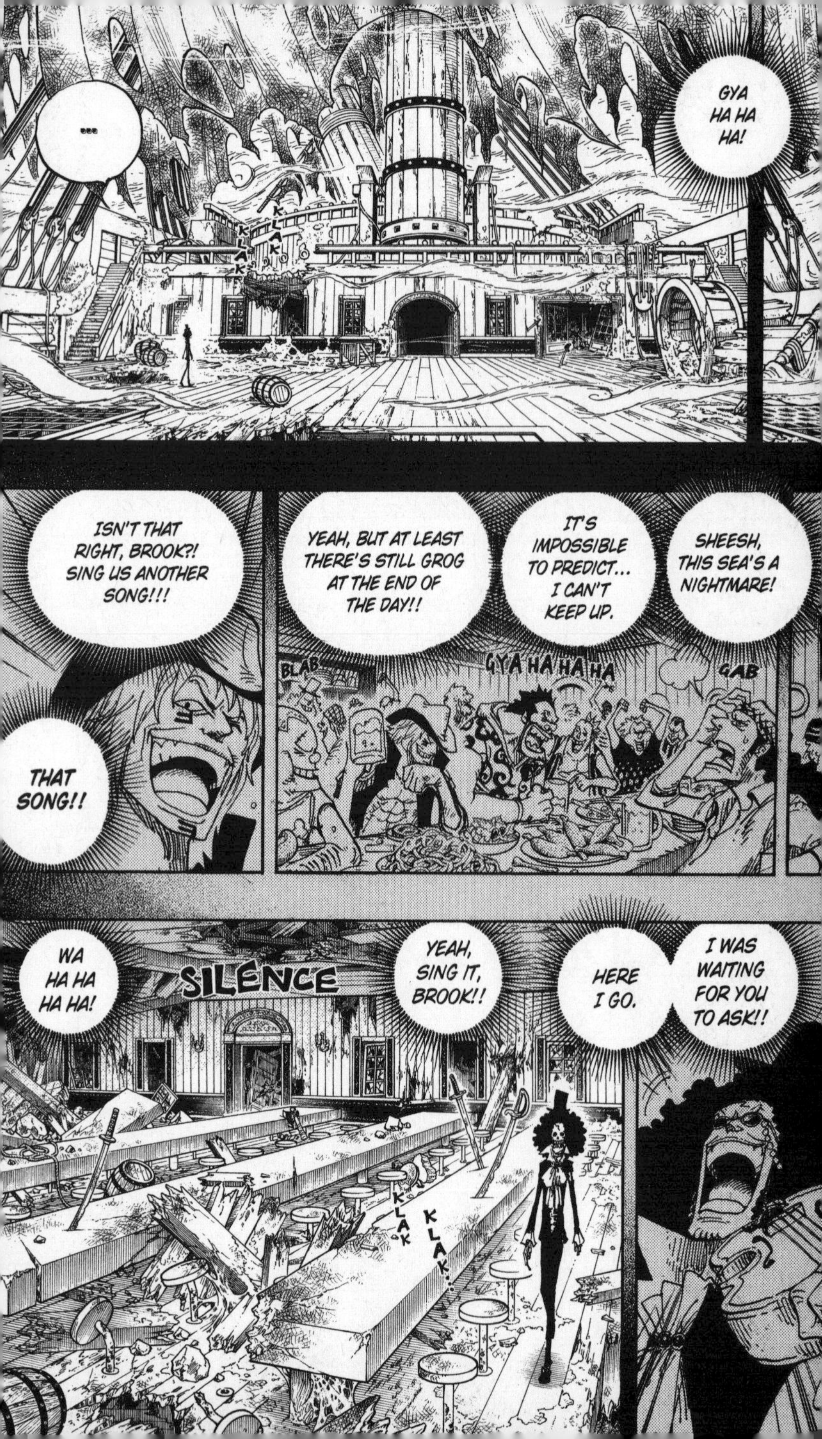
GYA HA HA HA!
KLAK KLAK
...
SHEESH, THIS SEA'S A NIGHTMARE!
IT'S IMPOSSIBLE TO PREDICT... I CAN'T KEEP UP.
YEAH, BUT AT LEAST THERE'S STILL GROG AT THE END OF THE DAY!!
GAB
GYA HA HA HA HA
BLAB
ISN'T THAT RIGHT, BROOK?! SING US ANOTHER SONG!!!
THAT SONG!!
I WAS WAITING FOR YOU TO ASK!!
HERE I GO.
YEAH, SING IT, BROOK!!
WA HA HA HA HA!
SILENCE
KLAK KLAK...

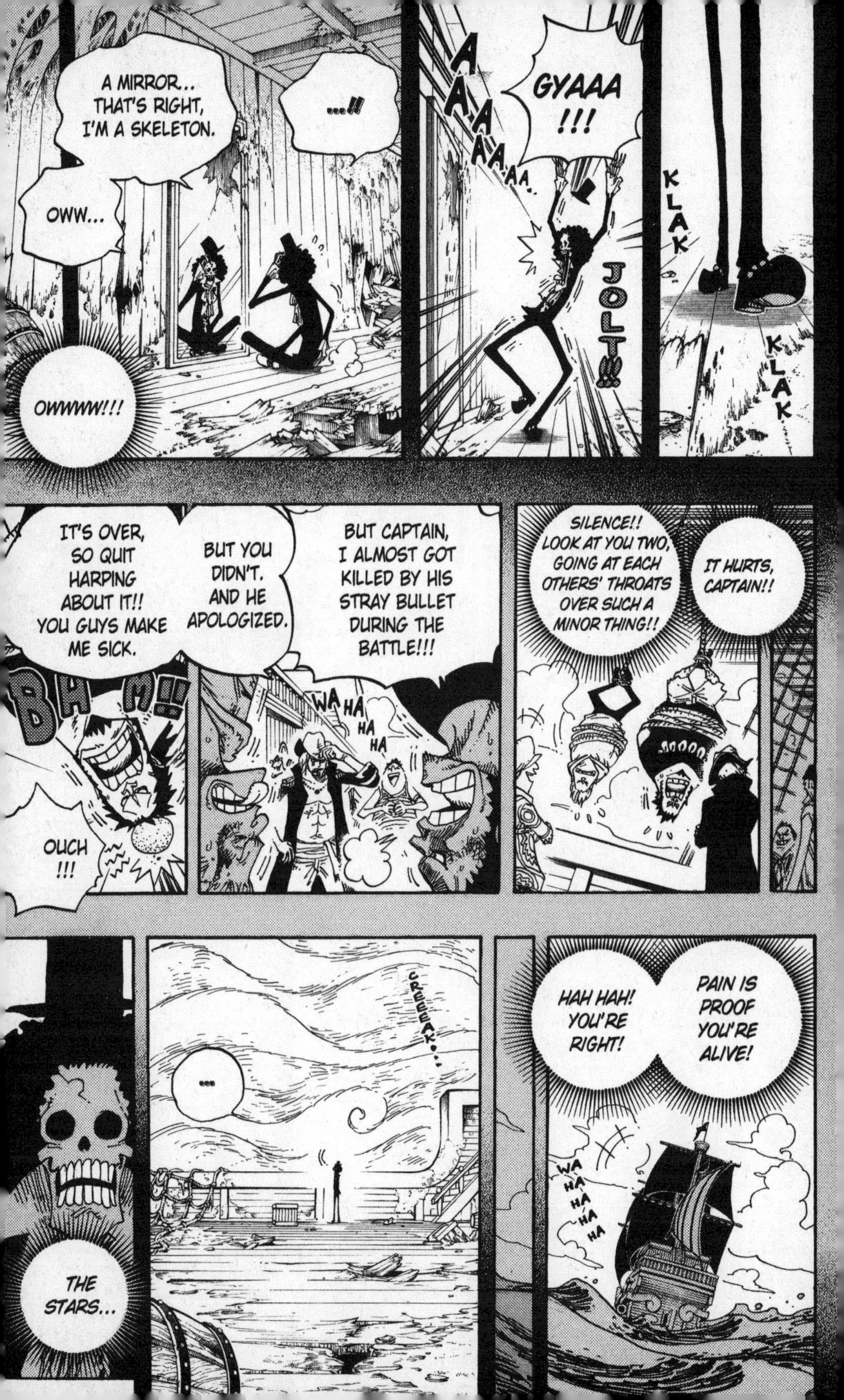

KLAK
KLAK KLAK
GYAAA!!!
AAAAAAAA...
JOLT!!
...!!
A MIRROR... THAT'S RIGHT, I'M A SKELETON.
OWW...
OWWW!!!
IT HURTS, CAPTAIN!!
SILENCE!! LOOK AT YOU TWO, GOING AT EACH OTHERS' THROATS OVER SUCH A MINOR THING!!
BUT CAPTAIN, I ALMOST GOT KILLED BY HIS STRAY BULLET DURING THE BATTLE!!!
WA HA HA HA
BUT YOU DIDN'T. AND HE APOLOGIZED.
IT'S OVER, SO QUIT HARPING ABOUT IT!! YOU GUYS MAKE ME SICK.
BAM!!
OUCH!!!
PAIN IS PROOF YOU'RE ALIVE!
HAH HAH! YOU'RE RIGHT!
WA HA HA HA HA HA
CREEEAK...
...
THE STARS...

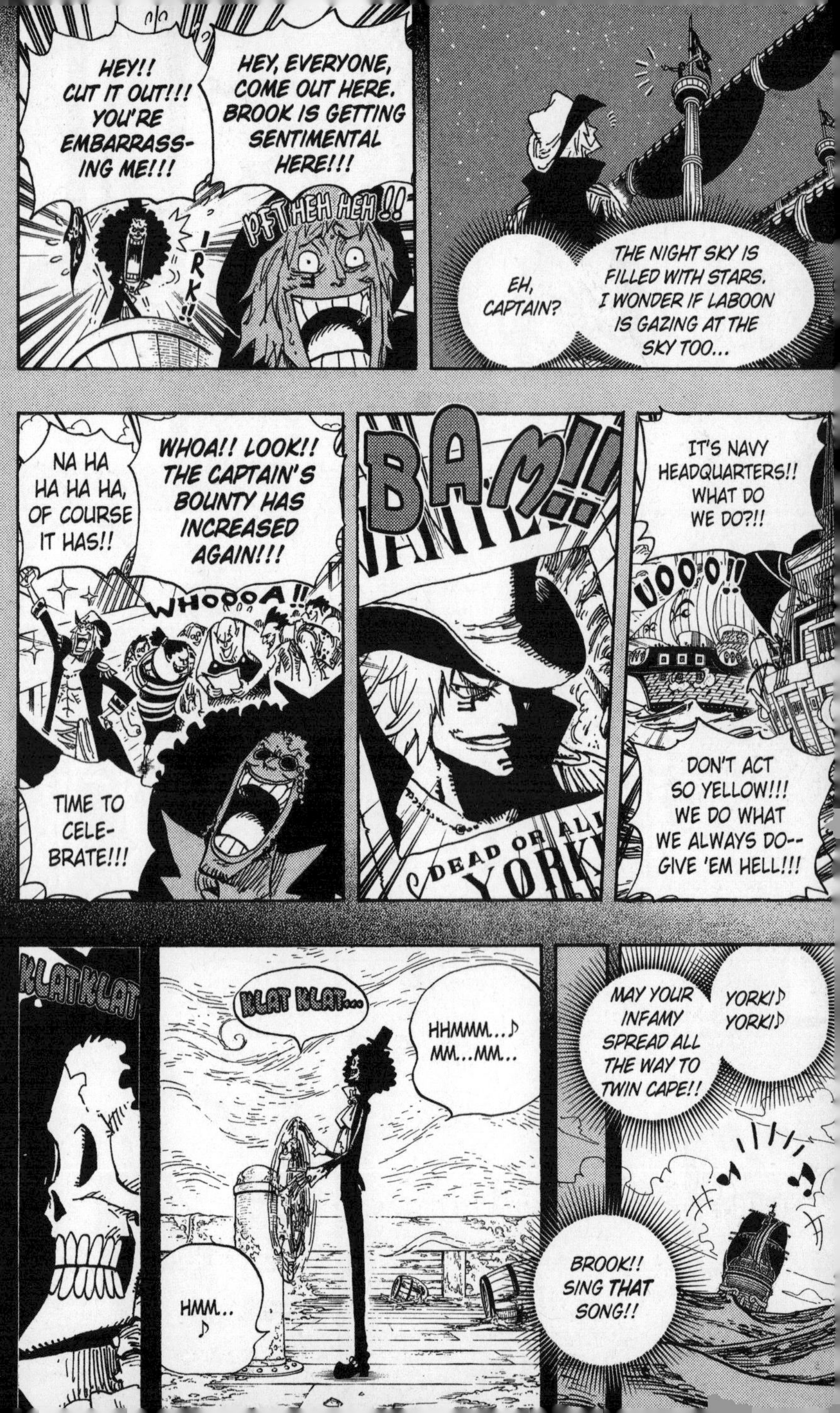
THE NIGHT SKY IS FILLED WITH STARS. I WONDER IF LABOON IS GAZING AT THE SKY TOO...
EH, CAPTAIN?
HEY, EVERYONE, COME OUT HERE. BROOK IS GETTING SENTIMENTAL HERE!!!
HEY!! CUT IT OUT!!! YOU'RE EMBARRASS-ING ME!!!
PFT HEH HEH!!
IRK!!
IT'S NAVY HEADQUARTERS!! WHAT DO WE DO?!!
UOOO!!
DON'T ACT SO YELLOW!!! WE DO WHAT WE ALWAYS DO-- GIVE 'EM HELL!!!
BAM!!
WHOA!! LOOK!! THE CAPTAIN'S BOUNTY HAS INCREASED AGAIN!!!
NA HA HA HA HA, OF COURSE IT HAS!!
WHOOOA!!
TIME TO CELE-BRATE!!!
YORKI♪ YORKI♪
MAY YOUR INFAMY SPREAD ALL THE WAY TO TWIN CAPE!!
BROOK!! SING THAT SONG!!
KLAT KLAT...
HHMMM...♪ MM...MM...
HMM... ♪
KLAT KLAT

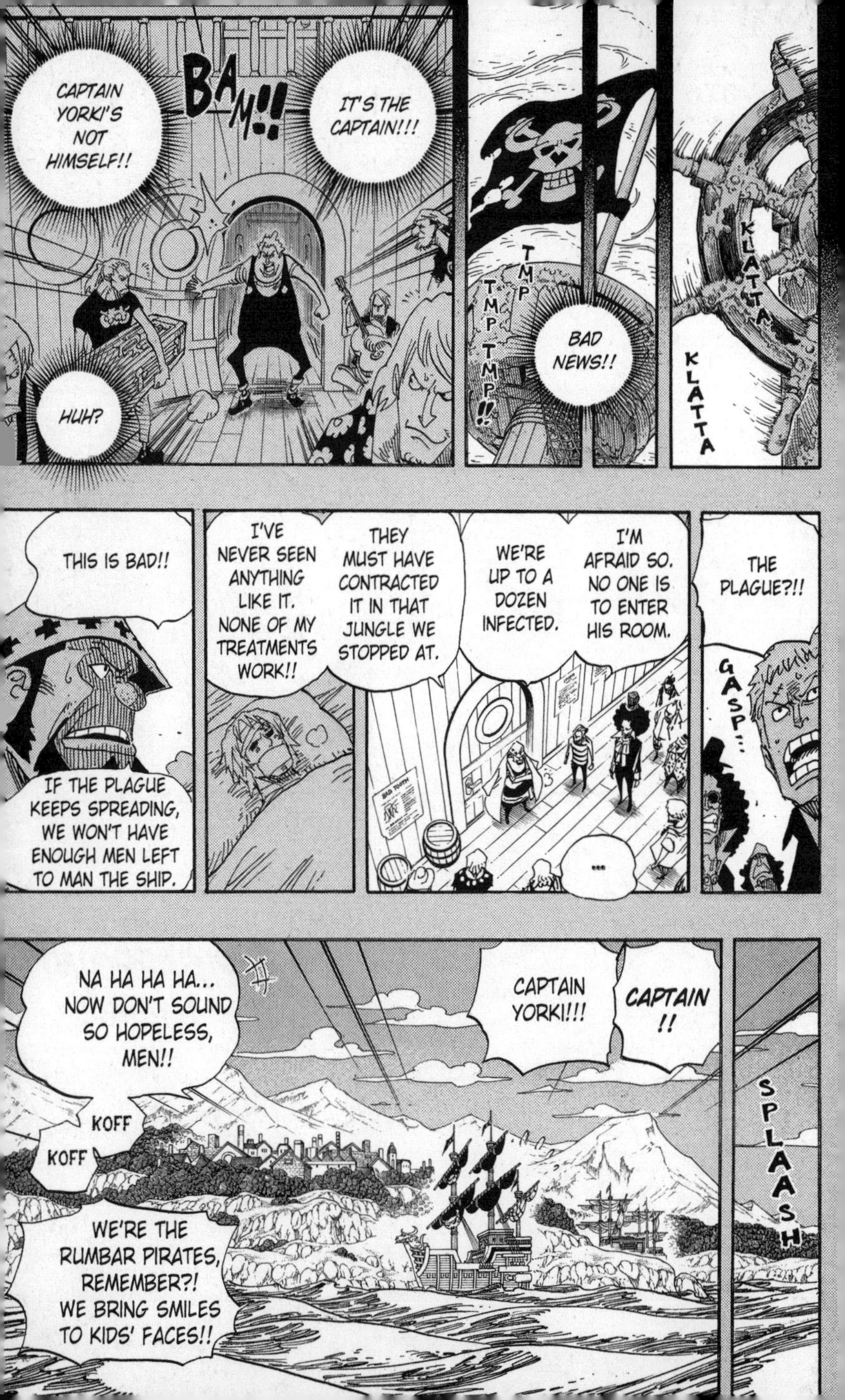
KLATTA
KLATTA
TMP TMP TMP TMP!!
BAD NEWS!!
IT'S THE CAPTAIN!!!
BAM!!
CAPTAIN YORKI'S NOT HIMSELF!!
HUH?
THE PLAGUE?!!
GASP...
I'M AFRAID SO. NO ONE IS TO ENTER HIS ROOM.
WE'RE UP TO A DOZEN INFECTED.
...
THEY MUST HAVE CONTRACTED IT IN THAT JUNGLE WE STOPPED AT.
I'VE NEVER SEEN ANYTHING LIKE IT. NONE OF MY TREATMENTS WORK!!
THIS IS BAD!!
IF THE PLAGUE KEEPS SPREADING, WE WON'T HAVE ENOUGH MEN LEFT TO MAN THE SHIP.
SPLAASH
CAPTAIN !!
CAPTAIN YORKI!!!
NA HA HA HA... NOW DON'T SOUND SO HOPELESS, MEN!!
KOFF
KOFF
WE'RE THE RUMBAR PIRATES, REMEMBER?! WE BRING SMILES TO KIDS' FACES!!

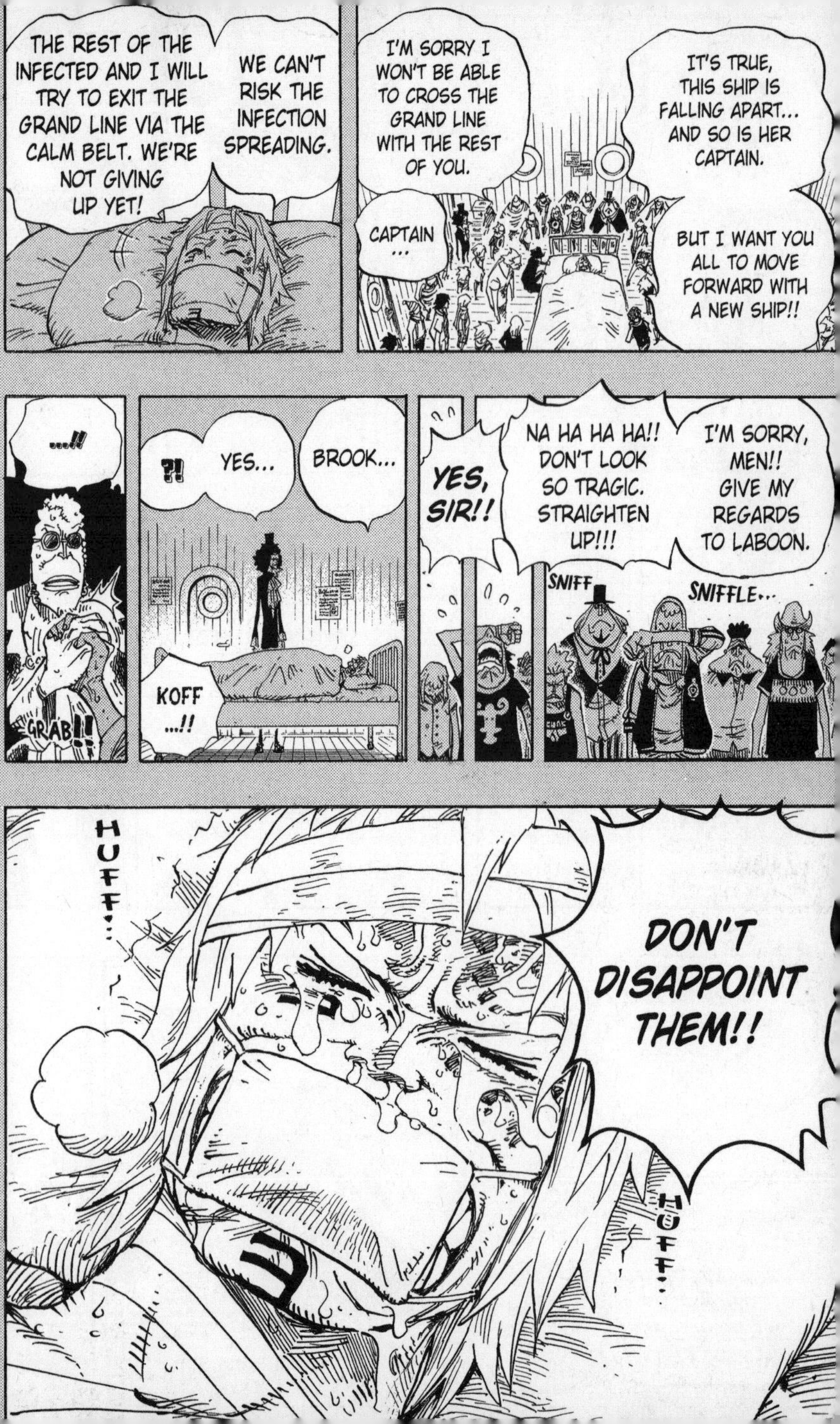
IT'S TRUE, THIS SHIP IS FALLING APART... AND SO IS HER CAPTAIN.
BUT I WANT YOU ALL TO MOVE FORWARD WITH A NEW SHIP!!
I'M SORRY I WON'T BE ABLE TO CROSS THE GRAND LINE WITH THE REST OF YOU.
CAPTAIN ...
WE CAN'T RISK THE INFECTION SPREADING.
THE REST OF THE INFECTED AND I WILL TRY TO EXIT THE GRAND LINE VIA THE CALM BELT. WE'RE NOT GIVING UP YET!
I'M SORRY, MEN!! GIVE MY REGARDS TO LABOON.
NA HA HA HA!! DON'T LOOK SO TRAGIC. STRAIGHTEN UP!!!
SNIFFLE...
SNIFF
YES, SIR!!
BROOK...
YES...
?!
KOFF ...!!
...!!
GRAB!!
DON'T DISAPPOINT THEM!!
HUFF...
HUFF...

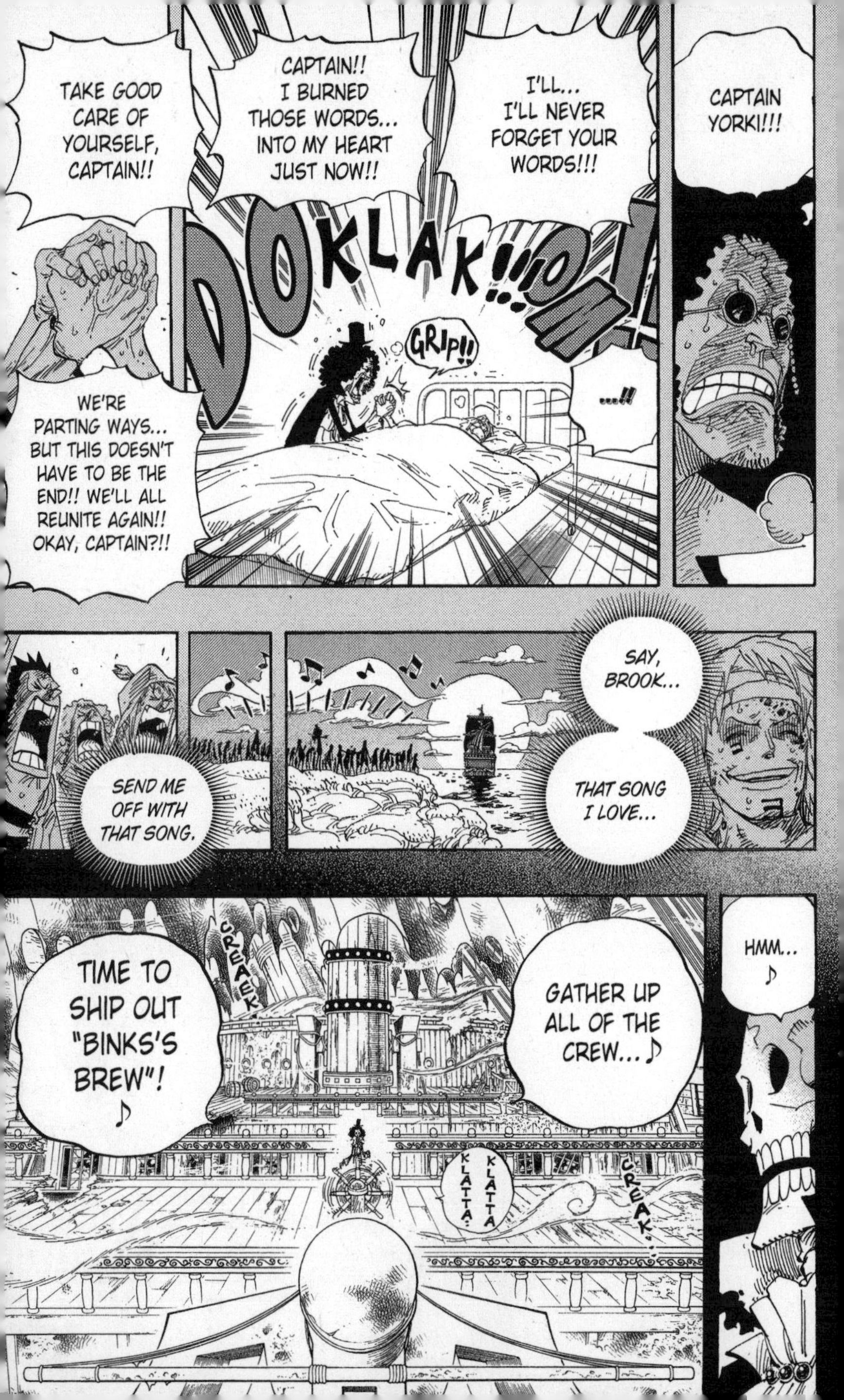
CAPTAIN YORKI!!!
I'LL... I'LL NEVER FORGET YOUR WORDS!!!
CAPTAIN!! I BURNED THOSE WORDS... INTO MY HEART JUST NOW!!
TAKE GOOD CARE OF YOURSELF, CAPTAIN!!
DOKLAK!!!
...!!
GRIP!!
WE'RE PARTING WAYS... BUT THIS DOESN'T HAVE TO BE THE END!! WE'LL ALL REUNITE AGAIN!! OKAY, CAPTAIN?!!
SAY, BROOK...
THAT SONG I LOVE...
SEND ME OFF WITH THAT SONG.
HMM... ♪
GATHER UP ALL OF THE CREW...♪
CREAK...
KLATTA KLATTA
CREAEK
TIME TO SHIP OUT "BINKS'S BREW"! ♪

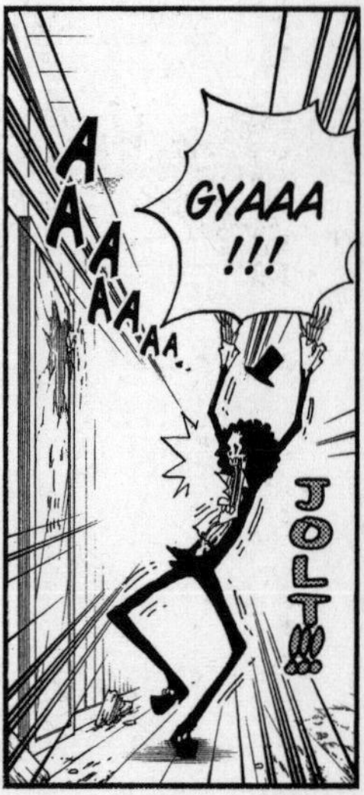
GYAAA
!!!
AAAAAAAA..
JOLT!!!

Chapter 488:
SONG OF LIFE

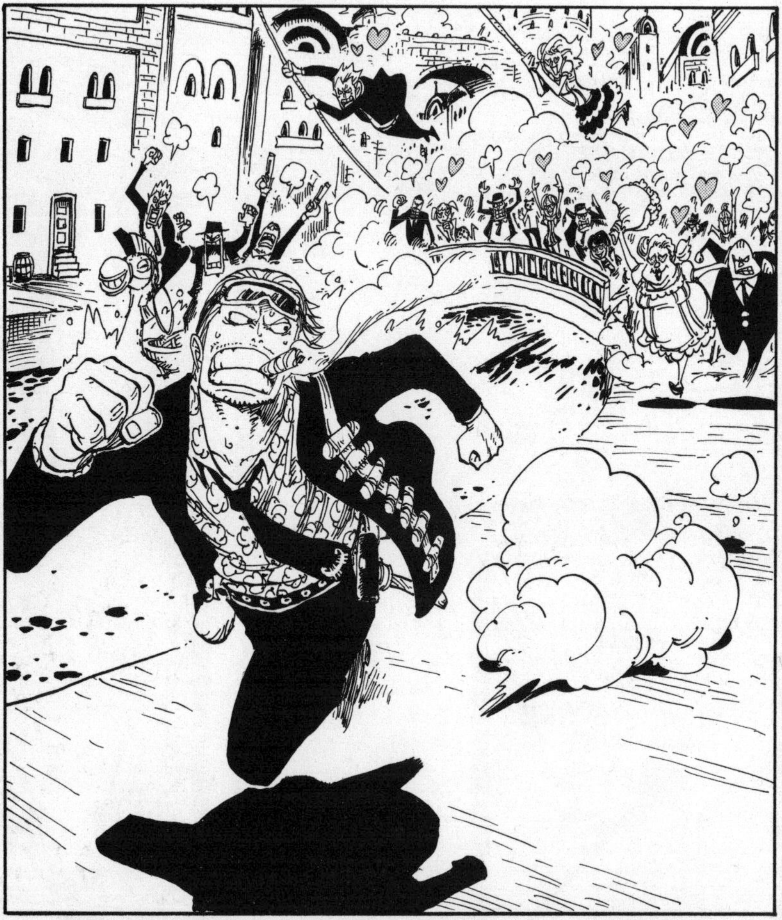

WHERE ARE THEY NOW? SHOT 6: "THE GALLEY-LA COMPANY'S VICE PRESIDENT BEING RUN DOWN BY FANS AND DEBT COLLECTORS"

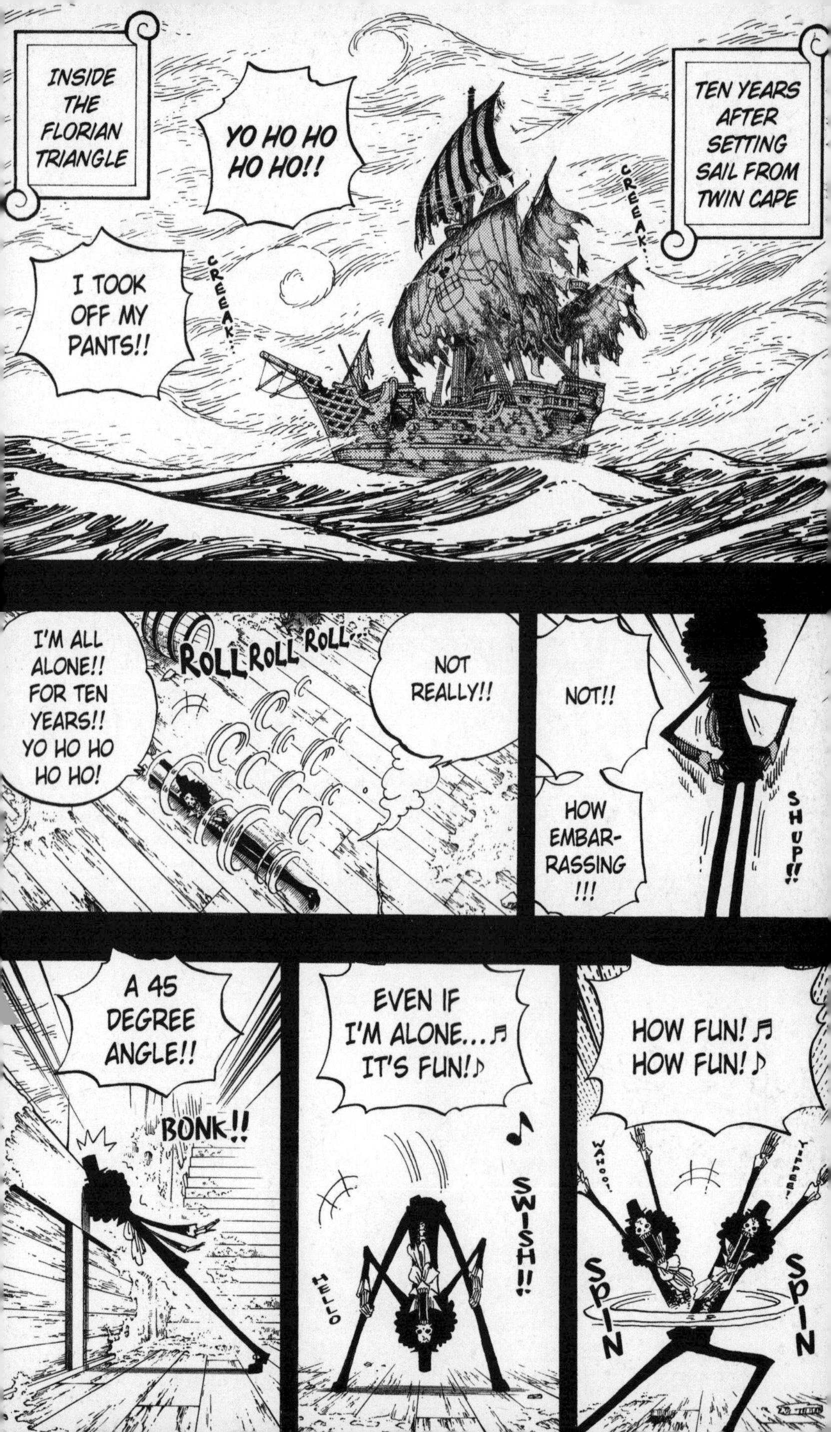
TEN YEARS AFTER SETTING SAIL FROM TWIN CAPE
CREEAK...
YO HO HO HO HO!!
INSIDE THE FLORIAN TRIANGLE
CREEAK...
I TOOK OFF MY PANTS!!
NOT!!
SHUP!!
HOW EMBARRASSING!!!
NOT REALLY!!
ROLL ROLL ROLL...
I'M ALL ALONE!! FOR TEN YEARS!! YO HO HO HO HO!
HOW FUN! ♬ HOW FUN! ♪
YIPPEE!
WAHOO!
SPIN
SPIN
EVEN IF I'M ALONE...♬ IT'S FUN!♪
SWISH!!
HELLO
A 45 DEGREE ANGLE!!
BONK!!

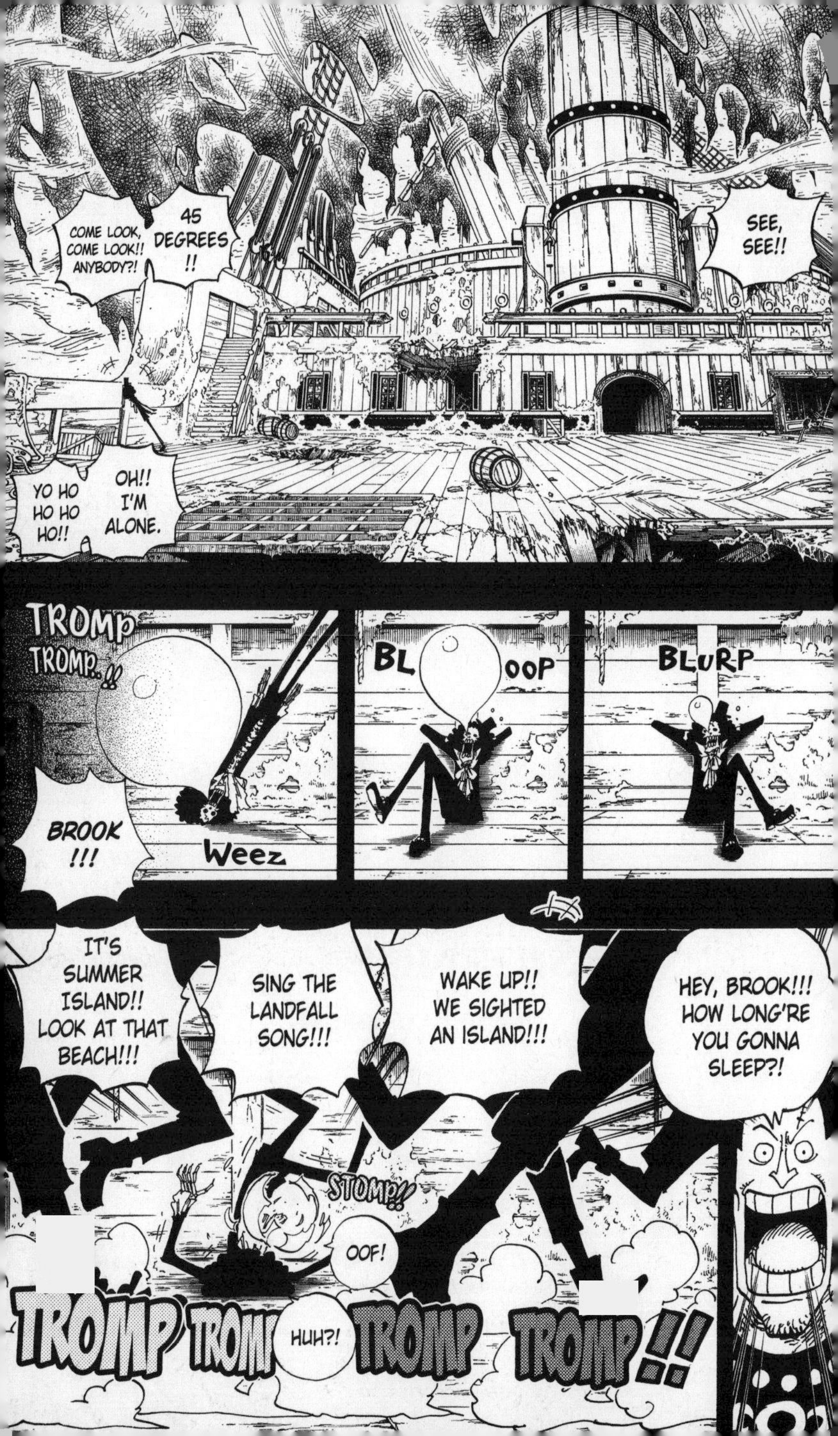
SEE, SEE!!
45 DEGREES!!
COME LOOK, COME LOOK!! ANYBODY?!
OH!! I'M ALONE.
YO HO HO HO HO!!
BLURP
BL OOP
TROMP TROMP..!!
BROOK!!!
Weez
HEY, BROOK!!! HOW LONG'RE YOU GONNA SLEEP?!
WAKE UP!! WE SIGHTED AN ISLAND!!!
SING THE LANDFALL SONG!!!
IT'S SUMMER ISLAND!! LOOK AT THAT BEACH!!!
STOMP!!
OOF!
HUH?!
TROMP
TROMP
TROMP
TROMP!!

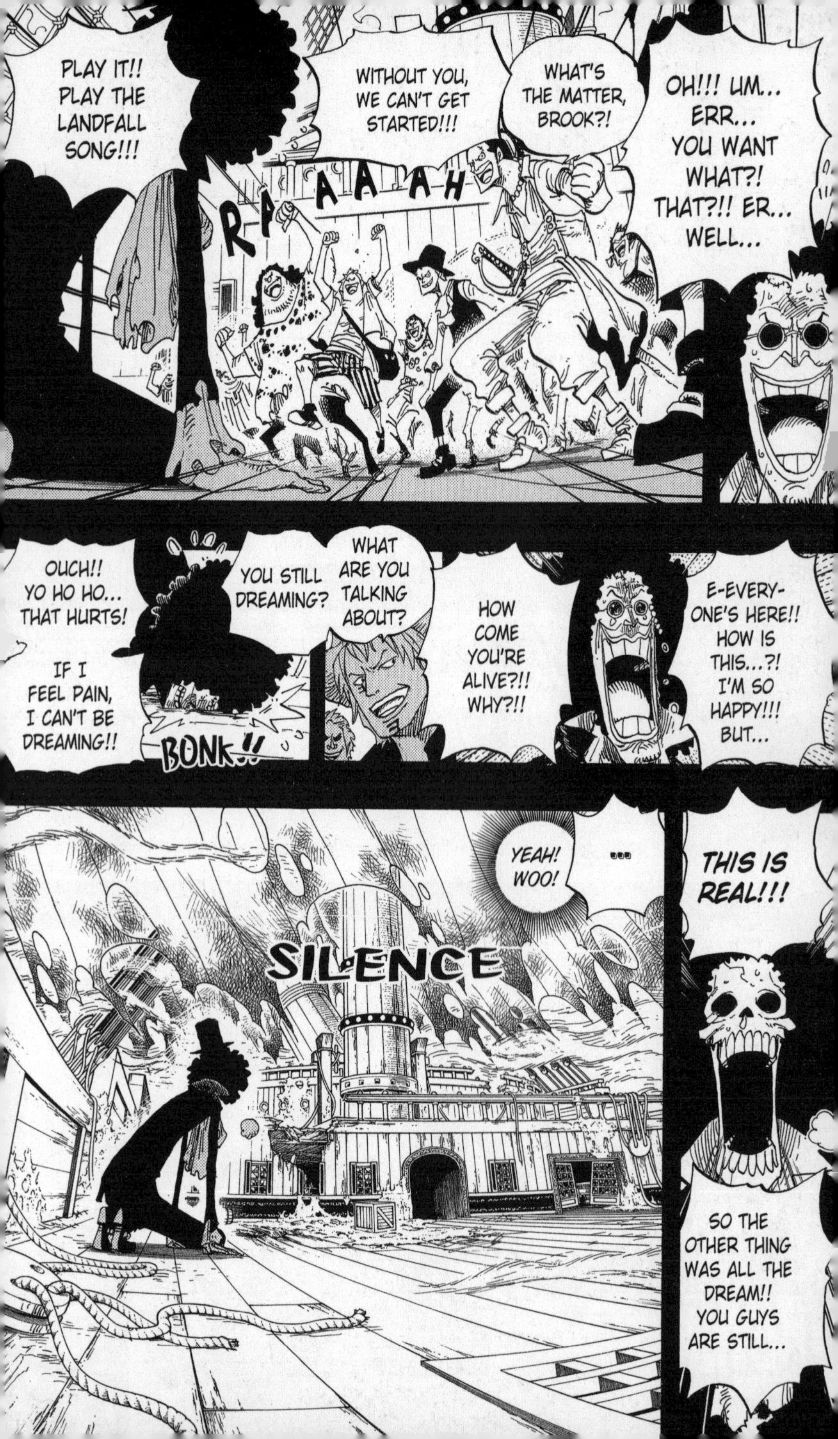
OH!!! UM... ERR... YOU WANT WHAT?! THAT?!! ER... WELL...
WHAT'S THE MATTER, BROOK?!
WITHOUT YOU, WE CAN'T GET STARTED!!!
PLAY IT!! PLAY THE LANDFALL SONG!!!
RAAAAH
E-EVERYONE'S HERE!! HOW IS THIS...?! I'M SO HAPPY!!! BUT...
HOW COME YOU'RE ALIVE?!! WHY?!!
WHAT ARE YOU TALKING ABOUT?
YOU STILL DREAMING?
OUCH!! YO HO HO... THAT HURTS!
IF I FEEL PAIN, I CAN'T BE DREAMING!!
BONK!!
THIS IS REAL!!!
SO THE OTHER THING WAS ALL THE DREAM!! YOU GUYS ARE STILL...
YEAH! WOO!
...
SILENCE

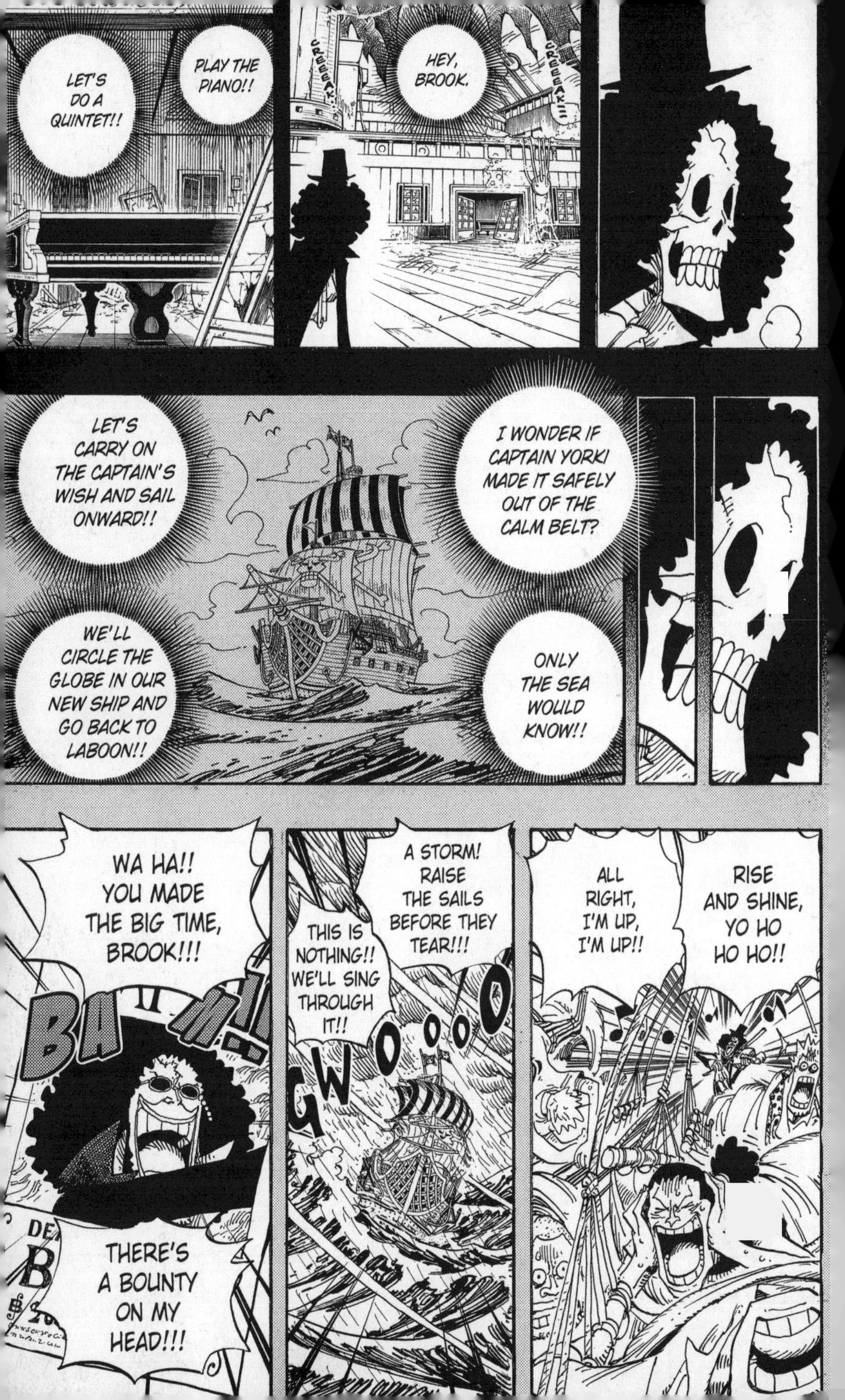

HEY, BROOK.
CREEEAK...
CREEEAK...
PLAY THE PIANO!!
LET'S DO A QUINTET!!
I WONDER IF CAPTAIN YORKI MADE IT SAFELY OUT OF THE CALM BELT?
ONLY THE SEA WOULD KNOW!!
LET'S CARRY ON THE CAPTAIN'S WISH AND SAIL ONWARD!!
WE'LL CIRCLE THE GLOBE IN OUR NEW SHIP AND GO BACK TO LABOON!!
RISE AND SHINE, YO HO HO HO!!
ALL RIGHT, I'M UP, I'M UP!!
A STORM! RAISE THE SAILS BEFORE THEY TEAR!!!
THIS IS NOTHING!! WE'LL SING THROUGH IT!!
GWOOOO
WA HA!! YOU MADE THE BIG TIME, BROOK!!!
BAM!!
THERE'S A BOUNTY ON MY HEAD!!!

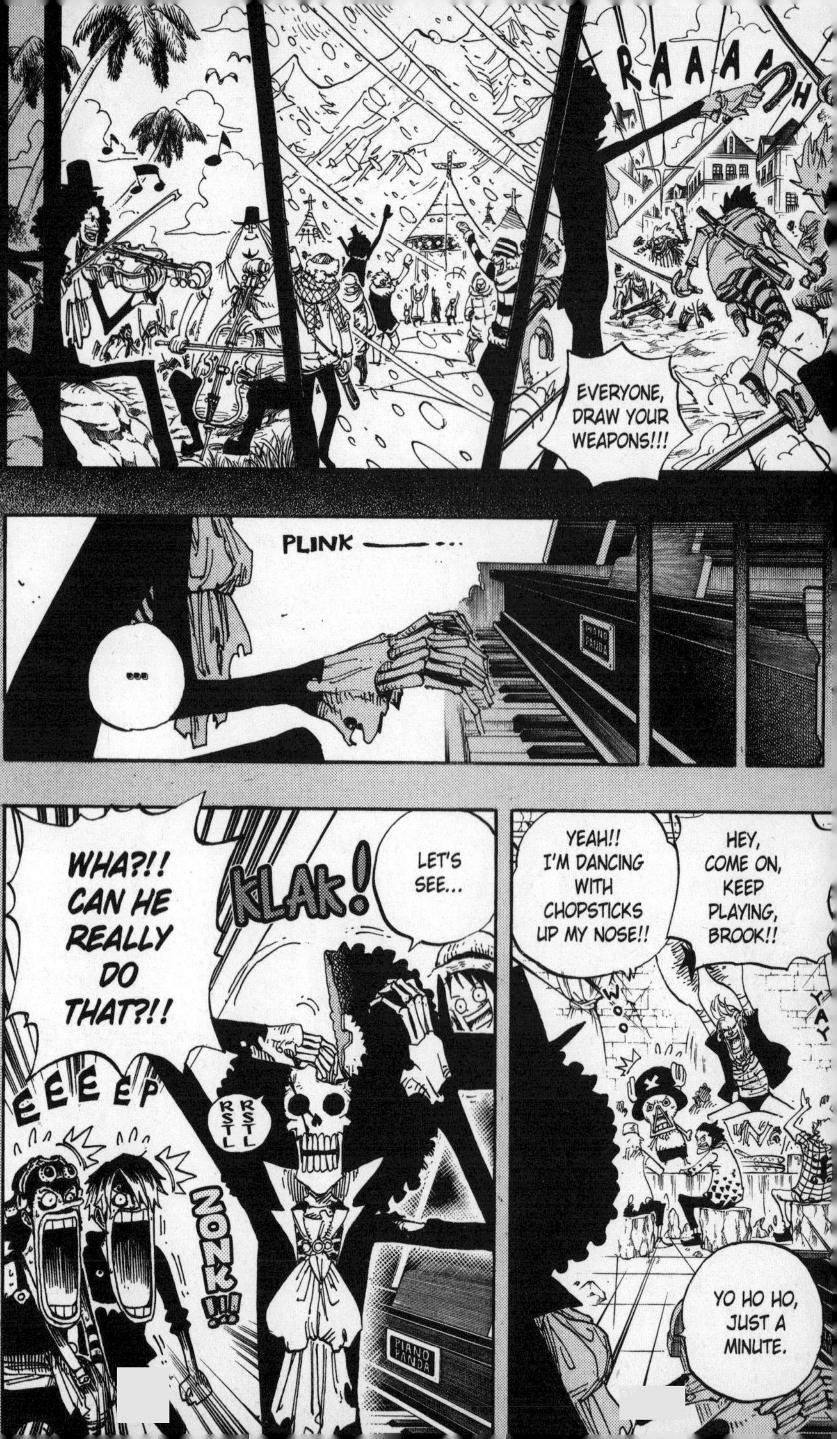
RAAAAH
EVERYONE, DRAW YOUR WEAPONS!!!
PLINK ——...
...
PIANO PANDA
HEY, COME ON, KEEP PLAYING, BROOK!!
YEAH!! I'M DANCING WITH CHOPSTICKS UP MY NOSE!!
WOO
YAY
YO HO HO, JUST A MINUTE.
LET'S SEE...
KLAK!
WHA?!! CAN HE REALLY DO THAT?!!
RSTL RSTL
EEEEP
ZONK!!!
PIANO PANDA

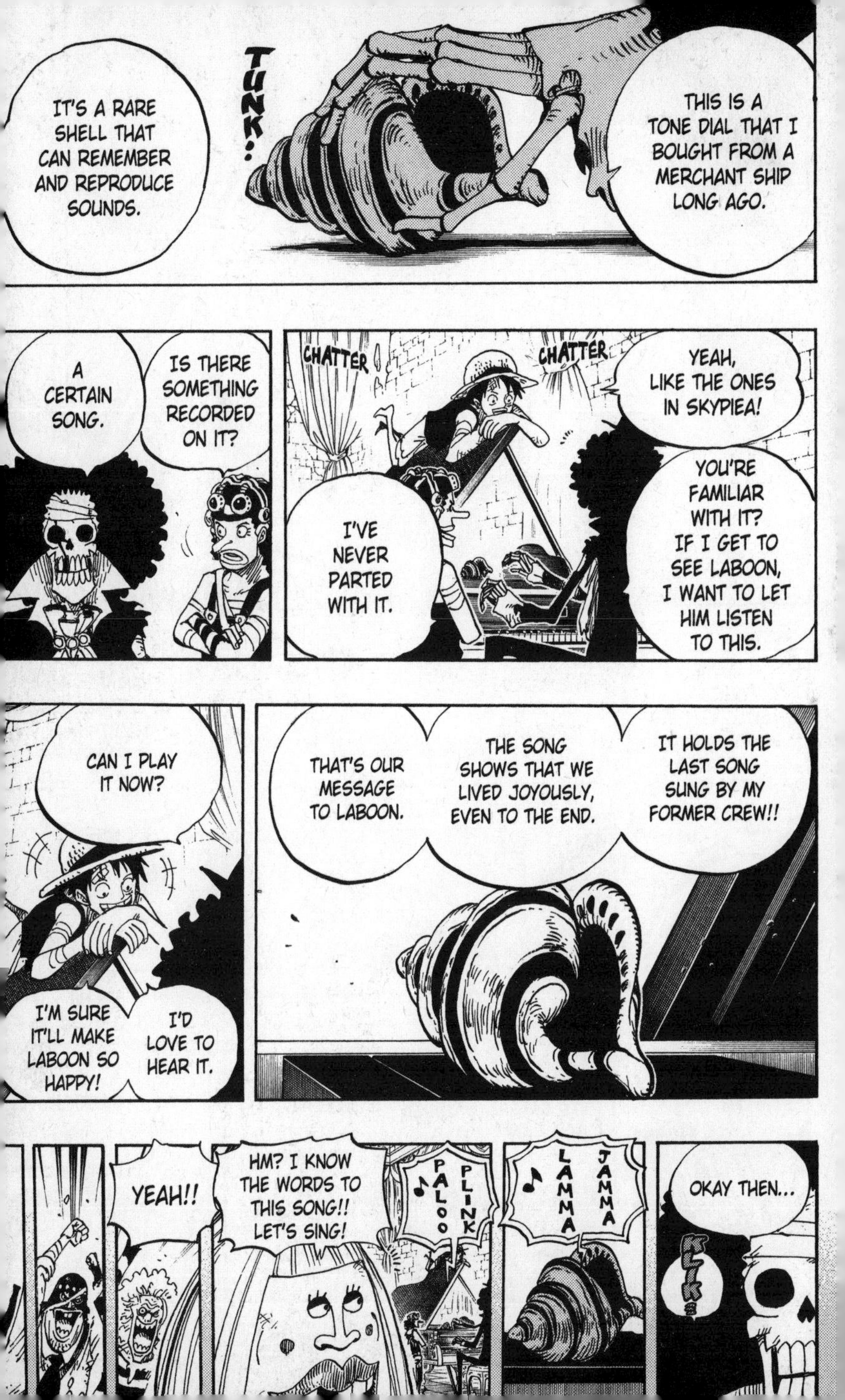
THIS IS A TONE DIAL THAT I BOUGHT FROM A MERCHANT SHIP LONG AGO.
TUNK
IT'S A RARE SHELL THAT CAN REMEMBER AND REPRODUCE SOUNDS.
YEAH, LIKE THE ONES IN SKYPIEA!
CHATTER
CHATTER
YOU'RE FAMILIAR WITH IT? IF I GET TO SEE LABOON, I WANT TO LET HIM LISTEN TO THIS.
I'VE NEVER PARTED WITH IT.
IS THERE SOMETHING RECORDED ON IT?
A CERTAIN SONG.
IT HOLDS THE LAST SONG SUNG BY MY FORMER CREW!!
THE SONG SHOWS THAT WE LIVED JOYOUSLY, EVEN TO THE END.
THAT'S OUR MESSAGE TO LABOON.
CAN I PLAY IT NOW?
I'D LOVE TO HEAR IT.
I'M SURE IT'LL MAKE LABOON SO HAPPY!
OKAY THEN...
KLIK
JAMMA
LAMMA
PLINK
PALOO
HM? I KNOW THE WORDS TO THIS SONG!! LET'S SING!
YEAH!!

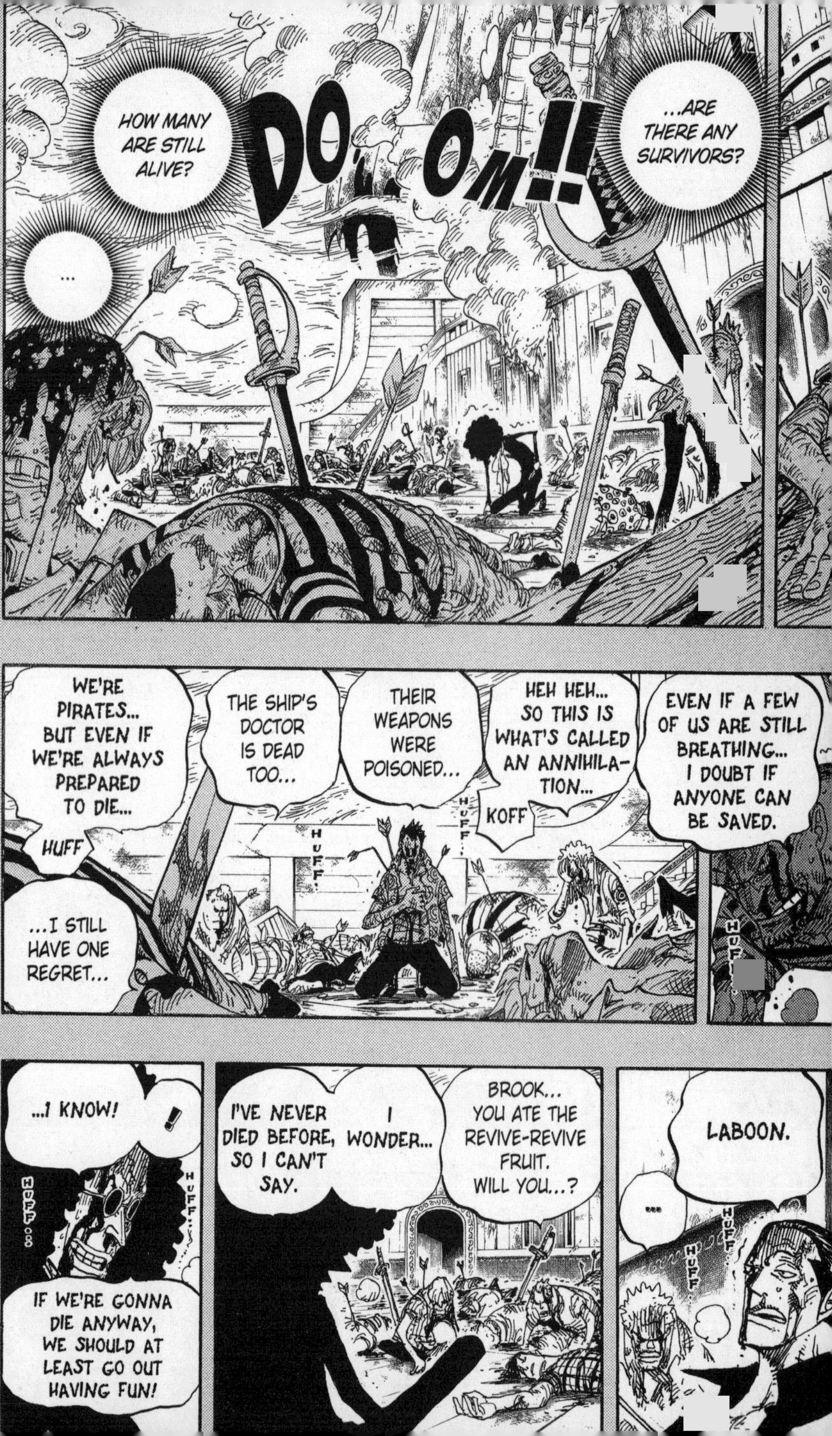
...ARE THERE ANY SURVIVORS?
DOOM!!
HOW MANY ARE STILL ALIVE?
...
EVEN IF A FEW OF US ARE STILL BREATHING... I DOUBT IF ANYONE CAN BE SAVED.
HUFF
HEH HEH... SO THIS IS WHAT'S CALLED AN ANNIHILATION...
KOFF
HUFF...
THEIR WEAPONS WERE POISONED...
THE SHIP'S DOCTOR IS DEAD TOO...
HUFF...
WE'RE PIRATES... BUT EVEN IF WE'RE ALWAYS PREPARED TO DIE...
HUFF
...I STILL HAVE ONE REGRET...
LABOON.
HUFF
HUFF
...
BROOK... YOU ATE THE REVIVE-REVIVE FRUIT. WILL YOU...?
I WONDER...
I'VE NEVER DIED BEFORE, SO I CAN'T SAY.
...I KNOW!
!
HUFF...
HUFF...
IF WE'RE GONNA DIE ANYWAY, WE SHOULD AT LEAST GO OUT HAVING FUN!

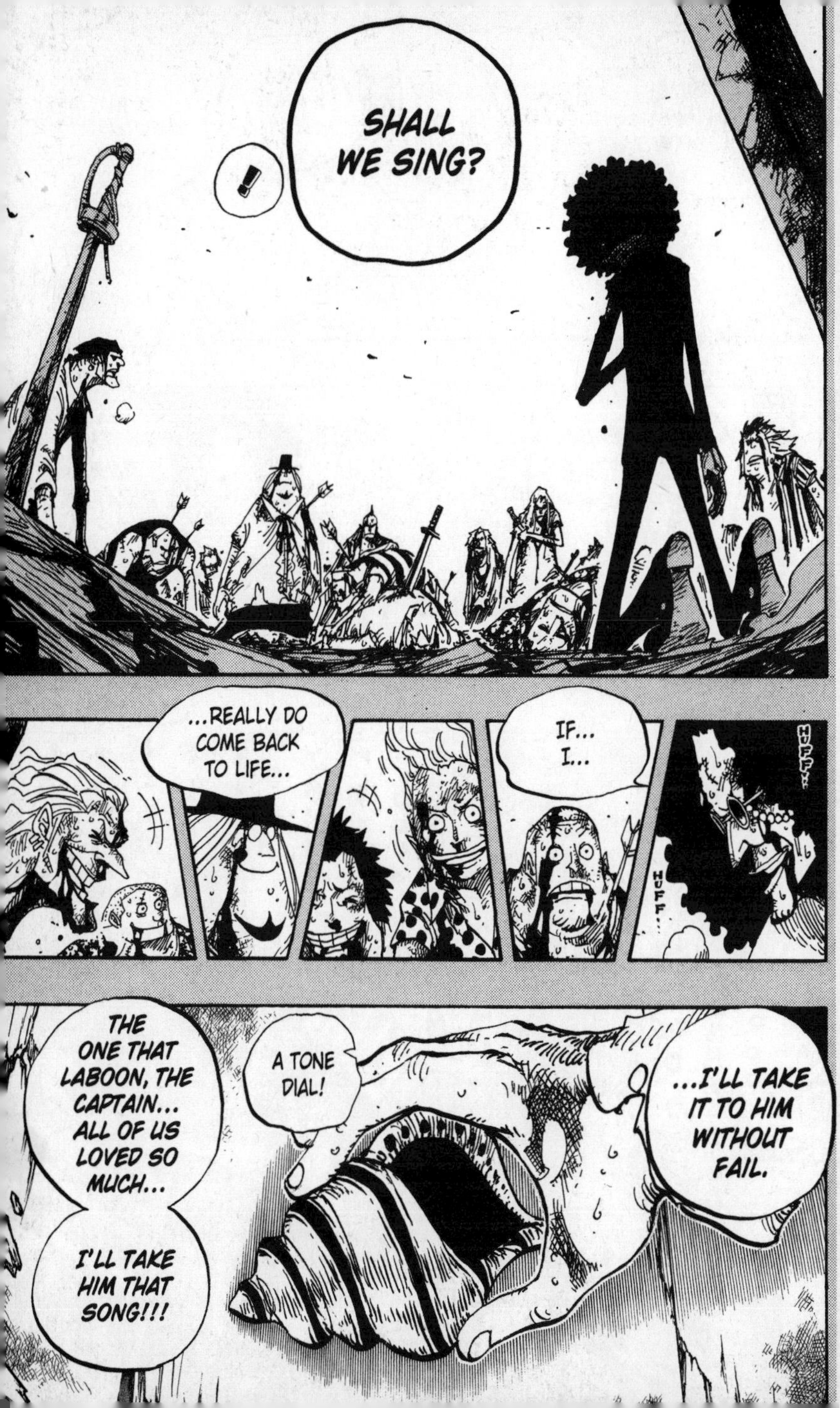
SHALL WE SING?
!
HUFF...
HUFF...
IF... I...
...REALLY DO COME BACK TO LIFE...
...I'LL TAKE IT TO HIM WITHOUT FAIL.
A TONE DIAL!
THE ONE THAT LABOON, THE CAPTAIN... ALL OF US LOVED SO MUCH...
I'LL TAKE HIM THAT SONG!!!

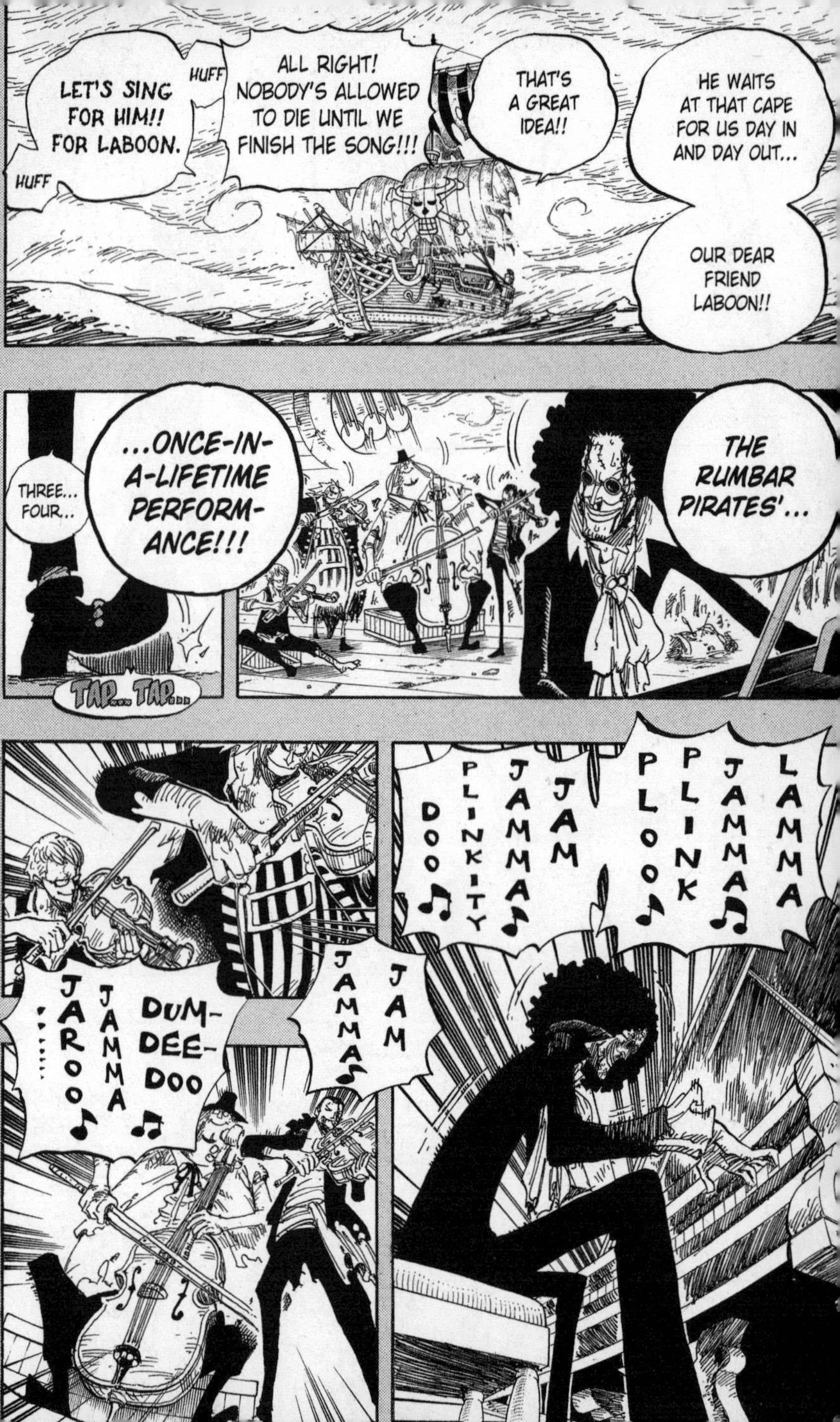

HE WAITS AT THAT CAPE FOR US DAY IN AND DAY OUT...
OUR DEAR FRIEND LABOON!!
THAT'S A GREAT IDEA!!
ALL RIGHT! NOBODY'S ALLOWED TO DIE UNTIL WE FINISH THE SONG!!!
HUFF
LET'S SING FOR HIM!! FOR LABOON.
HUFF
THE RUMBAR PIRATES'...
...ONCE-IN-A-LIFETIME PERFORMANCE!!!
THREE... FOUR...
TAP... TAP...
LAMMA JAMMA♫ PLINK PLOO♪ JAM JAMMA♪ PLINKITY DOO♫
JAM JAMMA♪
DUM-DEE-DOO♫ JAMMA JAROO♪ ......

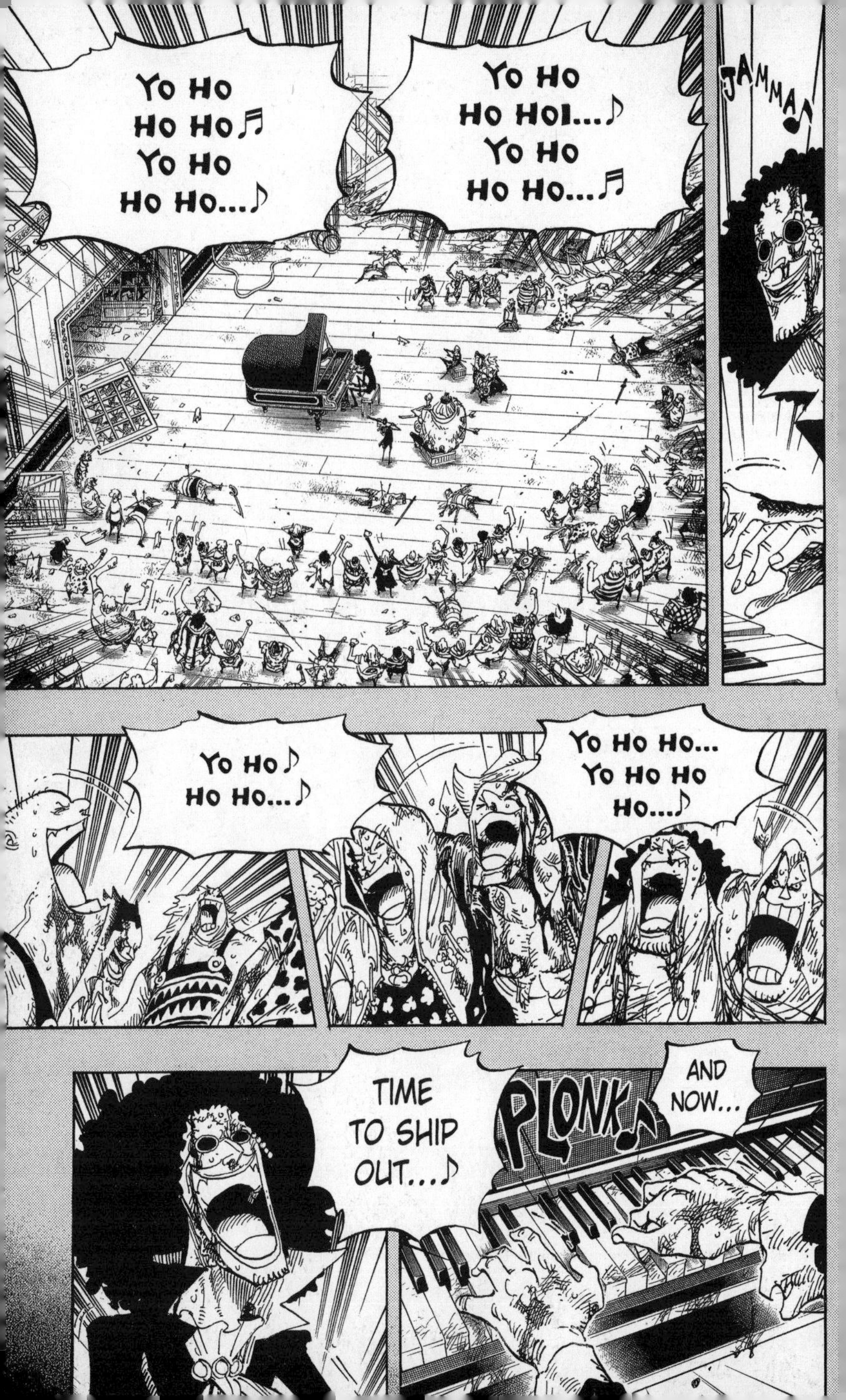
JAMMAN♪
YO HO HO HOI...♪ YO HO HO HO...♬
YO HO HO HO♬ YO HO HO HO...♪
YO HO HO... YO HO HO HO...♪
YO HO♪ HO HO...♪
AND NOW...
PLONK♪
TIME TO SHIP OUT...♪

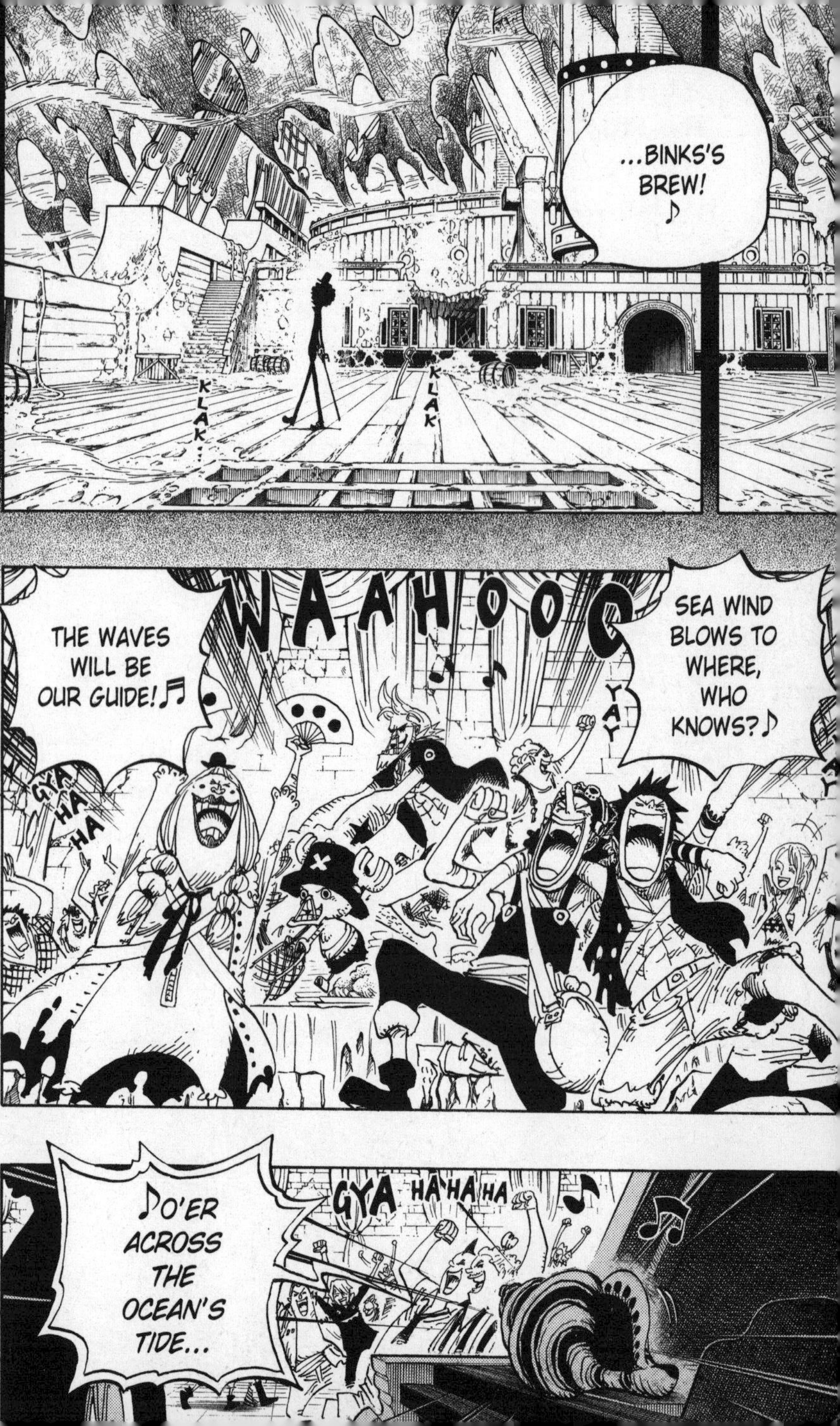
...BINKS'S BREW! ♪
KLAK...
KLAK
SEA WIND BLOWS TO WHERE, WHO KNOWS? ♪
YAY
WAAHOOO
THE WAVES WILL BE OUR GUIDE! ♬
GYA HA HA
GYA HA HA HA
♪O'ER ACROSS THE OCEAN'S TIDE...

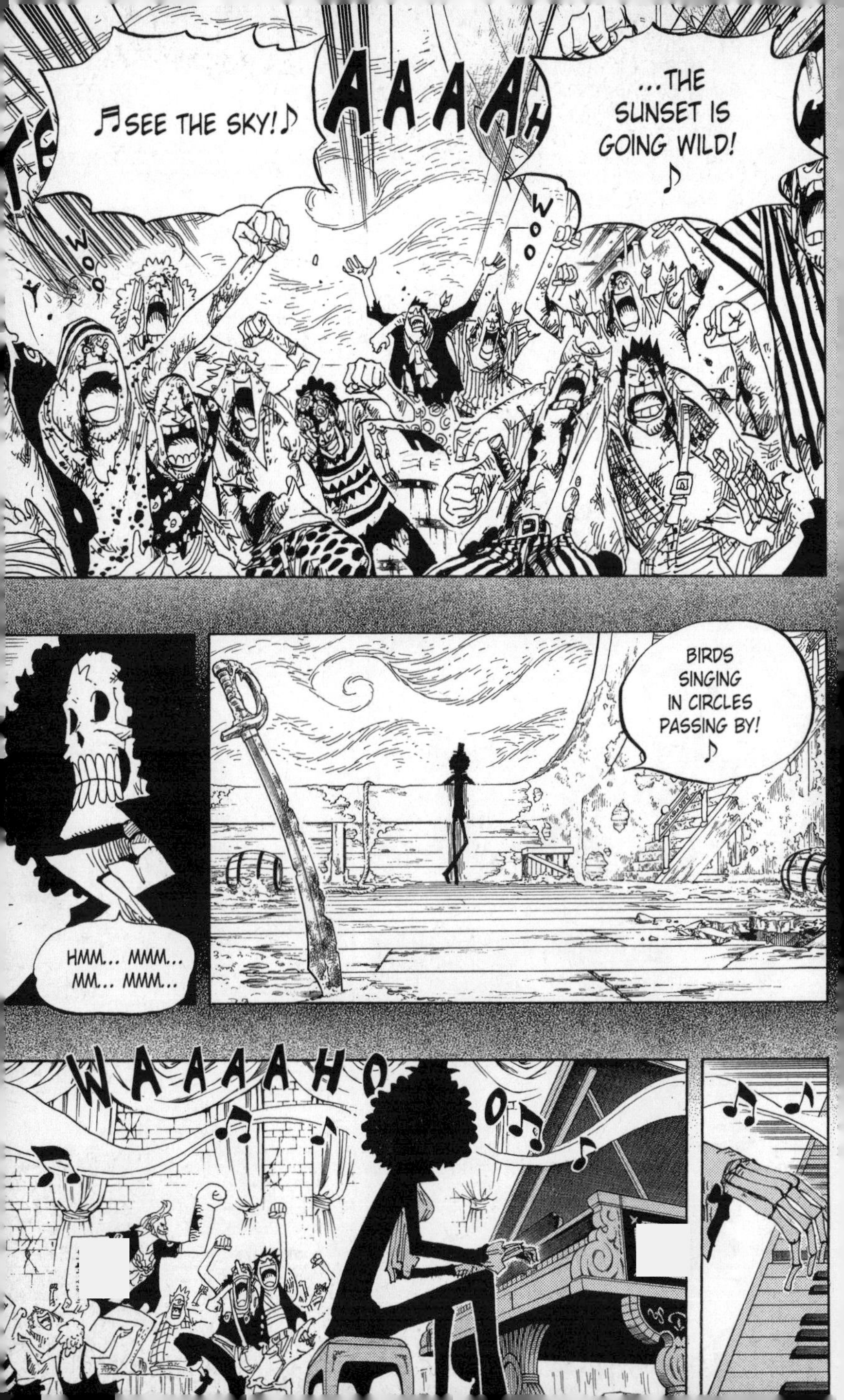
...THE SUNSET IS GOING WILD! ♪
AAAAH
WOO
♫SEE THE SKY!♪
WOO
BIRDS SINGING IN CIRCLES PASSING BY! ♪
HMM... MMM... MM... MMM...
WAAAAHOOO

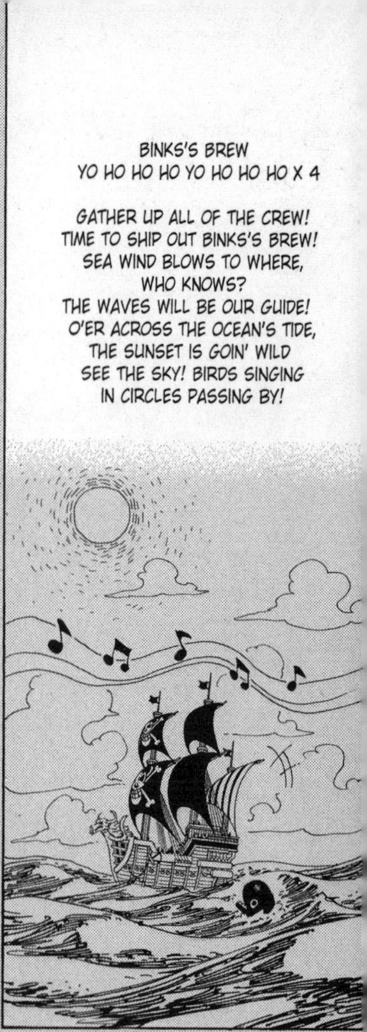
BINKS'S BREW
YO HO HO HO YO HO HO HO X 4
GATHER UP ALL OF THE CREW!
TIME TO SHIP OUT BINKS'S BREW!
SEA WIND BLOWS TO WHERE, WHO KNOWS?
THE WAVES WILL BE OUR GUIDE!
O'ER ACROSS THE OCEAN'S TIDE,
THE SUNSET IS GOIN' WILD
SEE THE SKY! BIRDS SINGING
IN CIRCLES PASSING BY!
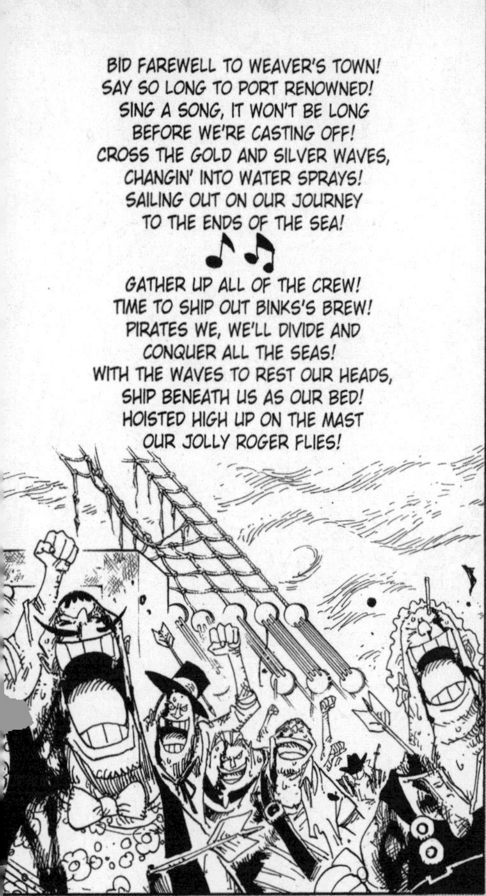
BID FAREWELL TO WEAVER'S TOWN!
SAY SO LONG TO PORT RENOWNED!
SING A SONG, IT WON'T BE LONG
BEFORE WE'RE CASTING OFF!
CROSS THE GOLD AND SILVER WAVES,
CHANGIN' INTO WATER SPRAYS!
SAILING OUT ON OUR JOURNEY
TO THE ENDS OF THE SEA!
GATHER UP ALL OF THE CREW!
TIME TO SHIP OUT BINKS'S BREW!
PIRATES WE, WE'LL DIVIDE AND
CONQUER ALL THE SEAS!
WITH THE WAVES TO REST OUR HEADS,
SHIP BENEATH US AS OUR BED!
HOISTED HIGH UP ON THE MAST
OUR JOLLY ROGER FLIES!
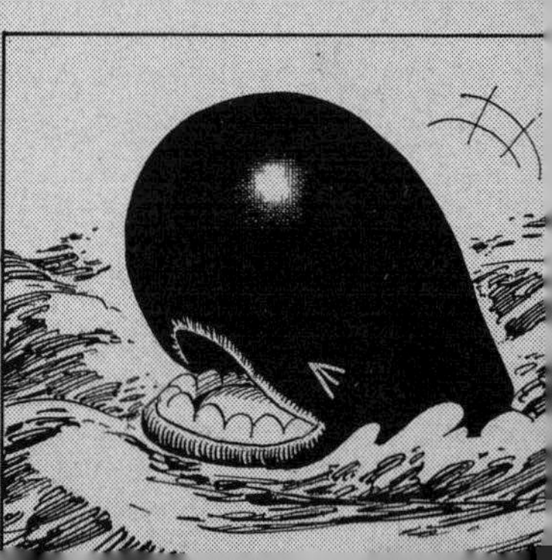
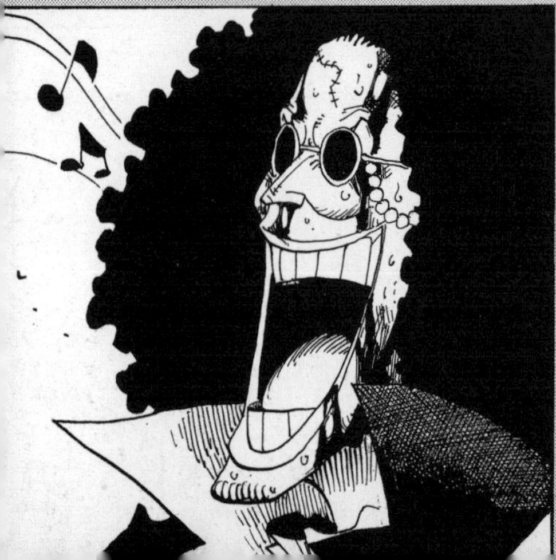

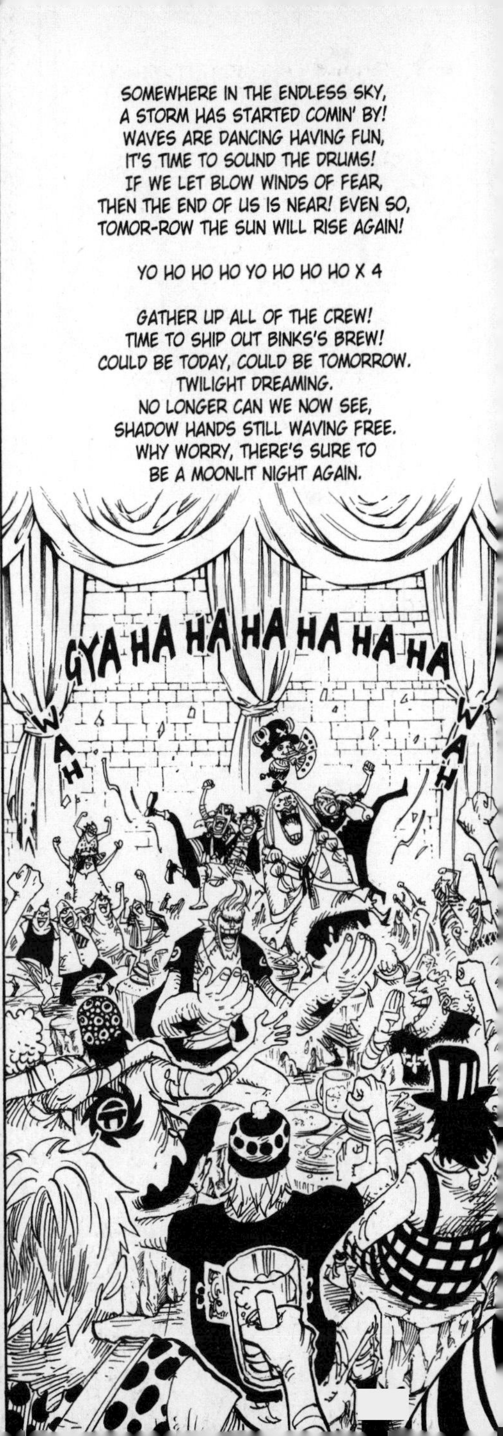
SOMEWHERE IN THE ENDLESS SKY,
A STORM HAS STARTED COMIN' BY!
WAVES ARE DANCING HAVING FUN,
IT'S TIME TO SOUND THE DRUMS!
IF WE LET BLOW WINDS OF FEAR,
THEN THE END OF US IS NEAR! EVEN SO,
TOMOR-ROW THE SUN WILL RISE AGAIN!
YO HO HO HO YO HO HO HO X 4
GATHER UP ALL OF THE CREW!
TIME TO SHIP OUT BINKS'S BREW!
COULD BE TODAY, COULD BE TOMORROW.
TWILIGHT DREAMING.
NO LONGER CAN WE NOW SEE,
SHADOW HANDS STILL WAVING FREE.
WHY WORRY, THERE'S SURE TO
BE A MOONLIT NIGHT AGAIN.
GYA HA HA HA HA HA HA
WAH
WAH

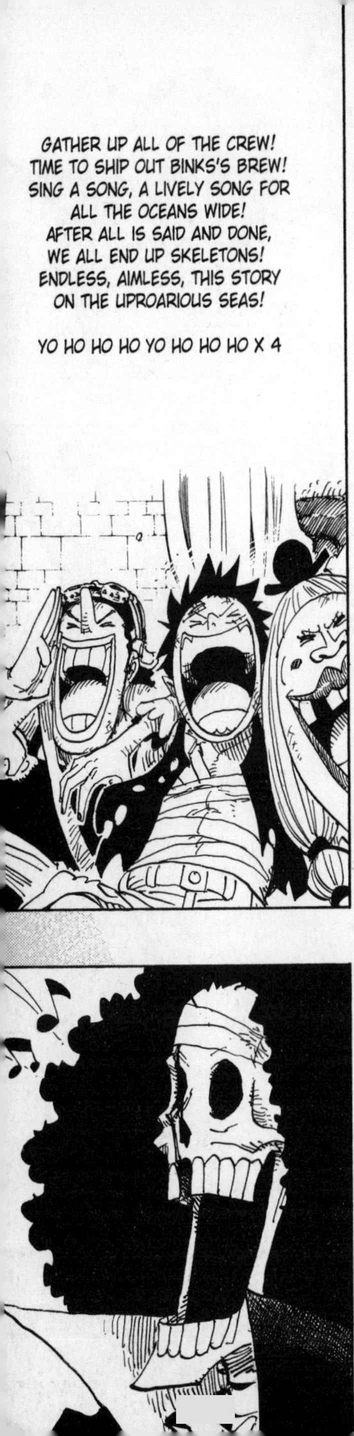
GATHER UP ALL OF THE CREW!
TIME TO SHIP OUT BINKS'S BREW!
SING A SONG, A LIVELY SONG FOR
ALL THE OCEANS WIDE!
AFTER ALL IS SAID AND DONE,
WE ALL END UP SKELETONS!
ENDLESS, AIMLESS, THIS STORY
ON THE UPROARIOUS SEAS!
YO HO HO HO YO HO HO HO X 4

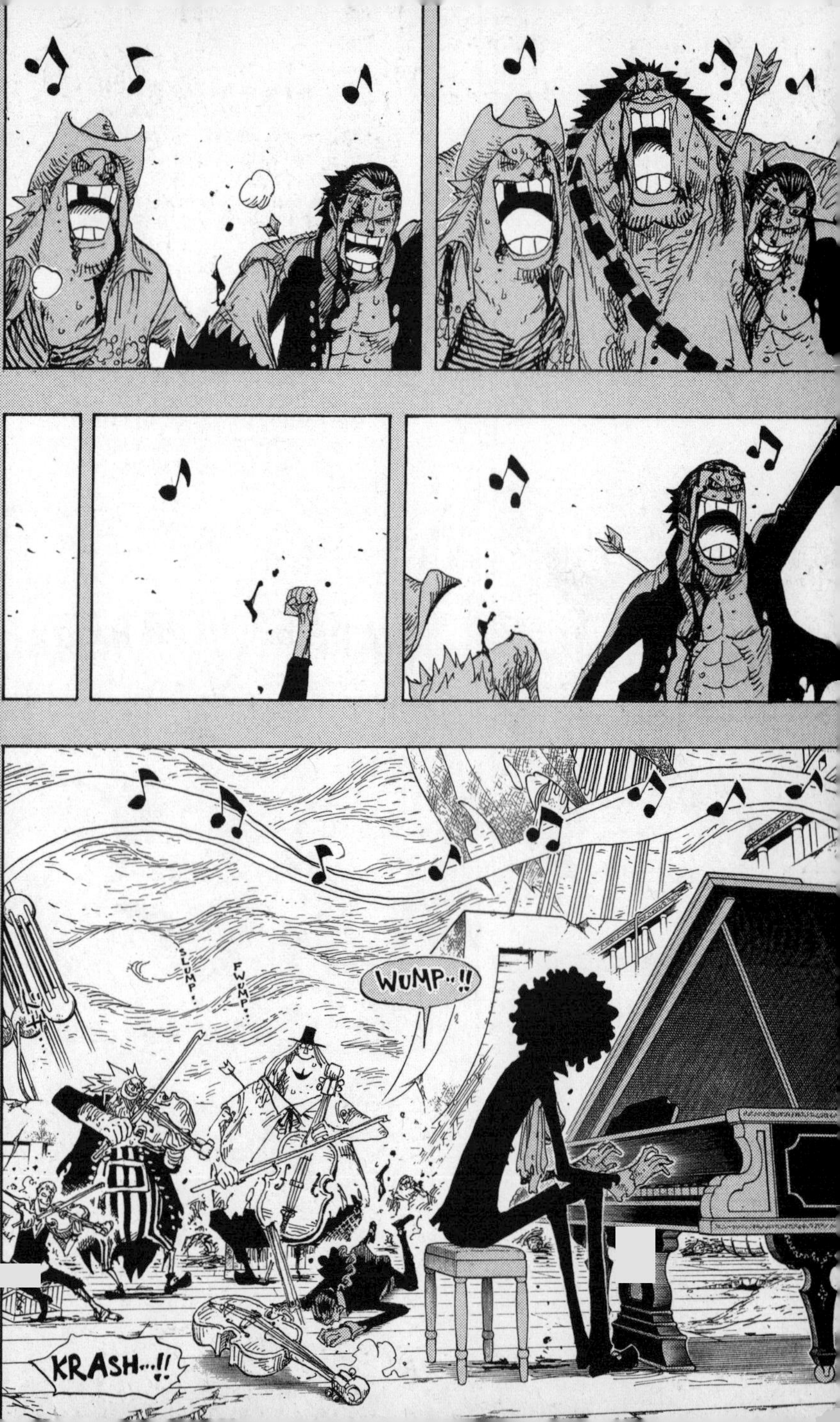
WUMP..!!
FWUMP...
SLUMP...
KRASH..!!

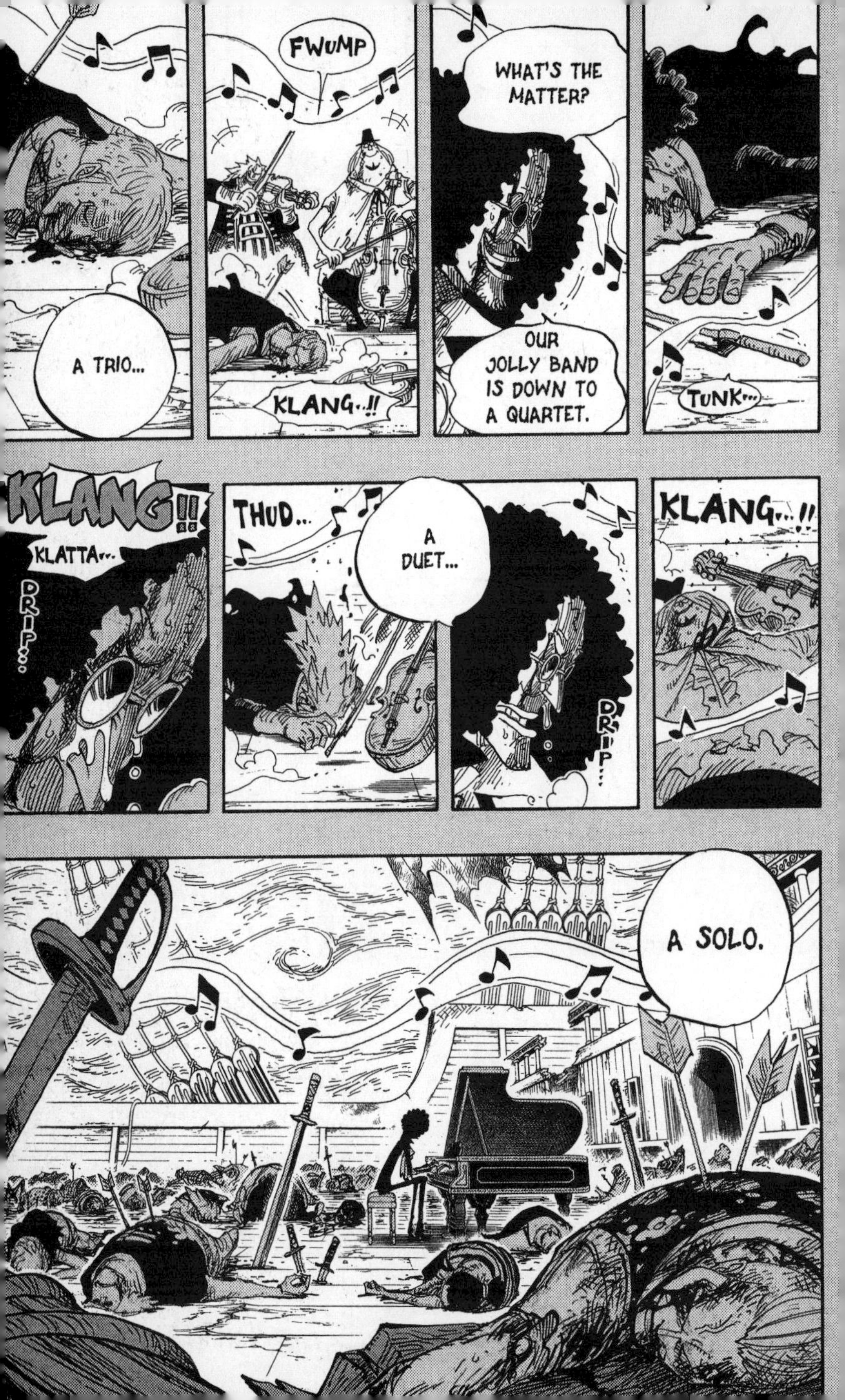
TUNK...
WHAT'S THE MATTER?
OUR JOLLY BAND IS DOWN TO A QUARTET.
FWUMP
KLANG..!!
A TRIO...
KLANG...!!
DRIP...
THUD...
A DUET...
KLANG!!
KLATTA...
DRIP...
A SOLO.

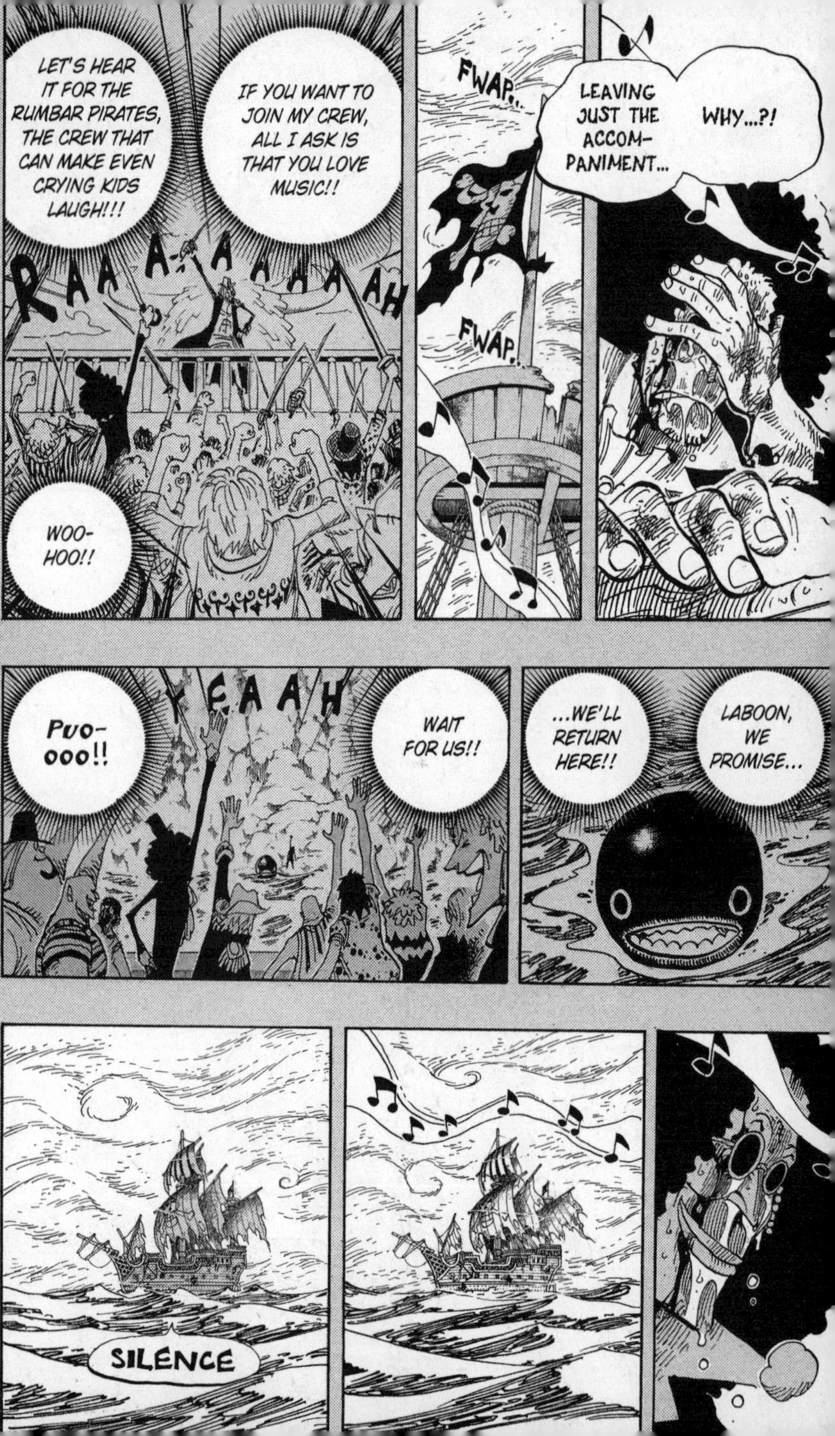
WHY...?!
LEAVING JUST THE ACCOMPANIMENT...
FWAP...
FWAP...
IF YOU WANT TO JOIN MY CREW, ALL I ASK IS THAT YOU LOVE MUSIC!!
LET'S HEAR IT FOR THE RUMBAR PIRATES, THE CREW THAT CAN MAKE EVEN CRYING KIDS LAUGH!!!
RAAAAAAAAH
WOO-HOO!!
LABOON, WE PROMISE...
...WE'LL RETURN HERE!!
WAIT FOR US!!
YEAAH
PUO-OOO!!
SILENCE

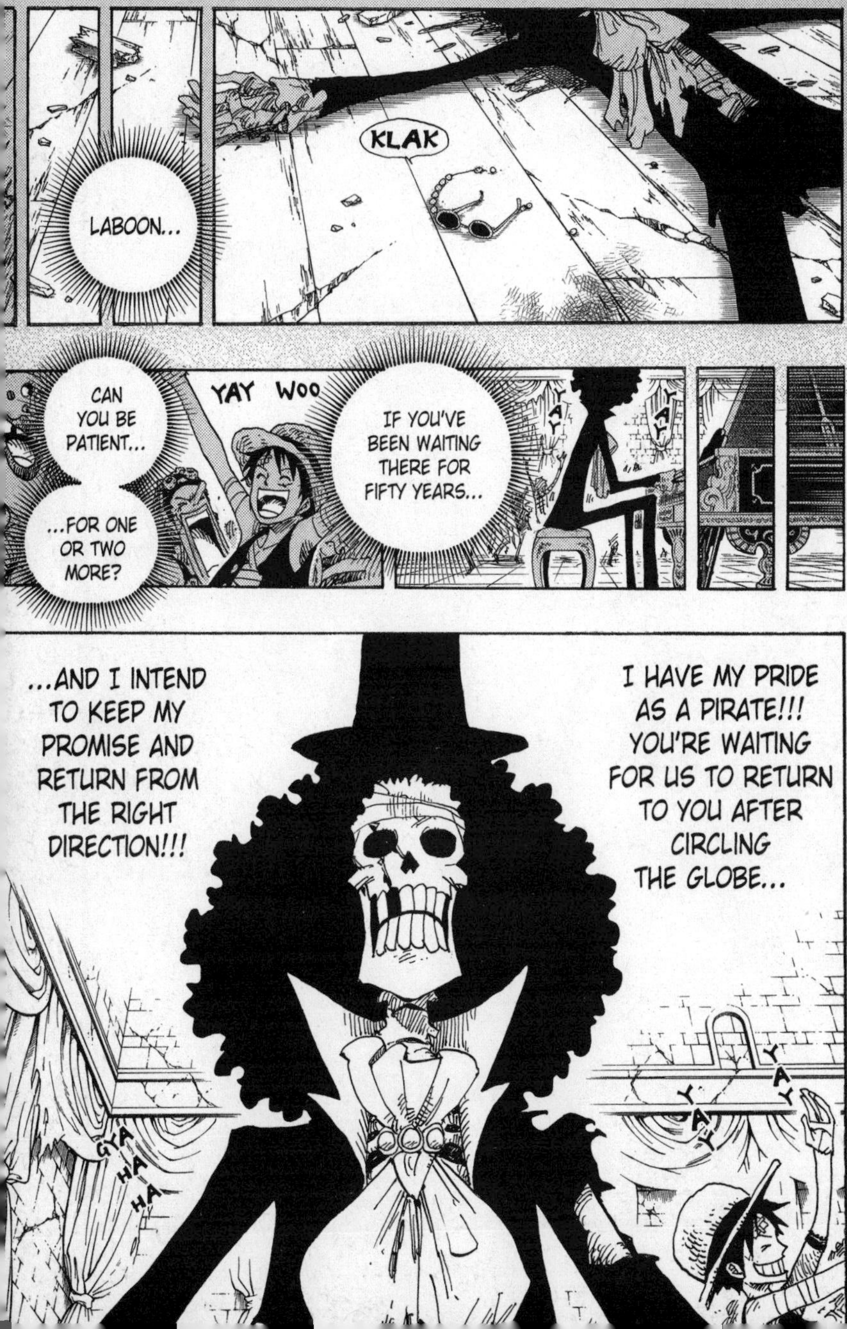
KLAK
LABOON...
YAY
YAY
IF YOU'VE BEEN WAITING THERE FOR FIFTY YEARS...
YAY WOO
CAN YOU BE PATIENT...
...FOR ONE OR TWO MORE?
I HAVE MY PRIDE AS A PIRATE!!! YOU'RE WAITING FOR US TO RETURN TO YOU AFTER CIRCLING THE GLOBE...
...AND I INTEND TO KEEP MY PROMISE AND RETURN FROM THE RIGHT DIRECTION!!!
YAY
YAY
GYA HA HA

EIGHTH PERSON

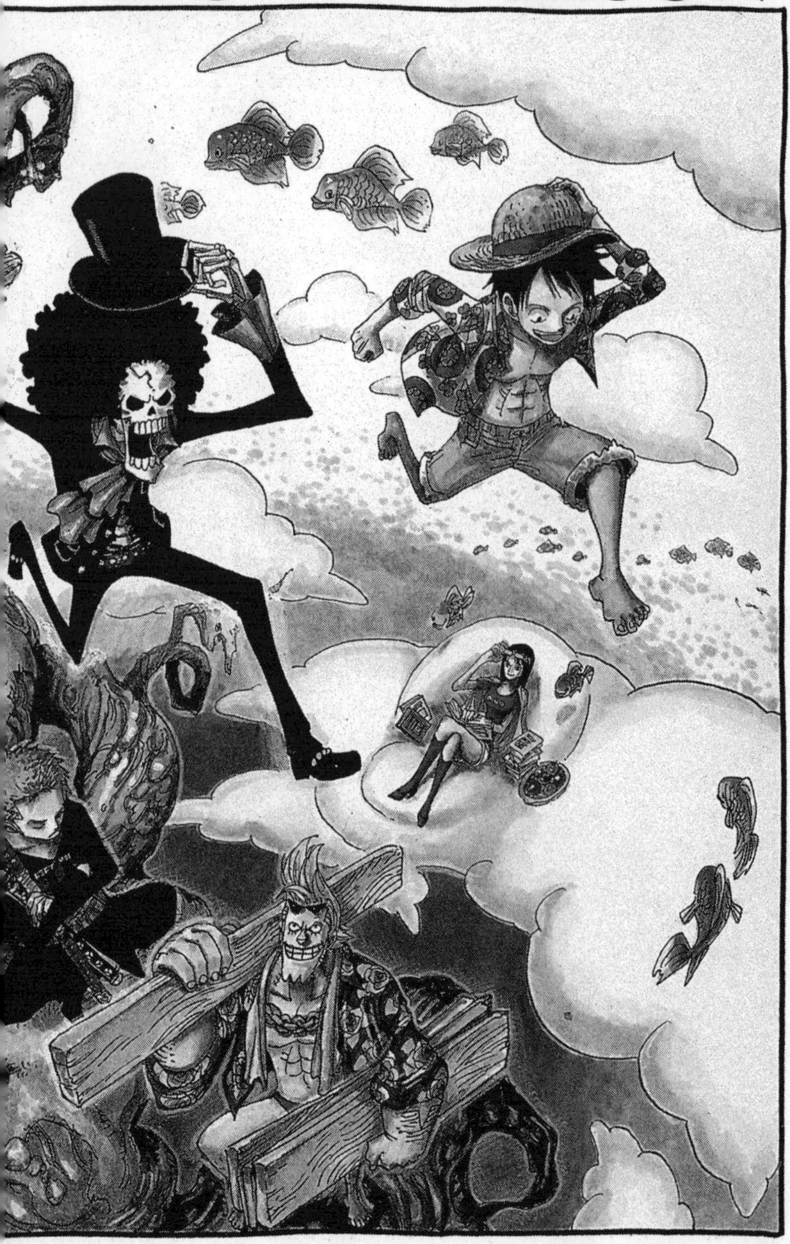

Chapter 489:

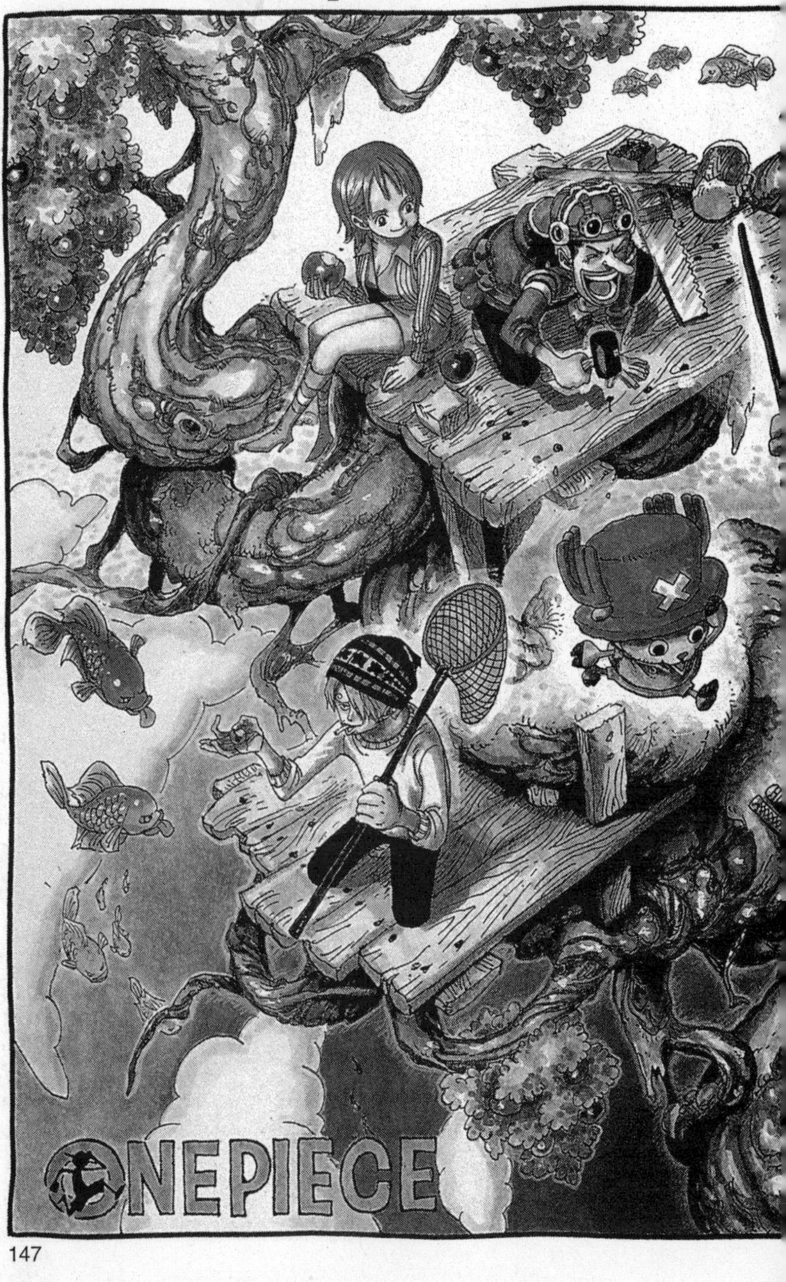
ONEPIECE

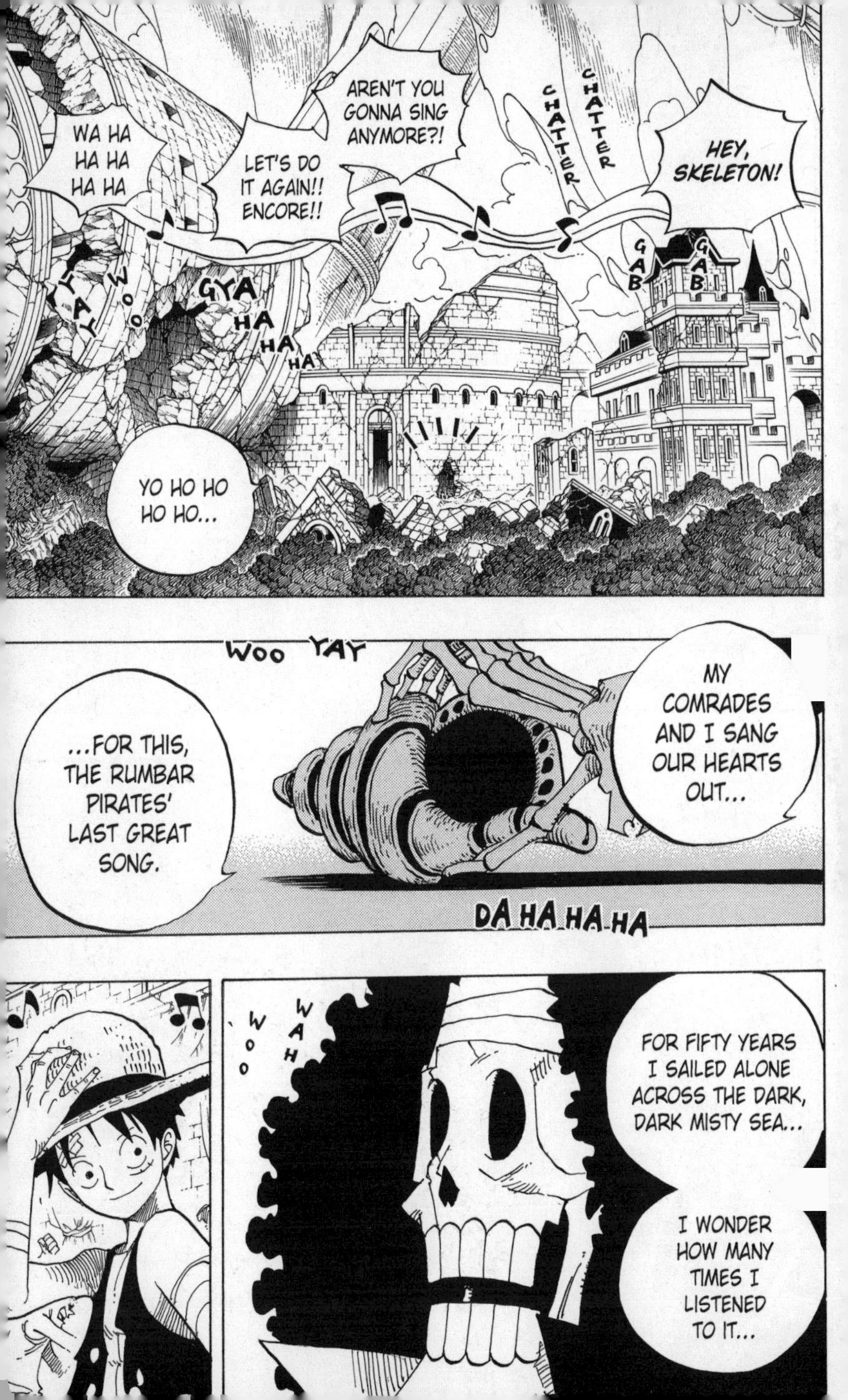
HEY, SKELETON!
GAB
GAB
CHATTER
CHATTER
AREN'T YOU GONNA SING ANYMORE?!
LET'S DO IT AGAIN!! ENCORE!!
WA HA HA HA HA HA
GYA HA HA HA
WOO YAY
YO HO HO HO HO...
MY COMRADES AND I SANG OUR HEARTS OUT...
WOO YAY
...FOR THIS, THE RUMBAR PIRATES' LAST GREAT SONG.
DA HA HA HA
FOR FIFTY YEARS I SAILED ALONE ACROSS THE DARK, DARK MISTY SEA...
I WONDER HOW MANY TIMES I LISTENED TO IT...
WAH
WOO

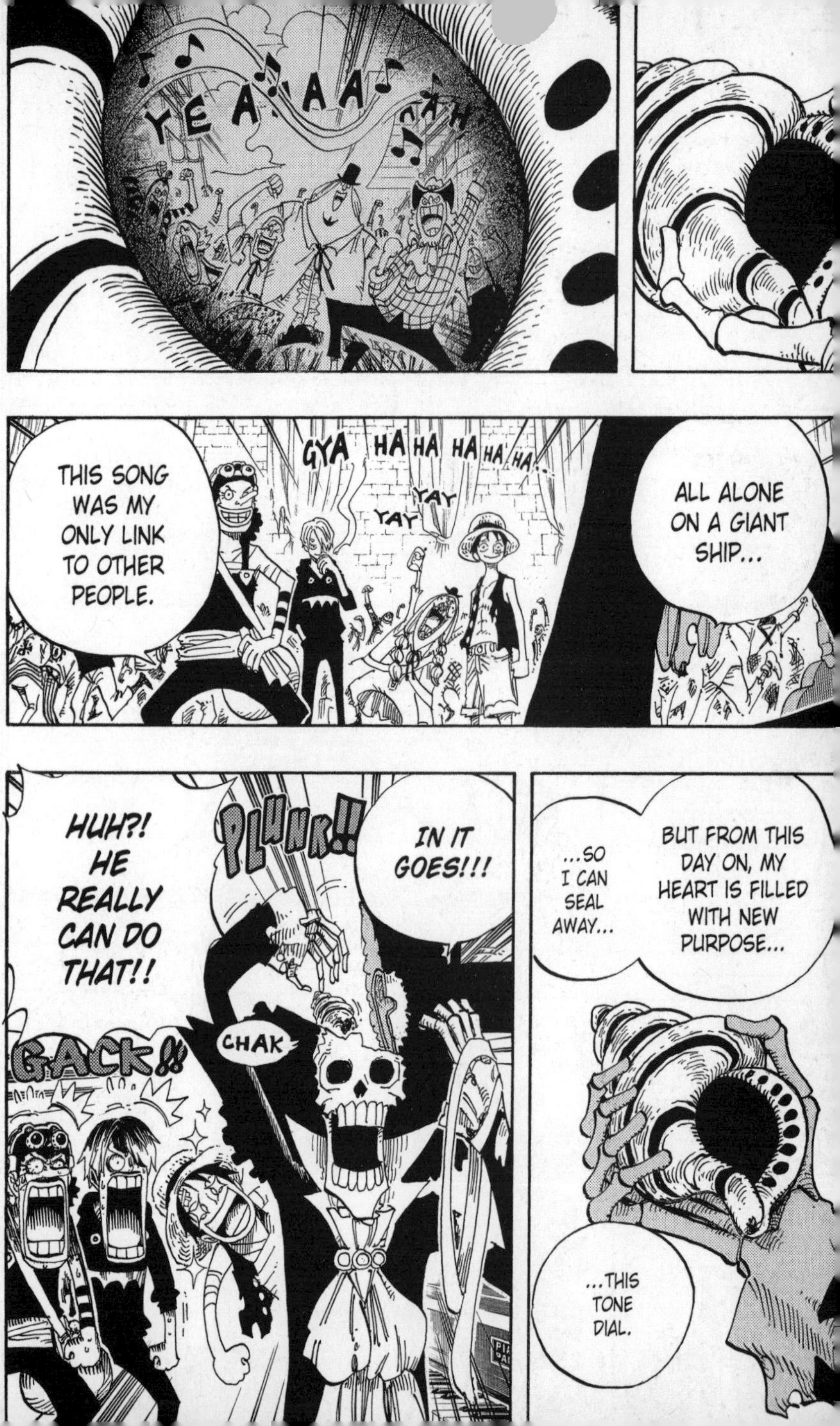
YEA AAA AAH
ALL ALONE ON A GIANT SHIP...
GYA HA HA HA HA HA...
YAY YAY
THIS SONG WAS MY ONLY LINK TO OTHER PEOPLE.
BUT FROM THIS DAY ON, MY HEART IS FILLED WITH NEW PURPOSE...
...SO I CAN SEAL AWAY...
...THIS TONE DIAL.
IN IT GOES!!!
PLUNK!!
HUH?! HE REALLY CAN DO THAT!!
CHAK
GACK!!

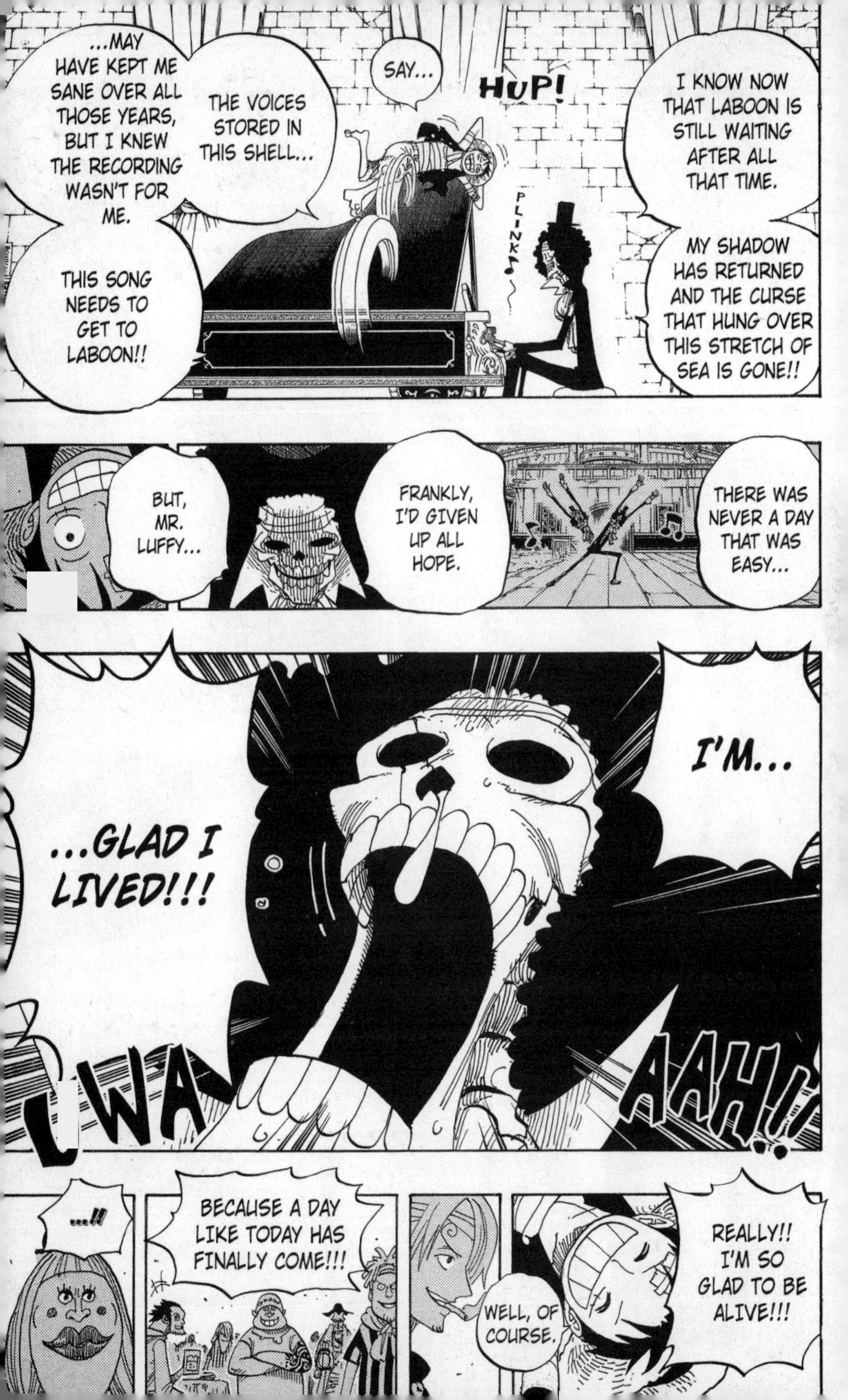
I KNOW NOW THAT LABOON IS STILL WAITING AFTER ALL THAT TIME.
MY SHADOW HAS RETURNED AND THE CURSE THAT HUNG OVER THIS STRETCH OF SEA IS GONE!!
PLINK
HUP!
SAY...
THE VOICES STORED IN THIS SHELL...
...MAY HAVE KEPT ME SANE OVER ALL THOSE YEARS, BUT I KNEW THE RECORDING WASN'T FOR ME.
THIS SONG NEEDS TO GET TO LABOON!!
THERE WAS NEVER A DAY THAT WAS EASY...
FRANKLY, I'D GIVEN UP ALL HOPE.
BUT, MR. LUFFY...
I'M...
...GLAD I LIVED!!!
WA
AAH!!
REALLY!! I'M SO GLAD TO BE ALIVE!!!
WELL, OF COURSE.
BECAUSE A DAY LIKE TODAY HAS FINALLY COME!!!
...!!

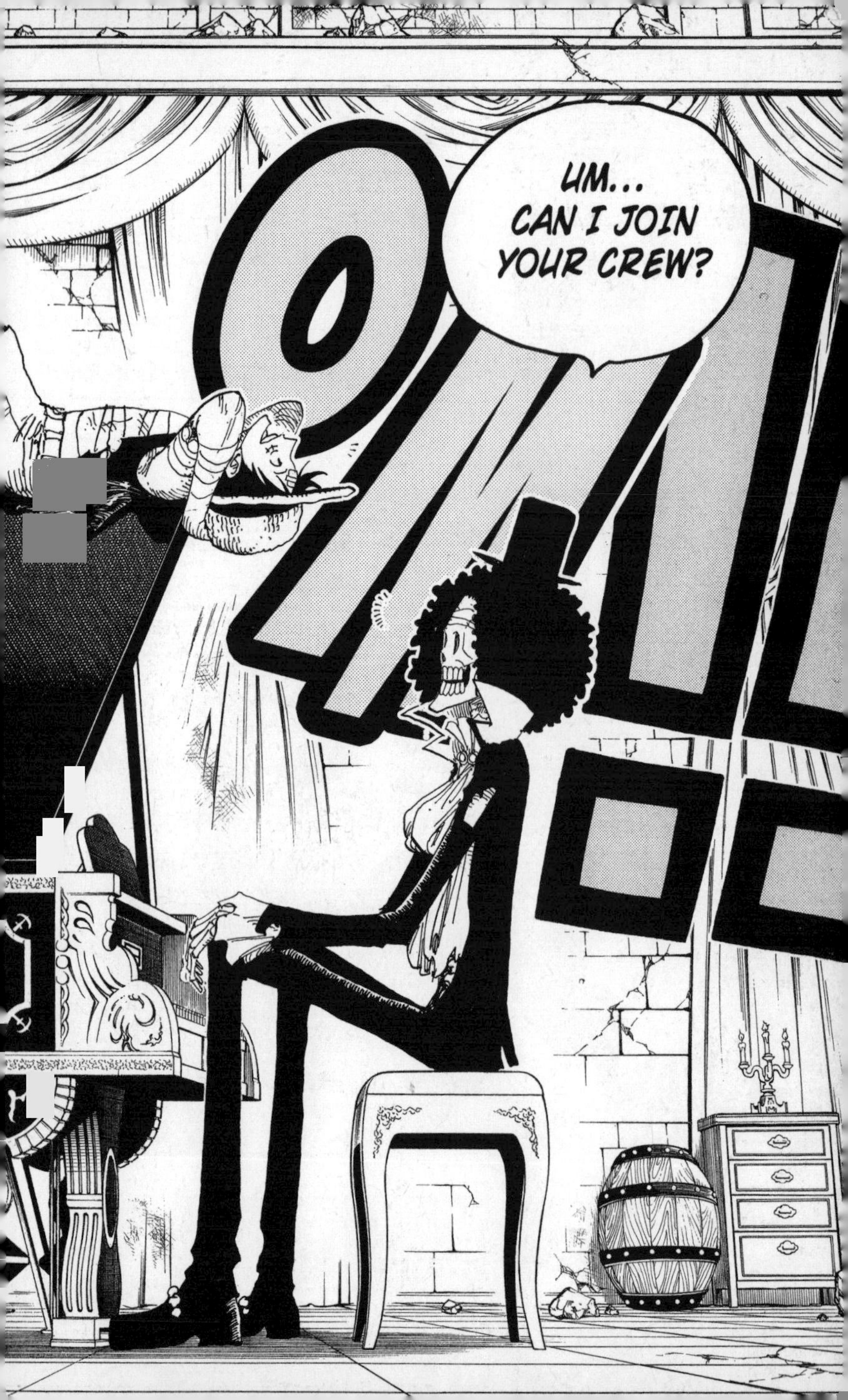
UM... CAN I JOIN YOUR CREW?

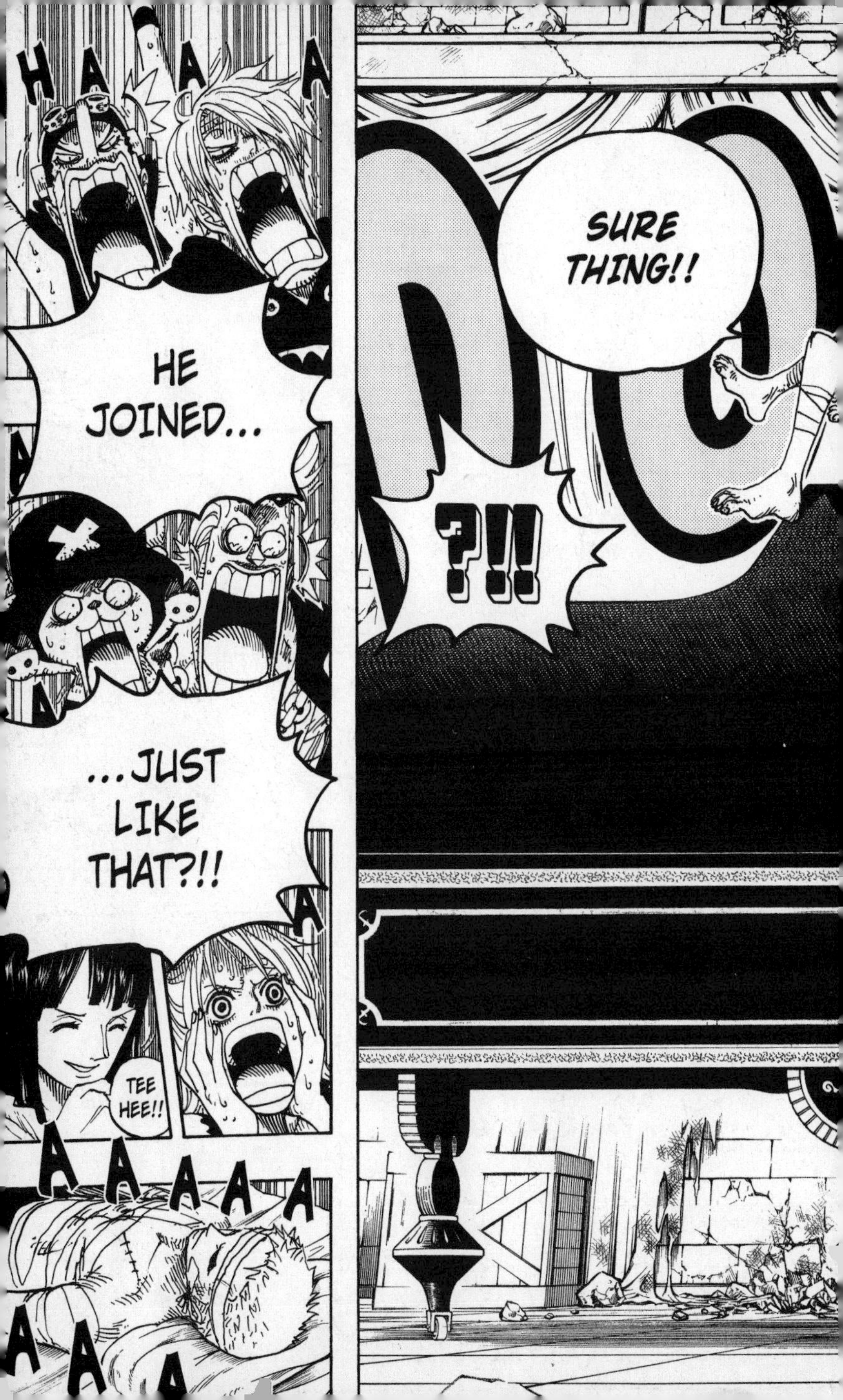
SURE THING!!
?!!
HA A A
HE JOINED...
...JUST LIKE THAT?!!
TEE HEE!!
A A A A A

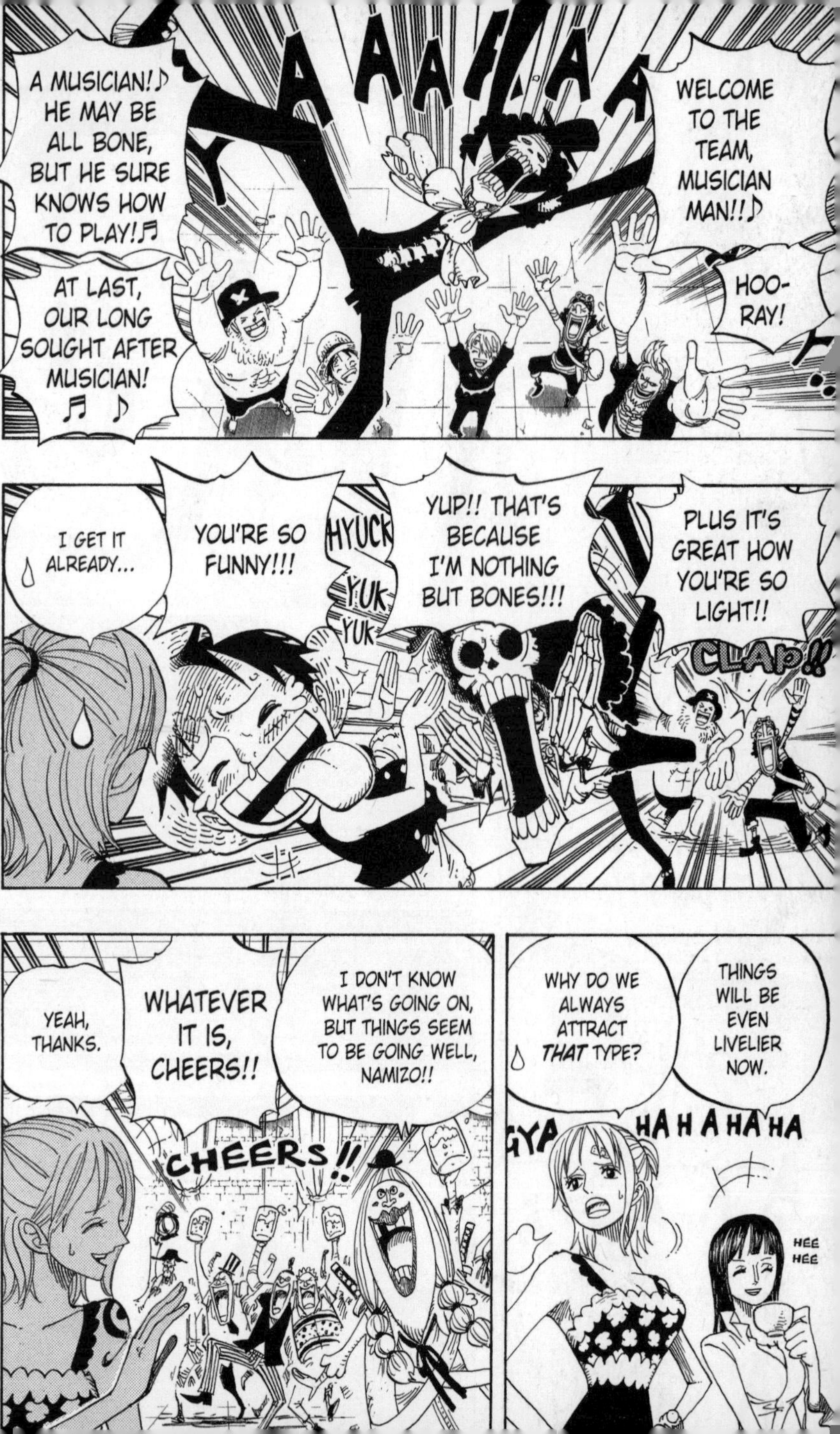
WELCOME TO THE TEAM, MUSICIAN MAN!!♪
HOO-RAY!
A MUSICIAN!♪ HE MAY BE ALL BONE, BUT HE SURE KNOWS HOW TO PLAY!♬
AT LAST, OUR LONG SOUGHT AFTER MUSICIAN! ♬ ♪
PLUS IT'S GREAT HOW YOU'RE SO LIGHT!!
CLAP!!
YUP!! THAT'S BECAUSE I'M NOTHING BUT BONES!!!
HYUCK YUK YUK
YOU'RE SO FUNNY!!!
I GET IT ALREADY...
THINGS WILL BE EVEN LIVELIER NOW.
WHY DO WE ALWAYS ATTRACT *THAT* TYPE?
GYA HA H A HA HA HA
HEE HEE
I DON'T KNOW WHAT'S GOING ON, BUT THINGS SEEM TO BE GOING WELL, NAMIZO!!
WHATEVER IT IS, CHEERS!!
CHEERS!!
YEAH, THANKS.

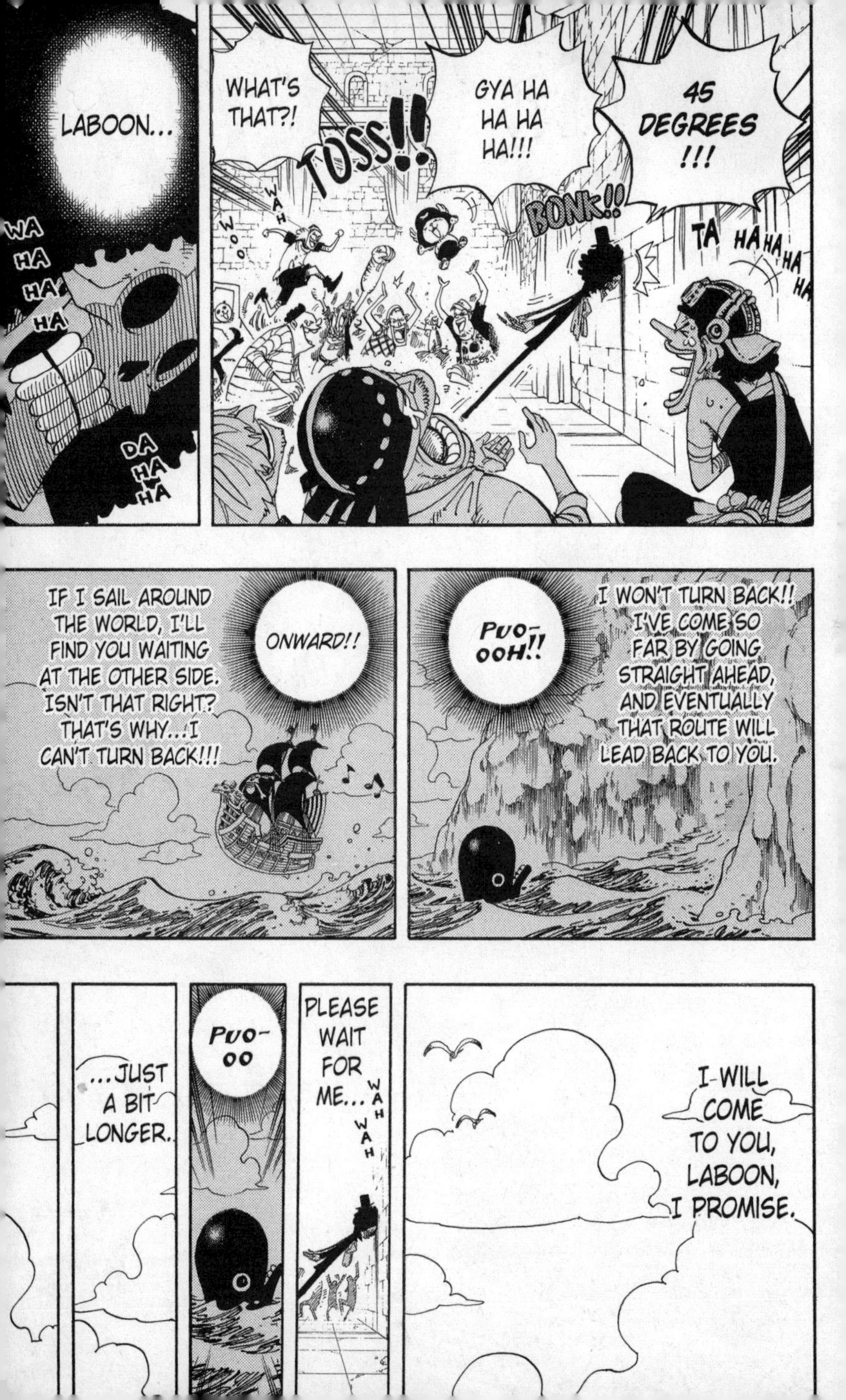
45 DEGREES!!!
TA HA HA HA HA HA
BONK!!
GYA HA HA HA HA!!!
TOSS!!
WHAT'S THAT?!
WAH
WOO
LABOON...
WA HA HA HA
DA HA HA HA
I WON'T TURN BACK!! I'VE COME SO FAR BY GOING STRAIGHT AHEAD, AND EVENTUALLY THAT ROUTE WILL LEAD BACK TO YOU.
PUO-OOH!!
ONWARD!!
IF I SAIL AROUND THE WORLD, I'LL FIND YOU WAITING AT THE OTHER SIDE. ISN'T THAT RIGHT? THAT'S WHY...I CAN'T TURN BACK!!!
I WILL COME TO YOU, LABOON, I PROMISE.
PLEASE WAIT FOR ME...
WAH WAH
PUO-OO
...JUST A BIT LONGER.

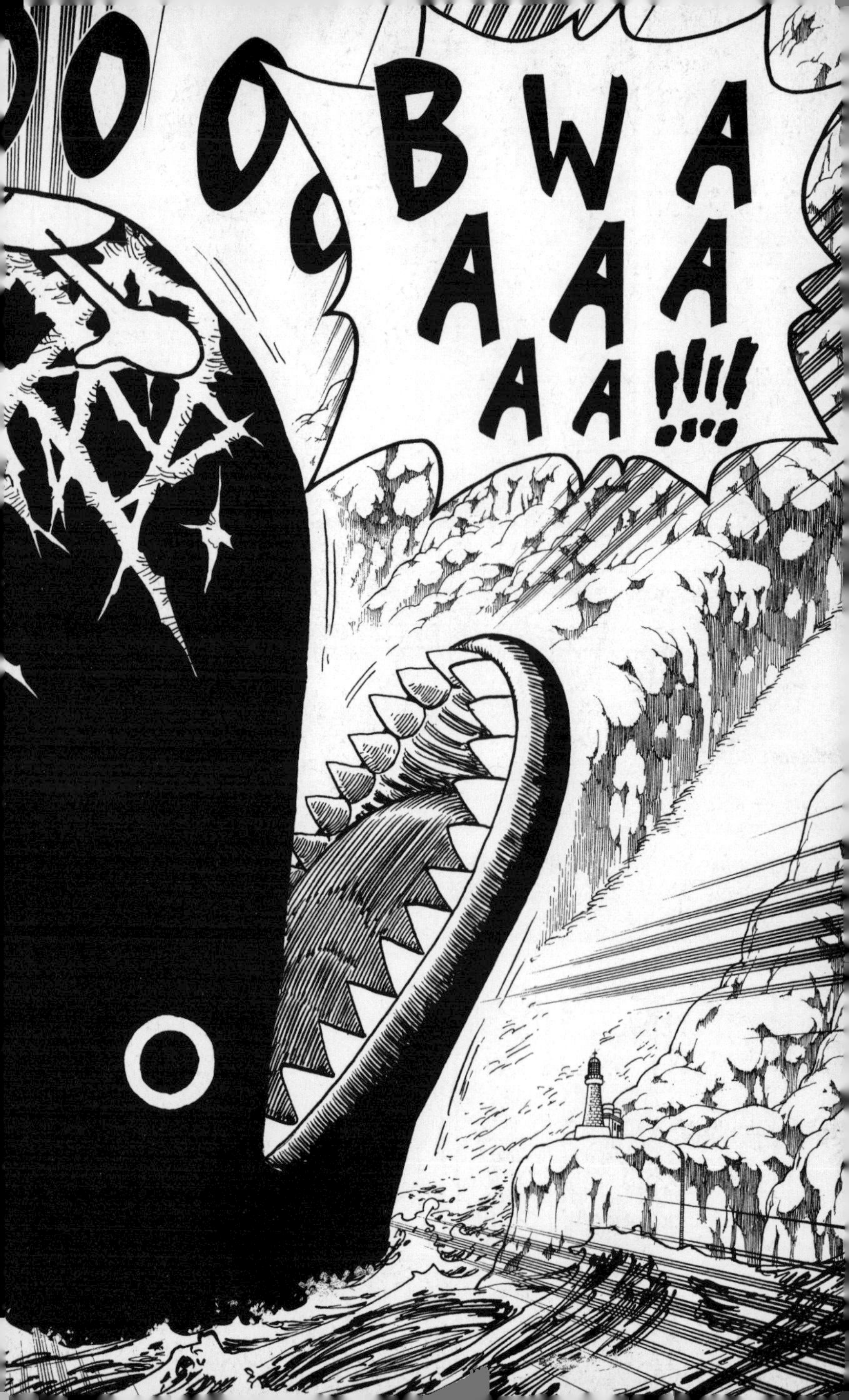
DOOOBWAAAAAA!!!!

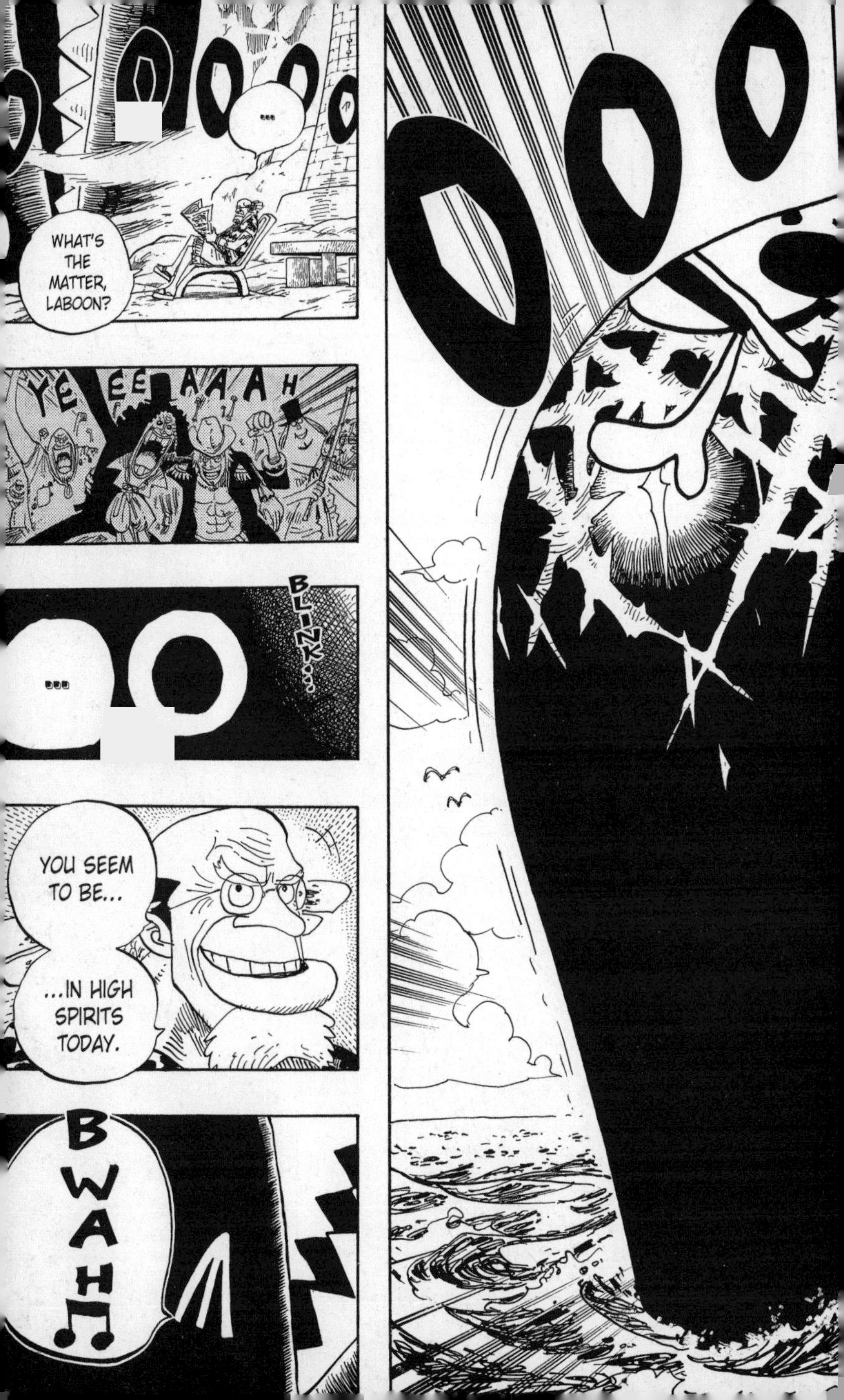
...
WHAT'S THE MATTER, LABOON?
YEEAAAH
...
BLINK...
YOU SEEM TO BE...
...IN HIGH SPIRITS TODAY.
BWAH♫

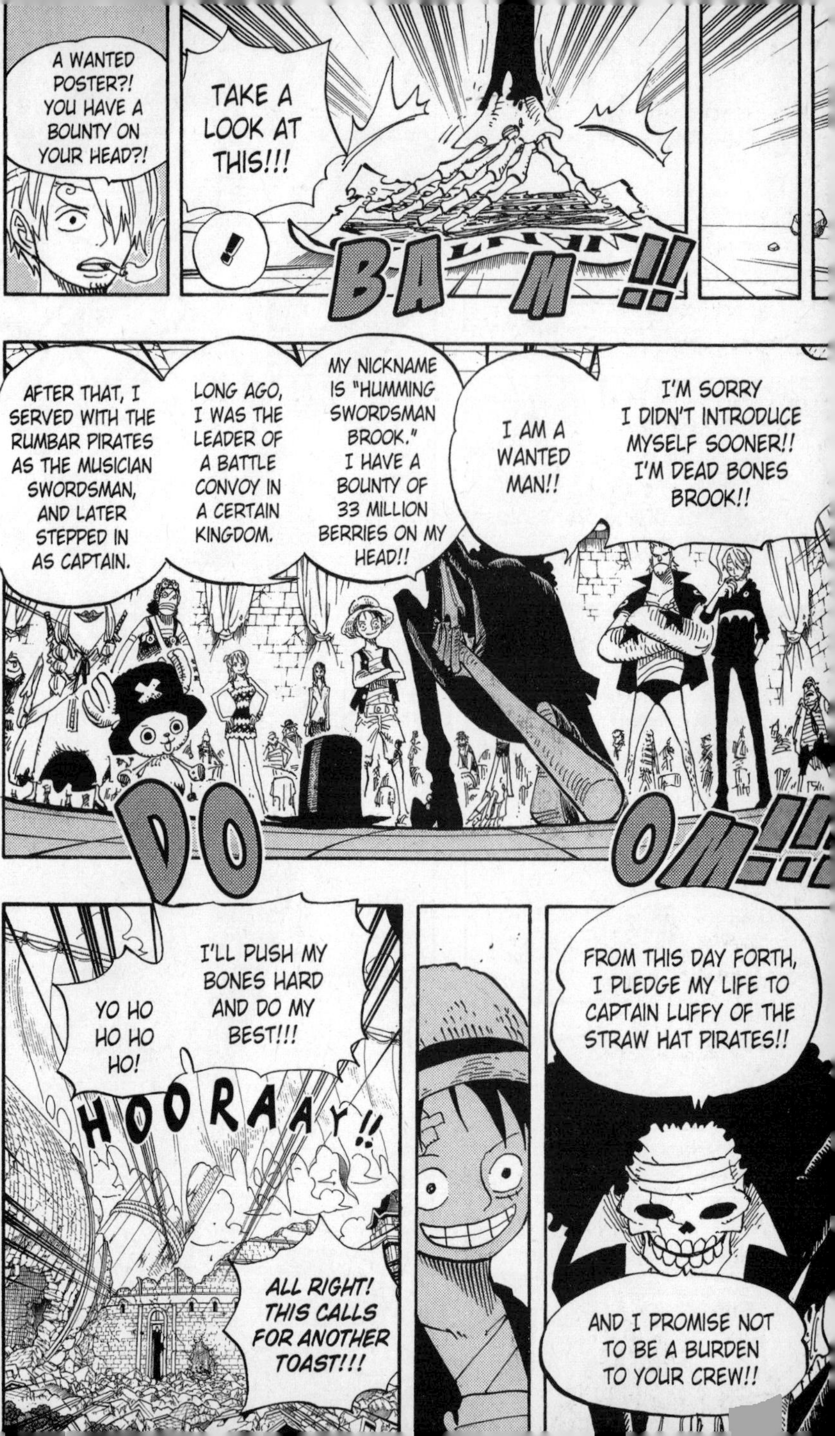
TAKE A LOOK AT THIS!!!
!
BAM!!
A WANTED POSTER?! YOU HAVE A BOUNTY ON YOUR HEAD?!
I'M SORRY I DIDN'T INTRODUCE MYSELF SOONER!! I'M DEAD BONES BROOK!!
I AM A WANTED MAN!!
MY NICKNAME IS "HUMMING SWORDSMAN BROOK." I HAVE A BOUNTY OF 33 MILLION BERRIES ON MY HEAD!!
LONG AGO, I WAS THE LEADER OF A BATTLE CONVOY IN A CERTAIN KINGDOM.
AFTER THAT, I SERVED WITH THE RUMBAR PIRATES AS THE MUSICIAN SWORDSMAN, AND LATER STEPPED IN AS CAPTAIN.
DOOM!!!
FROM THIS DAY FORTH, I PLEDGE MY LIFE TO CAPTAIN LUFFY OF THE STRAW HAT PIRATES!!
AND I PROMISE NOT TO BE A BURDEN TO YOUR CREW!!
I'LL PUSH MY BONES HARD AND DO MY BEST!!!
YO HO HO HO HO!
HOORAAY!!
ALL RIGHT! THIS CALLS FOR ANOTHER TOAST!!!

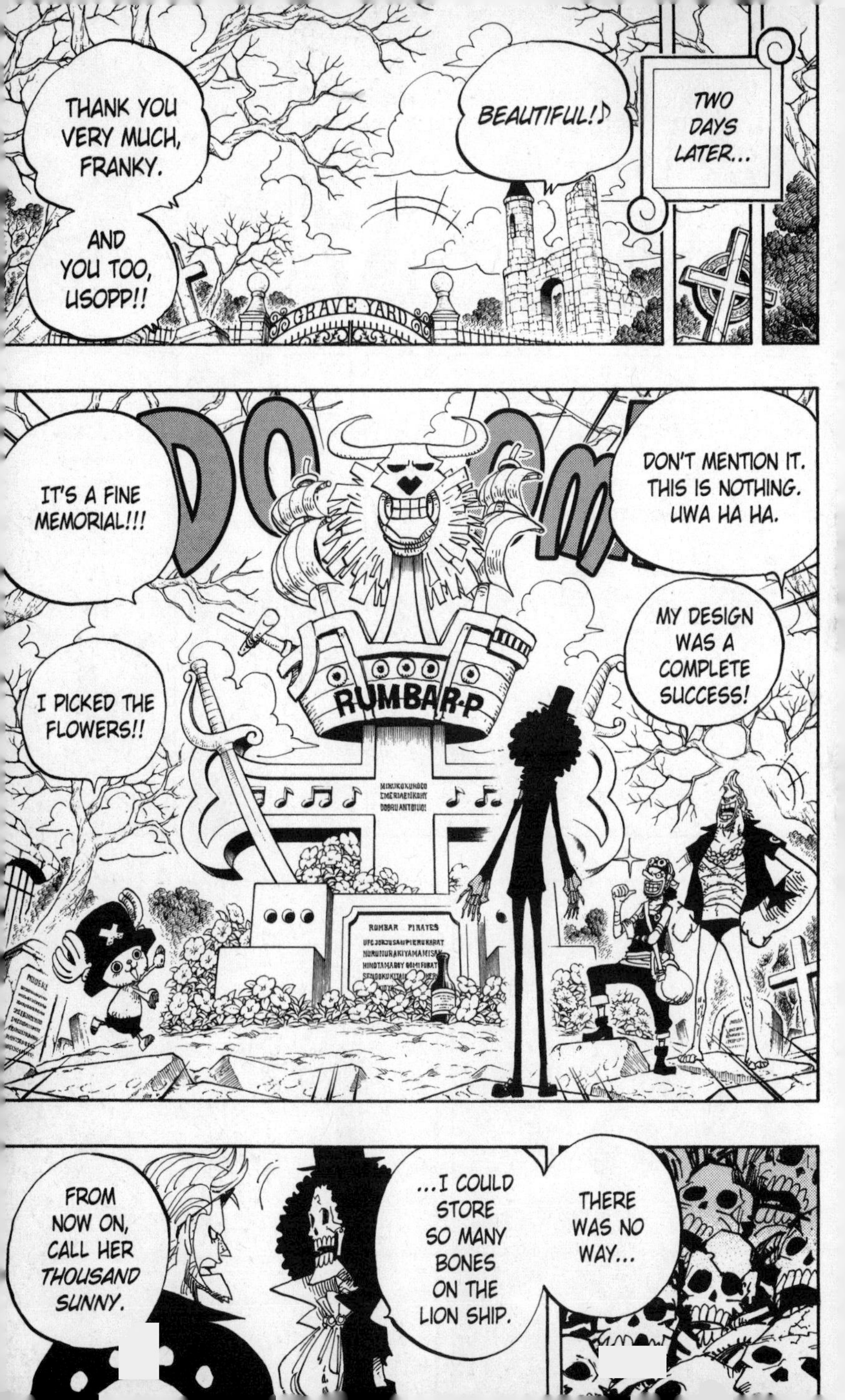
TWO DAYS LATER...
BEAUTIFUL!♪
THANK YOU VERY MUCH, FRANKY.
AND YOU TOO, USOPP!!
GRAVE YARD
DON'T MENTION IT. THIS IS NOTHING. UWA HA HA.
MY DESIGN WAS A COMPLETE SUCCESS!
IT'S A FINE MEMORIAL!!!
I PICKED THE FLOWERS!!
RUMBAR-P
RUMBAR PIRATES
THERE WAS NO WAY...
...I COULD STORE SO MANY BONES ON THE LION SHIP.
FROM NOW ON, CALL HER THOUSAND SUNNY.

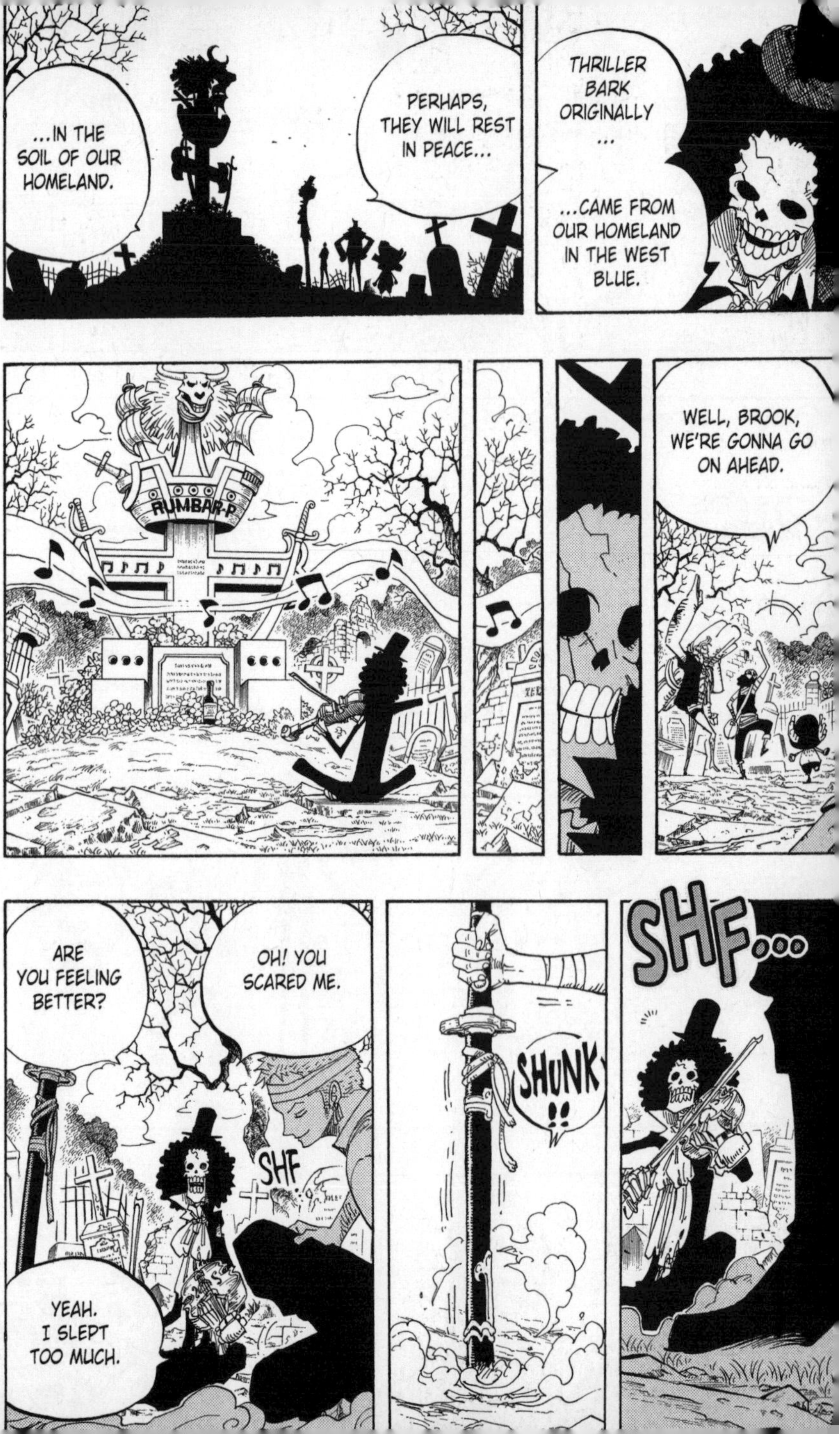
THRILLER BARK ORIGINALLY ...
...CAME FROM OUR HOMELAND IN THE WEST BLUE.
PERHAPS, THEY WILL REST IN PEACE...
...IN THE SOIL OF OUR HOMELAND.
WELL, BROOK, WE'RE GONNA GO ON AHEAD.
RUMBAR-P
SHF...
SHUNK!!
OH! YOU SCARED ME.
ARE YOU FEELING BETTER?
SHF
YEAH. I SLEPT TOO MUCH.

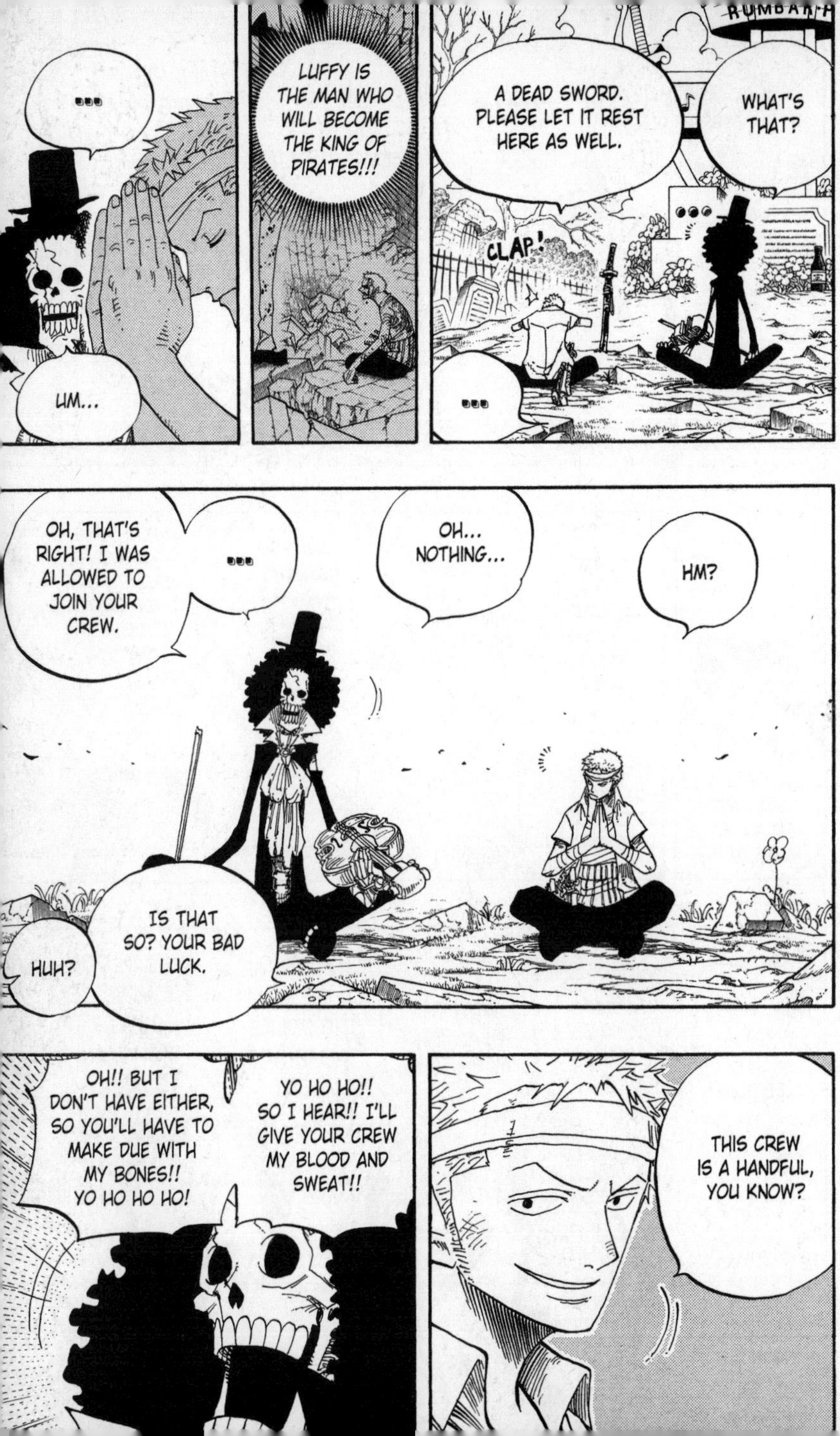
WHAT'S THAT?
A DEAD SWORD. PLEASE LET IT REST HERE AS WELL.
...
CLAP!
...
LUFFY IS THE MAN WHO WILL BECOME THE KING OF PIRATES!!!
...
UM...
HM?
OH... NOTHING...
...
OH, THAT'S RIGHT! I WAS ALLOWED TO JOIN YOUR CREW.
IS THAT SO? YOUR BAD LUCK.
HUH?
THIS CREW IS A HANDFUL, YOU KNOW?
YO HO HO!! SO I HEAR!! I'LL GIVE YOUR CREW MY BLOOD AND SWEAT!!
OH!! BUT I DON'T HAVE EITHER, SO YOU'LL HAVE TO MAKE DUE WITH MY BONES!! YO HO HO HO!

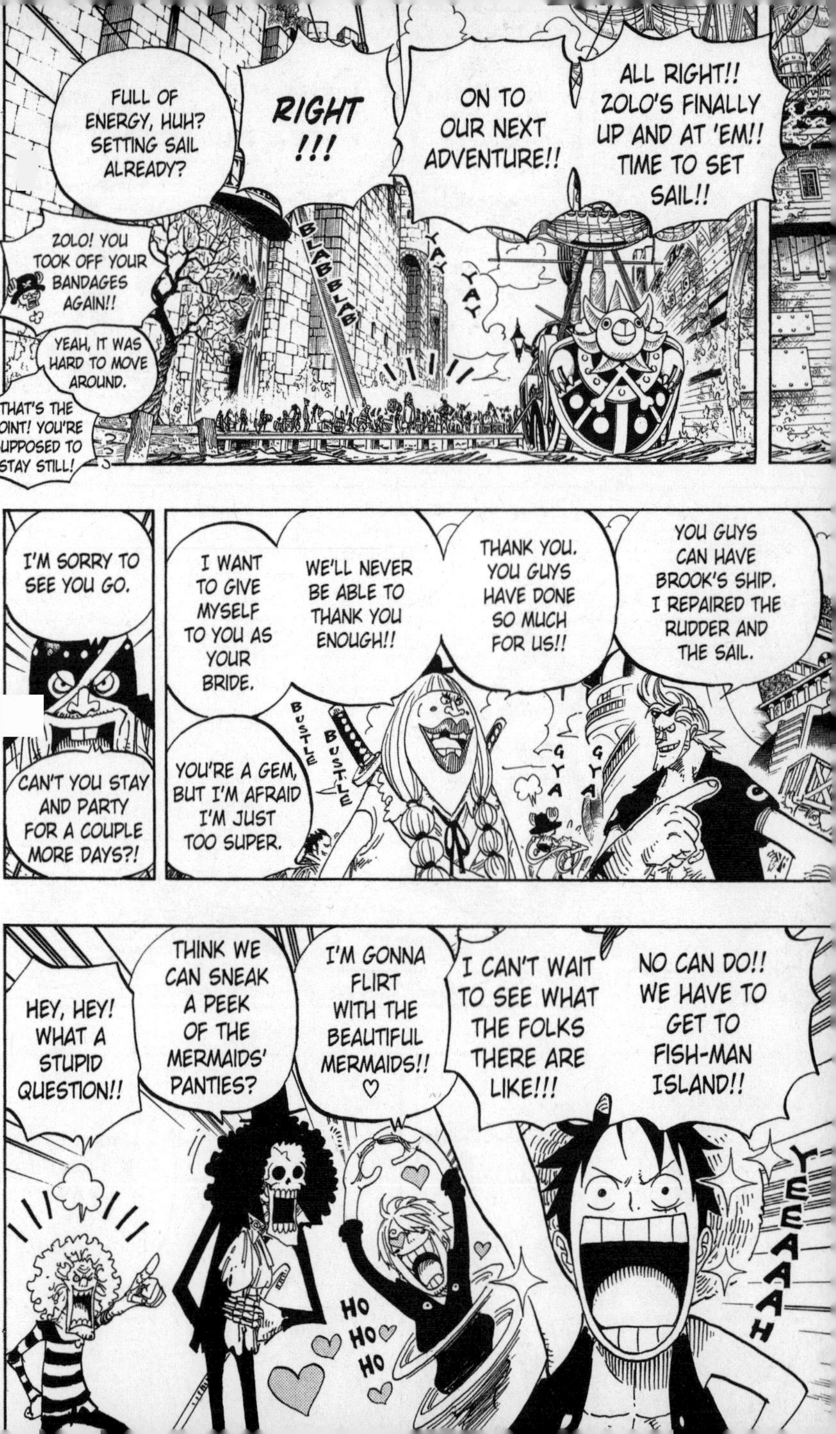
ALL RIGHT!! ZOLO'S FINALLY UP AND AT 'EM!! TIME TO SET SAIL!!
ON TO OUR NEXT ADVENTURE!!
RIGHT !!!
FULL OF ENERGY, HUH? SETTING SAIL ALREADY?
YAY YAY
BLAB BLAB
ZOLO! YOU TOOK OFF YOUR BANDAGES AGAIN!!
YEAH, IT WAS HARD TO MOVE AROUND.
THAT'S THE POINT! YOU'RE SUPPOSED TO STAY STILL!
YOU GUYS CAN HAVE BROOK'S SHIP. I REPAIRED THE RUDDER AND THE SAIL.
THANK YOU. YOU GUYS HAVE DONE SO MUCH FOR US!!
WE'LL NEVER BE ABLE TO THANK YOU ENOUGH!!
I WANT TO GIVE MYSELF TO YOU AS YOUR BRIDE.
GYA GYA
BUSTLE BUSTLE
YOU'RE A GEM, BUT I'M AFRAID I'M JUST TOO SUPER.
I'M SORRY TO SEE YOU GO.
CAN'T YOU STAY AND PARTY FOR A COUPLE MORE DAYS?!
NO CAN DO!! WE HAVE TO GET TO FISH-MAN ISLAND!!
YEEAAAAH
I CAN'T WAIT TO SEE WHAT THE FOLKS THERE ARE LIKE!!!
I'M GONNA FLIRT WITH THE BEAUTIFUL MERMAIDS!! ♡
HO HO HO
THINK WE CAN SNEAK A PEEK OF THE MERMAIDS' PANTIES?
HEY, HEY! WHAT A STUPID QUESTION!!

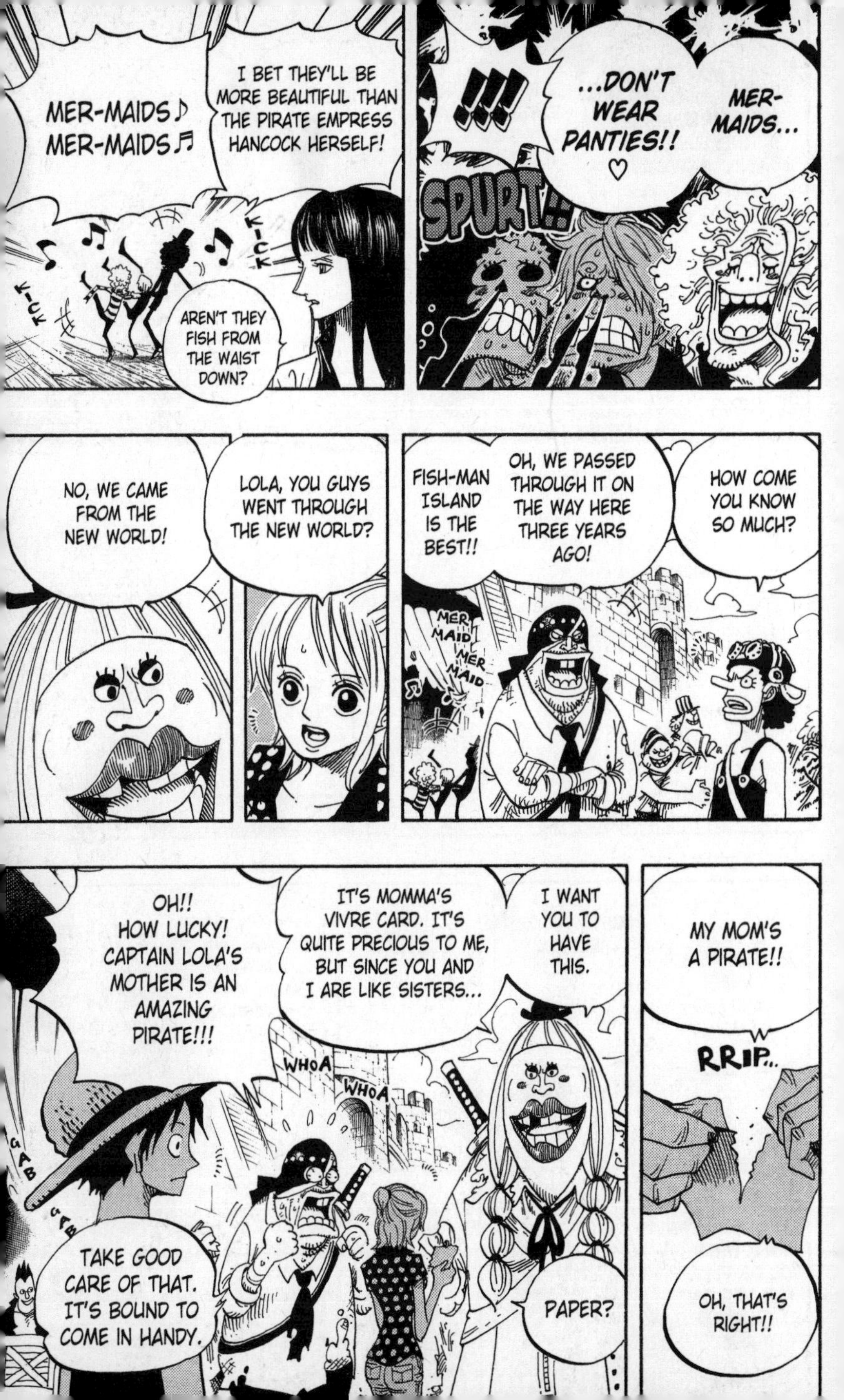
!!!
MER-MAIDS...
...DON'T WEAR PANTIES!! ♥
SPURT!!
I BET THEY'LL BE MORE BEAUTIFUL THAN THE PIRATE EMPRESS HANCOCK HERSELF!
MER-MAIDS♪ MER-MAIDS♬
KICK
KICK
AREN'T THEY FISH FROM THE WAIST DOWN?
HOW COME YOU KNOW SO MUCH?
OH, WE PASSED THROUGH IT ON THE WAY HERE THREE YEARS AGO!
FISH-MAN ISLAND IS THE BEST!!
MER MAID MER MAID
LOLA, YOU GUYS WENT THROUGH THE NEW WORLD?
NO, WE CAME FROM THE NEW WORLD!
MY MOM'S A PIRATE!!
RRIP..
OH, THAT'S RIGHT!!
I WANT YOU TO HAVE THIS.
IT'S MOMMA'S VIVRE CARD. IT'S QUITE PRECIOUS TO ME, BUT SINCE YOU AND I ARE LIKE SISTERS...
PAPER?
OH!! HOW LUCKY! CAPTAIN LOLA'S MOTHER IS AN AMAZING PIRATE!!!
WHOA
WHOA
GAB
GAB
TAKE GOOD CARE OF THAT. IT'S BOUND TO COME IN HANDY.

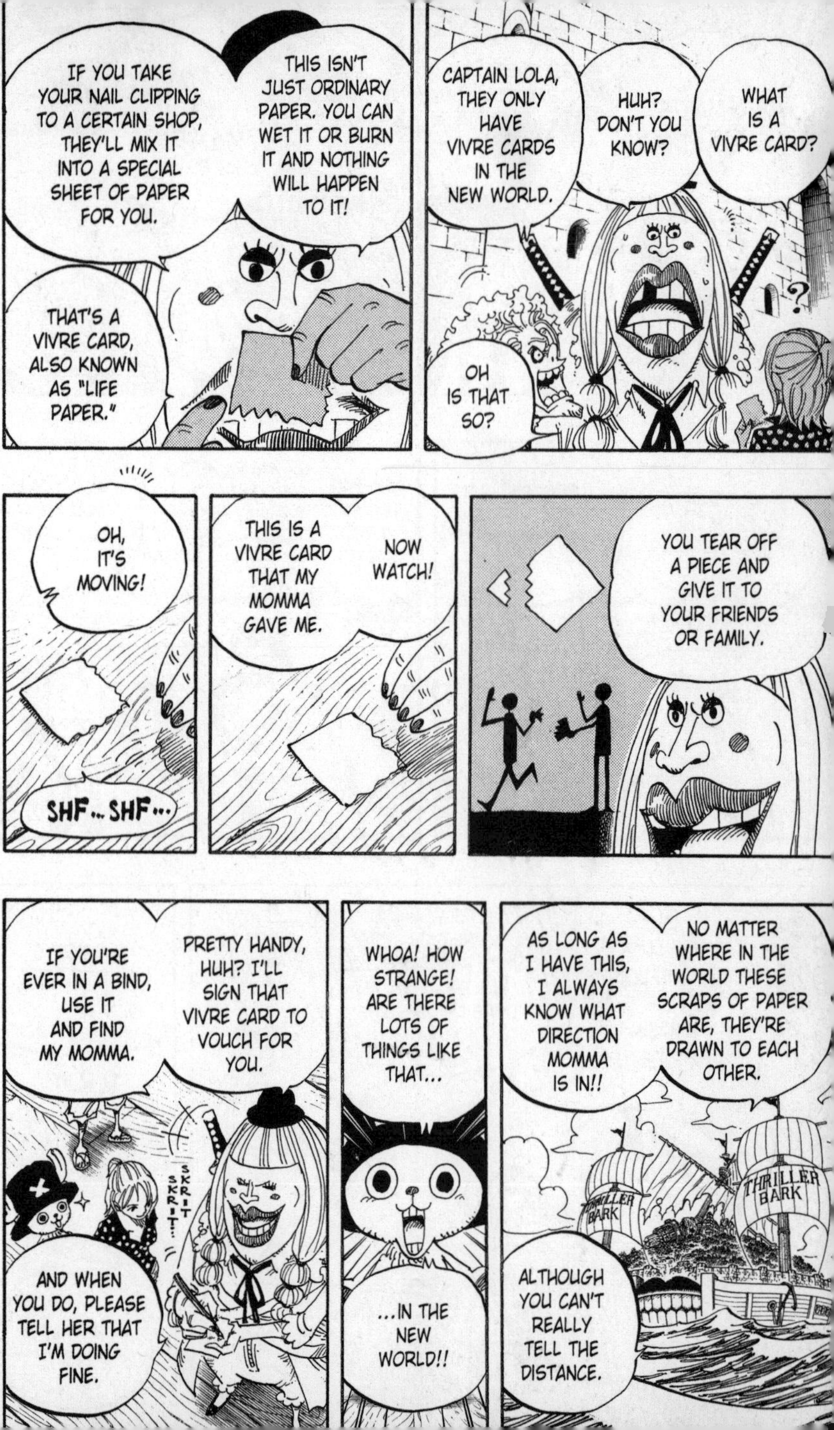
WHAT IS A VIVRE CARD?
HUH? DON'T YOU KNOW?
CAPTAIN LOLA, THEY ONLY HAVE VIVRE CARDS IN THE NEW WORLD.
OH IS THAT SO?
THIS ISN'T JUST ORDINARY PAPER. YOU CAN WET IT OR BURN IT AND NOTHING WILL HAPPEN TO IT!
IF YOU TAKE YOUR NAIL CLIPPING TO A CERTAIN SHOP, THEY'LL MIX IT INTO A SPECIAL SHEET OF PAPER FOR YOU.
THAT'S A VIVRE CARD, ALSO KNOWN AS "LIFE PAPER."
YOU TEAR OFF A PIECE AND GIVE IT TO YOUR FRIENDS OR FAMILY.
NOW WATCH!
THIS IS A VIVRE CARD THAT MY MOMMA GAVE ME.
OH, IT'S MOVING!
SHF... SHF...
NO MATTER WHERE IN THE WORLD THESE SCRAPS OF PAPER ARE, THEY'RE DRAWN TO EACH OTHER.
AS LONG AS I HAVE THIS, I ALWAYS KNOW WHAT DIRECTION MOMMA IS IN!!
THRILLER BARK
THRILLER BARK
ALTHOUGH YOU CAN'T REALLY TELL THE DISTANCE.
WHOA! HOW STRANGE! ARE THERE LOTS OF THINGS LIKE THAT...
...IN THE NEW WORLD!!
PRETTY HANDY, HUH? I'LL SIGN THAT VIVRE CARD TO VOUCH FOR YOU.
IF YOU'RE EVER IN A BIND, USE IT AND FIND MY MOMMA.
SKRIT SKRIT
AND WHEN YOU DO, PLEASE TELL HER THAT I'M DOING FINE.

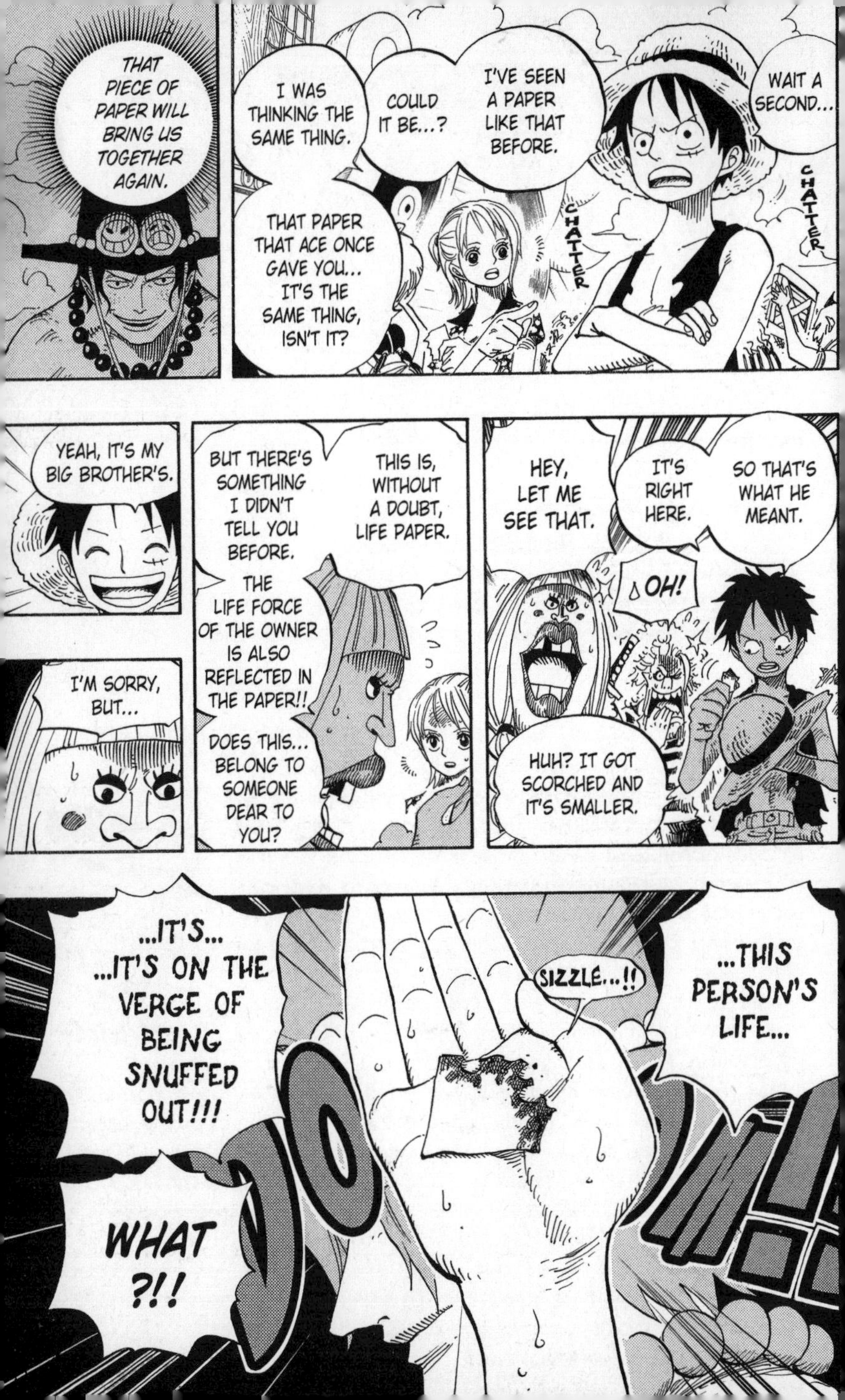

WAIT A SECOND...
CHATTER
I'VE SEEN A PAPER LIKE THAT BEFORE.
COULD IT BE...?
I WAS THINKING THE SAME THING.
THAT PAPER THAT ACE ONCE GAVE YOU... IT'S THE SAME THING, ISN'T IT?
CHATTER
THAT PIECE OF PAPER WILL BRING US TOGETHER AGAIN.
SO THAT'S WHAT HE MEANT.
IT'S RIGHT HERE.
HEY, LET ME SEE THAT.
OH!
HUH? IT GOT SCORCHED AND IT'S SMALLER.
THIS IS, WITHOUT A DOUBT, LIFE PAPER.
BUT THERE'S SOMETHING I DIDN'T TELL YOU BEFORE.
THE LIFE FORCE OF THE OWNER IS ALSO REFLECTED IN THE PAPER!!
DOES THIS... BELONG TO SOMEONE DEAR TO YOU?
YEAH, IT'S MY BIG BROTHER'S.
I'M SORRY, BUT...
...THIS PERSON'S LIFE...
SIZZLE...!!
...IT'S... ...IT'S ON THE VERGE OF BEING SNUFFED OUT!!!
WHAT ?!!

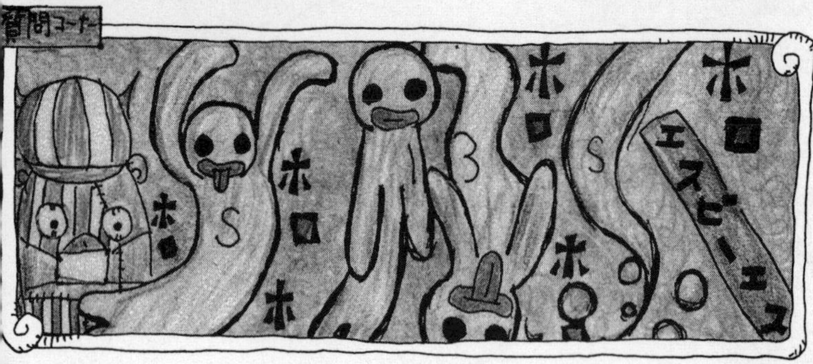

(I'll Knock Out the Strong Ones, Kanagawa)

Q: I know this is out of the blue, Odacchi… I understand that when you eat four Rumble Balls, Odacchi, you go wild. And if a reader eats five, we go wild?
(Like me…)
YAAAAAH~~~~~~~!!!
P.S. All Question Corner Readers Must Eat Five

A: Yikes!! He's looking so strange!! That's one scary Chopper!! I see. So everyone who sends a postcard to the Question Corner is eating too many Rumble Balls… Now I understand.

Q: Please release a CD of "Binks's Brew." With lyrics by Eiichiro Oda!
--Fusion!!! Hah!!!

A: Yes, I think "Binks's Brew" will be released. Or at least in time it will be. That sailor's anthem was already composed when Brook debuted and sang it. I went to Kouhei Tanaka, a mainstay in the world of anime music, to compose a melody, explaining that I had this idea for a story, and I didn't want to get bogged down with setting music to it later on. I had told him, "the Thriller Bark arc will start in about a year," but it ended up coming four, five years later? (lol) Well, it took me about an hour, but my lyrics made it in time for chapter 488, "Song of Life." It sounds a bit scary at first, but when the melody changes it sounds pretty neat. I must say, Kouhei Tanaka did wonders with my request, and I'm so grateful for his work on Thriller Bark., Please look forward to the anime too!! My aim was to create a sailor's song which would make it into music lesson books, but I used the word "brew," so I'm resigned to the fact that it won't be used. But I'd still like everyone to sing it. And on that note, we'll end the Question Corner!! See you in the next volume!!!

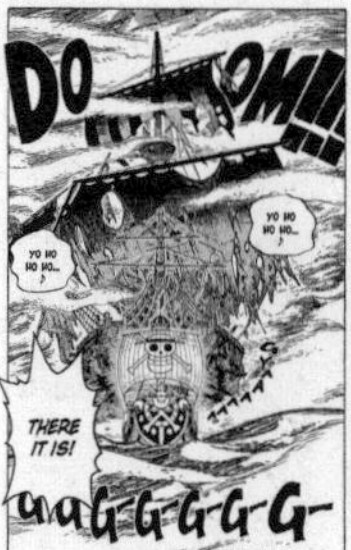
THERE IT IS!

Chapter 490:
ARRIVING AGAIN

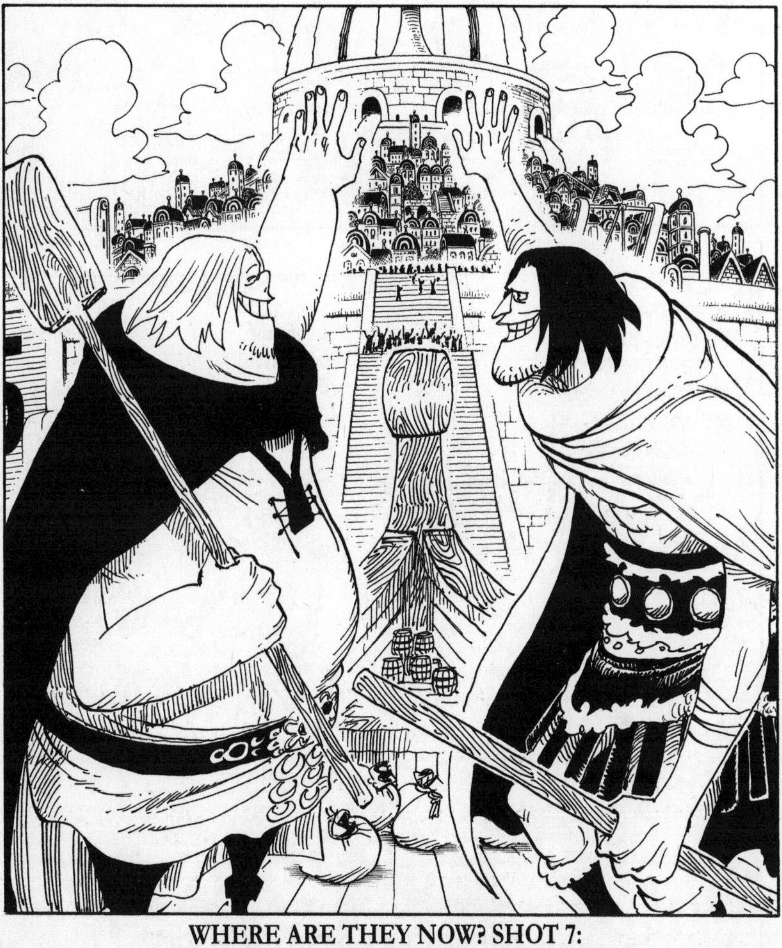

WHERE ARE THEY NOW? SHOT 7:
"OIMO AND KASHII RETURN TO ELBAPH"

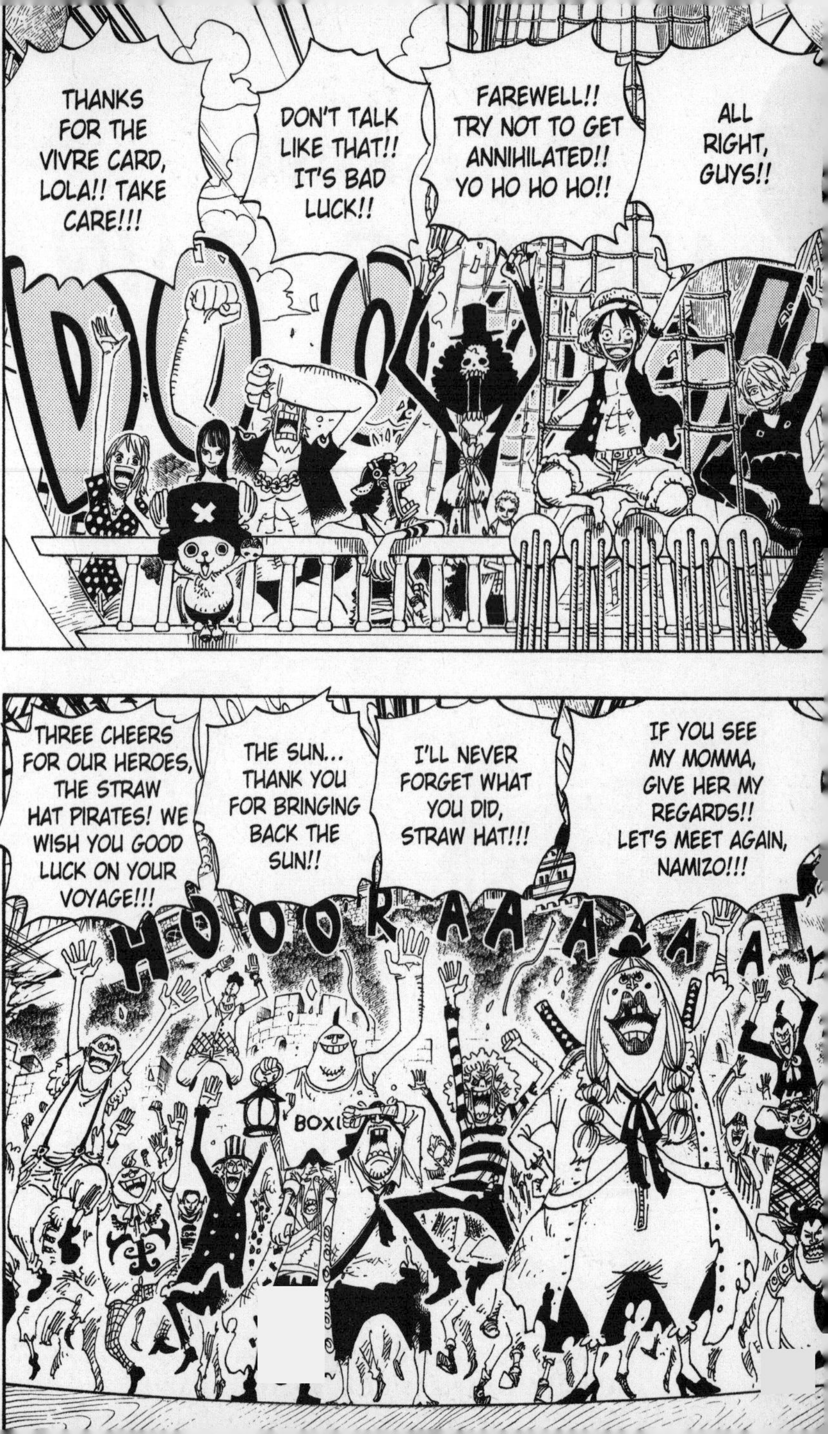
ALL RIGHT, GUYS!!
FAREWELL!! TRY NOT TO GET ANNIHILATED!! YO HO HO HO!!
DON'T TALK LIKE THAT!! IT'S BAD LUCK!!
THANKS FOR THE VIVRE CARD, LOLA!! TAKE CARE!!!
IF YOU SEE MY MOMMA, GIVE HER MY REGARDS!! LET'S MEET AGAIN, NAMIZO!!!
I'LL NEVER FORGET WHAT YOU DID, STRAW HAT!!!
THE SUN... THANK YOU FOR BRINGING BACK THE SUN!!
THREE CHEERS FOR OUR HEROES, THE STRAW HAT PIRATES! WE WISH YOU GOOD LUCK ON YOUR VOYAGE!!!
HOOORAAAAAAY
BOXI

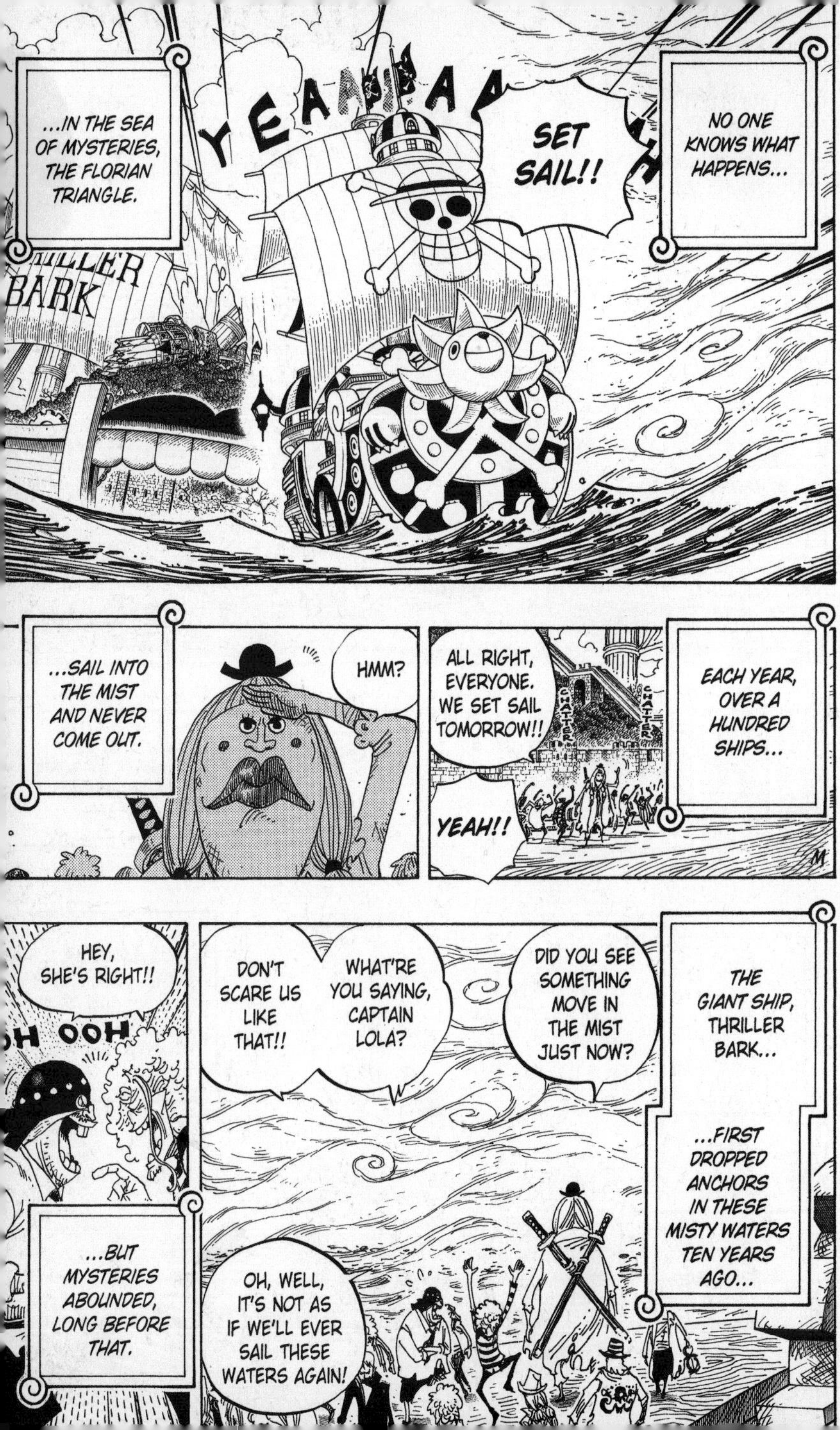
NO ONE KNOWS WHAT HAPPENS...
SET SAIL!!
YEAAAAAH
...IN THE SEA OF MYSTERIES, THE FLORIAN TRIANGLE.
EACH YEAR, OVER A HUNDRED SHIPS...
ALL RIGHT, EVERYONE. WE SET SAIL TOMORROW!!
CHATTER
CHATTER
YEAH!!
...SAIL INTO THE MIST AND NEVER COME OUT.
HMM?
THE GIANT SHIP, THRILLER BARK...
...FIRST DROPPED ANCHORS IN THESE MISTY WATERS TEN YEARS AGO...
DID YOU SEE SOMETHING MOVE IN THE MIST JUST NOW?
WHAT'RE YOU SAYING, CAPTAIN LOLA?
DON'T SCARE US LIKE THAT!!
OH, WELL, IT'S NOT AS IF WE'LL EVER SAIL THESE WATERS AGAIN!
HEY, SHE'S RIGHT!!
OOH
...BUT MYSTERIES ABOUNDED, LONG BEFORE THAT.

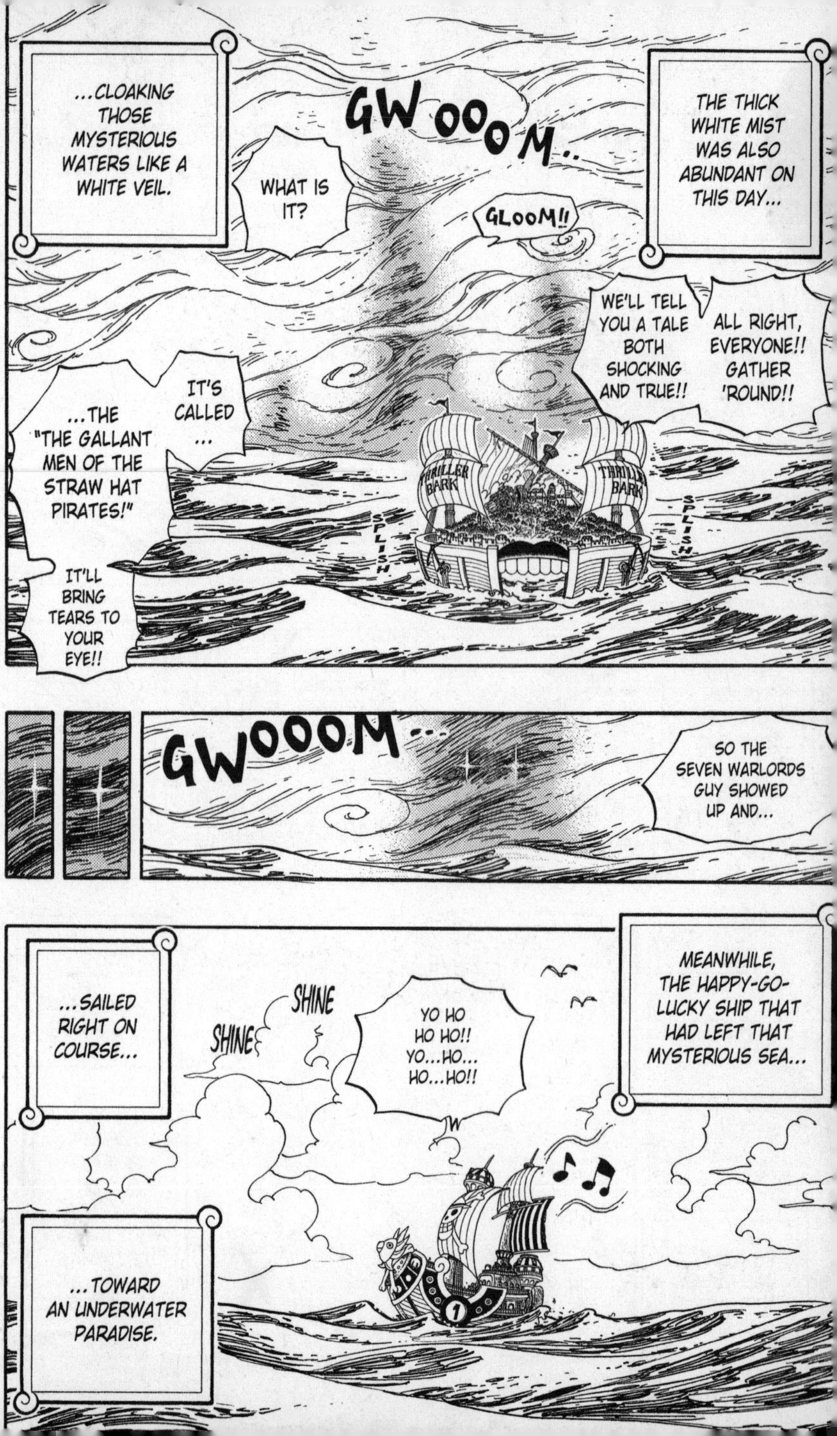
THE THICK WHITE MIST WAS ALSO ABUNDANT ON THIS DAY...
GW OOO M..
GLOOM!!
WHAT IS IT?
...CLOAKING THOSE MYSTERIOUS WATERS LIKE A WHITE VEIL.
ALL RIGHT, EVERYONE!! GATHER 'ROUND!!
WE'LL TELL YOU A TALE BOTH SHOCKING AND TRUE!!
THRILLER BARK
THRILLER BARK
SPLISH
SPLISH
IT'S CALLED...
...THE "THE GALLANT MEN OF THE STRAW HAT PIRATES!"
IT'LL BRING TEARS TO YOUR EYE!!
SO THE SEVEN WARLORDS GUY SHOWED UP AND...
GWOOOM...
MEANWHILE, THE HAPPY-GO-LUCKY SHIP THAT HAD LEFT THAT MYSTERIOUS SEA...
YO HO HO HO!! YO...HO... HO...HO!!
SHINE
SHINE
...SAILED RIGHT ON COURSE...
...TOWARD AN UNDERWATER PARADISE.

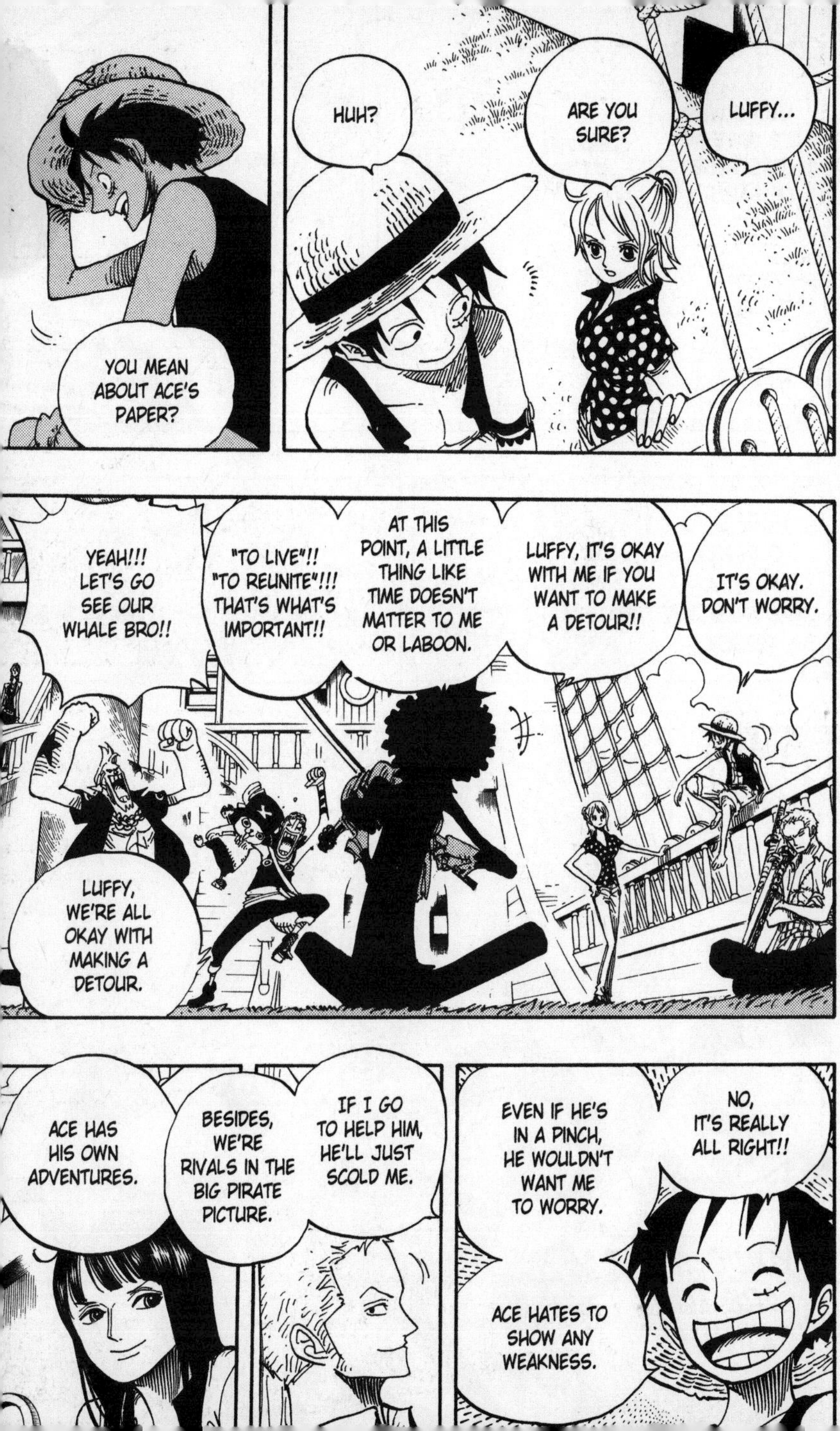
LUFFY...
ARE YOU SURE?
HUH?
YOU MEAN ABOUT ACE'S PAPER?
IT'S OKAY. DON'T WORRY.
LUFFY, IT'S OKAY WITH ME IF YOU WANT TO MAKE A DETOUR!!
AT THIS POINT, A LITTLE THING LIKE TIME DOESN'T MATTER TO ME OR LABOON.
"TO LIVE"!! "TO REUNITE"!!! THAT'S WHAT'S IMPORTANT!!
YEAH!!! LET'S GO SEE OUR WHALE BRO!!
LUFFY, WE'RE ALL OKAY WITH MAKING A DETOUR.
NO, IT'S REALLY ALL RIGHT!!
EVEN IF HE'S IN A PINCH, HE WOULDN'T WANT ME TO WORRY.
ACE HATES TO SHOW ANY WEAKNESS.
IF I GO TO HELP HIM, HE'LL JUST SCOLD ME.
BESIDES, WE'RE RIVALS IN THE BIG PIRATE PICTURE.
ACE HAS HIS OWN ADVENTURES.

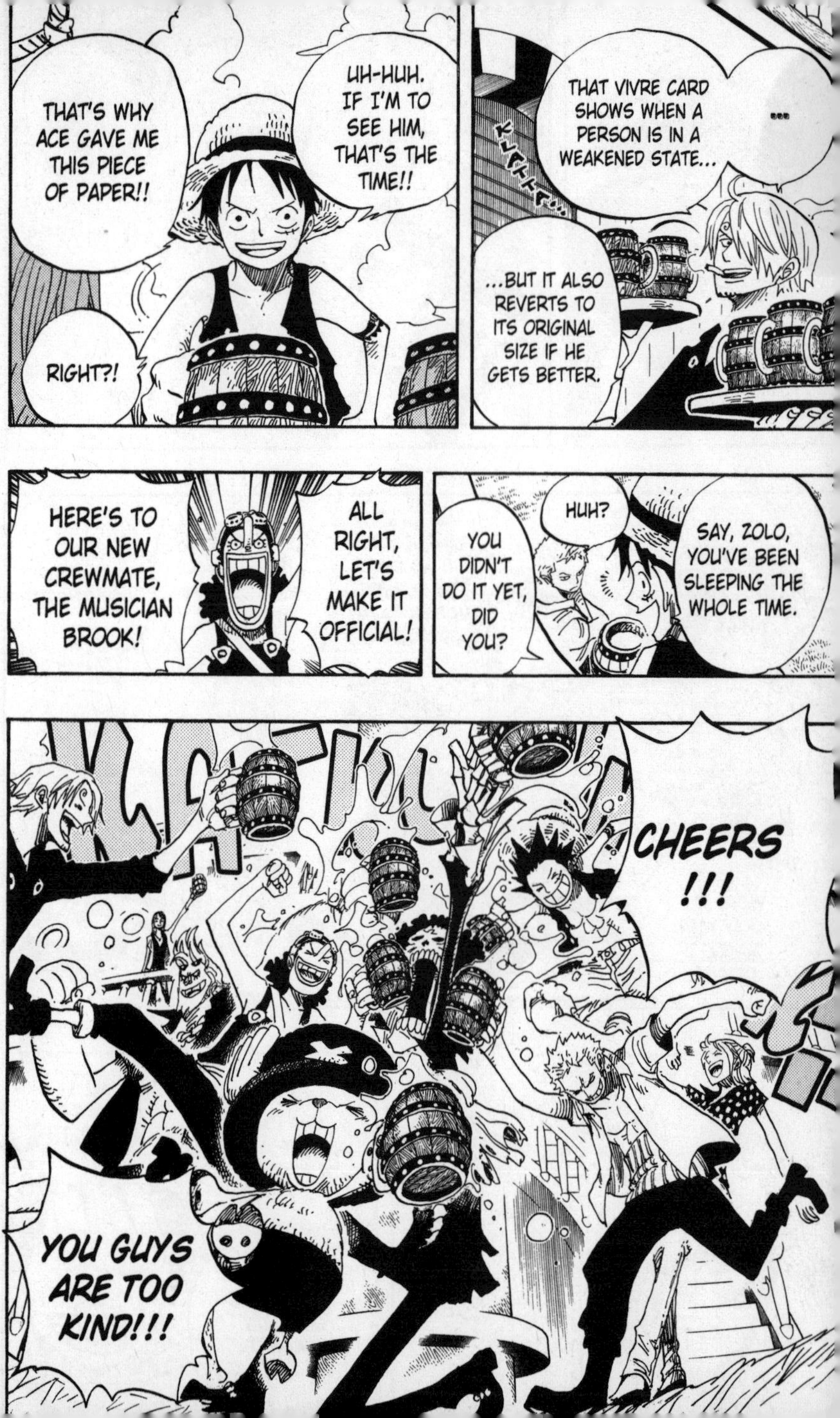
...
THAT VIVRE CARD SHOWS WHEN A PERSON IS IN A WEAKENED STATE...
...BUT IT ALSO REVERTS TO ITS ORIGINAL SIZE IF HE GETS BETTER.
UH-HUH. IF I'M TO SEE HIM, THAT'S THE TIME!!
THAT'S WHY ACE GAVE ME THIS PIECE OF PAPER!!
RIGHT?!
SAY, ZOLO, YOU'VE BEEN SLEEPING THE WHOLE TIME.
HUH?
YOU DIDN'T DO IT YET, DID YOU?
ALL RIGHT, LET'S MAKE IT OFFICIAL!
HERE'S TO OUR NEW CREWMATE, THE MUSICIAN BROOK!
CHEERS !!!
YOU GUYS ARE TOO KIND!!!

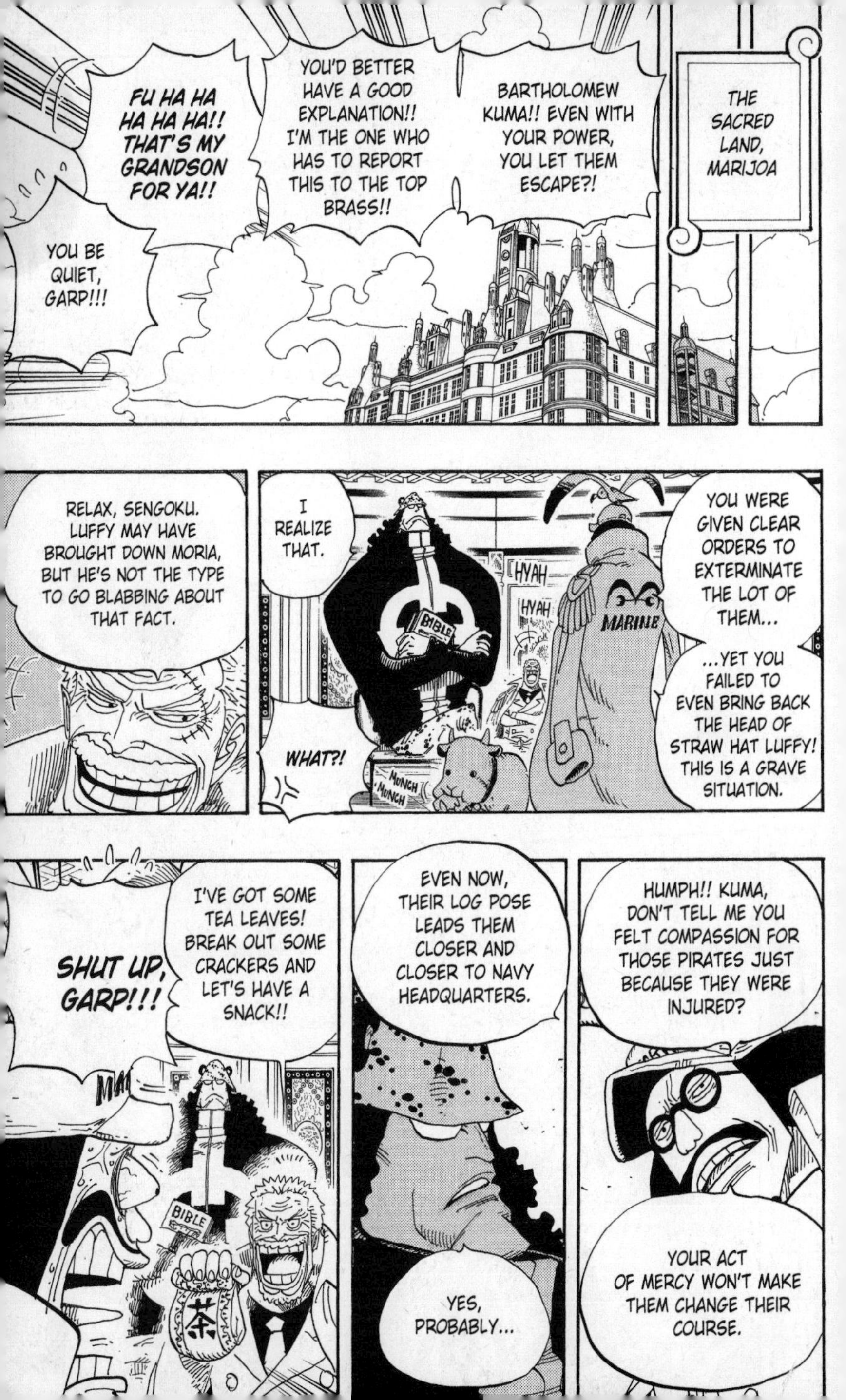
THE SACRED LAND, MARIJOA
BARTHOLOMEW KUMA!! EVEN WITH YOUR POWER, YOU LET THEM ESCAPE?!
YOU'D BETTER HAVE A GOOD EXPLANATION!! I'M THE ONE WHO HAS TO REPORT THIS TO THE TOP BRASS!!
FU HA HA HA HA HA!! THAT'S MY GRANDSON FOR YA!!
YOU BE QUIET, GARP!!!
YOU WERE GIVEN CLEAR ORDERS TO EXTERMINATE THE LOT OF THEM...
...YET YOU FAILED TO EVEN BRING BACK THE HEAD OF STRAW HAT LUFFY! THIS IS A GRAVE SITUATION.
MARINE
HYAH
HYAH
I REALIZE THAT.
BIBLE
WHAT?!
MUNCH MUNCH
RELAX, SENGOKU. LUFFY MAY HAVE BROUGHT DOWN MORIA, BUT HE'S NOT THE TYPE TO GO BLABBING ABOUT THAT FACT.
HUMPH!! KUMA, DON'T TELL ME YOU FELT COMPASSION FOR THOSE PIRATES JUST BECAUSE THEY WERE INJURED?
YOUR ACT OF MERCY WON'T MAKE THEM CHANGE THEIR COURSE.
EVEN NOW, THEIR LOG POSE LEADS THEM CLOSER AND CLOSER TO NAVY HEADQUARTERS.
YES, PROBABLY...
I'VE GOT SOME TEA LEAVES! BREAK OUT SOME CRACKERS AND LET'S HAVE A SNACK!!
SHUT UP, GARP!!!
MM
BIBLE
茶

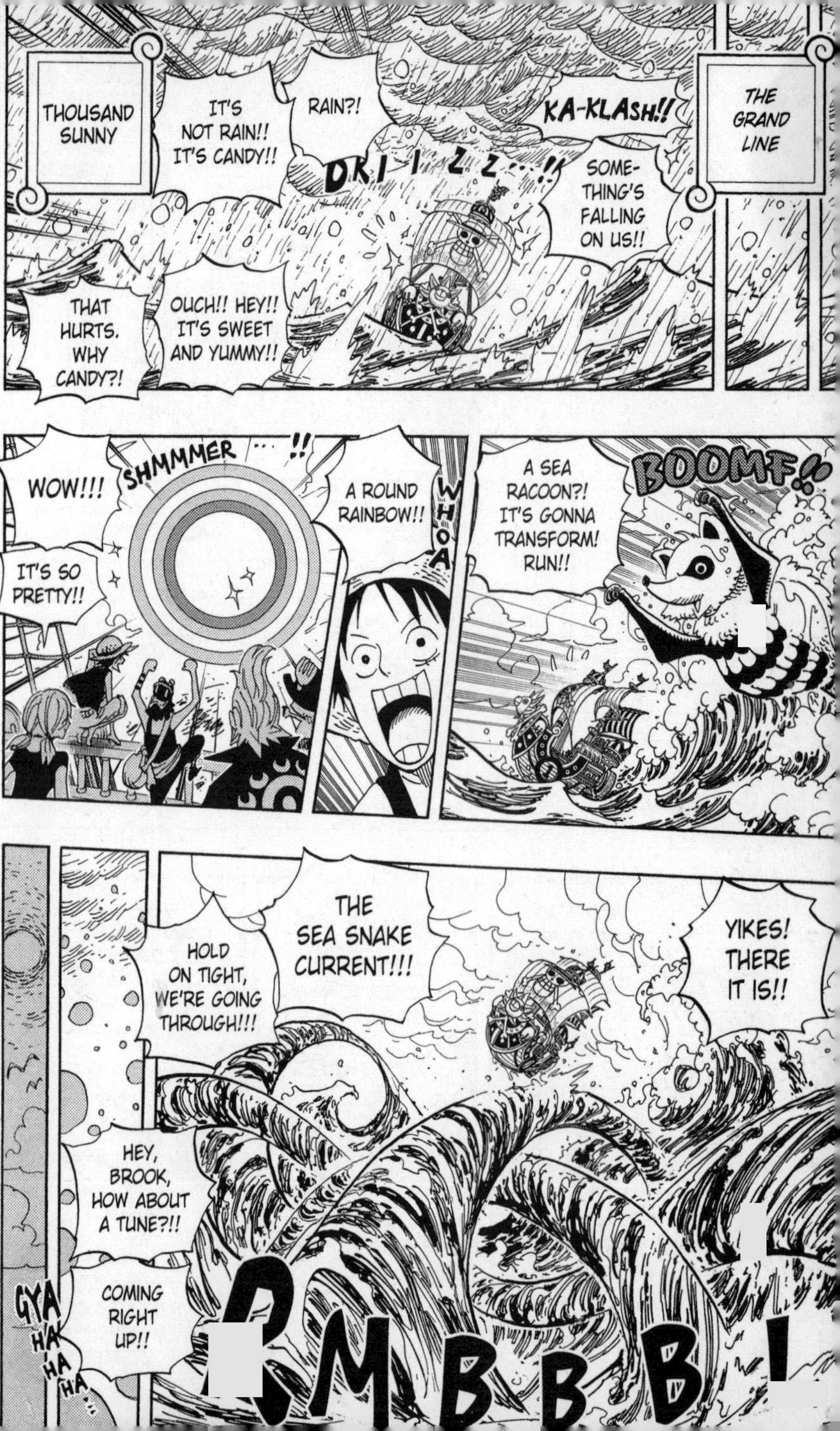
THE GRAND LINE
KA-KLASH!!
SOME-THING'S FALLING ON US!!
RAIN?!
DRIZZZ...!!
IT'S NOT RAIN!! IT'S CANDY!!
THOUSAND SUNNY
OUCH!! HEY!! IT'S SWEET AND YUMMY!!
THAT HURTS. WHY CANDY?!
BOOMF!!
A SEA RACOON?! IT'S GONNA TRANSFORM! RUN!!
WHOA
A ROUND RAINBOW!!
...!!
SHMMMER
WOW!!!
IT'S SO PRETTY!!
YIKES! THERE IT IS!!
THE SEA SNAKE CURRENT!!!
HOLD ON TIGHT, WE'RE GOING THROUGH!!!
HEY, BROOK, HOW ABOUT A TUNE?!!
COMING RIGHT UP!!
GYAHAHAHAHA...

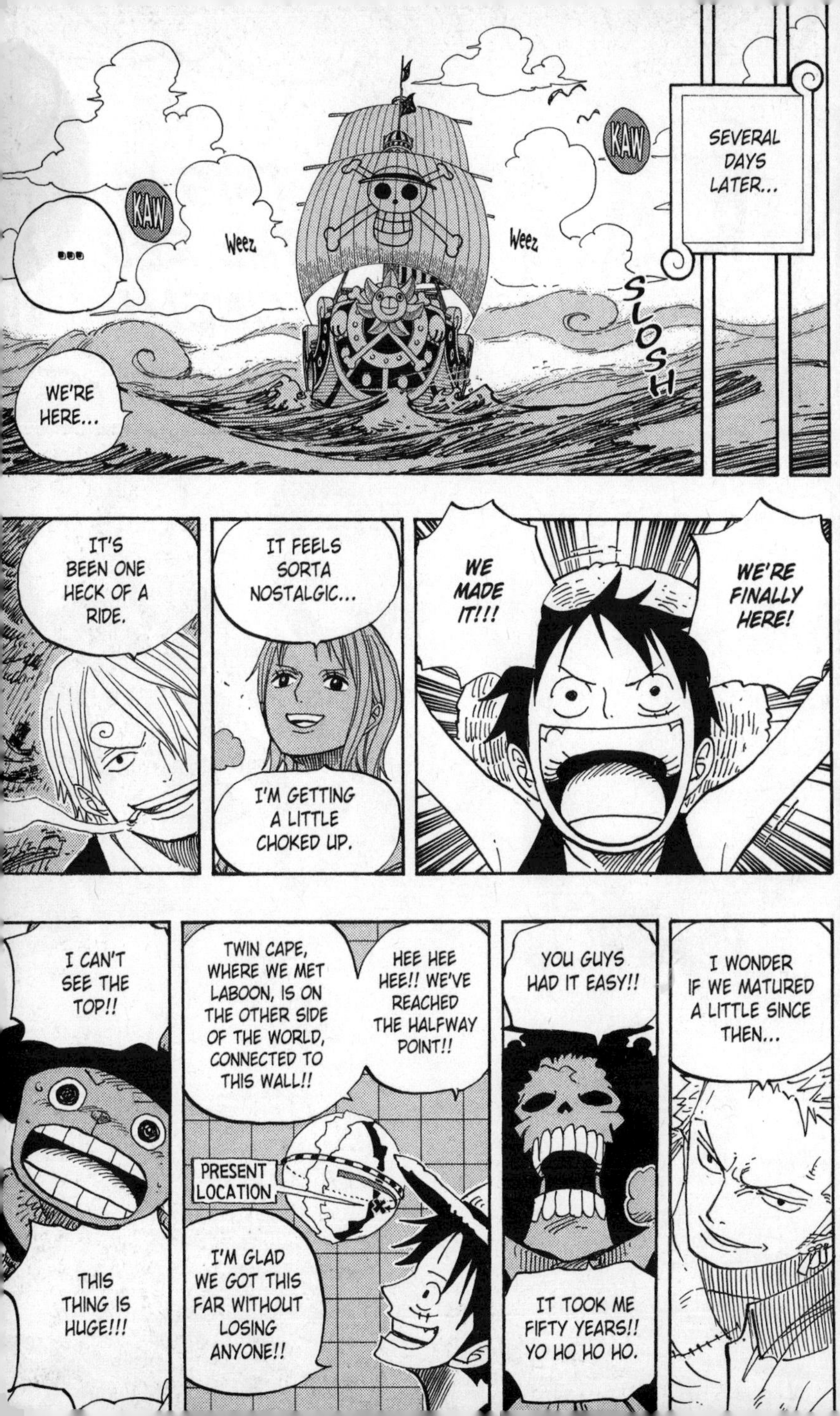

SEVERAL DAYS LATER...
KAW
Weez
SLOSH
Weez
KAW
...
WE'RE HERE...
WE'RE FINALLY HERE!
WE MADE IT!!!
IT FEELS SORTA NOSTALGIC...
I'M GETTING A LITTLE CHOKED UP.
IT'S BEEN ONE HECK OF A RIDE.
I WONDER IF WE MATURED A LITTLE SINCE THEN...
YOU GUYS HAD IT EASY!!
IT TOOK ME FIFTY YEARS!! YO HO HO HO.
HEE HEE HEE!! WE'VE REACHED THE HALFWAY POINT!!
TWIN CAPE, WHERE WE MET LABOON, IS ON THE OTHER SIDE OF THE WORLD, CONNECTED TO THIS WALL!!
PRESENT LOCATION
I'M GLAD WE GOT THIS FAR WITHOUT LOSING ANYONE!!
I CAN'T SEE THE TOP!!
THIS THING IS HUGE!!!

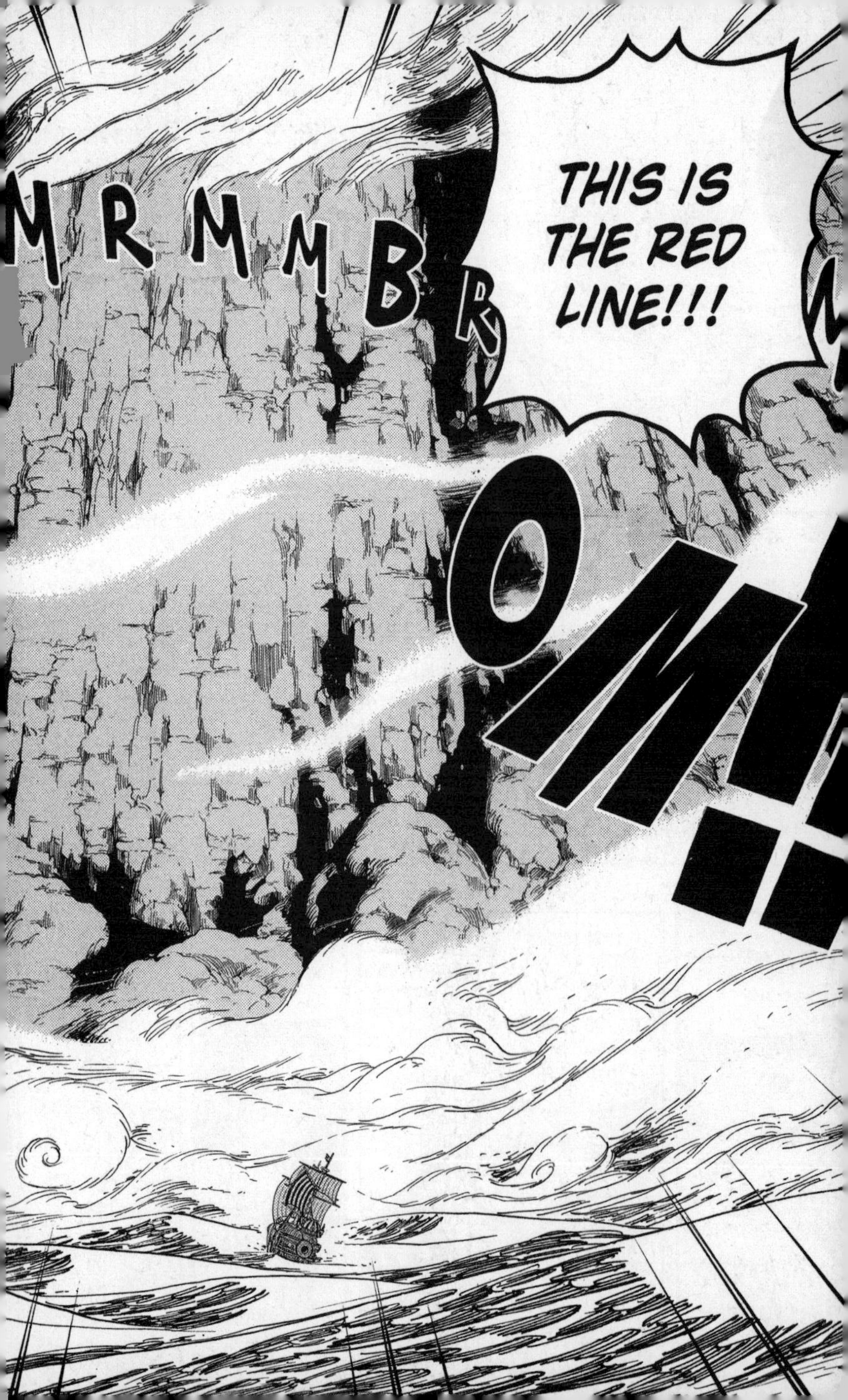
THIS IS THE RED LINE!!!
MRMMBROM!!

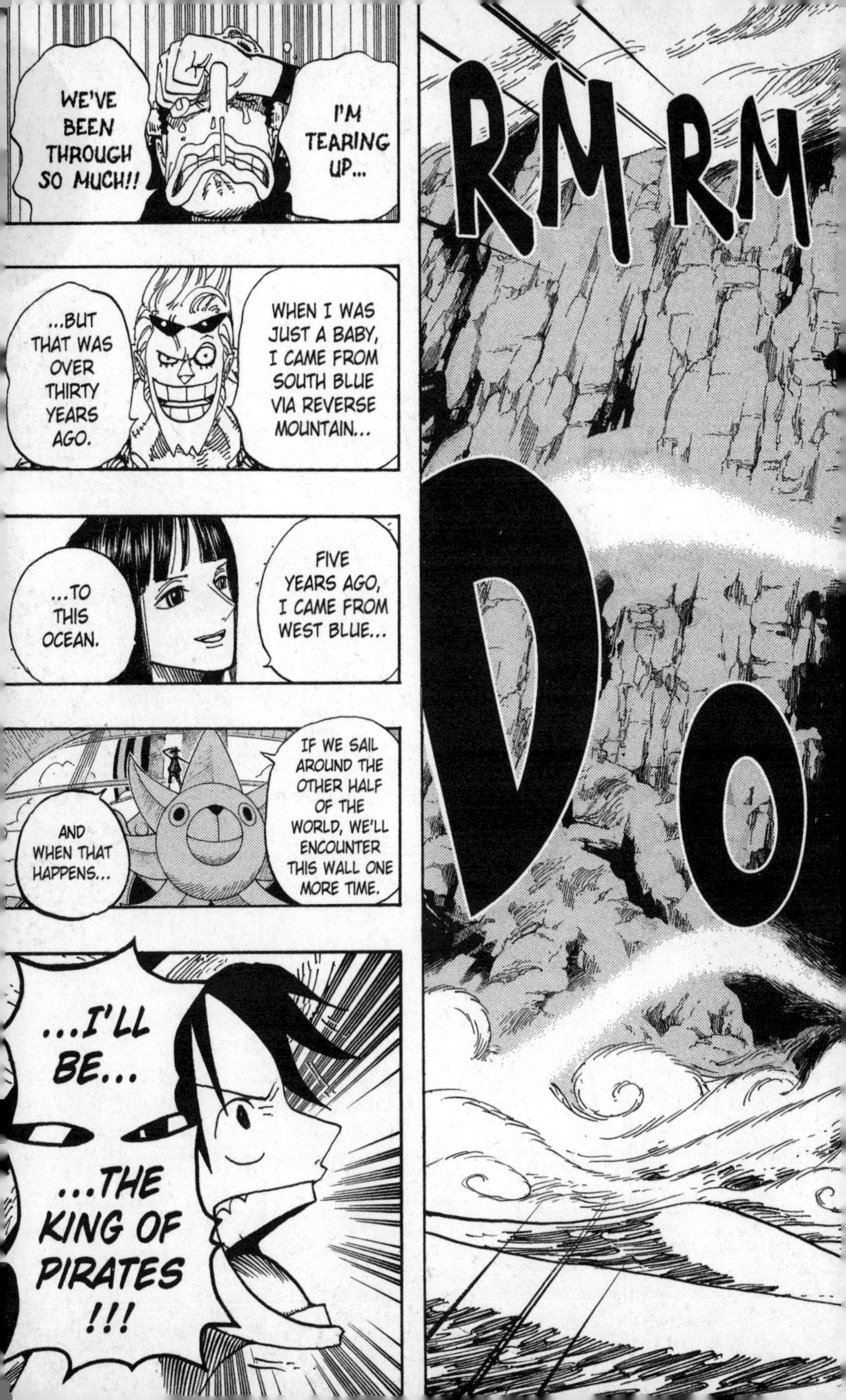
RM RM
DO
I'M TEARING UP...
WE'VE BEEN THROUGH SO MUCH!!
WHEN I WAS JUST A BABY, I CAME FROM SOUTH BLUE VIA REVERSE MOUNTAIN...
...BUT THAT WAS OVER THIRTY YEARS AGO.
FIVE YEARS AGO, I CAME FROM WEST BLUE...
...TO THIS OCEAN.
IF WE SAIL AROUND THE OTHER HALF OF THE WORLD, WE'LL ENCOUNTER THIS WALL ONE MORE TIME.
AND WHEN THAT HAPPENS...
...I'LL BE...
...THE KING OF PIRATES!!!

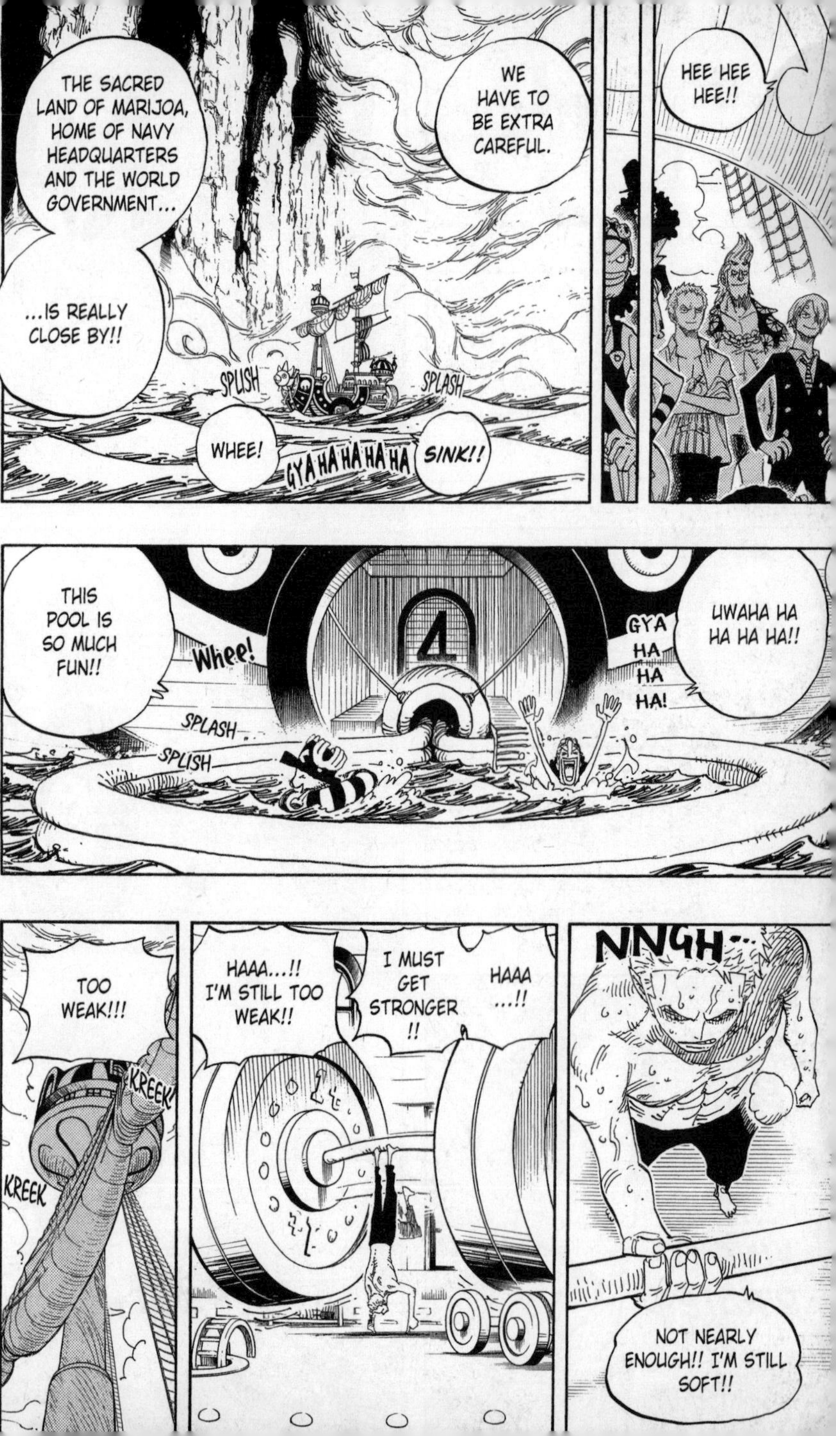
HEE HEE HEE!!
WE HAVE TO BE EXTRA CAREFUL.
THE SACRED LAND OF MARIJOA, HOME OF NAVY HEADQUARTERS AND THE WORLD GOVERNMENT...
...IS REALLY CLOSE BY!!
SPLASH
SINK!!
GYA HA HA HA HA
SPLUSH
WHEE!
UWAHA HA HA HA HA!!
GYA HA HA HA!
Whee!
THIS POOL IS SO MUCH FUN!!
SPLASH
SPLISH
NNGH...
NOT NEARLY ENOUGH!! I'M STILL SOFT!!
HAAA ...!!
I MUST GET STRONGER !!
HAAA...!! I'M STILL TOO WEAK!!
TOO WEAK!!!
KREEK
KREEK

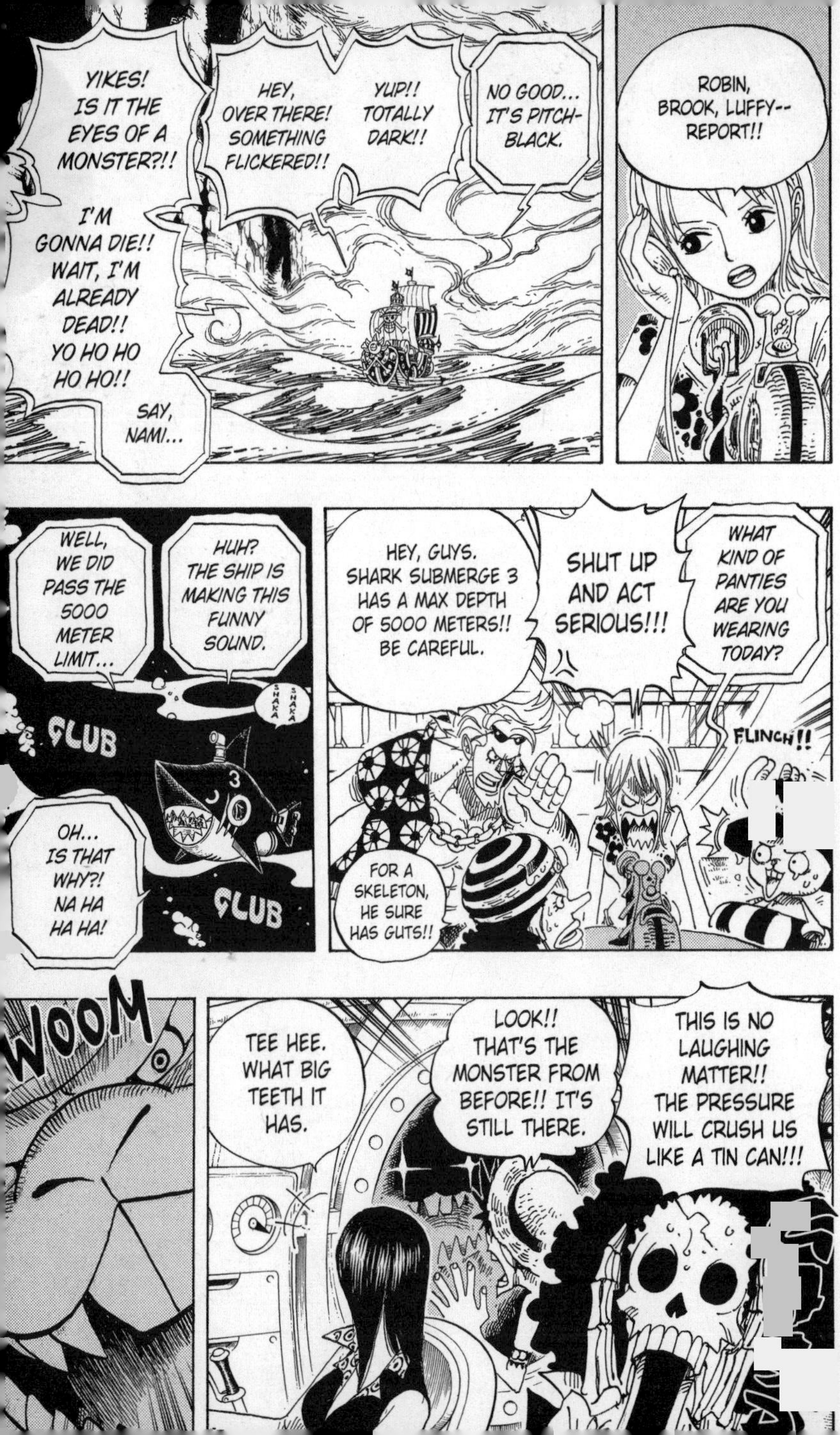

ROBIN, BROOK, LUFFY-- REPORT!!
NO GOOD... IT'S PITCH-BLACK.
YUP!! TOTALLY DARK!!
HEY, OVER THERE! SOMETHING FLICKERED!!
YIKES! IS IT THE EYES OF A MONSTER?!!
I'M GONNA DIE!! WAIT, I'M ALREADY DEAD!! YO HO HO HO HO!!
SAY, NAMI...
WHAT KIND OF PANTIES ARE YOU WEARING TODAY?
SHUT UP AND ACT SERIOUS!!!
FLINCH!!
HEY, GUYS. SHARK SUBMERGE 3 HAS A MAX DEPTH OF 5000 METERS!! BE CAREFUL.
FOR A SKELETON, HE SURE HAS GUTS!!
HUH? THE SHIP IS MAKING THIS FUNNY SOUND.
WELL, WE DID PASS THE 5000 METER LIMIT...
SHAKA SHAKA
GLUB
OH... IS THAT WHY?! NA HA HA HA!
GLUB
THIS IS NO LAUGHING MATTER!! THE PRESSURE WILL CRUSH US LIKE A TIN CAN!!!
LOOK!! THAT'S THE MONSTER FROM BEFORE!! IT'S STILL THERE.
TEE HEE. WHAT BIG TEETH IT HAS.
WOOM

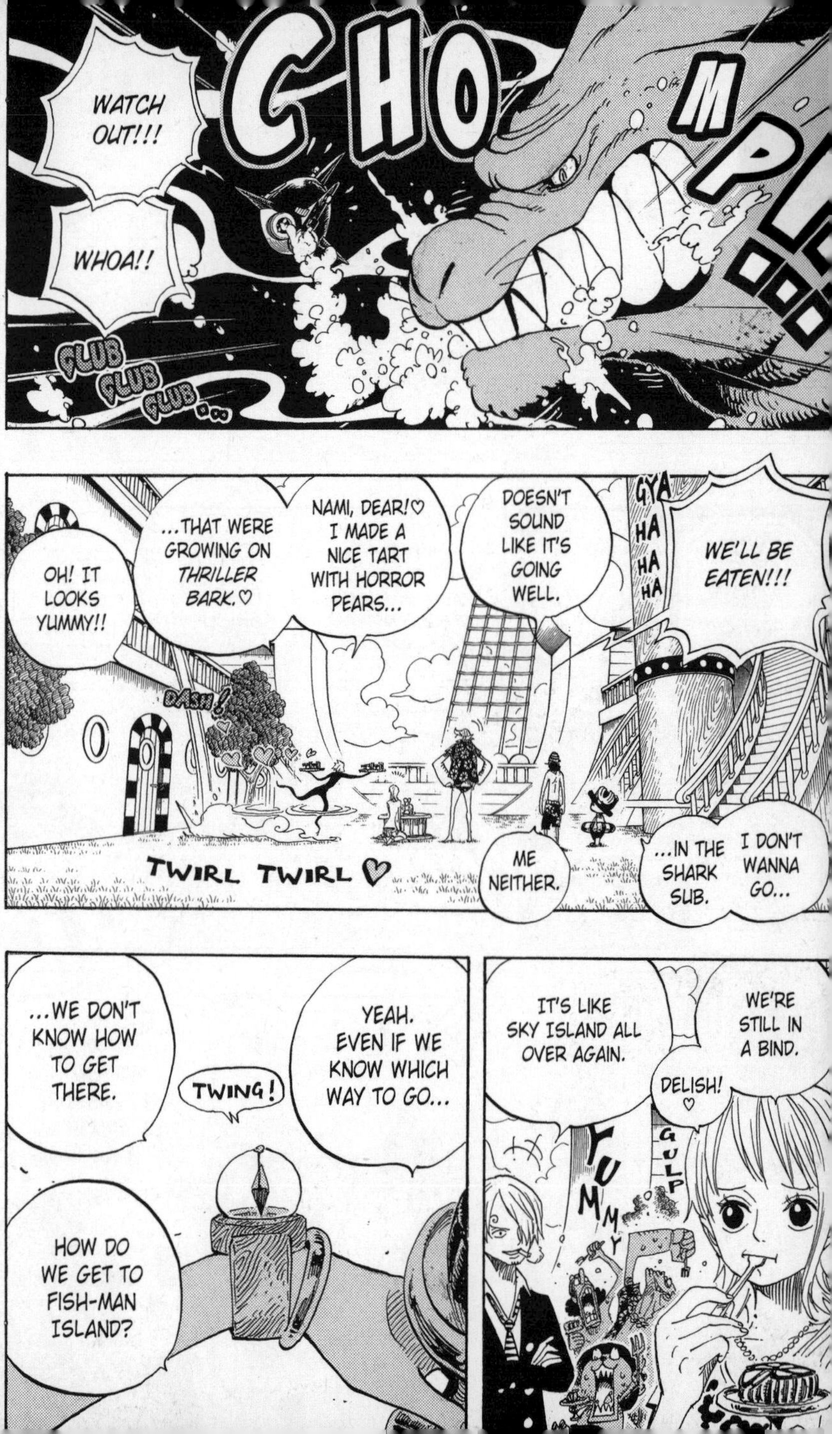
CHOMP...
WATCH OUT!!!
WHOA!!
GLUB GLUB GLUB...
WE'LL BE EATEN!!!
GYA HA HA HA HA
DOESN'T SOUND LIKE IT'S GOING WELL.
NAMI, DEAR!♡ I MADE A NICE TART WITH HORROR PEARS...
...THAT WERE GROWING ON THRILLER BARK.♡
OH! IT LOOKS YUMMY!!
DASH!
I DON'T WANNA GO...
...IN THE SHARK SUB.
ME NEITHER.
TWIRL TWIRL ♡
WE'RE STILL IN A BIND.
IT'S LIKE SKY ISLAND ALL OVER AGAIN.
DELISH!♡
GULP
YUMMMY
YEAH. EVEN IF WE KNOW WHICH WAY TO GO...
...WE DON'T KNOW HOW TO GET THERE.
TWING!
HOW DO WE GET TO FISH-MAN ISLAND?

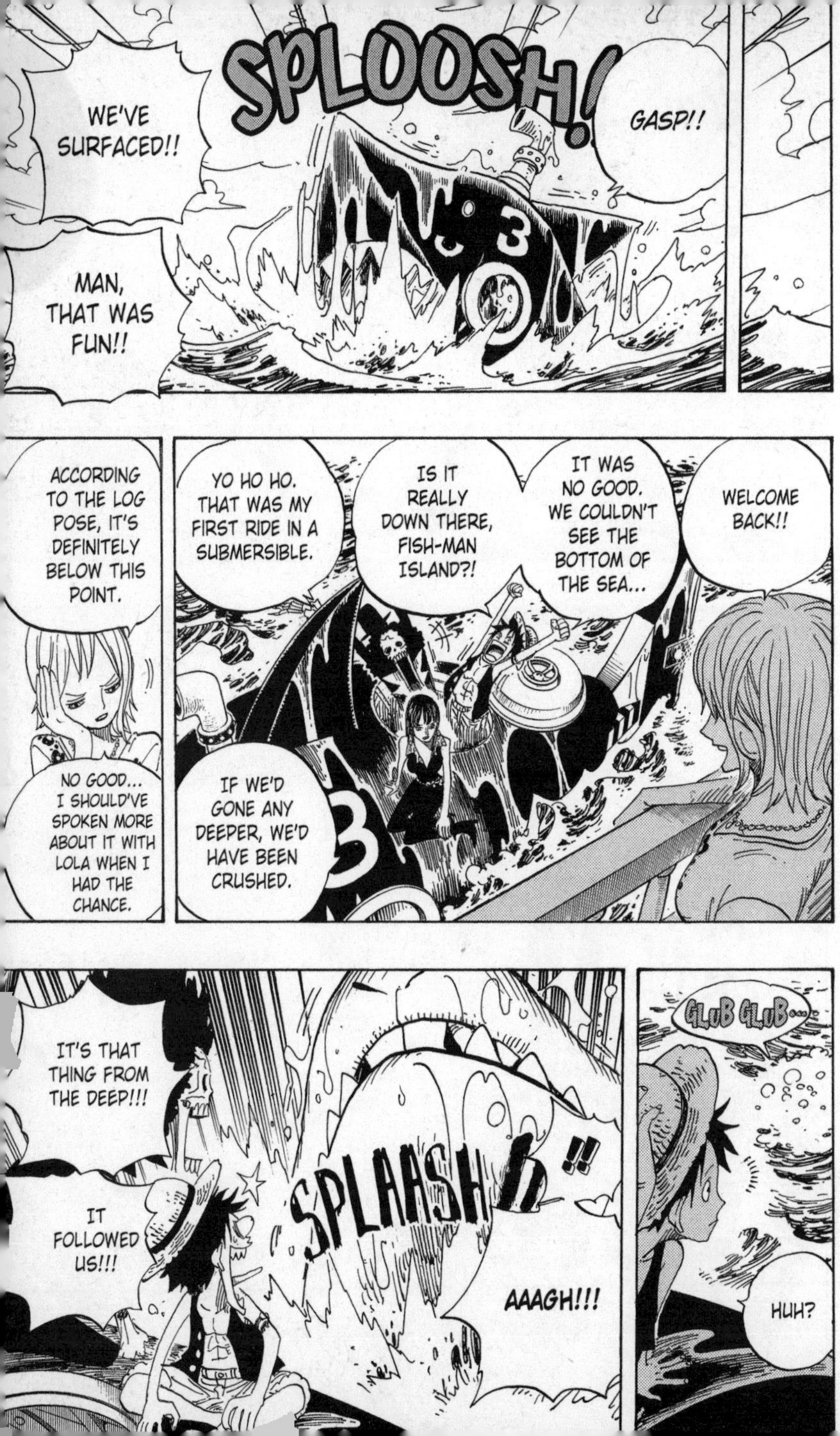
SPLOOSH!
GASP!!
WE'VE SURFACED!!
MAN, THAT WAS FUN!!
WELCOME BACK!!
IT WAS NO GOOD. WE COULDN'T SEE THE BOTTOM OF THE SEA...
IS IT REALLY DOWN THERE, FISH-MAN ISLAND?!
YO HO HO. THAT WAS MY FIRST RIDE IN A SUBMERSIBLE.
IF WE'D GONE ANY DEEPER, WE'D HAVE BEEN CRUSHED.
ACCORDING TO THE LOG POSE, IT'S DEFINITELY BELOW THIS POINT.
NO GOOD... I SHOULD'VE SPOKEN MORE ABOUT IT WITH LOLA WHEN I HAD THE CHANCE.
GLUB GLUB...
HUH?
SPLAASH!!
IT'S THAT THING FROM THE DEEP!!!
AAAGH!!!
IT FOLLOWED US!!!

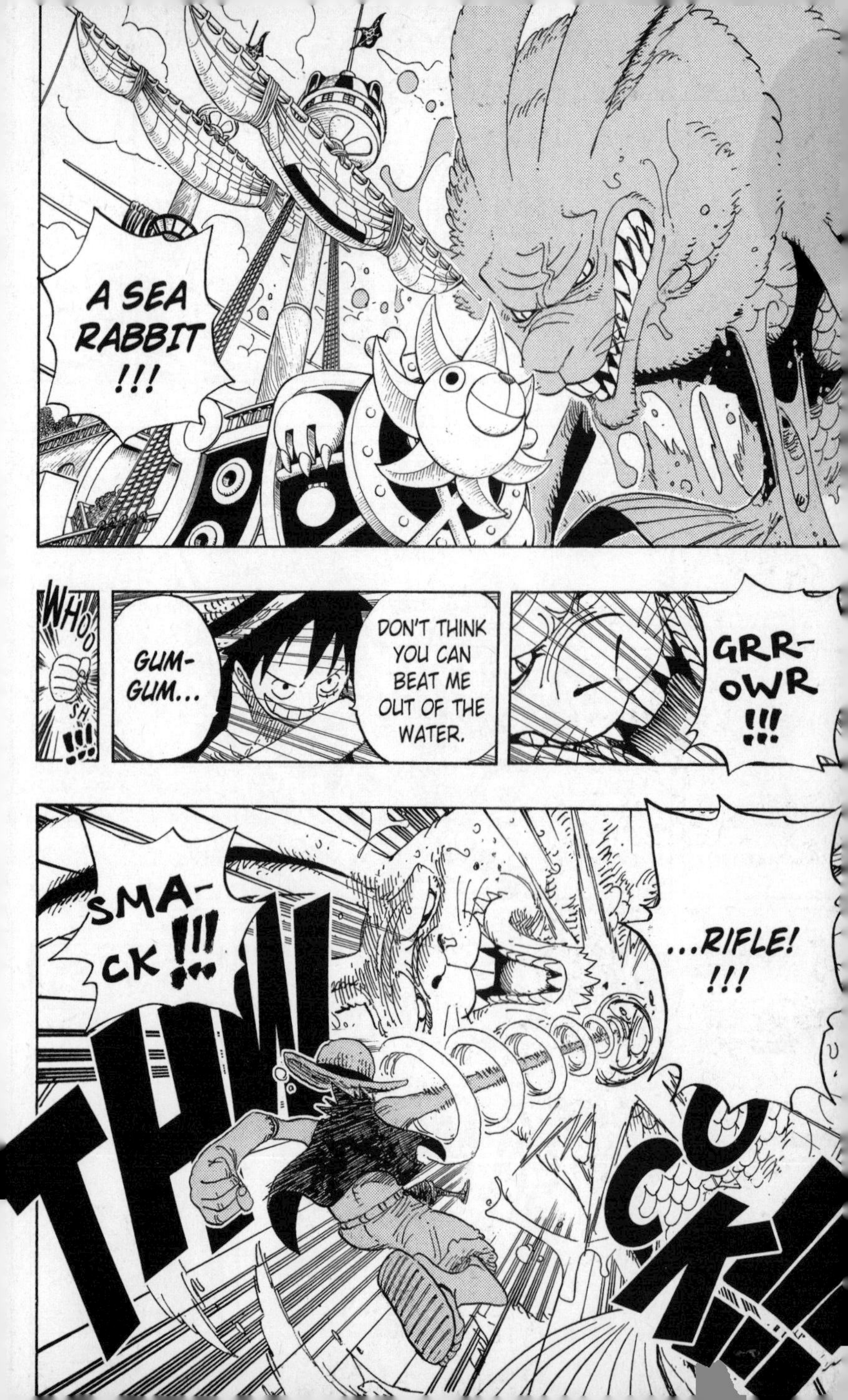
A SEA RABBIT!!!
GRR-OWR!!!
DON'T THINK YOU CAN BEAT ME OUT OF THE WATER.
GUM-GUM...
WHOOSH!!!
...RIFLE! !!!
SMA-CK!!!
THW
CK

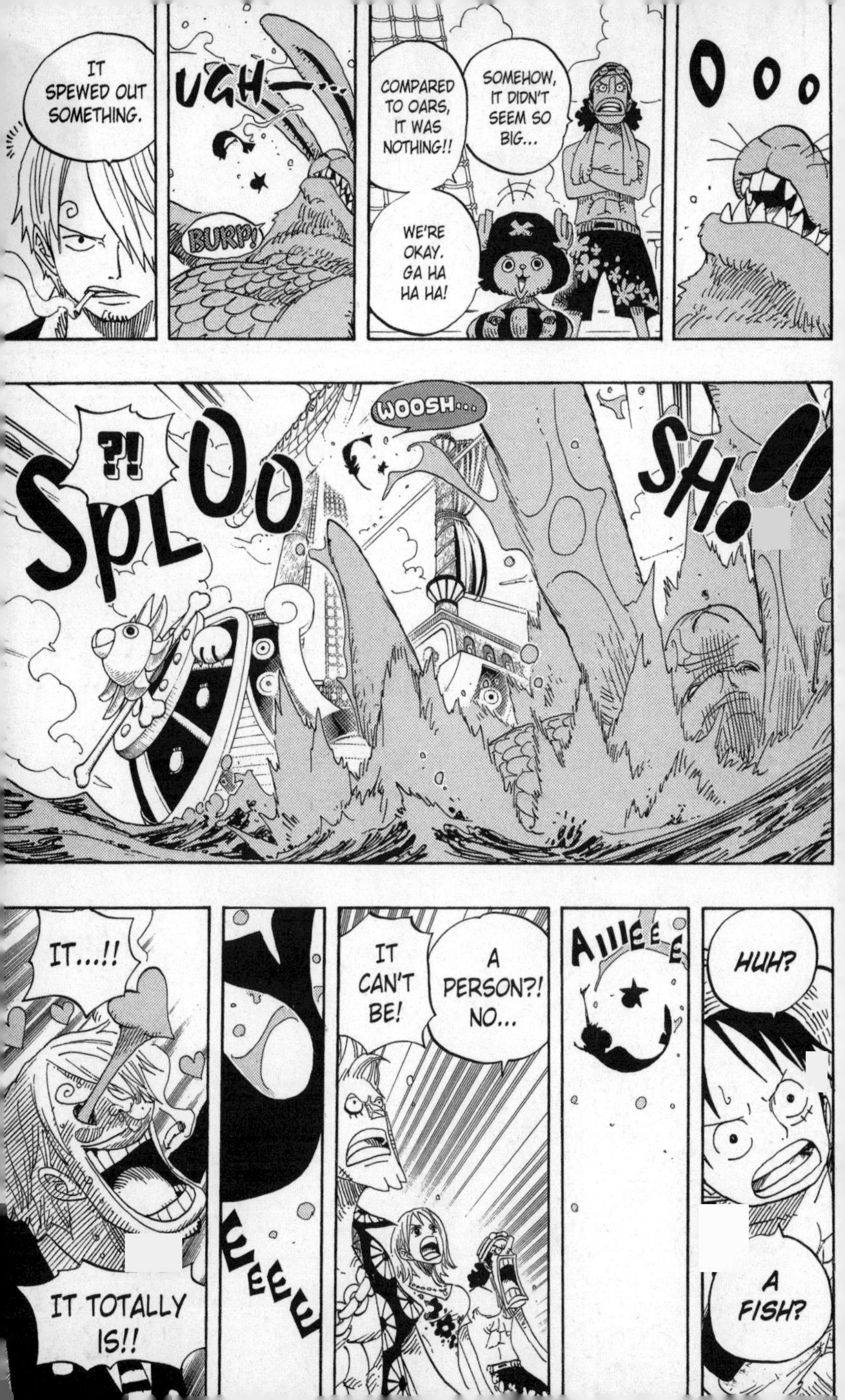
O O O
SOMEHOW, IT DIDN'T SEEM SO BIG...
COMPARED TO OARS, IT WAS NOTHING!!
WE'RE OKAY. GA HA HA HA!
UGH—...
BURP!
IT SPEWED OUT SOMETHING.
SHO
WOOSH...
?!
SPLOO
HUH?
A FISH?
AIIIEEE
A PERSON?! NO...
IT CAN'T BE!
EEEW
IT...!!
IT TOTALLY IS!!

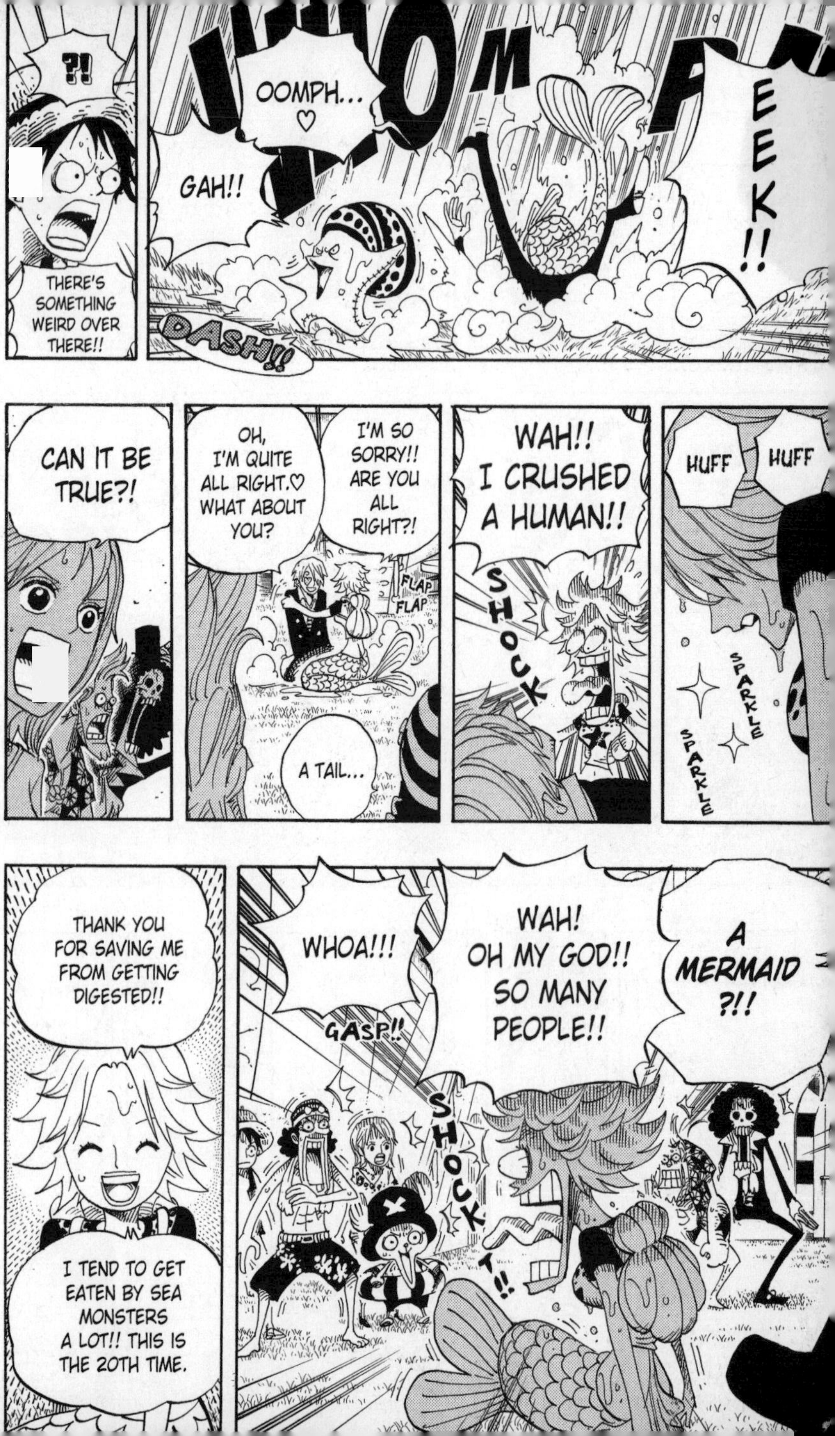
EEK!!
OOMPH... ♡
GAH!!
DASH!!
?!
THERE'S SOMETHING WEIRD OVER THERE!!
HUFF
HUFF
SPARKLE
SPARKLE
WAH!! I CRUSHED A HUMAN!!
SHOCK
I'M SO SORRY!! ARE YOU ALL RIGHT?!
OH, I'M QUITE ALL RIGHT.♡ WHAT ABOUT YOU?
FLAP
FLAP
A TAIL...
CAN IT BE TRUE?!
A MERMAID?!!
WAH! OH MY GOD!! SO MANY PEOPLE!!
WHOA!!!
GASP!!
SHOCK!!
THANK YOU FOR SAVING ME FROM GETTING DIGESTED!!
I TEND TO GET EATEN BY SEA MONSTERS A LOT!! THIS IS THE 20TH TIME.

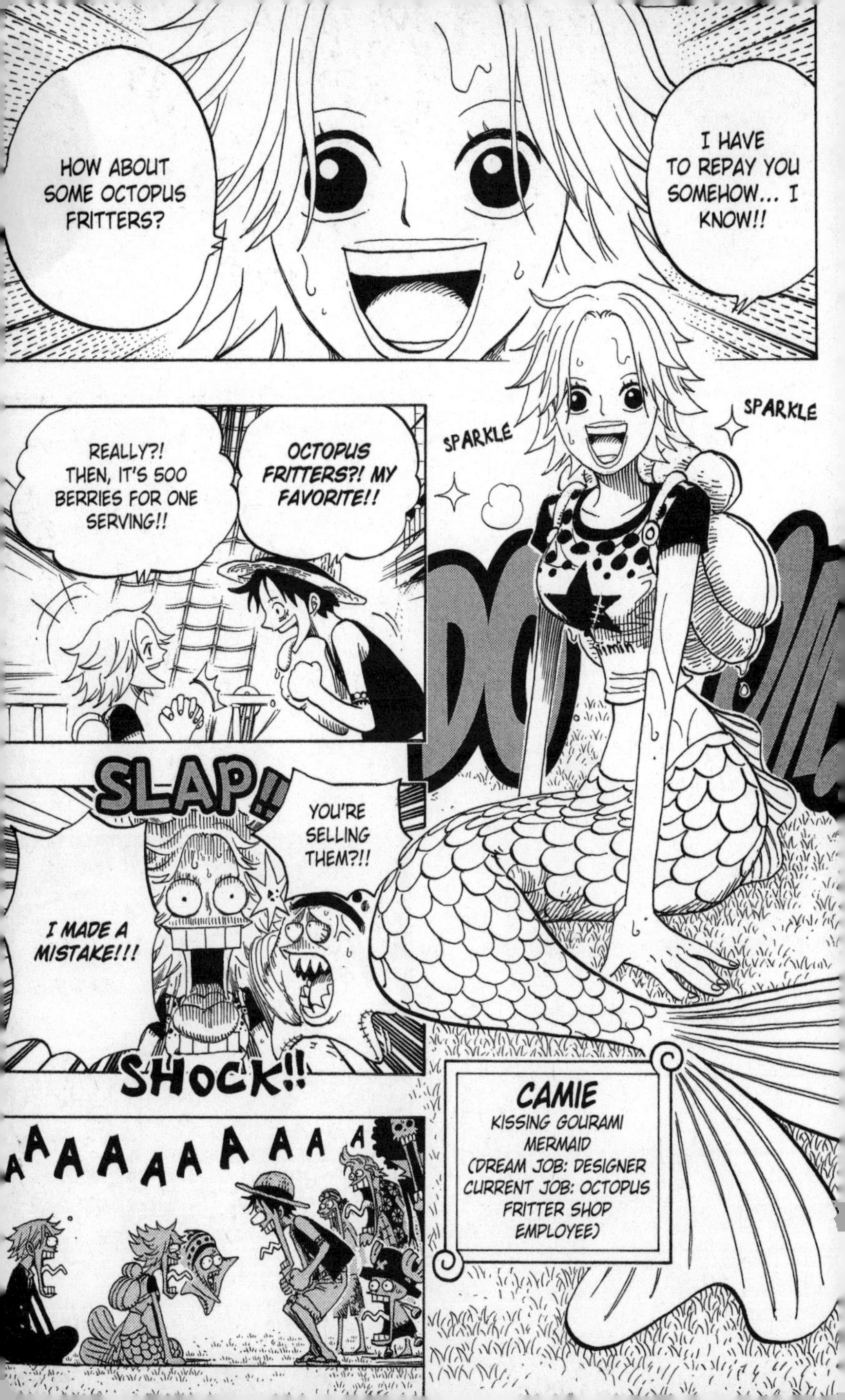

I HAVE TO REPAY YOU SOMEHOW... I KNOW!!
HOW ABOUT SOME OCTOPUS FRITTERS?
SPARKLE
SPARKLE
CAMIE
KISSING GOURAMI MERMAID
(DREAM JOB: DESIGNER CURRENT JOB: OCTOPUS FRITTER SHOP EMPLOYEE)
OCTOPUS FRITTERS?! MY FAVORITE!!
REALLY?! THEN, IT'S 500 BERRIES FOR ONE SERVING!!
SLAP!!
YOU'RE SELLING THEM?!!
I MADE A MISTAKE!!!
SHOCK!!
AAAAAAAAAAA

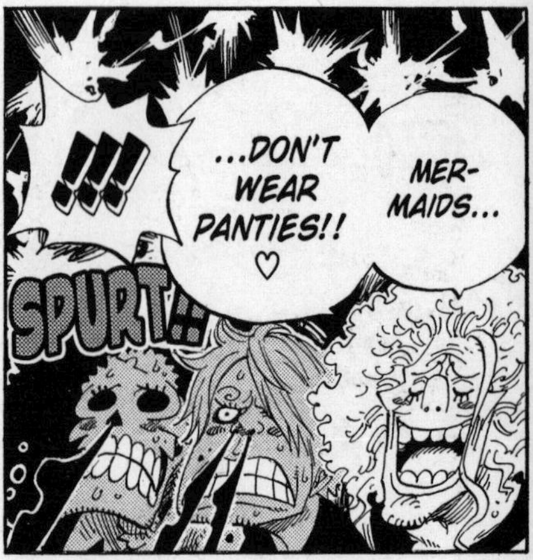
MER-
MAIDS...
...DON'T
WEAR
PANTIES!!
♡
!!!
SPURT!!

Chapter 491:
FLYING FISH RIDERS

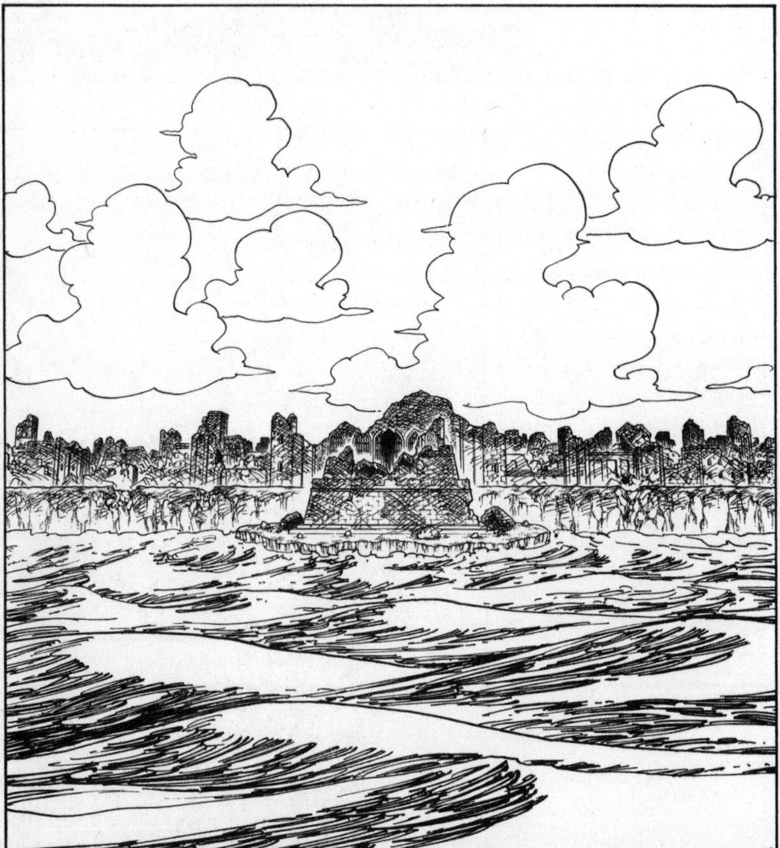

LIMITED COVER SERIES, NO. 10:
"ISLAND OF NO SURVIVORS"

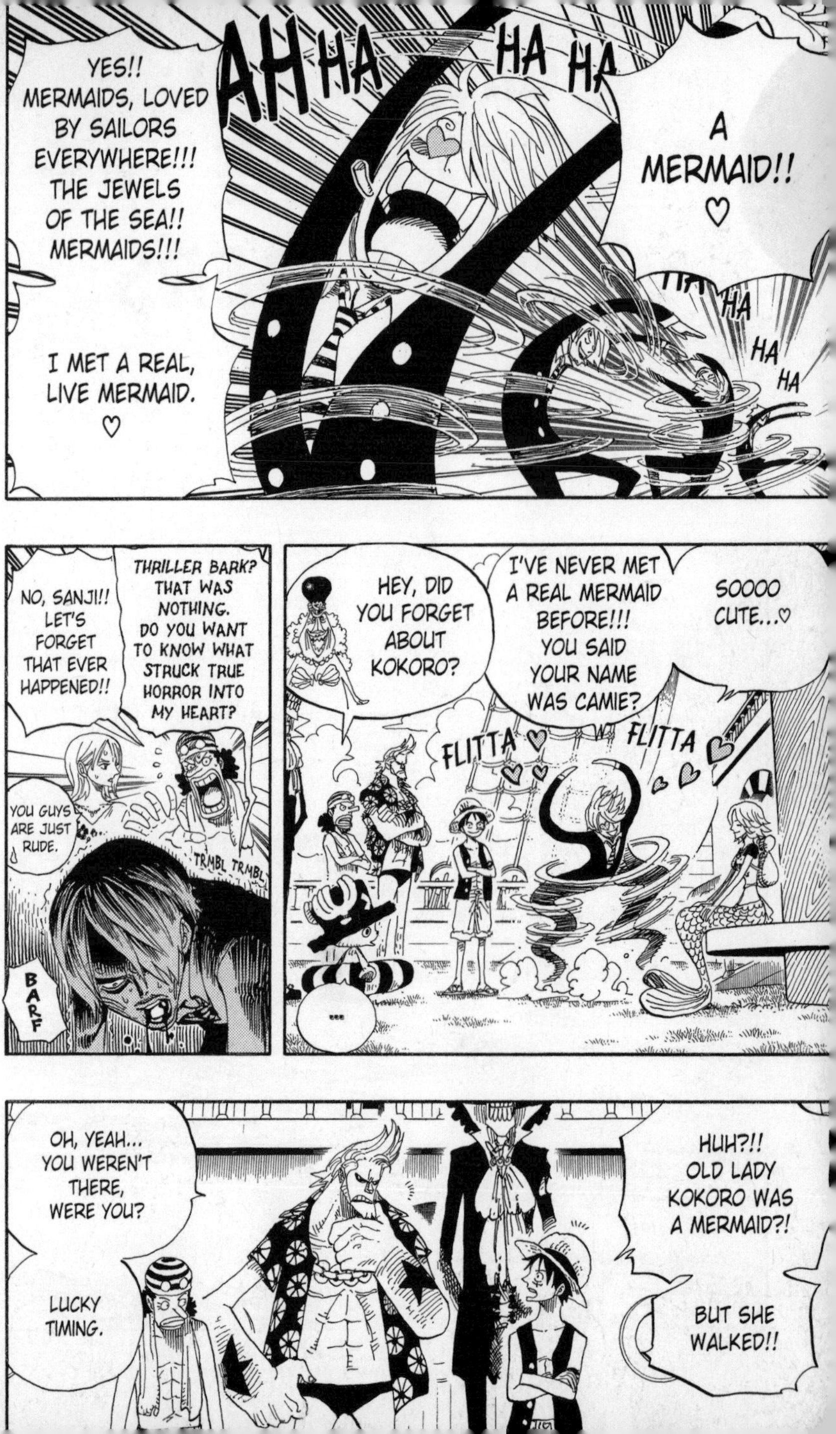
A MERMAID!! ♡
HA HA HA HA
AHHA HA HA HA
YES!! MERMAIDS, LOVED BY SAILORS EVERYWHERE!!! THE JEWELS OF THE SEA!! MERMAIDS!!!
I MET A REAL, LIVE MERMAID. ♡
SOOOO CUTE...♡
I'VE NEVER MET A REAL MERMAID BEFORE!!! YOU SAID YOUR NAME WAS CAMIE?
HEY, DID YOU FORGET ABOUT KOKORO?
FLITTA
FLITTA
...
THRILLER BARK? THAT WAS NOTHING. DO YOU WANT TO KNOW WHAT STRUCK TRUE HORROR INTO MY HEART?
NO, SANJI!! LET'S FORGET THAT EVER HAPPENED!!
YOU GUYS ARE JUST RUDE.
TRMBL TRMBL
BARF
HUH?!! OLD LADY KOKORO WAS A MERMAID?!
BUT SHE WALKED!!
OH, YEAH... YOU WEREN'T THERE, WERE YOU?
LUCKY TIMING.

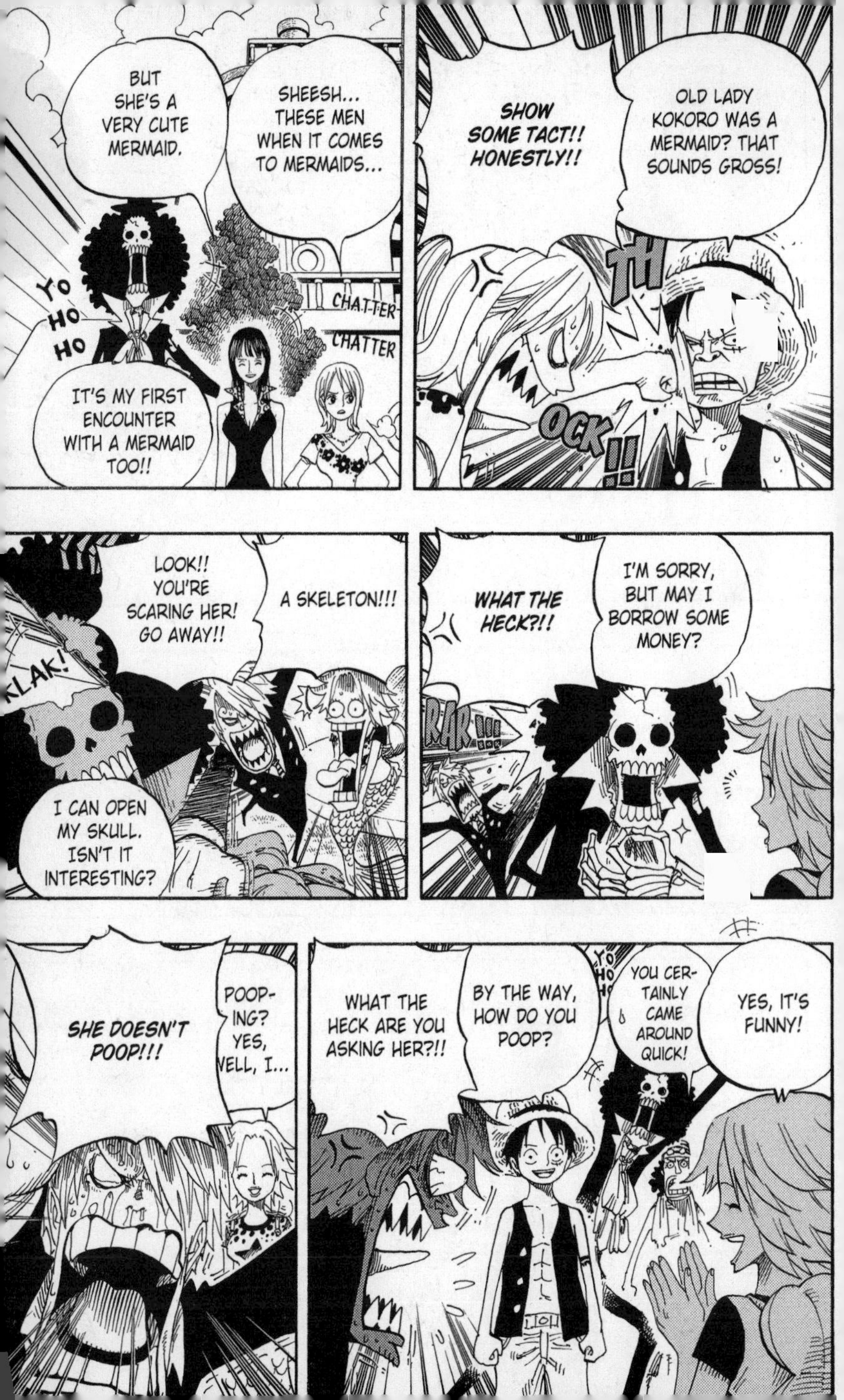
OLD LADY KOKORO WAS A MERMAID? THAT SOUNDS GROSS!
SHOW SOME TACT!! HONESTLY!!
TH
OCK!!
SHEESH... THESE MEN WHEN IT COMES TO MERMAIDS...
BUT SHE'S A VERY CUTE MERMAID.
CHATTER
CHATTER
YO HO HO
IT'S MY FIRST ENCOUNTER WITH A MERMAID TOO!!
I'M SORRY, BUT MAY I BORROW SOME MONEY?
WHAT THE HECK?!!
RAR!!!
A SKELETON!!!
LOOK!! YOU'RE SCARING HER! GO AWAY!!
KLAK!
I CAN OPEN MY SKULL. ISN'T IT INTERESTING?
YES, IT'S FUNNY!
YOU CERTAINLY CAME AROUND QUICK!
BY THE WAY, HOW DO YOU POOP?
WHAT THE HECK ARE YOU ASKING HER?!!
POOPING? YES, WELL, I...
SHE DOESN'T POOP!!!

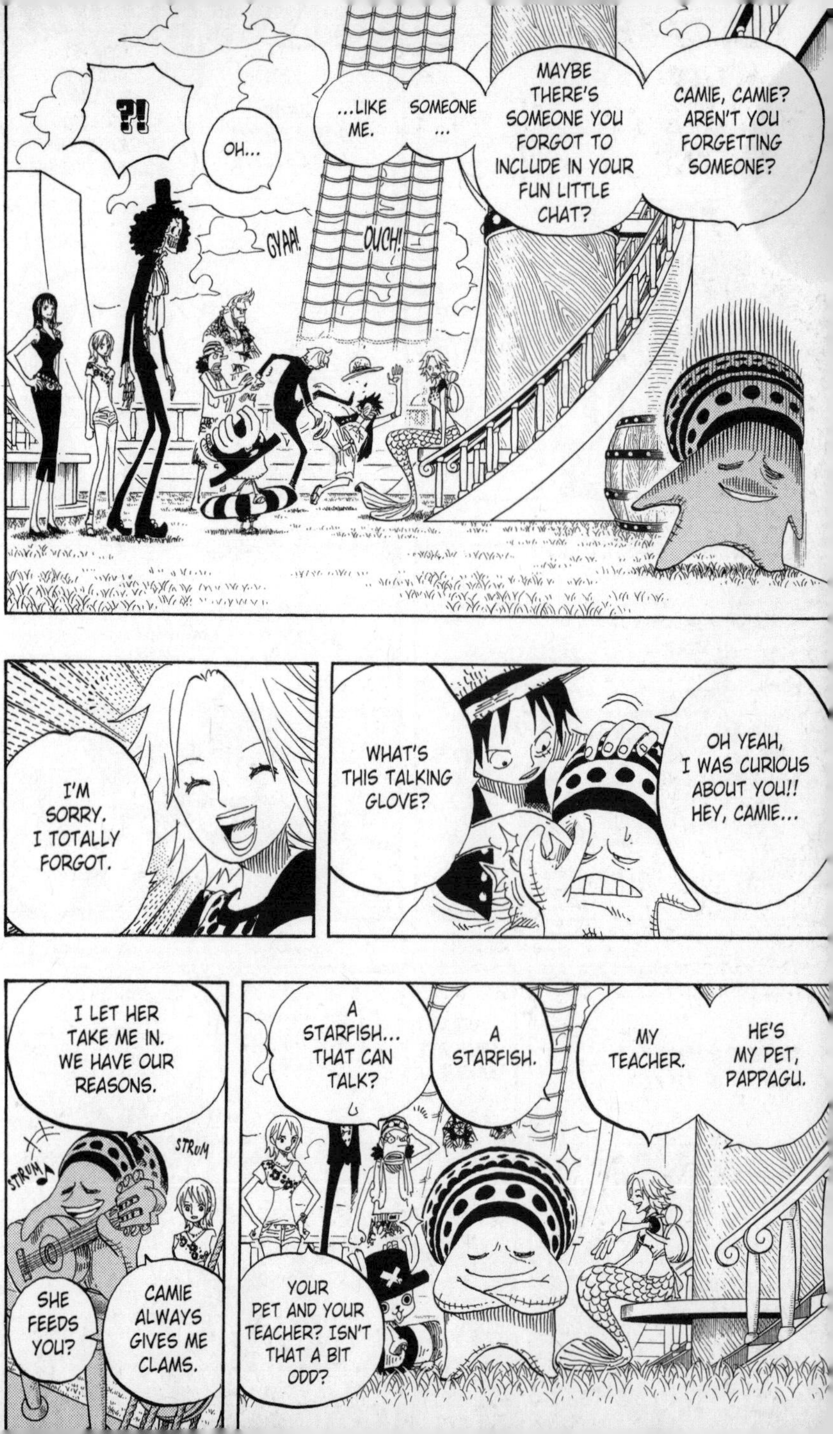
CAMIE, CAMIE? AREN'T YOU FORGETTING SOMEONE?
MAYBE THERE'S SOMEONE YOU FORGOT TO INCLUDE IN YOUR FUN LITTLE CHAT?
SOMEONE ...
...LIKE ME.
OH...
?!
OUCH!
GYAA!
OH YEAH, I WAS CURIOUS ABOUT YOU!! HEY, CAMIE...
WHAT'S THIS TALKING GLOVE?
I'M SORRY. I TOTALLY FORGOT.
HE'S MY PET, PAPPAGU.
MY TEACHER.
A STARFISH.
A STARFISH... THAT CAN TALK?
YOUR PET AND YOUR TEACHER? ISN'T THAT A BIT ODD?
I LET HER TAKE ME IN. WE HAVE OUR REASONS.
STRUM
STRUM
CAMIE ALWAYS GIVES ME CLAMS.
SHE FEEDS YOU?

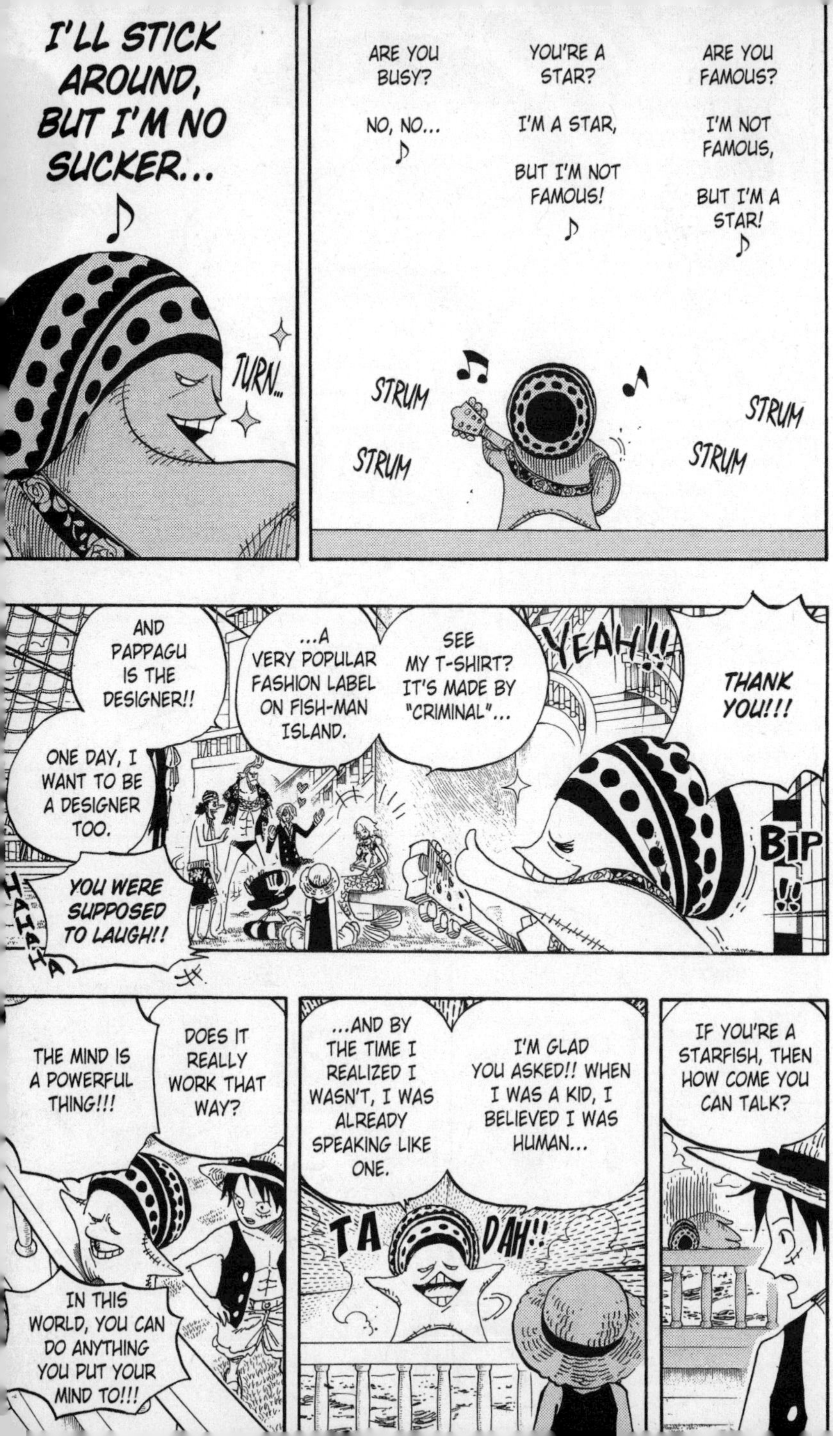
ARE YOU FAMOUS?
I'M NOT FAMOUS,
BUT I'M A STAR! ♪
YOU'RE A STAR?
I'M A STAR,
BUT I'M NOT FAMOUS! ♪
ARE YOU BUSY?
NO, NO... ♪
STRUM
STRUM
STRUM
STRUM
I'LL STICK AROUND, BUT I'M NO SUCKER... ♪
TURN...
YEAH!!
THANK YOU!!!
BIP!!
SEE MY T-SHIRT? IT'S MADE BY "CRIMINAL"...
...A VERY POPULAR FASHION LABEL ON FISH-MAN ISLAND.
AND PAPPAGU IS THE DESIGNER!!
ONE DAY, I WANT TO BE A DESIGNER TOO.
YOU WERE SUPPOSED TO LAUGH!!
HAHAHA
IF YOU'RE A STARFISH, THEN HOW COME YOU CAN TALK?
I'M GLAD YOU ASKED!! WHEN I WAS A KID, I BELIEVED I WAS HUMAN...
...AND BY THE TIME I REALIZED I WASN'T, I WAS ALREADY SPEAKING LIKE ONE.
TA DAH!!
DOES IT REALLY WORK THAT WAY?
THE MIND IS A POWERFUL THING!!!
IN THIS WORLD, YOU CAN DO ANYTHING YOU PUT YOUR MIND TO!!!

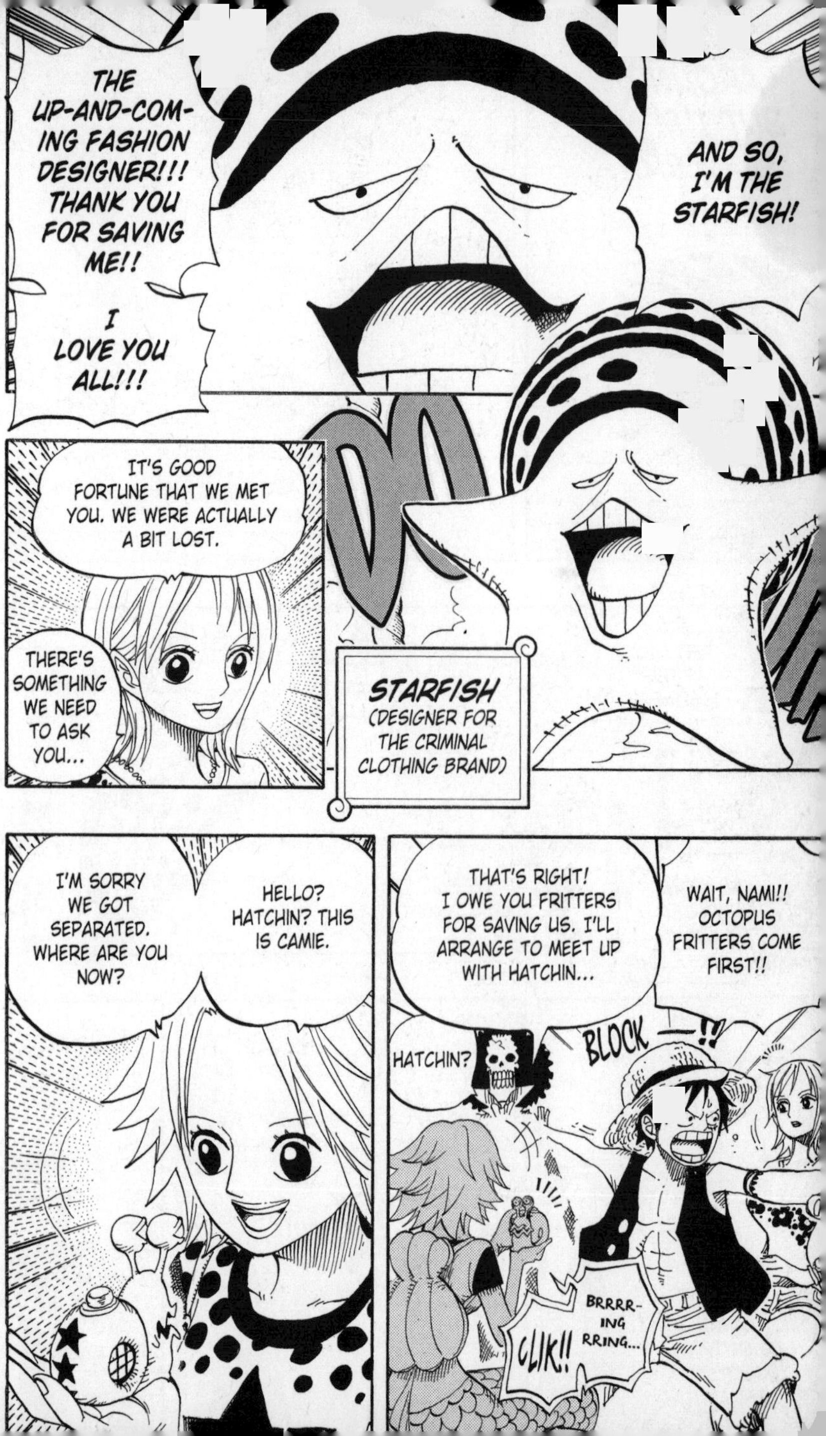
AND SO, I'M THE STARFISH!
THE UP-AND-COMING FASHION DESIGNER!!! THANK YOU FOR SAVING ME!!
I LOVE YOU ALL!!!
STARFISH (DESIGNER FOR THE CRIMINAL CLOTHING BRAND)
IT'S GOOD FORTUNE THAT WE MET YOU. WE WERE ACTUALLY A BIT LOST.
THERE'S SOMETHING WE NEED TO ASK YOU...
THAT'S RIGHT! I OWE YOU FRITTERS FOR SAVING US. I'LL ARRANGE TO MEET UP WITH HATCHIN...
WAIT, NAMI!! OCTOPUS FRITTERS COME FIRST!!
BLOCK—!!
HATCHIN?
BRRRR-ING RRING...
CLIK!!
HELLO? HATCHIN? THIS IS CAMIE.
I'M SORRY WE GOT SEPARATED. WHERE ARE YOU NOW?

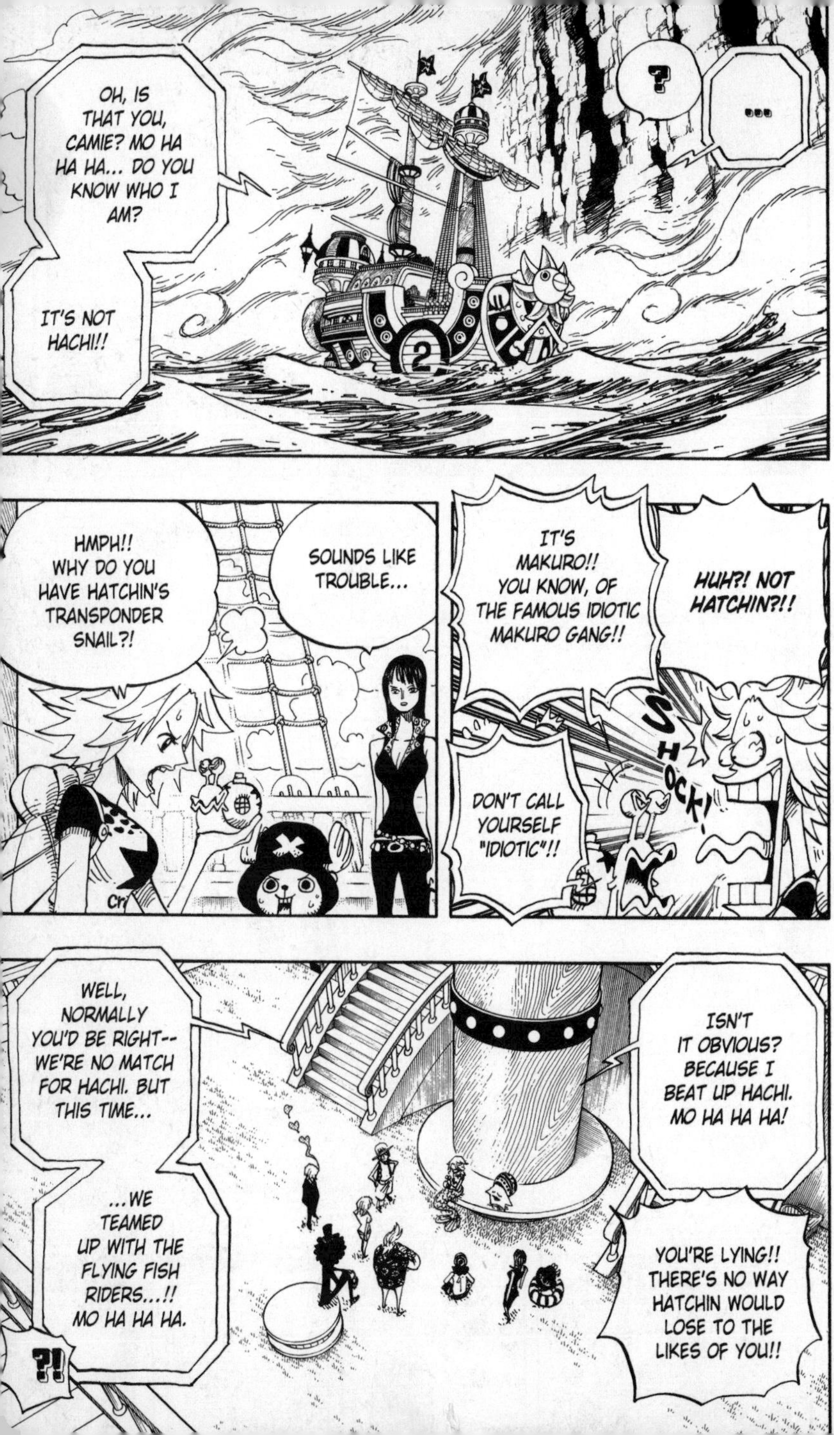
...
?
OH, IS THAT YOU, CAMIE? MO HA HA... DO YOU KNOW WHO I AM?
IT'S NOT HACHI!!
HUH?! NOT HATCHIN?!!
IT'S MAKURO!! YOU KNOW, OF THE FAMOUS IDIOTIC MAKURO GANG!!
SHOCK!
DON'T CALL YOURSELF "IDIOTIC"!!
SOUNDS LIKE TROUBLE...
HMPH!! WHY DO YOU HAVE HATCHIN'S TRANSPONDER SNAIL?!
ISN'T IT OBVIOUS? BECAUSE I BEAT UP HACHI. MO HA HA HA!
YOU'RE LYING!! THERE'S NO WAY HATCHIN WOULD LOSE TO THE LIKES OF YOU!!
WELL, NORMALLY YOU'D BE RIGHT-- WE'RE NO MATCH FOR HACHI. BUT THIS TIME...
...WE TEAMED UP WITH THE FLYING FISH RIDERS...!! MO HA HA HA.
?!

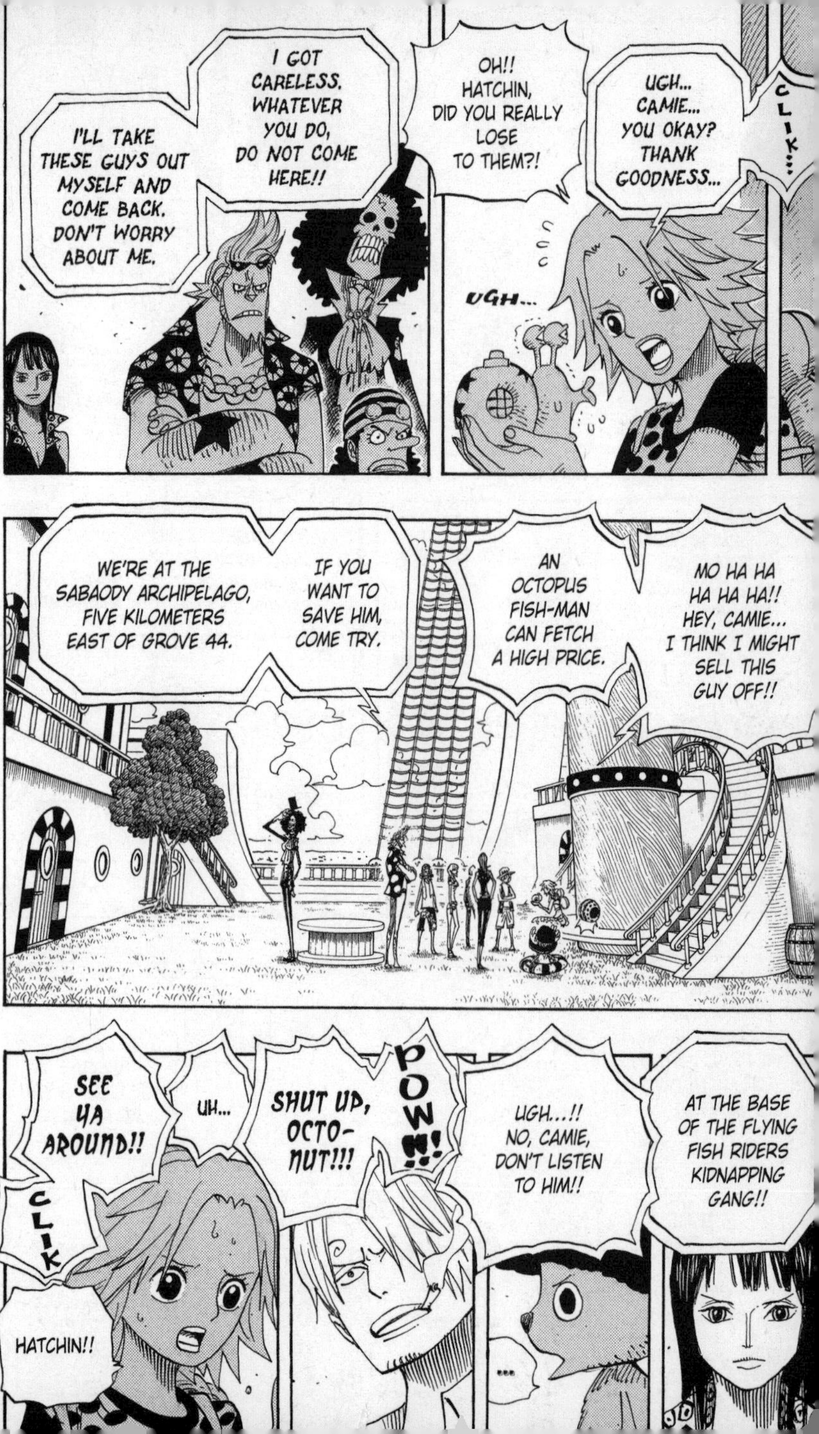
CLIK...
UGH... CAMIE... YOU OKAY? THANK GOODNESS...
OH!! HATCHIN, DID YOU REALLY LOSE TO THEM?!
UGH...
I GOT CARELESS. WHATEVER YOU DO, DO NOT COME HERE!!
I'LL TAKE THESE GUYS OUT MYSELF AND COME BACK. DON'T WORRY ABOUT ME.
MO HA HA HA HA HA!! HEY, CAMIE... I THINK I MIGHT SELL THIS GUY OFF!!
AN OCTOPUS FISH-MAN CAN FETCH A HIGH PRICE.
IF YOU WANT TO SAVE HIM, COME TRY.
WE'RE AT THE SABAODY ARCHIPELAGO, FIVE KILOMETERS EAST OF GROVE 44.
AT THE BASE OF THE FLYING FISH RIDERS KIDNAPPING GANG!!
UGH...!! NO, CAMIE, DON'T LISTEN TO HIM!!
...
POW!!
SHUT UP, OCTO-NUT!!!
UH...
SEE YA AROUND!!
CLIK
HATCHIN!!

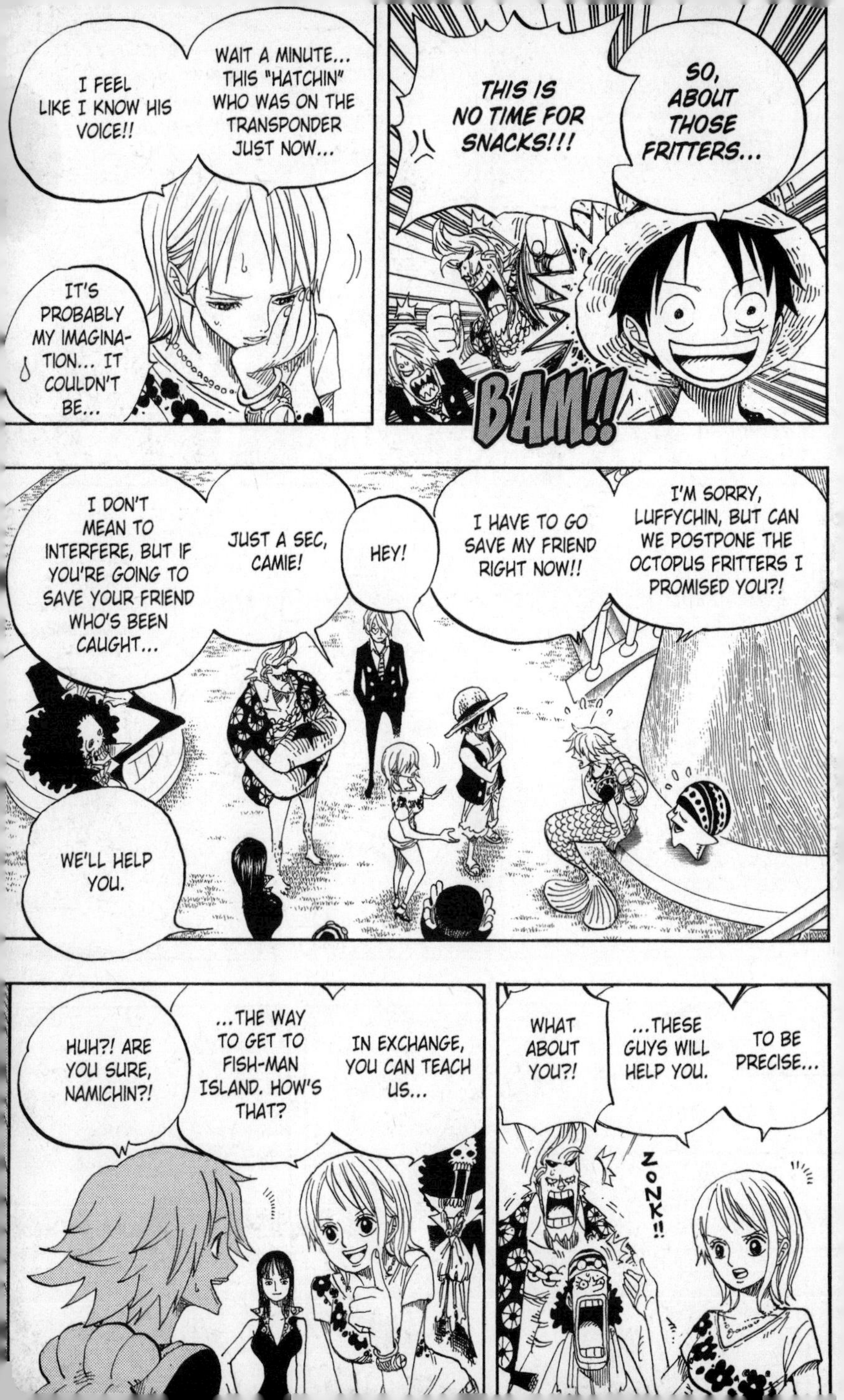
SO, ABOUT THOSE FRITTERS...
THIS IS NO TIME FOR SNACKS!!!
BAM!!
WAIT A MINUTE... THIS "HATCHIN" WHO WAS ON THE TRANSPONDER JUST NOW...
I FEEL LIKE I KNOW HIS VOICE!!
IT'S PROBABLY MY IMAGINATION... IT COULDN'T BE...
I'M SORRY, LUFFYCHIN, BUT CAN WE POSTPONE THE OCTOPUS FRITTERS I PROMISED YOU?!
I HAVE TO GO SAVE MY FRIEND RIGHT NOW!!
HEY!
JUST A SEC, CAMIE!
I DON'T MEAN TO INTERFERE, BUT IF YOU'RE GOING TO SAVE YOUR FRIEND WHO'S BEEN CAUGHT...
WE'LL HELP YOU.
TO BE PRECISE...
...THESE GUYS WILL HELP YOU.
WHAT ABOUT YOU?!
ZONK!!
IN EXCHANGE, YOU CAN TEACH US...
...THE WAY TO GET TO FISH-MAN ISLAND. HOW'S THAT?
HUH?! ARE YOU SURE, NAMICHIN?!

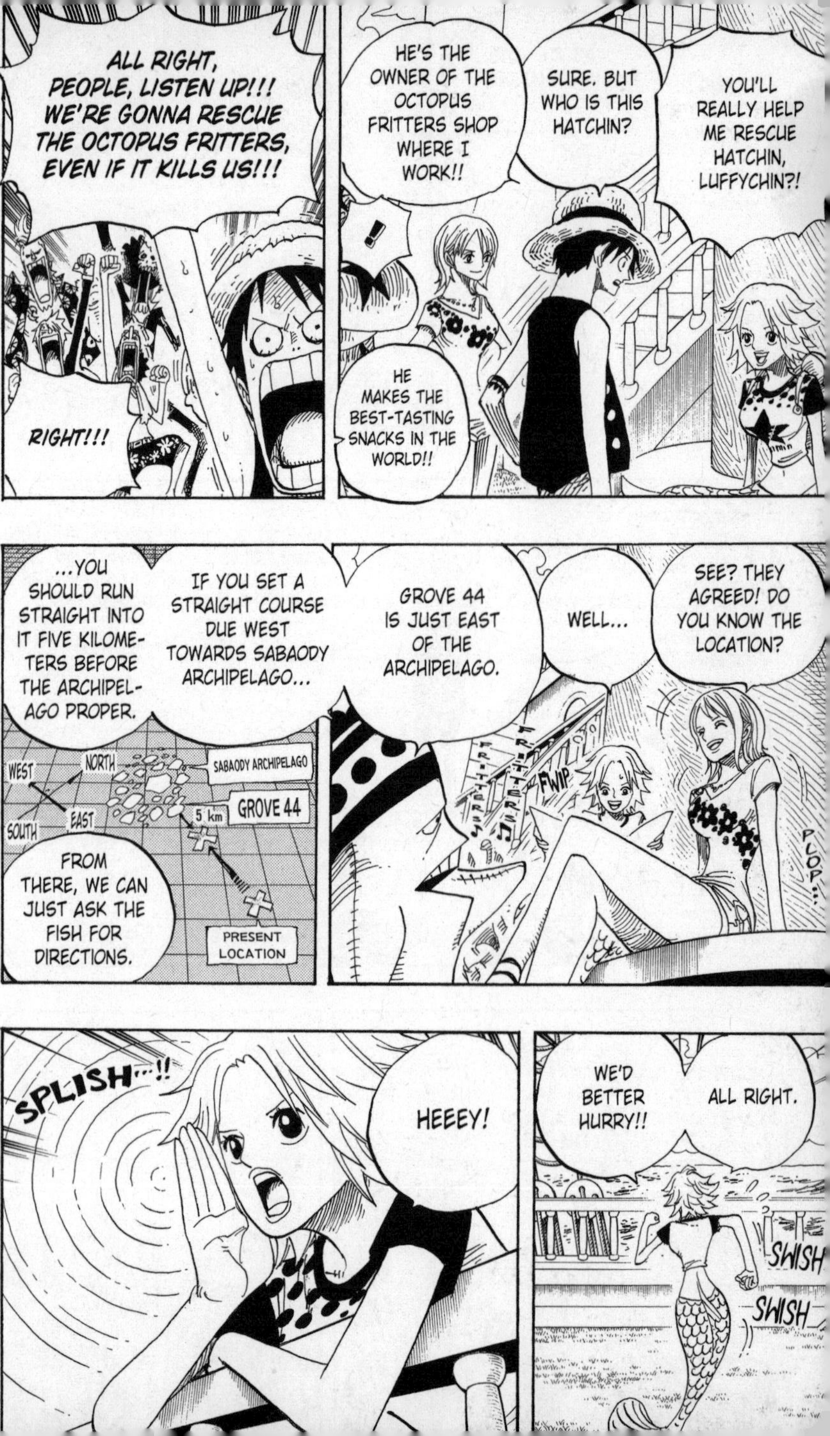
YOU'LL REALLY HELP ME RESCUE HATCHIN, LUFFYCHIN?!
SURE. BUT WHO IS THIS HATCHIN?
HE'S THE OWNER OF THE OCTOPUS FRITTERS SHOP WHERE I WORK!!
!
HE MAKES THE BEST-TASTING SNACKS IN THE WORLD!!
ALL RIGHT, PEOPLE, LISTEN UP!!! WE'RE GONNA RESCUE THE OCTOPUS FRITTERS, EVEN IF IT KILLS US!!!
RIGHT!!!
SEE? THEY AGREED! DO YOU KNOW THE LOCATION?
WELL...
GROVE 44 IS JUST EAST OF THE ARCHIPELAGO.
FRITTERS
FRITTERS
FWIP
PLOP...
IF YOU SET A STRAIGHT COURSE DUE WEST TOWARDS SABAODY ARCHIPELAGO...
...YOU SHOULD RUN STRAIGHT INTO IT FIVE KILOMETERS BEFORE THE ARCHIPELAGO PROPER.
WEST
NORTH
SOUTH
EAST
SABAODY ARCHIPELAGO
GROVE 44
5 km
PRESENT LOCATION
FROM THERE, WE CAN JUST ASK THE FISH FOR DIRECTIONS.
ALL RIGHT.
WE'D BETTER HURRY!!
SWISH
SWISH
HEEEY!
SPLISH...!!

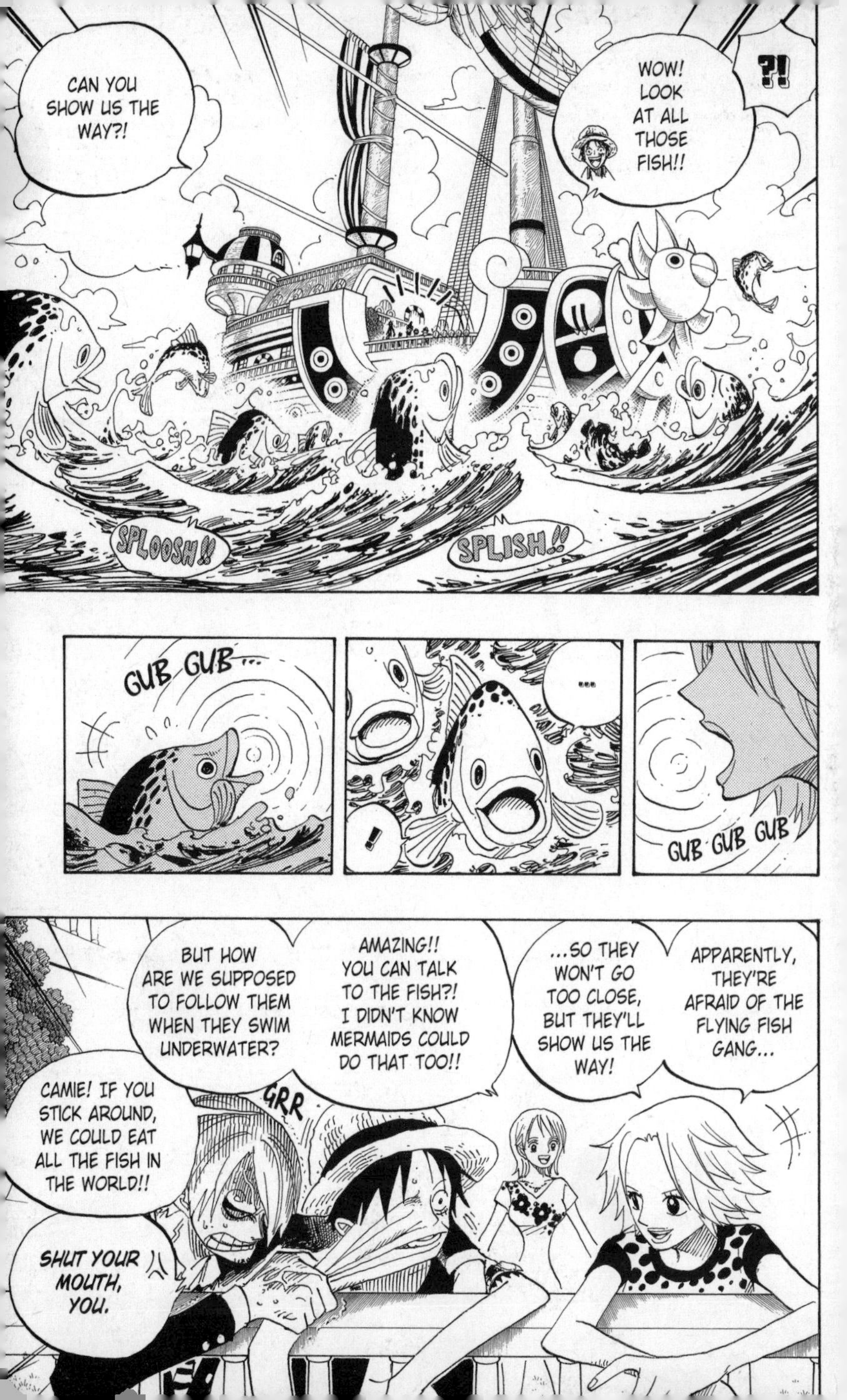
?!
WOW! LOOK AT ALL THOSE FISH!!
CAN YOU SHOW US THE WAY?!
SPLISH!!
SPLOOSH!!
GUB GUB GUB
...
!
GUB GUB...
APPARENTLY, THEY'RE AFRAID OF THE FLYING FISH GANG...
...SO THEY WON'T GO TOO CLOSE, BUT THEY'LL SHOW US THE WAY!
AMAZING!! YOU CAN TALK TO THE FISH?! I DIDN'T KNOW MERMAIDS COULD DO THAT TOO!!
BUT HOW ARE WE SUPPOSED TO FOLLOW THEM WHEN THEY SWIM UNDERWATER?
GRR
CAMIE! IF YOU STICK AROUND, WE COULD EAT ALL THE FISH IN THE WORLD!!
SHUT YOUR MOUTH, YOU.

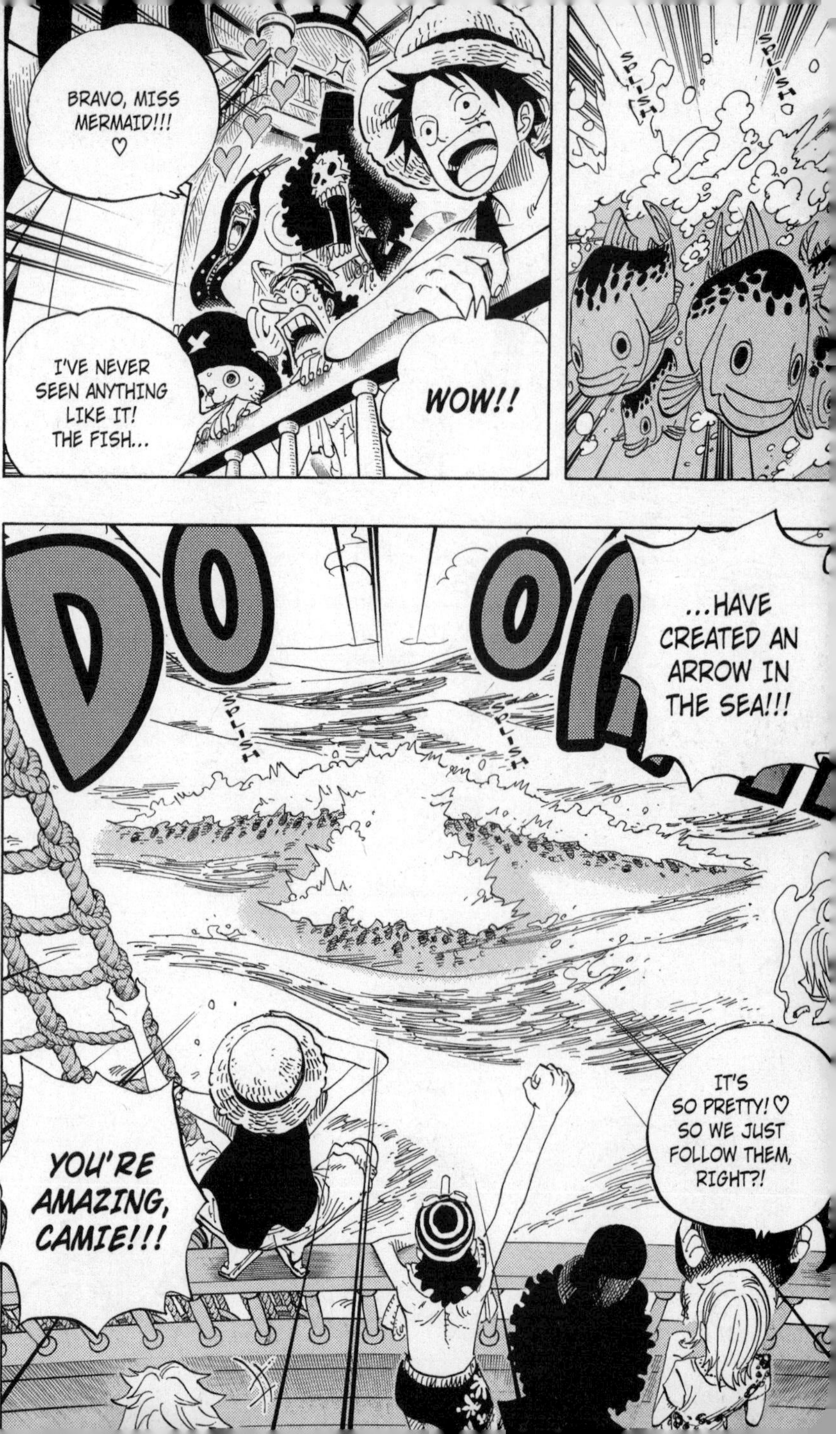
SPLISH
SPLISH
BRAVO, MISS MERMAID!!! ♡
WOW!!
I'VE NEVER SEEN ANYTHING LIKE IT! THE FISH...
...HAVE CREATED AN ARROW IN THE SEA!!!
SPLISH
SPLISH
IT'S SO PRETTY! ♡ SO WE JUST FOLLOW THEM, RIGHT?!
YOU'RE AMAZING, CAMIE!!!

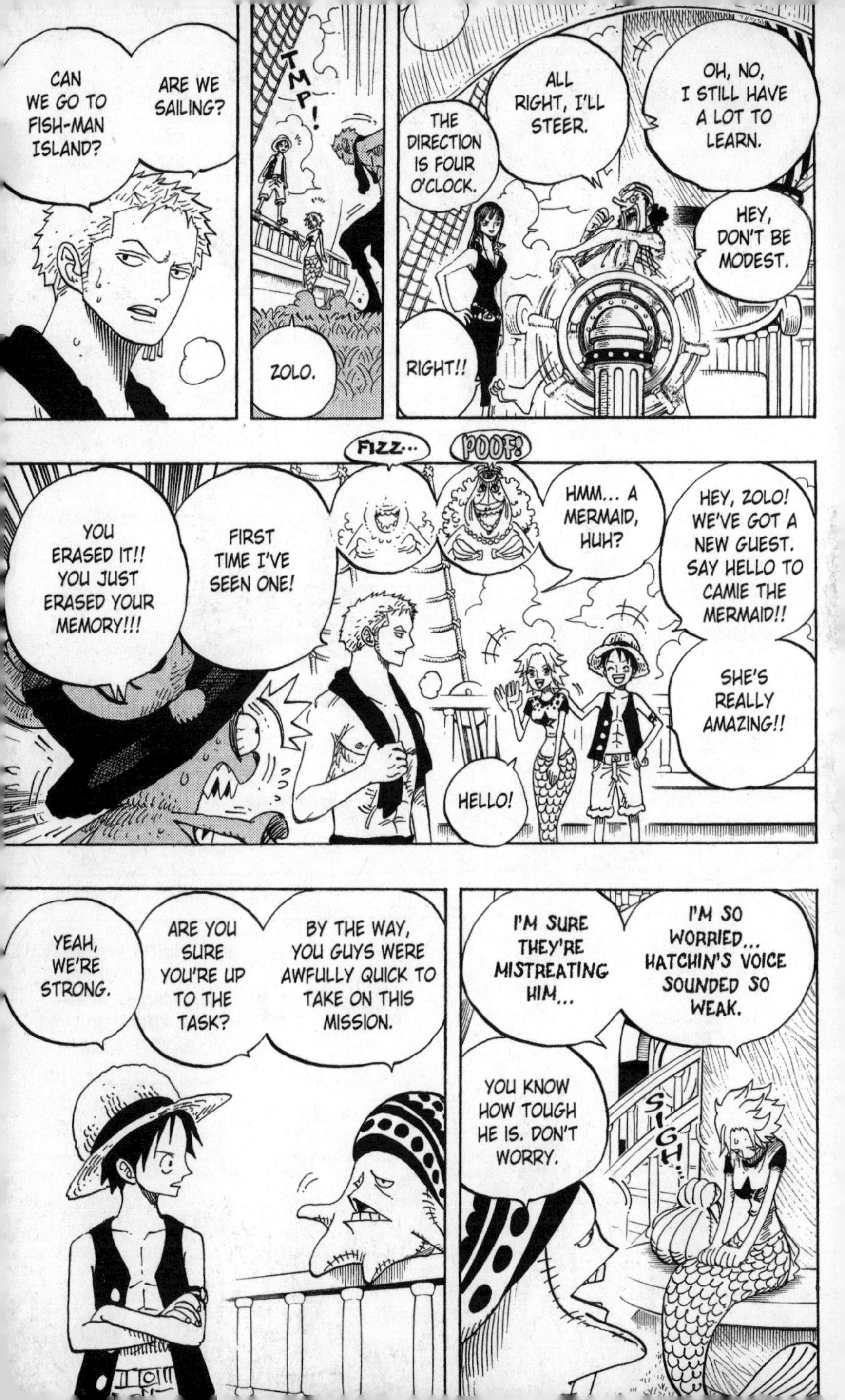

OH, NO, I STILL HAVE A LOT TO LEARN.
ALL RIGHT, I'LL STEER.
THE DIRECTION IS FOUR O'CLOCK.
HEY, DON'T BE MODEST.
RIGHT!!
TMP!
ZOLO.
ARE WE SAILING?
CAN WE GO TO FISH-MAN ISLAND?
HEY, ZOLO! WE'VE GOT A NEW GUEST. SAY HELLO TO CAMIE THE MERMAID!!
SHE'S REALLY AMAZING!!
HMM... A MERMAID, HUH?
POOF!
FIZZ...
HELLO!
FIRST TIME I'VE SEEN ONE!
YOU ERASED IT!! YOU JUST ERASED YOUR MEMORY!!!
I'M SO WORRIED... HATCHIN'S VOICE SOUNDED SO WEAK.
I'M SURE THEY'RE MISTREATING HIM...
SIGH...
YOU KNOW HOW TOUGH HE IS. DON'T WORRY.
BY THE WAY, YOU GUYS WERE AWFULLY QUICK TO TAKE ON THIS MISSION.
ARE YOU SURE YOU'RE UP TO THE TASK?
YEAH, WE'RE STRONG.

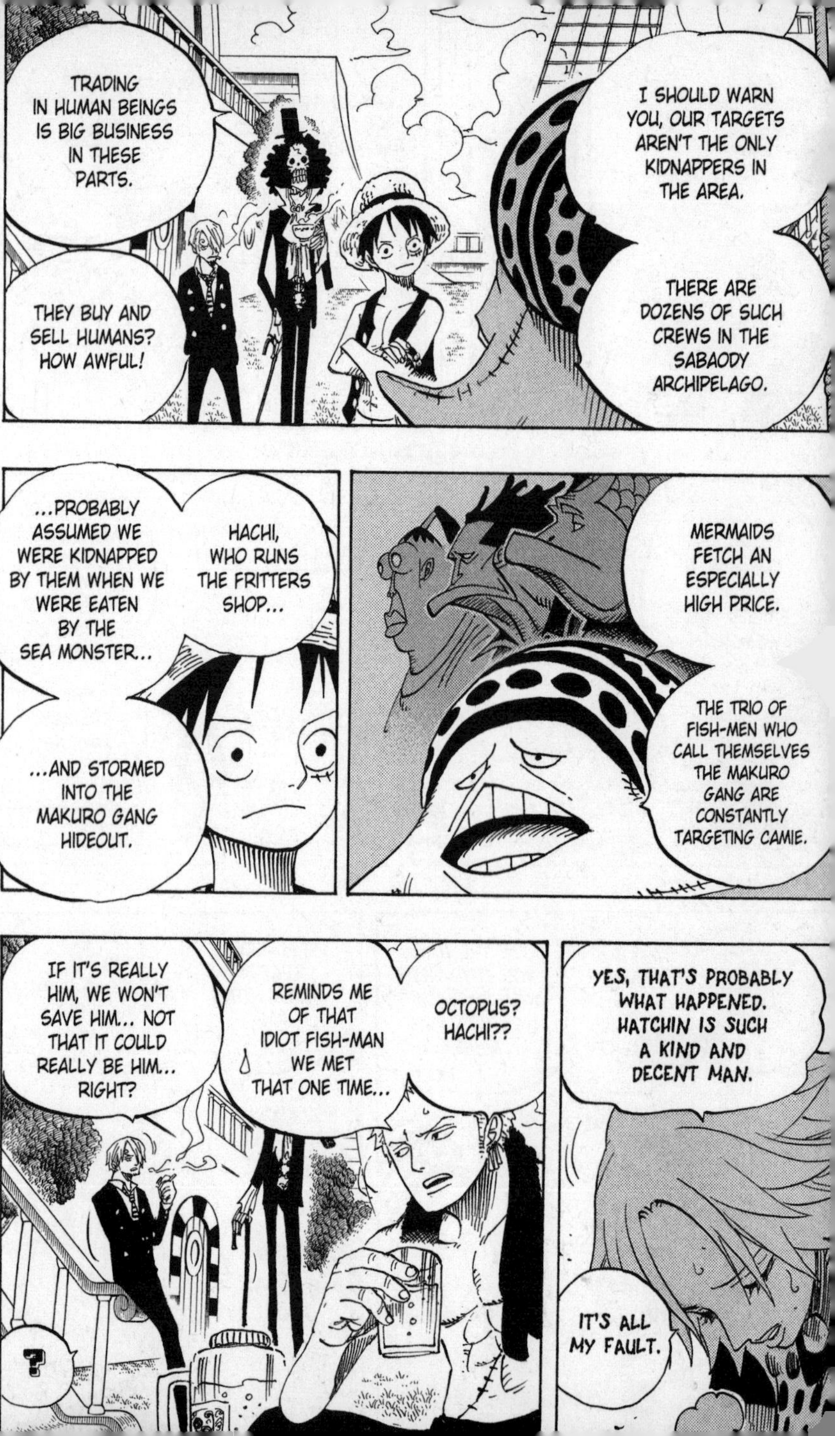
I SHOULD WARN YOU, OUR TARGETS AREN'T THE ONLY KIDNAPPERS IN THE AREA.
THERE ARE DOZENS OF SUCH CREWS IN THE SABAODY ARCHIPELAGO.
TRADING IN HUMAN BEINGS IS BIG BUSINESS IN THESE PARTS.
THEY BUY AND SELL HUMANS? HOW AWFUL!
MERMAIDS FETCH AN ESPECIALLY HIGH PRICE.
THE TRIO OF FISH-MEN WHO CALL THEMSELVES THE MAKURO GANG ARE CONSTANTLY TARGETING CAMIE.
HACHI, WHO RUNS THE FRITTERS SHOP...
...PROBABLY ASSUMED WE WERE KIDNAPPED BY THEM WHEN WE WERE EATEN BY THE SEA MONSTER...
...AND STORMED INTO THE MAKURO GANG HIDEOUT.
YES, THAT'S PROBABLY WHAT HAPPENED. HATCHIN IS SUCH A KIND AND DECENT MAN.
IT'S ALL MY FAULT.
OCTOPUS? HACHI??
REMINDS ME OF THAT IDIOT FISH-MAN WE MET THAT ONE TIME...
IF IT'S REALLY HIM, WE WON'T SAVE HIM... NOT THAT IT COULD REALLY BE HIM... RIGHT?
?

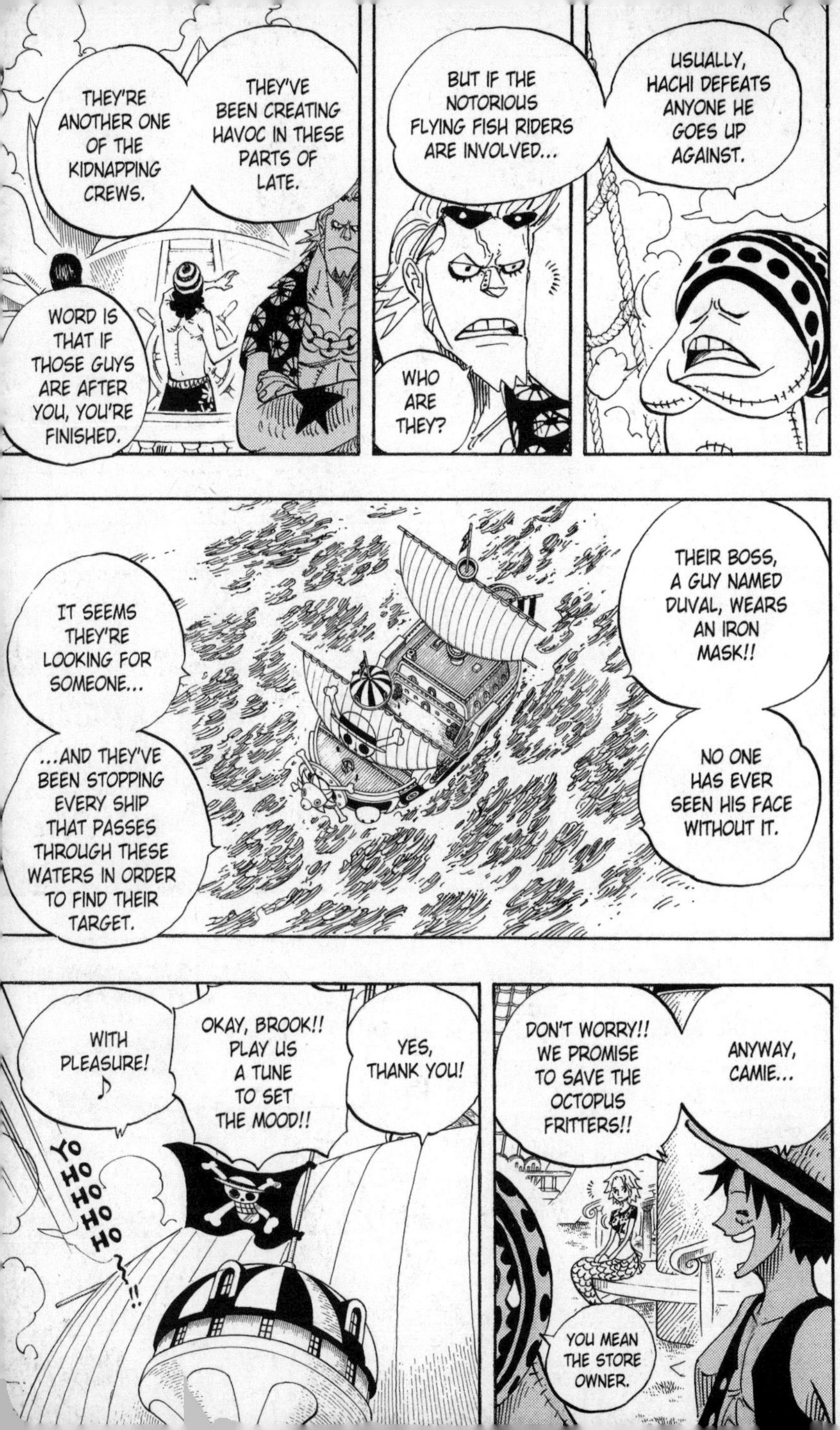
USUALLY, HACHI DEFEATS ANYONE HE GOES UP AGAINST.
BUT IF THE NOTORIOUS FLYING FISH RIDERS ARE INVOLVED...
WHO ARE THEY?
THEY'VE BEEN CREATING HAVOC IN THESE PARTS OF LATE.
THEY'RE ANOTHER ONE OF THE KIDNAPPING CREWS.
WORD IS THAT IF THOSE GUYS ARE AFTER YOU, YOU'RE FINISHED.
THEIR BOSS, A GUY NAMED DUVAL, WEARS AN IRON MASK!!
NO ONE HAS EVER SEEN HIS FACE WITHOUT IT.
IT SEEMS THEY'RE LOOKING FOR SOMEONE...
...AND THEY'VE BEEN STOPPING EVERY SHIP THAT PASSES THROUGH THESE WATERS IN ORDER TO FIND THEIR TARGET.
ANYWAY, CAMIE...
DON'T WORRY!! WE PROMISE TO SAVE THE OCTOPUS FRITTERS!!
YOU MEAN THE STORE OWNER.
YES, THANK YOU!
OKAY, BROOK!! PLAY US A TUNE TO SET THE MOOD!!
WITH PLEASURE! ♪
YO HO HO HO HO HO~!!

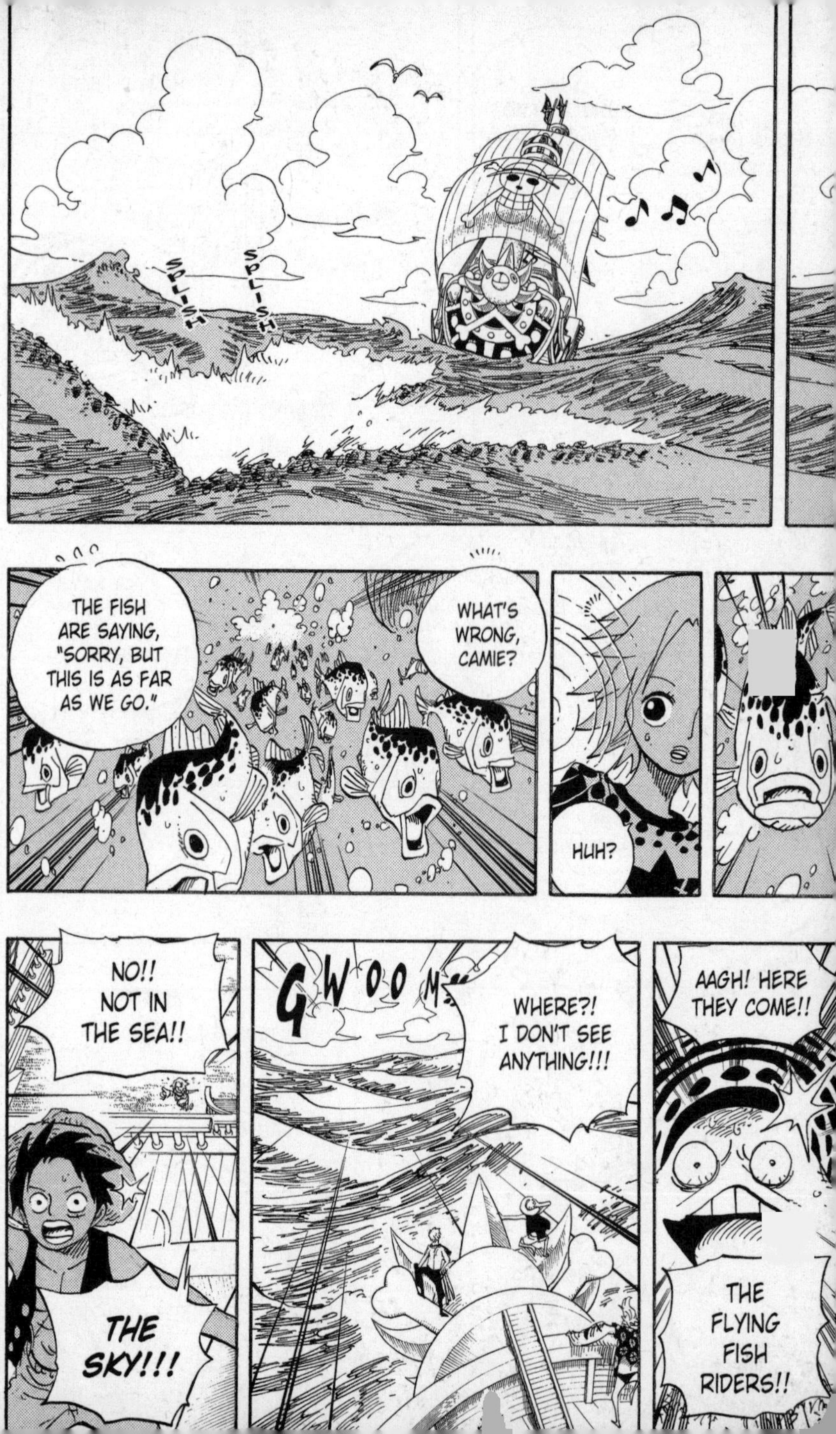
SPLISH
SPLISH
HUH?
WHAT'S WRONG, CAMIE?
THE FISH ARE SAYING, "SORRY, BUT THIS IS AS FAR AS WE GO."
AAGH! HERE THEY COME!!
THE FLYING FISH RIDERS!!
GWOOM
WHERE?! I DON'T SEE ANYTHING!!!
NO!! NOT IN THE SEA!!
THE SKY!!!

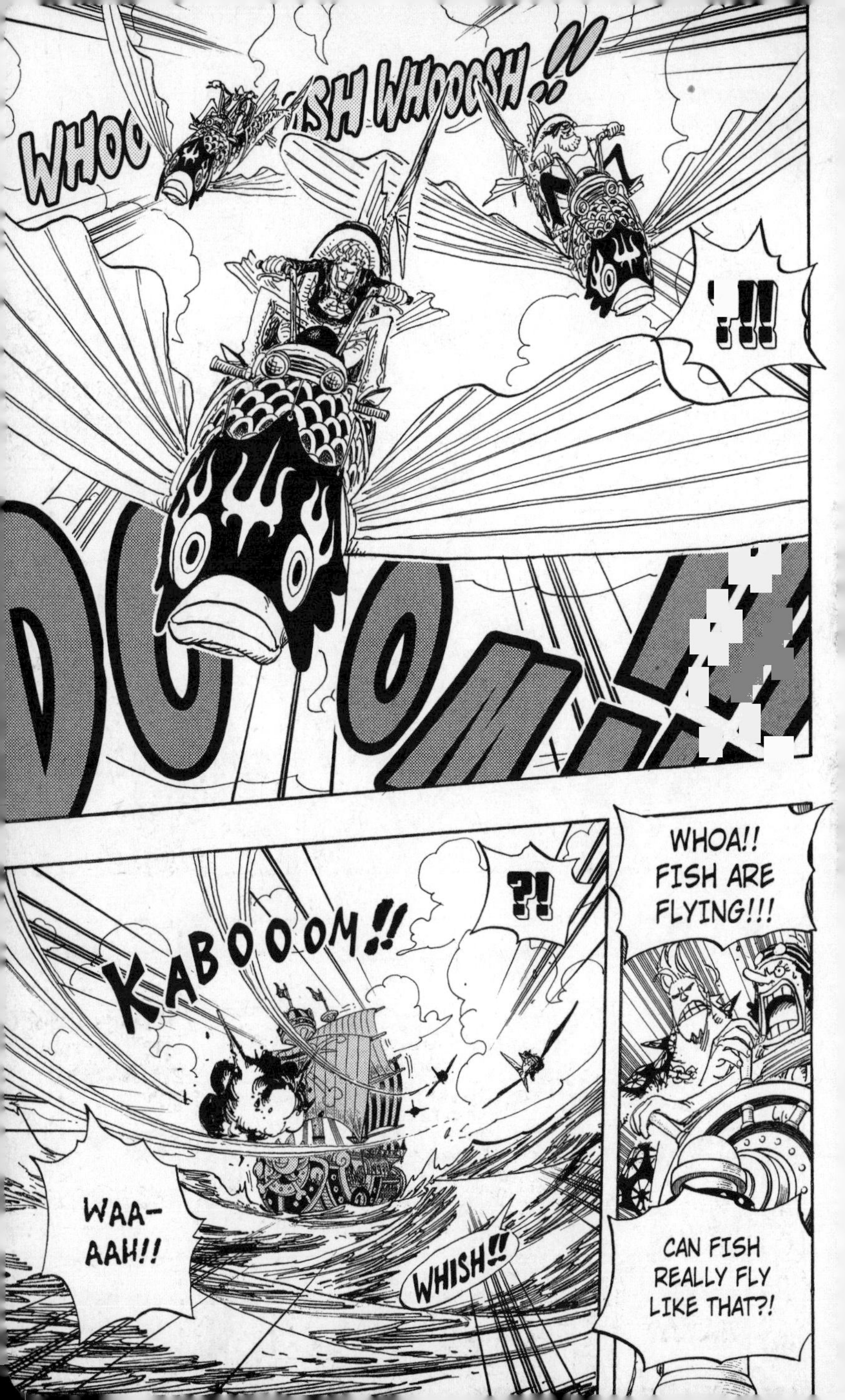

WHOOOSH!!
?!!
WHOA!! FISH ARE FLYING!!!
CAN FISH REALLY FLY LIKE THAT?!
?!
KABOOOM!!
WAA-AAH!!
WHISH!!

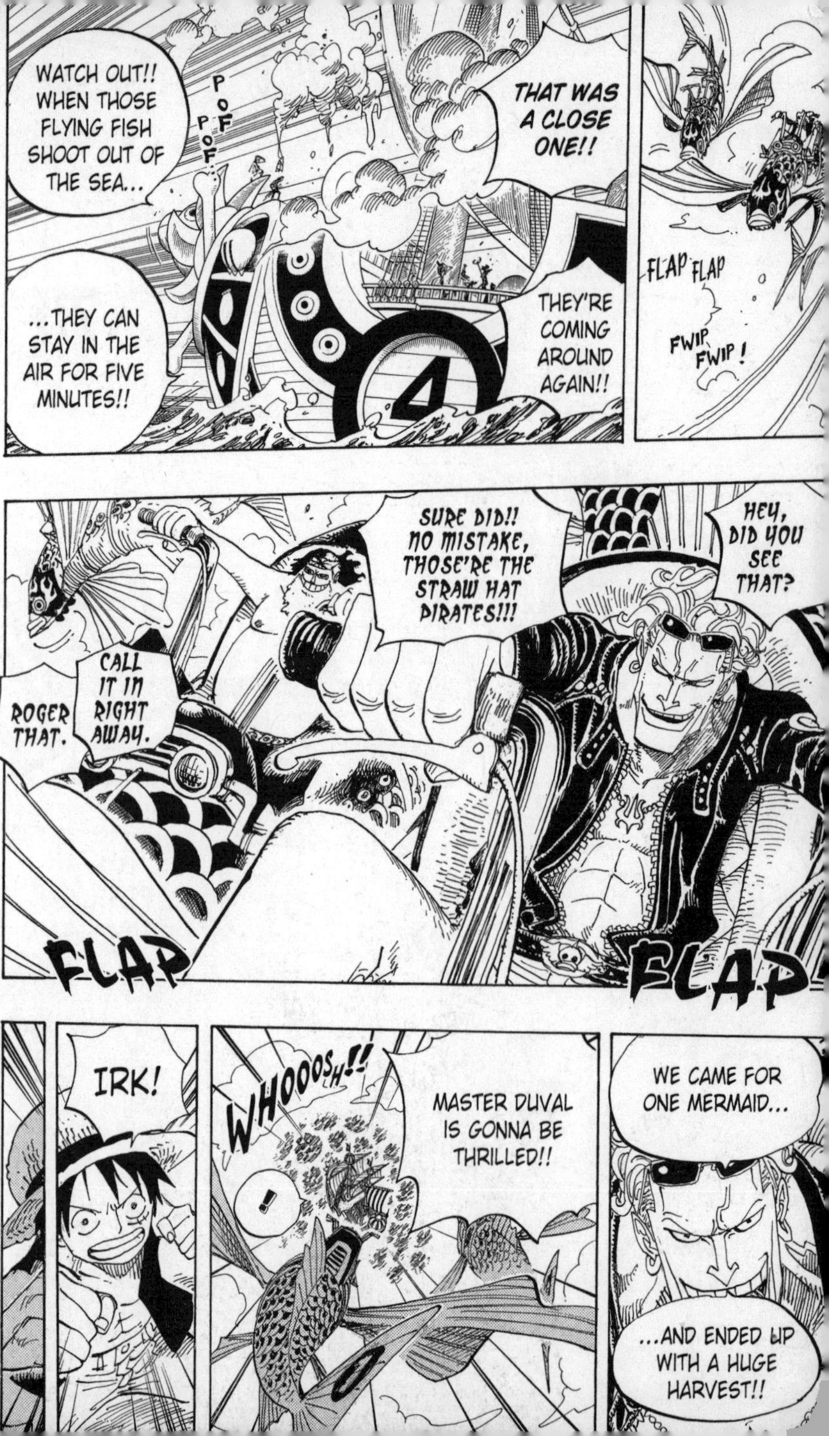
FLAP FLAP
FWIP FWIP!
THAT WAS A CLOSE ONE!!
WATCH OUT!! WHEN THOSE FLYING FISH SHOOT OUT OF THE SEA...
POF POF POF
THEY'RE COMING AROUND AGAIN!!
...THEY CAN STAY IN THE AIR FOR FIVE MINUTES!!
HEY, DID YOU SEE THAT?
SURE DID!! NO MISTAKE, THOSE'RE THE STRAW HAT PIRATES!!!
CALL IT IN RIGHT AWAY.
ROGER THAT.
FLAP
FLAP
WE CAME FOR ONE MERMAID...
...AND ENDED UP WITH A HUGE HARVEST!!
MASTER DUVAL IS GONNA BE THRILLED!!
WHOOOSH!!
!
IRK!

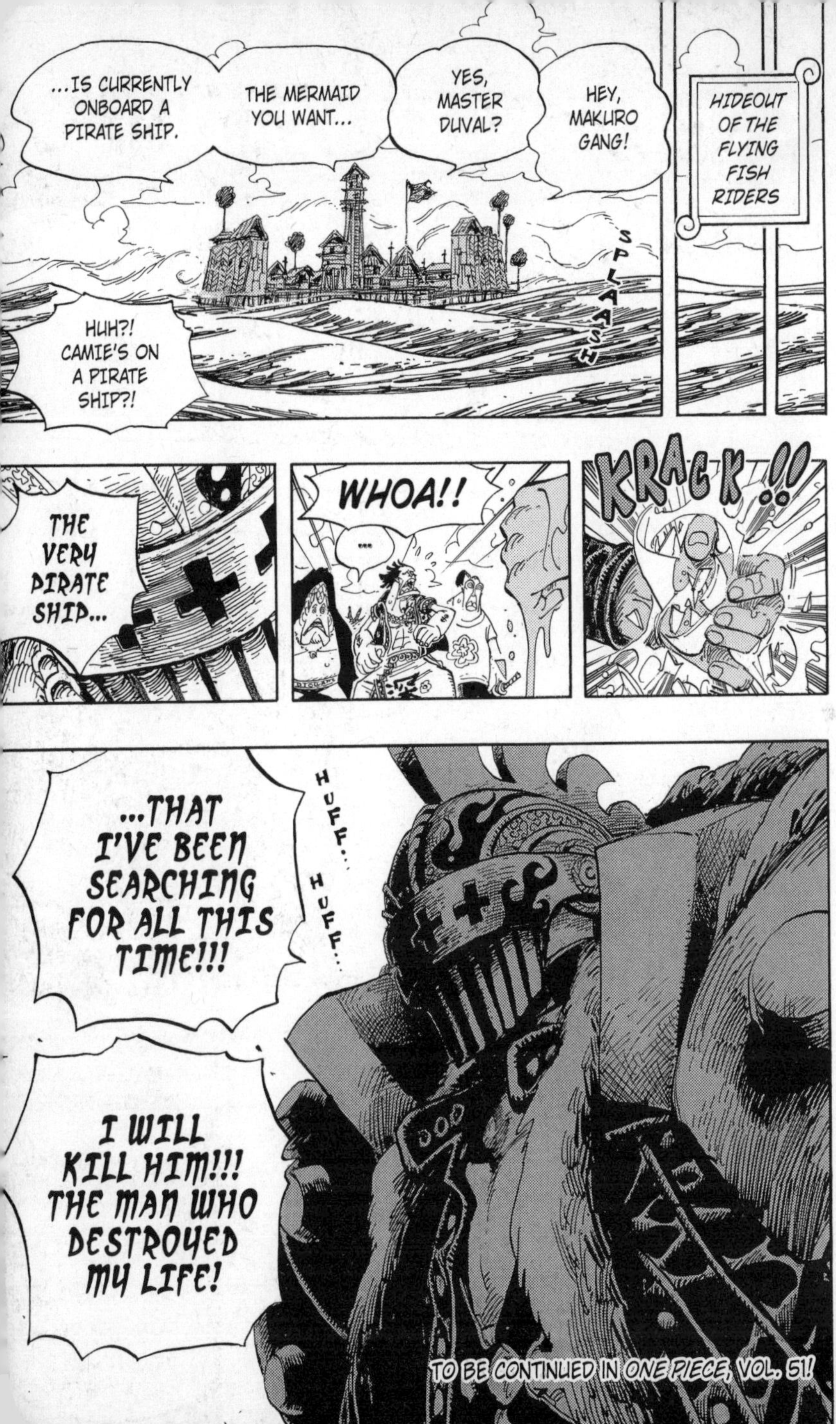
HIDEOUT OF THE FLYING FISH RIDERS
HEY, MAKURO GANG!
YES, MASTER DUVAL?
THE MERMAID YOU WANT...
...IS CURRENTLY ONBOARD A PIRATE SHIP.
SPLAAASH
HUH?! CAMIE'S ON A PIRATE SHIP?!
KRACK!!
WHOA!!
...
THE VERY PIRATE SHIP...
HUFF... HUFF...
...THAT I'VE BEEN SEARCHING FOR ALL THIS TIME!!!
I WILL KILL HIM!!! THE MAN WHO DESTROYED MY LIFE!
TO BE CONTINUED IN ONE PIECE, VOL. 51!

COMING NEXT VOLUME:

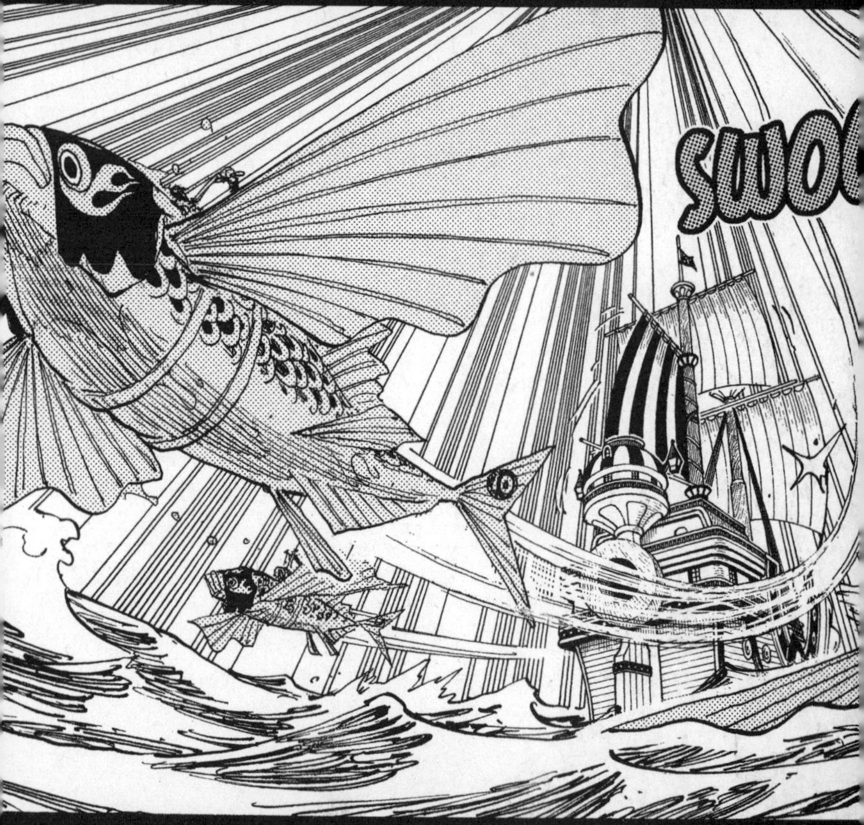

Camie the mermaid offers to take Luffy and the crew to Fish-Man Island if they'll help rescue her boss Hachi from the notorious Flying Fish Riders. Ignoring all of the warning signs, the crew agrees to help their mermaid friend, only to face a totally unexpected new foe.

ON SALE NOW!

Set Sail with

Read all about **MONKEY D. LUFFY**'s adventures as he sails around the world assembling a motley crew to join him on his search for the legendary treasure "**ONE PIECE**." For more information, check out **onepiece.viz.com**.

EAST BLUE
(Vols. 1-12)
Available now!

See where it all began! One man, a dinghy and a dream. Or rather… a rubber man who can't swim, setting out in a tiny boat on the vast seas without any navigational skills. What are the odds that his dream of becoming King of the Pirates will ever come true?

BAROQUE WORKS
(Vols. 12-24)
Available now!

Friend or foe? Ms. Wednesday is part of a group of bounty hunters—or isn't she? The Straw Hats get caught up in a civil war when they find a princess in their midst. But can they help her stop the revolution in her home country before the evil Crocodile gets his way?!

SKYPIEA
(Vols. 24-32)
Available now!

Luffy's quest to become King of the Pirates and find the elusive treasure known as "One Piece" continues…in the sky! The Straw Hats sail to Skypiea, an airborne island in the midst of a territorial war and ruled by a short-fused megalomaniac!

WATER SEVEN
(Vols. 32-46)
Available now!

The *Merry Go* has been a stalwart for the Straw Hats since the beginning, but countless battles have taken their toll on the ship. Luckily, their next stop is Water Seven, where a rough-and-tumble crew of shipwrights awaits their arrival!

THRILLER BARK
(Vols. 46-50)
Available now!

Luffy and crew get more than they bargained for when their ship is drawn toward haunted Thriller Bark. When Gecko Moria, one of the Warlords of the Sea, steals the crew's shadows, they'll have to get them back before the sun rises or else they'll all turn into zombies!

SABAODY
(Vols. 50-54)
Available now!

On the way to Fish-Man Island, the Straw Hats disembark on the Sabaody archipelago to get soaped up for their undersea adventure! But it's not too long before they get caught up in trouble! Luffy's made an enemy of an exalted World Noble when he saves Camie the mermaid from being sold on the slave market, and now he's got the Navy after him too!

IMPEL DOWN
(Vols. 54-56)
Available now!

Luffy's brother Ace is about to be executed! Held in the Navy's maximum security prison Impel Down, Luffy needs to find a way to break in to help Ace escape. But with murderous fiends for guards inside, the notorious prisoners start to seem not so bad. Some are even friendly enough to give Luffy a helping hand!

You're Reading in the Wrong Direction!!

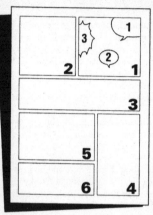

Whoops! Guess what? You're starting at the wrong end of the comic!

…It's true! In keeping with the original Japanese format, **One Piece** is meant to be read from right to left, starting in the upper-right corner.

Unlike English, which is read from left to right, Japanese is read from right to left, meaning that action, sound effects and word-balloon order are completely reversed…something which can make readers unfamiliar with Japanese feel pretty backwards themselves. For this reason, manga or Japanese comics published in the U.S. in English have sometimes been published "flopped"—that is, printed in exact reverse order, as though seen from the other side of a mirror.

By flopping pages, U.S. publishers can avoid confusing readers, but the compromise is not without its downside. For one thing, a character in a flopped manga series who once wore in the original Japanese version a T-shirt emblazoned with "M A Y" (as in "the merry month of") now wears one which reads "Y A M"! Additionally, many manga creators in Japan are themselves unhappy with the process, as some feel the mirror-imaging of their art skews their original intentions.

We are proud to bring you Eiichiro Oda's **One Piece** in the original unflopped format. For now, though, turn to the other side of the book and let the journey begin…!

—Editor